D0013211

# the middle east

## an
## anthropological
## approach

**dale f. eickelman**

*new york university*

prentice-hall, inc.
englewood cliffs, new jersey 07632

*Library of Congress Cataloging in Publication Data*

Eickelman, Dale F (date)
  The Middle East.

  Includes bibliographical references and index.
    1. Ethnology—Near East.    2. Ethnology—Africa,
North.    3. Near East—Social life and customs.
4. Africa, North—Social life and customs.    I. Title.
GN635.N42E38          956          80-19547
ISBN  0-13-581629-7

*Editorial/production supervision and interior
design by Linda Schuman
Cover design by Edsal Enterprises
Manufacturing buyer: Edmund W. Leone*

Prentice-Hall Series in Anthropology
  David M. Schneider, Editor

©1981 by Prentice-Hall, Inc., Englewood Cliffs, N.J. 07632

*All rights reserved. No part of this book
may be reproduced in any form or
by any means without permission in writing
from the publisher.*

Printed in the United States of America

10   9   8   7   6   5   4   3

PRENTICE-HALL INTERNATIONAL, INC., *London*
PRENTICE-HALL OF AUSTRALIA PTY. LIMITED, *Sydney*
PRENTICE-HALL OF CANADA, LTD., *Toronto*
PRENTICE-HALL OF INDIA PRIVATE LIMITED, *New Delhi*
PRENTICE-HALL OF JAPAN, INC., *Tokyo*
PRENTICE-HALL OF SOUTHEAST ASIA PTE. LTD., *Singapore*
WHITEHALL BOOKS LIMITED, *Wellington, New Zealand*

GN
635
.N42
E38

*To*

*Abdul Hamid M. El-Zein*
*(1934 - 1979)*

# contents

# preface

This book is intended as an anthropological introduction to the Middle East. This goal is inseparable from a second, complementary one, that of indicating the contribution which the study of the Middle East is making to the main currents of anthropology, especially those which relate to the analysis of complex societies. As anthropological scholarship on the major civilizational areas of the world has reached a critical intensity, certain themes have been more emphasized than others. In research on Black Africa in the 1940s and early 1950s, the nature of political order to be found in "stateless" societies was a predominant question. Much of the anthropological study of India has focused on the cultural and social aspects of inequality, and this literature has profoundly influenced the consideration of stratification and social class elsewhere.

Research on the Middle East is beginning to reach a similar critical intensity and several interrelated themes prevail. One group of problems is suggested by the study of Islam and the means by which a world religion is to be understood simultaneously as a universal ideological force and in its rich local manifestations. How does a world religion such as Islam maintain its vitality in rapidly evolving economic and political contexts, and how do local understandings of Islam affect the wider currents of Islamic civilization?

Another set of problems deals with ideas which people hold of their cultural identity. In a region as complex as the Middle East, with interlocking linguistic, ethnic, religious, kin, and class distinctions, the problems of how personal and collective identities are asserted and what they mean in differing historical and political contexts are especially crucial. Such distinctions are much more plastic than earlier stereotypes concerning their cultural bases have allowed.

A third emerging research focus concerns economic activities—the production and consumption of goods and services. At a general level, shared with other disciplines, this focus involves analyzing the social and cultural impact of developments such as massive labor emigration from poorer countries, the influx of oil and mineral wealth to others, urbanization and land reform, and the shifting circumstances of international politics. A specifically anthropological contribution to these issues concerns the analysis of the cultural values and systems of social relationships associated with forms of economic activity ranging from the Middle Eastern bazaar to "modern" forms of industrial and commercial activities and what happens to values and social relationships in the context of rapid economic and social change.

A fourth research focus concerns changing *interpretations* of Middle Eastern societies and cultures by Westerners and by Middle Easterners themselves. This problem, once regarded as an historiographic one related only indirectly to "real" anthropological inquiry, is now regarded as implicit in any problem in the human sciences. Ideas concerning what constitutes valid description and interpretation of any culture and society have changed dramatically over the last two centuries, especially as social science has ceased to be primarily a Western or European enterprise.

This book is intended both as a textbook and as an interpretative essay. It is a textbook insofar as it is intended as a self-contained book to introduce students and colleagues to the basic ethnographic themes of the Middle East and the theoretical questions that have been and are being developed by specialists in the region. Although this book is in part necessarily a synthesis of major research, I seek to develop a particular style of anthropological inquiry and show its contribution to the study of a region of complex civilization rather than provide an exhaustive review of the literature. Many textbooks are derivative and unconvincing in that they rarely convey the sense of discovery which leaps from the pages of the more extensive monographs which constitute the central substance of anthropological inquiry. I hope that this book contains enough of the sense of discovery that I have felt in creating it so that readers will be prompted to read it in conjunction with some of the monographs and articles indicated in the footnotes. The footnotes to each section and chapter are designed to be a guide to further readings on particular topics, and for this reason no separate list of further readings is included. To enhance the value of this book as a guide to contemporary anthropological research, I have indicated the best available sources, even when they are in foreign languages. This is deliberately contrary to some of the established conventions of textbook writing. My purpose is to indicate the cutting edge of anthropological and related research for those who wish to pursue given topics.

The outline of this book first took form when I was asked to prepare a series on Middle Eastern anthropology for CBS-TV's "Sunrise Semester." As the title of the general series implies, these programs did not exactly reach a prime time audience, but writing them brought me directly in contact with the evasive "general" audience so often evoked but never clearly delineated by academics. I wrote for the series as I would for graduate and undergraduate students (in my own experience the distinction between writing and teaching for these two categories of students is often exaggerated because the critical talents of undergraduates are often not fully appreciated) and for anyone interested in the region and civilizations of the Middle East. From correspondence and conversations it gradually emerged that the decision not to seek to popularize by softening the edges of difficult problems was enthusiastically received by an audience wider than one interested simply in the Middle East or in how anthropology as a discipline can contribute to the study of complex societies. I have tried to use the same approach in this book.

In writing this essay, I have benefited substantially from the critical comments and advice of a number of colleagues and friends. Hildred Geertz of Princeton University read the entire manuscript with a critical intensity which enabled me to strengthen and clarify key points of the essay, especially the sections concerning kinship and cultural identity. Paul J. Sanfaçon of the American Museum of Natural History also commented with insight upon the manuscript and coordinated key editorial tasks at a time when my absence from the country might have delayed the appearance of the book. My colleague Karen I. Blu at New York University provided timely and detailed suggestions on most of the manuscript. Jon Anderson, Richard T. Antoun, T. O. Beidelman, Vincent Crapanzano, Bouzekri Draiouiy, Christine Eickelman, Clifford Geertz, Abdellah Hammoudi, Nicholas S. Hopkins, Michael Marcus, Kenneth Sandbank, David M. Schneider, and Delores Walters have also offered useful advice. Except where otherwise noted in the text, the maps have been prepared by Danny Cornyetz. Numerous colleagues have generously allowed me to use photographs and other materials, and such assistance is acknowledged at appropriate places in the text. This book is dedicated to the late Abdul Hamid M. el-Zein, a friend who in his own work sought to make anthropology a self-renewing form of philosophical and social inquiry which could transcend the intellectual traditions of "East" and "West," an aspiration which I fully share.

Dale F. Eickelman
Ḥamrā', Sultanate of Oman

# note on transliteration

One of the first books which I read on the Middle East was Carleton Coon's *Caravan*.[1] As a beginning student of Arabic, I appreciated his careful transcription. It facilitated my identification of unfamiliar terms, and for languages that I did not speak it gave me a general idea of how words were spoken. In a time of publishing economies, the willingness of Prentice-Hall to allow the full transcription of terms from Middle Eastern languages, particularly Arabic, reflects a concern for editorial quality that can no longer be taken for granted. I have in general followed the conventions of the *International Journal of Middle East Studies,* although in deciding on how to transliterate colloquial terms I have attempted to follow the pronunciation of the area being discussed. For Arabic, the stroke over a vowel indicates it is lengthened: $\bar{a}$ as in ma, $\bar{\imath}$ as in bean, and $\bar{u}$ as in noon; *ay* as in pay is a diphthong. The emphatic consonants (*ḍ, ṣ, ṭ, ẓ, ḥ*) are indicated by dots under them; *kh* is pronounced as in Bach; *gh* as the *r* of Parisian French. The ᶜayn has been rendered with a small, raised ᶜ, and the *hamza,* a glottal stop as in the Brooklynese "bottle," with an apostrophe ('). Often in spoken language, even in educated speech, the *hamza* is dropped; but I have included it in transliteration in those instances where it seemed necessary to do so. Except where otherwise noted, only the singular form of Arabic words is indicated, with -*s* added for plurals. Adjectival forms of many

[1] Carleton S. Coon, *Caravan: The Story of the Middle East,* rev. ed. (New York: Holt, Rinehart and Winston, Inc., 1961).

Arabic place names and words are indicated with an ī at the end of the word, as in Arabic. Words and place names with common English forms appear as they do in English and are not fully transliterated. Thus Mecca, not Makka; Fez, not Fās; Quran, not Qur'ān; Allah, not Allāh; Islam, not Islām; and sultan, not sulṭān. Richard Bulliet of Columbia University has kindly checked the accuracy of transliterated Persian and Turkish words.

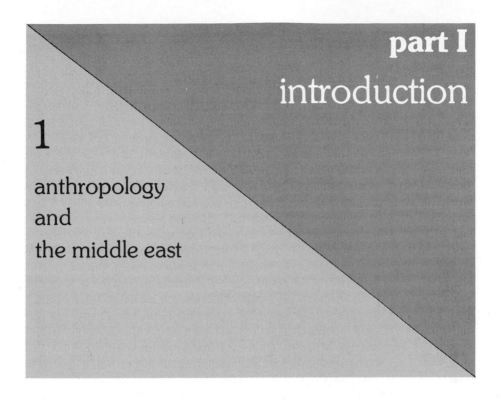

# part I
# introduction

## 1

## anthropology
## and
## the middle east

### THE MIDDLE EAST DEFINED

The term "Middle East" appears clear when it is employed in general common-sense contexts, especially those which imply a contrast with other regions of the world. Yet scholars interested in the region are usually ambivalent about the term. The late Marshall Hodgson reluctantly conceded that of all the terms used to describe the area it was probably the best, but nonetheless proceeded to banish it from his majestic *Venture of Islam* in favor of a private terminology which he considered to be free of all traces of Western ethnocentrism.[1] Another historian recently expressed dissatisfaction with the term in an article entitled "Is There a Middle East?" but concluded, after a useful excursus on the characteristics which unite and divide the region, that it remains the best term available.[2]

The specialist's reluctance to speak of a "Middle East" without providing an extensive gloss on the term is due to the circumstances surrounding its origins. Just like older, more geographically limited labels such as "the Near East" and "the Levant" that remain in use, the term "Middle East" was not coined by inhabitants of the region. It originated with nineteenth-century European military strategists

---

[1] Marshall G. S. Hodgson, *The Venture of Islam,* Vol. 1 (Chicago: University of Chicago Press, 1974), pp. 60-62.
[2] Nikki R. Keddie, "Is There a Middle East?" *International Journal of Middle East Studies,* 4 (1973), 255-71.

and thus is unabashedly Euro-centered. In the geopolitics of the English military, for example, the "Middle East" meant the command responsible for the region from the Nile to the Oxus; the lands to the east of the Oxus belonged to their Indian command.[3] In terms of civilizational boundaries such a division made little sense since it cut the historically united (or at least interacting) Iranian plateau in two, but after all the term was not coined with scholars in mind.

In contrast, the terms most commonly used to describe North Africa are more sharply defined, although once again this is largely due to the manner in which the region was divided by European colonial powers. In the first place, the term "North Africa" should not be taken literally. It is almost never used by area specialists to include Egypt. It is generally taken to mean Morocco, Algeria, Tunisia, and Libya. For Arab-speakers this region is generally known as the "Maghrib," a term which literally means the West and, more poetically, the land where the sun sets. This usage clearly indicates the geopolitics of an earlier epoch, that of the first waves of Muslim invaders in the seventh and eighth centuries. The term "Maghrib" is popularly used in French as well, largely because the region, less Libya and a narrow mountainous zone in northern Morocco ceded by the French to Spain, was under French colonial domination until recent times. Even in this more compact region, the imposition of colonial boundaries created distinctions which are still significant even though the period of European colonial domination is over. The country known today as the Islamic Republic of Mauritania was considered by Arab geographers as part of the Maghrib and toward the beginning of the twentieth century also came under effective French rule. Yet because it was attached to French West Africa and administered from Dakar it is often considered not to be part of the Middle East, despite the fact that the majority of its population is Muslim and Arabic-speaking, and the country is a member of the Arab League. The Sudan, despite its large non-Muslim, non-Arabic-speaking minority, has no such difficulty in being considered part of the Middle East, but again this is largely due to the accident of spheres of colonial rule—it fell under Egyptian rule about 1830, and by the end of the nineteenth century was ruled by what was formerly an Anglo-Egyptian condominium.

In contemporary usage the "Middle East" is taken to encompass the region stretching from Rabat to Tehran, a distance of roughly 3,400 miles. This is equal to the distance from New York City to Fairbanks, Alaska. To give another indication of its vastness the Middle East includes territory on the three continents of Africa, Asia, and Europe (the European section of Turkey). When certain features of the linguistic, religious, political, and historical complexities of the region are emphasized, it is often extended to encompass Afghanistan, Pakistan, and, at least in the recent historical past, the states of Soviet Central Asia that are heavily influenced by Islam.

In this broader sense the Middle East has often been characterized as a "mosaic." Despite the popularity of this metaphor, it has significant drawbacks for

[3]Hodgson, *Venture*, pp. 60-61.

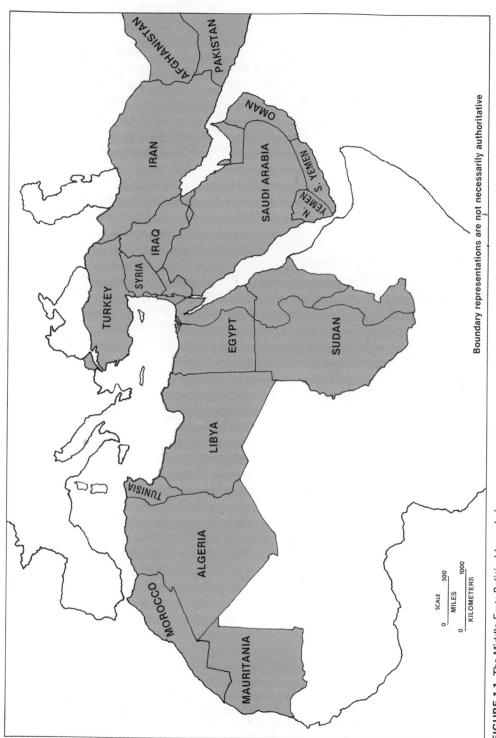

Boundary representations are not necessarily authoritative

**FIGURE 1-1** The Middle East: Political boundaries.

the purposes of modern social anthropology, for it does little more than indicate the fact of significant internal regional differentiation. One of the basic arguments of this book is that the juxtaposition of a range of cultural and noncultural features in the Middle East does not in itself make the region unique. Such a "mosaic" characterization can be equally applied to the Indian subcontinent, Southeast Asia, the Balkans, and the Soviet Union, among other locales. Rather, it is the presence throughout the area of key cultural symbols and their variants and through shared historical circumstances that this region can justifiably be considered as a single sociocultural area.

In historical terms the area designated by this broader, contemporary usage of the term "Middle East" coincides roughly with the first wave of Arab invasions and with the three largest Muslim empires at their greatest extent—the Umayyad (661-750), the early Abbasid (750-ca.-800), and the Ottoman as it was from the six-teenth through the eighteenth centuries. Geographically the region also shares common characteristics. As a whole, it is semiarid and characterized by the prevalence of irrigation agriculture and pastoral nomadism. However, it is not fully delineated by natural frontiers. Although the region is partially cut off from sub-Saharan Africa and from the Indo-Pakistani subcontinent by mountains and deserts, its present northern boundaries with the Soviet Muslim territories, for example, are more political than natural.

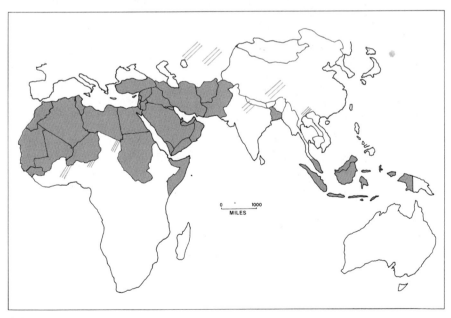

**FIGURE 1-2** Muslims in the world today. Shaded areas: majority population; areas with tranverse lines: minority population. (Adapted from *Aramco Handbook,* rev. ed. [Dhahran: Arabian American Oil Company, 1968] , p. 230.)

Seen in terms of social and cultural features, the boundaries of the Middle East are more elusive. The region is closely identified with Islam and is where Islam won its first adherents, but thinking of it as a heartland of Islam can lead to a distorted view of Islamic civilization. Muslims today are situated in a wide band which ranges from Indonesia and the Philippines through the Indo-Pakistani sub-continent, Soviet Central Asia, Iran, and Turkey to the Arabic-speaking regions of the Middle East and North Africa and Black Africa. The epicenter of the total Muslim population lies between Iran and Pakistan, on the eastern edge of the area with which this book is concerned.

Similarly, Arabic is often thought of as the language principally identified with Islam and the Middle East, yet unless qualified this assumption also engenders serious distortions, one of which is to diminish the role attributed to Persian culture in Islamic civilization. Although Arabic today is the principal language of the largest part of the Middle East, this was not always the case. For a considerable period after the initial Islamic conquests of the seventh century, Arabic had still not become the principal language of either commoners or the indigenous elite of many of the conquered regions. Likewise, during the period of the hegemony of the Ottoman Empire from the fifteenth through the eighteenth centuries, Ottoman Turkish tended to be the principal lingua franca of the elite in much of the region. Persian was also commonly employed in a similar role in regions beyond those where it is spoken today.

The majority of the region's inhabitants are Muslim, but only occasionally has this fact provided a base of common sentiment and identity. Currently an ethnic irredentism based upon common language is on the upsurge in the Middle East as elsewhere in the world, but this was not always the case. Thus for over half a century the elite of Turkey have stressed their ties with Europe more than those with their Muslim neighbors. Egyptian elites prior to the 1950s, and again in this decade in certain contexts, stressed the Mediterranean identity of their country as much as its Arab or Middle Eastern identity. The same is true for the various countries of North Africa. Historians such as Fernand Braudel have persuasively argued the case for considering the countries on both sides of the Mediterranean as a single society for extended historical periods.[4]

To sum up, despite its drawbacks, the term "Middle East" continues to be the most acceptable of available terms, provided that it is not taken unreflectively to indicate a homogeneity which the region does not possess, much as is suggested by the misleading concept of the "Arab mind" which has recently resurfaced in some popular literature. Alternatives are occasionally introduced, such as the acronym SWANA (South West Asia and North Africa), and justified on the ground that they are completely devoid of all historical, political, and religious assumptions. Yet all such terms suffer equally from unfamiliarity. Furthermore, it is precisely the shifting cultural and historical realities that must be taken into account in any meaning-

---

[4]Fernand Braudel, *The Mediterranean and the Mediterranean World in the Age of Philip II* (New York: Harper & Row, 1975).

ful study of the region, whatever initial difficulties such complexities may offer. In any case, whatever the origin of the term "Middle East," it is now employed in a fairly neutral, descriptive sense by Middle Easterners themselves and is used in the same way in this book.


## ANTHROPOLOGY: SOME PRACTICAL ASSUMPTIONS

Anthropology as an academic discipline is notoriously difficult to define, yet a brief sketch of its nature is essential to indicate its unique contribution to the study of a region such as the Middle East. Many of the anthropological studies referred to in this book use specialized terms in different and occasionally incompatible ways. By indicating some of the broader theoretical issues which are implicit in such usages, these differences can be seen for what they are—references to broader intellectual concerns rather than being inconsistencies of writing or thought.

In an earlier, theoretically less reflective era, social anthropology was commonly—although imprecisely—defined as that branch of sociology most concerned with the study of small-scale, technologically simple, nonliterate societies. Now that sociologists, political scientists, economists, and historians rub elbows with anthropologists in the study of both complex and "simple" societies, such a casual division of labor—always a questionable one—is now fully inadequate. Hence two questions must be raised. The first concerns the nature of an *anthropological* study of a complex or simple society and the extent to which such a study can be differentiated from those of history and the other disciplines of the social sciences. A second issue, introduced here and implicitly answered by the structure of this book, is the means by which anthropological techniques developed largely in the context of the study of small-scale societies and small groups can contribute to the study of major civilizational areas. By specifying some of the central concerns of anthropological inquiry or, to be more precise, the style of anthropological inquiry developed in this book, I suggest a view of anthropology less heroic than a literal reading of our discipline's name—the science of man—implies, but which at the same time more accurately represents its unique contribution to the human sciences.

The difficulty in defining anthropology reflects less a confusion on the part of its practitioners than the nature of anthropological inquiry itself. The discipline does not exhibit the features of what Thomas Kuhn calls a "normal" science. There is no clear agreement among its leading practitioners upon a central paradigm for research or upon the nature of the questions to be asked.[5] For this reason the discipline is intractable to ordinary textbook treatment. Indeed, it is one of the few major disciplines for which even the Educational Testing Service appears to have despaired, at least for the time being, of determining a body of orthodox

[5] Thomas S. Kuhn, *The Structure of Scientific Revolutions,* 2nd ed. (Chicago: University of Chicago Press, 1970).

knowledge for which competence can be measured by objective testing. To adapt Kuhn's concepts to my immediate argument, anthropology is an anormal science.[6] In an anormal field of inquiry, competence in the discipline is acquired by joining its central debates at any given moment.

In England and the United States, anthropology has existed as a formal academic discipline only since the turn of the century but had been a clearly demarcated field of inquiry for several decades before then. Since that time, like the other human sciences, its central concerns have shifted. In the late nineteenth century, anthropology was closely linked with Darwinian concepts of human evolution, so that the techniques and data of what are today separate subdisciplines— social and cultural anthropology (then less grandly known as *ethnography*), linguistics, archaeology, and physical anthropology—were all loosely united. New frames of reference and methodologies have tended to draw these subdisciplines apart for many purposes although the departmental structure of most American universities still reflects the nineteenth century organization of the discipline.

The lack of a common central paradigm in anthropology makes it difficult to convey the concerns of the anthropologists, especially a sociocultural anthropologist, to nonspecialists. In 1950 Edward Evans-Pritchard, a leading British anthropologist, sought to depict the nature of social anthropology to the English public in a series of radio lectures. He began by admitting that for most persons, anthropology still conjures up hazy connotations of apes and skulls, primitive rites, and curious superstitions.[7] This image of anthropology is of course far from reality; although, given the lack of theoretical orthodoxy, hard and fast characterizations are difficult to make. Thus, the account of the discipline that follows should be considered as a set of working guidelines rather than dogma.

A cultural or social anthropologist studies contemporary or historically well-known societies and is concerned with describing, analyzing, and comparing patterns of order in them. *Cultural* anthropologists have tended to be concerned with the key symbols through which persons in a given society make sense of the world about them and proceed to act in it. Until the last two decades, this emphasis upon the study of patterns of meaning has been the dominant American contribution to anthropology. *Social* anthropologists have traditionally been more concerned with the study of regularities in observed social organization and in the ideas held by a society about such organization—how the domestic and public activities of social groups are organized and the consequences of this organization. A concern with such issues has been until recently a dominant characteristic of British anthropology. It is true that the monographs of most anthropologists emphasize one concern or the other, but in practice the distinction that used to be made between

---

[6]I prefer the neologism *anormal* to *abnormal* because the latter term implies that an established body of orthodoxy is necessary and desirable in all the sciences and an indication of disciplinary health.

[7]E. E. Evans-Pritchard, *Social Anthropology and Other Essays* (New York: The Free Press, 1964), p. 1.

social and cultural anthropology has become increasingly blurred in recent years as the practitioners of the discipline have begun to converge in their key theoretical assumptions. For all practical purposes, the labels of *social* and *cultural* anthropology are now interchangeable and are used to encompass more recent theoretical developments as well. My own preference is to use the term *social anthropology* to encompass what others now designate by the compromise term of *sociocultural* anthropology. I spell out these flexible usages to avoid unnecessary terminological confusion.

As an enthusiast of my discipline, I recognize that I am passing over several lively theoretical debates of the moment. I am doing this so as not to get bogged down in a technical discussion of the merits of Levi-Straussian structuralism, the nearly cryptological study of symbols favored by others, the reemergence of a somewhat musty evolutionary perspective to the study of society, or other sets of concerns. Instead, I briefly sketch the nature of the discipline as it specifically relates to the study of the Middle East, although throughout the text I refer to other approaches.

In the first place, anthropology, or at least a major tradition within it, is a human science—and as such shares many common features with history, the other major discipline through which the study of major civilizational areas is undertaken. Some anthropologists seek legitimacy for their enterprise by claiming that their goal is to develop universal "laws" of social organization or of cultural order which are somehow independent of specific societies or historical realities. Despite occasional programmatic essays proclaiming this goal, the enduring core of the discipline is contained in detailed, monographic studies of specific societies and cultures. Admittedly, one leading anthropologist, Edmund Leach, has written that he finds the details of ethnography dull, especially the details of other persons' ethnographies. Yet he is also the first to admit that such details, and the means by which they are interconnected, are the essence of anthropological inquiry.[8]

Comparative studies of societies and cultures are possible on the basis of such ethnographic studies, but the order thus discerned is not of the sort discerned by the natural scientist. In some sciences, such as physics, chemistry, and geology, the patterns of order which are described and analyzed are the products of communication among fellow specialists. There is no question of their speaking with the objects of their study. In anthropology and the other human sciences, like history, the notion of objectivity acquires a special meaning, since the anthropologist must discern the meaning behind a social act in order to comprehend it. Briefly stated, humans are cultural animals. They communicate with others and comprehend the world through ordered, shared systems of symbols. Anthropologists are usually much more concerned with making explicit the underlying logic of these shared patterns of meaning and codes of conduct than are historians, but such patterns must be presumed to exist in the work of both disciplines.

---

[8] Leach first expressed this opinion in 1954 and reiterated it in *Culture and Communication* (New York: Cambridge University Press, 1976), p. 1.

The problem of making explicit such shared meanings has been called the "translation of cultures." This problem is most vivid in working with the small-scale, relatively isolated groups which have traditionally been the concern of anthropologists, for in such societies such basic concepts as *time, space,* and *person,* along with other aspects of the nature of the social order, are likely to be substantially removed from our own concepts. At the same time, such notions are often so taken-for-granted that they usually are not fully expressed by those who share a given cultural tradition. Yet the explanation of such implicit concepts is central to making sense of other societies and cultures. Such problems of translation are just as real for anthropologists studying the rich, complex civilizations of the Middle East; although at first sight there is much more that is at least superficially known about shared patterns of meaning and social action in such societies. The same problem equally exists for a contemporary historian studying, for example, early nineteenth-century sectarian movements in upstate New York when he or she seeks to determine exactly what was the significance to audiences in that period of the frenzied descriptions of the terrors of hell contained in surviving written copies of sermons. In the New York case, the problem of translation initially appears less obvious, as the historian can "get by," although imperfectly, through a substitution of contemporary attitudes. My point is that *some* set of hypotheses as to the underlying patterns of the social order must be made in order to render such evidence intelligible. Thus, the historian will seek systematically to state what is known or knowable about the beliefs and the social order of the earlier period, just as the anthropologist does in the study of any contemporary society, including his own.

So far I have concentrated on the similarities between history and social anthropology. Both entail abstractions from social reality and the comprehension of the shared social meanings which constitute such reality. History differs from social anthropology in the type of abstraction which is made from this reality, although this is more a difference of degree than of kind. A common-sense way of conceiving history has been to consider it as simply a record of what happened in the past along with the discipline concerned in eliciting this record. Yet a moment's reflection (as Malinowski was fond of saying) makes it clear that any coherent narrative concerning the past requires abstractions from reality. Sartre has aphoristically defined history as "the deliberate resumption of the past by the present" and thus captures at least part of the enterprise involved.[9] Whether the historian is concerned with the Battle of Algiers or the 1933 World Series, no account would be duller or less meaningful than one which naively attempted to gather all relevant documents while imposing no order upon them. The historian must sift through what is known of events and then abstract from them, discarding data that fail to contribute to a "story." The historian's primary goal is to elicit the circumstances that are unique to a given event or to a sequence of events. The

---

[9] Jean Paul Sartre, *Literary and Philosophic Essays* (New York: Collier Books, 1962), p. 206.

resulting explanations only partially entail the determination of fact: The more difficult issue, as the French sociologist Raymond Aron has emphasized, is in deciding the best way of arranging the facts to make them intelligible. Unlike scientific explanations, which can be tested and confirmed through success with parallel cases, historical explanations cannot be tested in the same way. Instead, the best historical explanation is the one which is "most consistent, plausible, and in accordance with all the evidence."[10]

The historian may seek primarily to explain specific events but must still rely upon sociological (or social anthropological) abstractions about the nature of religious beliefs, political relations, and the like in a given society in order to proceed with his narrative. The goal of the social anthropologist is complementary to that of the historian in that the social anthropologist is primarily interested in attempts to elicit and to confirm recurrent regularities in a society—such as the relation of certain systems of belief to social action, the nature of symbol systems, and the relation of types of political authority to various ideas of social inequality. Such explanations are closely intertwined with the understanding of specific historical events. Raymond Aron has gone so far as to say that the job of the sociologist—and sociology as he uses the term encompasses social anthropology as well—is "to render social or historical content more intelligible than it was in the experience of those who lived it."[11]

The relation between history and social anthropology has often been obscured by theorists who presume that because historical and sociological explanations are separable as ideal types, the actual work of historians and sociologists is equally separable.[12] Even a casual comparison of key monographs in social anthropology and in history indicates that the two forms of explanation are necessarily complementary. Marc Bloch's *Feudal Society* contains long sections on the ideas of fealty and kinship and notions of equality and hierarchy in the social order of Europe over a specific historical period that are as sociological in character as similar passages in Edmund Leach's *Political Systems of Highland Burma.*[13] At the risk of shocking my anthropological colleagues, I think that Bloch's study can even be considered the superior of the two studies because the nature of his documentation is more carefully described and integrated into his principal conceptual argu-

---

[10] Raymond Aron, *Introduction to the Philosophy of History* (London: Weidenfeld and Nicolson, 1961), p. 124.

[11] Raymond Aron, *Main Currents in Sociological Thought,* Vol. 2, trans. Richard Howard and Helen Weaver (New York: Doubleday/Anchor Books, 1970), p. 245. A similar argument, based in part upon the arguments of classic anthropological monographs, can be found in W. G. Runciman, *Sociology in Its Place and Other Essays* (Cambridge: Cambridge University Press, 1970), pp. 1-44.

[12] An extreme formulation of this notion which for a time blocked a more sophisticated consideration of the nature of anthropological thought can be found in A. R. Radcliffe-Brown, *Structure and Function in Primitive Society* (London: Cohen and West, Ltd., 1952), pp. 1-3.

[13] Marc Bloch, *Feudal Society* (Chicago: University of Chicago Press, 1964 [orig. 1939-1940]); Edmund Leach, *Political Systems of Highland Burma* (Boston: Beacon Press, 1965 [orig. 1954]).

ment, while the argument in *Political Systems,* for all its iconoclastic brilliance, is more crudely drawn.

Some forms of anthropological explanation at first appear to fall outside the general framework sketched above, such as the seminal example of "pure" symbolic analysis provided by David Schneider's *American Kinship: A Cultural Account.*[14] For the sake of clarity, Schneider deliberately set aside questions of historical development in order to concentrate upon the logical interrelations among the key cultural symbols of kinship. Such an approach does not deny the importance of historical context. Moreover, as Schneider emphasizes, the *style* of analysis which he used to delineate relations among the key symbols which define ideas of kinship in American culture can be applied to other cultures as well—many such studies now have been carried out—but the direct comparisons of symbols and clusters of symbols about kinship in two or more societies does not lead to any meaningful generalizations which can be applied to cultures in general. A comparison of American cultural ideas of kinship with those held, for instance, by Moroccans facilitates an understanding of what is unique and distinctive about ideas of person and of relationships among them in each case. Such implicit and explicit comparisons are, of course, also used by historians in making sense of their data.

So far I have discussed the nature of historical and sociological explanation in general, but I have not indicated what is distinctly "anthropological" about anthropological research. In terms of the theoretical base upon which anthropologists draw, there is little that is unique to our discipline or to any of the other social sciences. All draw equally upon the works of Marx, Weber, Durkheim, Simmel, and their successors. As I indicated earlier, the study of distinctively "primitive" societies is no longer the hallmark of the discipline, nor is the intensive research technique called "fieldwork" exclusive to us. Yet, because anthropologists emphasize fieldwork as a principal technique, a description of anthropology in terms of what anthropologists do may facilitate distinguishing it from neighboring disciplines.

To prepare for fieldwork, in addition to immersion in anthropological monographs and sociological theory, an anthropologist characteristically, or at least ideally, spends several years learning the language and history of a region. Fieldwork itself generally lasts for a year or two and concentrates upon a particular small-scale group or groups. Evans-Pritchard's definition of anthropology as that branch of sociology concerned with small-scale societies is now dated, although it reflects the primary concern of the discipline until the early 1950s. The reason for this emphasis on small-scale, "primitive" societies was that in them most significant social relations were assumed to be face-to-face and geographically self-contained. Under these circumstances it was easier for the anthropologist to see the links between institutions—family and kinship relations, friendship and patron-client ties, land tenure, inheritance rules and practices, religious rituals, beliefs, politics, and, most importantly, the shared symbolic conceptions of the world that underlie these

[14] David M. Schneider, *American Kinship: A Cultural Account* (Englewood Cliffs, N.J.: Prentice-Hall, Inc., 1968).

various forms of behavior.[15] On the basis of the intensive study of such societies (or, increasingly today, of small groups within larger societies), the anthropologist then proceeds to the hardest job, that of creating out of the record of research a coherent representation of a society and the general principles of order within it. More self-consciously than most historians, the anthropologist relates this task to general theoretical issues.

Now that anthropologists are, or try to be, as much at home in cities, towns, villages, and regions encapsulated within modern and complex societies, as in the rapidly disappearing isolated and small-scale societies, the question of how the microsociological technique of fieldwork—the intensive, totalistic study of social forms—contributes to understanding larger units of society becomes more pressing than when they could claim the study of certain types of society for their own. How can the microsociological study of an anthropologist contribute to the understanding of larger entities such as nation-states? As Clifford Geertz has asked with characteristic irony: "Are the petty squabbles of barnyard notables really what we mean by politics? Are mud huts and goat-skin tents really where the action is?"[16] Is there not the danger of getting lost in "mindless descriptivism" in the study of a pilgrimage center in Morocco or a tribe in the Yemen, or at least of learning more about these entities than one really wants to know?

A constant theme of this book is to demonstrate that anthropologists, or most anthropologists anyway, study specific places not for themselves or for the love of minute description of routine events in exotic places, but in order to learn something beyond them. We do intensive analyses of political, economic, symbolic, and historical processes on a small scale. Like all other disciplines in the social sciences, we use our data as a means of making hypotheses about larger wholes. As Geertz emphasizes, the question is not whether we generalize—any science generalizes—but *how* we generalize. And that is important. In the human sciences, the microsociological technique of anthropology offers an alternative to the tendency to speak of tribe and peasants, of rulers and ruled, as if they were stock characters in a sociological morality play.[17]

Anthropologists are particularly concerned with eliciting the taken-for-granted, shared meanings that underlie conduct in given societies and are so familiar

[15]The definition of *institution* varies significantly in the social sciences. By the term I mean customary, accepted ways of doing things in a given society. The emphasis in this definition is upon the culturally shared patterns of meaning and mutual expectations which underlie such conventions. For what I regard as the best account of the *psychological* aspect of the relations of the anthropologist and those cultures studied, and the consequences of this relationship for how the anthropologist conceptualizes social experience, see Vincent Crapanzano, *Tuhami: Portrait of a Moroccan* (Chicago and London: University of Chicago Press, 1980).

[16]Clifford Geertz, "Comments," in *Rural Politics and Social Change in the Middle East,* eds. Richard Antoun and Iliya Harik (Bloomington and London: Indiana University Press, 1972), p. 460. The discussion of these issues which follows owes much to Geertz's succinct presentation of the issues in pp. 460-67 of the Antoun and Harik volume.

[17]Geertz, *ibid.,* p. 463.

a part of routine that they are taken to be "natural." It is against such undramatic backgrounds that citizens participate in nation-states or have contact with the governments of such entities, or even form a part of such governments. The petty squabbles of barnyard notables, as Geertz says, may not in themselves be of compelling interest, but they frequently offer a more advantageous means of determining the components of a political style than do the more formal and generally less accessible deliberations of parliaments and cabinet meetings. The link between the unit of the anthropologist's study and the larger whole is not that of microcosm to macrocosm—as an earlier generation of community studies often naively assumed—but merely that of an arena the study of which permits the elaboration of hypotheses about certain social and cultural processes. Through the study of such mundane events as patterns of naming, seeking a husband or wife, the ways in which sickness is cured, the selling of a sheep, local elections, and religious ceremonies, anthropologists seek to grasp what is distinctly Moroccan about Moroccan markets, Lebanese about Lebanese political factionalism, Alevi about Alevi conceptions of Islam, Omani about Omani notions of honor, or Egyptian about Egyptian styles of etiquette and deference. Even the citizens of nation-states find themselves living most of their lives in the sets of microcosms that make up such larger entities. The microsociological perspective of the anthropologist can often provide valuable insights into just how participation in such larger entities is experienced.

To sum up the argument so far, social anthropologists and historians pursue styles of explanation that are complementary and interchangeable in many respects. Just as in history the search for universal laws devoid of specific content leads only to trivial or false generalizations, similarly the search for laws in social anthropological research is unfruitful. Yet, through comparison of different societies and cultures and through careful attention to technique and theoretical assumptions, anthropologists seek an understanding of what is distinctive about general processes operating in specific historical and culture settings. Some anthropologists conduct research within less comprehensive but nonetheless useful theoretical frameworks. Cultural ecologists, for instance, are primarily interested in the relations between individuals and their environment in societies that generally are technologically simple and for such a purpose do not require a broader theoretical base. This book makes reference to such approaches in appropriate contexts.

Having briefly stated what is characteristic of the anthropological approach to the study of society, we now consider the ways in which this approach contributes to an understanding of the Middle East and the particular anthropological themes most fully developed in the study of the region.

## FIRST APPROXIMATIONS

Not long after the French Protectorate over Morocco began in 1912, a popular scholarly literature on Islam and on Arabs in that country began to flourish in the French language. By the 1920s the production of popular books on Islam and

Morocco had become a minor industry, so that Georges Hardy, a prominent colonial administrator of the period, was able to publish a synthesis of the vast literature. Hardy's chapter on Moroccan "character" gives some indication of the approach which was used to grasp the "mysteries" of the Orient of which Morocco was considered a part. Hardy juxtaposed a series of contrasts: Moroccans were said to be both individualistic and gregarious, anarchic and despotic, intellectually lethargic and avidly pragmatic, serene and impulsive, reliable and fickle, artistic and uncreative, Muslims and animists, morally scrupulous and evasive.[18] An equivalent juxtaposition of opposites was used to describe such mundane things as climate and geography.

A consideration of these earlier colonial images of Morocco is important because of their influence on later attempts to characterize the Middle East as a whole. Carleton Coon, who wrote the first general anthropological survey of the region, lived and worked for extended periods in Morocco in the 1930s. When he came to write the first edition of *Caravan* in the late 1940s, he used the image of the mosaic, implicit in earlier writing on Morocco, as his guiding metaphor in order to highlight the geographic, linguistic, religious, and ethnic complexities of the region in general.[19] In a descriptive sense the mosaic metaphor is useful, although its major shortcomings are discussed in Chapter 3.

The object of the rest of this chapter is to indicate some of the general characteristics of the Middle East, beginning with certain geographic factors. This is because, at least traditionally, geographic factors have formed broad constraints within which the societies of the Middle East have developed.

As a whole, the Middle East can be characterized by three basic geographical features: It is semiarid (although there are local exceptions to this condition); it is a region which since antiquity has been one of agriculture (since at least 8000 B.C.) and empire; and, as mentioned earlier, it lacks sharply defined natural boundaries, so that it has always been accessible to conquest by land and sea, and it has long served as a crossroads of long-distance trade. Of course, the same is true of most other major sociocultural regions of the world. These characteristics thus do not serve to distinguish the Middle East from other major sociocultural areas, but they do constitute major factors of relevance to historical developments and the kinds of lives lived in the region.

As Figure 1-3 indicates, few places in the Middle East receive the forty to fifty inches of rainfall which is characteristic of the eastern United States and the richer agricultural regions of Europe. Some coastal and mountain areas receive up to twenty inches annually, but many other regions receive as little as four to eight inches annually (Saudi Arabia) or less than one inch a year (southern Egypt). Rainfall-fed, or nonirrigated, farming is possible only in relatively narrow belts of Syria, Turkey, Lebanon, Iran, Jordan, and the countries of the Maghrib. Even in these

---

[18] Georges Hardy, *L'Ame Marocaine d'après la Littérature Française* (Paris: Librairie Larose, 1926), pp. 20-67.
[19] Carleton S. Coon, *Caravan: The Story of the Middle East,* rev. ed. (New York: Holt, Rinehart and Winston, Inc., 1961 [orig. 1951]).

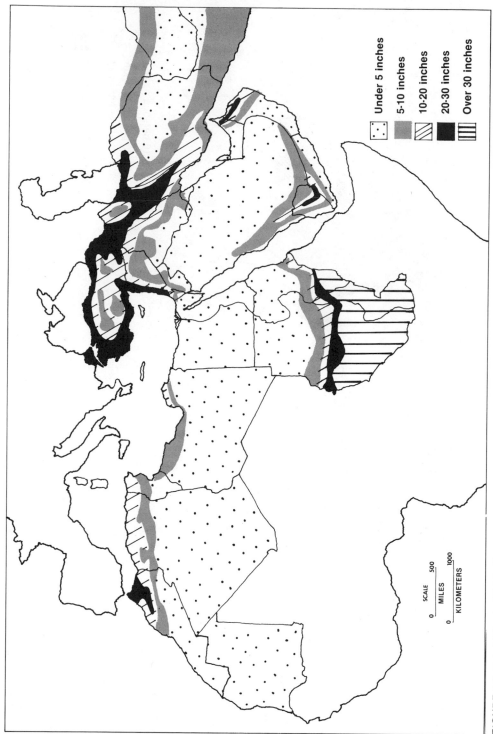

Under 5 inches
5-10 inches
10-20 inches
20-30 inches
Over 30 inches

SCALE
0 ___500
MILES
0 ___1000
KILOMETERS

FIGURE 1-3 Rainfall in the Middle East.

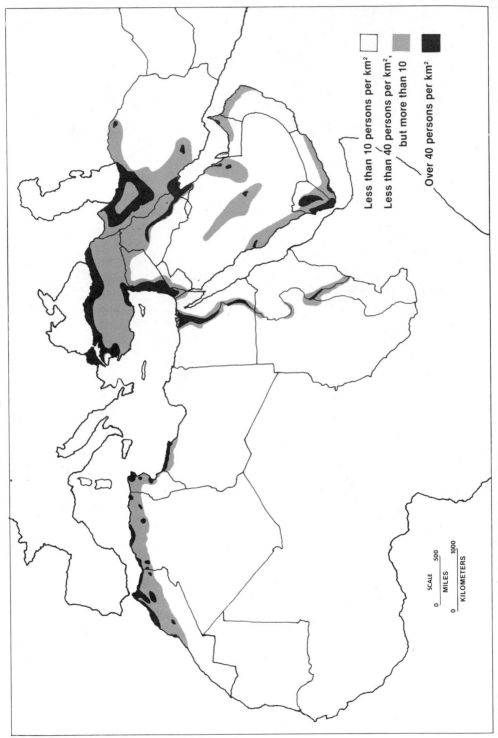

**FIGURE 1-4** Population density of the Middle East, c. 1970.

Less than 10 persons per km²

Less than 40 persons per km², but more than 10

Over 40 persons per km²

SCALE
0        500
MILES
0        1000
KILOMETERS

cases, the amount of rain varies substantially from year to year and radical annual shifts in rainfall and climatic conditions are the rule. Where there is heavy rainfall, as in the Rif mountains of northern Morocco, the soils are often too poor to permit regular, adequate agricultural yields.

Nonetheless, agriculture is important throughout the region. By 1970 figures, over 95 percent of the Middle East's rural population is sedentary and lives from agriculture, although only 14 percent of the total land surface is arable.[20] Thus the popular image of the Middle East as nomads traveling between oases on the desert is misleading. To a large extent, however, agriculture is dependent upon irrigation. A glance at the population map of the Middle East indicates how dramatically many of the centers of population cluster around sources of water for agriculture. Thus for Egypt, cultivation is confined to a few miles on either side of the Nile, although on the Nile Delta and in Iraq between the Tigris and Euphrates rivers, there are intricate webs of irrigation channels that support relatively dense populations. Elsewhere throughout the Middle East there are other sorts of irrigation systems, both traditional and modern, adapted to local circumstances. Wells often are a source of water, although in Iran and in regions of Morocco such as Marrakesh, there are elaborate underground canals (called *ghaṭṭāra* in Morocco, *qanāt* in Iran, and *aflāj* in Oman) that carry water from underground streams in nearby mountain regions to the rich oases of the plains. Modern technology has greatly expanded the regions that have been brought under cultivation.

Because it is semiarid, large parts of the Middle East traditionally have been given over to a mode of livelihood that combines the extensive seasonal cultivation of crops such as wheat and barley with semitranshumant pastoralism, especially of sheep and goats. Pastoral nomadism as the sole or predominant activity of certain groups to the full exclusion of cultivation is today relatively rare; although when considered together with transhumant pastoralists, nomads still form a significant (although rapidly declining) minority in such countries as Saudi Arabia (probably between 11 and 20 percent), Iran (10 percent), Afghanistan (16 percent or more), and less than 5 percent of the population of the countries of North Africa, with the exception of Libya and Mauritania. Only in Somalia have nomads until recently constituted a majority of the population (about 75 percent in the early 1970s).[21]

---

[20] Peter Beaumont, Gerald H. Blake, and J. Malcolm Wagstaff, *The Middle East: A Geographical Study* (New York: John Wiley & Sons, 1976), pp. 160, 184-85. The limits of the Middle East as defined by Beaumont, Blake, and Wagstaff exclude all of the Maghrib except Libya, so these statistics should be regarded as approximate.

[21] These figures are derived from Donald Powell Cole, *Nomads of the Nomads* (Chicago: Aldine Publishing Company, 1975), p. 143, and Beaumont, Blake, and Wagstaff, *The Middle East*, p. 185. The tentative nature of all such overall estimates should always be kept in mind. To cite two extreme examples, population estimates for Afghanistan in 1968 ranged from 7 to 17 million. A census in Saudi Arabia in 1962-1963 (the results of which were never officially recognized) revealed the population to be only 3.9 million as opposed to earlier estimates of 7 million and a 1972 estimate of 8 million. See Beaumont, Blake, and Wagstaff, *The Middle East*, pp. 176-77, and Robert J. Lapham, "Population Policies in the Middle East and North Africa," *Middle East Studies Association Bulletin*, 11, no. 2 (May 1977), 16.

The significance of transhumant pastoralists and nomads has often been exaggerated as a factor in Middle Eastern history. Nonetheless, such groups have traditionally constituted political and military threats to effective central government in many regions, including Morocco and Iran. From at least 1500 to 1917 the Iranian polity was to some extent limited by the power of pastoral tribal groups. In the case of Morocco it was not so much the strength of pastoral groups as the strength of tribally organized societies, not necessarily pastoral, that limited the control of the central government until the effective imposition of the Protectorate.

Most Middle Eastern countries also possess mountainous regions—Kuwait and certain other Gulf states are some of the few exceptions. From premodern times to the present these regions have served as zones of refuge from central government control. Thus the Kurds of Iraq, Iran, and Turkey have been able to preserve a degree of autonomy, and Berber-speaking tribal groups in Algeria's Kabylia mountains and Morocco's Rif and Atlas mountain chains have managed to do so until the relatively recent past.

Traditionally, the Middle East may have been a region of irrigation agriculture and pastoralism, but for many of the countries of the region a significant mineral wealth, especially in oil, has created the potential for significant economic growth. Revenues from such resources have dramatically increased in recent years and have made possible substantial alterations in the social and material life of some of the region's inhabitants, especially in the cities.

The Middle East is a region of intense urban and commercial life, with ancient cities as Damascus, Cairo, and Istanbul, as well as those of much more recent origin, such as Riyadh and Casablanca. Over 40 percent of the region's inhabitants were urban dwellers in 1970, as opposed to roughly 10 percent in 1900.[22] The transformations occurring in these cities are not unique to the Middle East. The rapid rate of urbanization, for instance, is occurring throughout the Third World. In the chapters of this book concerned with the nature of cities these more general trends are considered, but the emphasis is upon the extent to which certain features of urban life continue to make these cities distinctly Turkish, Egyptian, Muslim, or Middle Eastern and how these culturally unique attributes influence and are affected by more general processes such as population growth and world economic currents.

In terms of religion, the Middle East as a whole is predominantly Muslim. One of the major issues that must be faced is how a world religion such as Islam has remained a vital force for over a millennium in such a wide range of cultural and social contexts. Islam has retained its significance because of its capacity to be reinterpreted in a variety of ways in different cultural contexts and in different strata of society. The mosaic metaphor sufficiently indicates some of these major contrasts in belief and ritual; although by and large this has not led to a more analytic consideration of their implications.

The Middle Eastern mosaic also contains significant Christian and Jewish minorities, with the obvious exception of the state of Israel in which Jews con-

[22] Lapham, *ibid.*, p. 4, and Beaumont, Blake, and Wagstaff, *The Middle East*, p. 185.

stitute a majority of the population. To consider Christians first, roughly 8 percent of Egypt's population is Christian (mostly Coptic), 20 percent of Syria and Iraq, and perhaps 40 percent of Lebanon. Exact statistics on the size of this minority are hard to obtain, especially in the case of Lebanon, where no census has been conducted since 1932 in an effort (which largely succeeded until 1975) to preserve a delicate political balance between various ethnic and religious groups: Maronite Christian, Armenian Greek Orthodox, Greek Catholic, Sunnī Muslim, Shīʿī Muslim, Palestinian Christians and Muslims, Druze, and other smaller groups. A significant question in this book is to determine precisely how such complex ethnic and religious identities are socially maintained in various situations.

Most of the countries of the Middle East have also possessed significant Jewish minorities, with the exception of Saudi Arabia and the states of the Persian/ Arab Gulf (which, however, have Hindu minorities). Jewish communities contracted in size after the creation of the state of Israel in 1948 and (more significantly in terms of sheer numbers) with the collapse of the colonial regimes of North Africa in the 1950s and 1960s and, in the east, the Iraqi revolution of 1958. Sizeable Jewish minorities remain, however, in Iran, Turkey, Tunisia, and Morocco. Another significant minority in many of the countries of North Africa were colonial settlers, who were predominantly, although not exclusively, of French, Spanish, and Italian origin. Elsewhere in the Middle East there have traditionally been thriving Greek and Armenian communities, especially in Egypt and Turkey, although since the beginning of this century their numbers have considerably diminished.

The major language groups of the Middle East have already been mentioned, but in many areas a number of languages and dialects of more limited scope also exist. In a small town of 12,000 inhabitants in northwestern Turkey recently studied by an anthropologist, virtually the entire population spoke mutually intelligible dialects of Turkish, but the older generation in the town continued to speak Circassian and Georgian.[23] Kurdish is widely spoken elsewhere in Turkey, which also has an Arabic-speaking minority. In northern Iraq, there is a bewildering array of ethnolinguistic communities: Kurdish-speaking gypsies, Kurds, Arabic-speaking pastoralists, and a range of groups with finely distinguished religious, ethnic, and linguistic identities. Similarly, in many border areas of the Middle East, such as between Iraq and Iran, most of the population is bilingual—Arabic and Persian in the case of the southerly portions of that particular border and trilingual (Arabic, Persian, and Kurdish) along its northernmost sections.

Similarly, there are large Berber-speaking populations in North Africa, although most of these are becoming increasingly bilingual in Arabic. In other regions, such as Egyptian and Sudanese Nubia, most of the male population is

---

[23] Paul Magnarella, *Tradition and Change in a Turkish Town* (New York: Halstead Press, 1974), p. 33. For a fuller account of Middle Eastern languages, see Gernot L. Windfuhr, "Linguistics," in *The Study of the Middle East*, ed. Leonard Binder (New York: John Wiley & Sons, 1976), pp. 347-97.

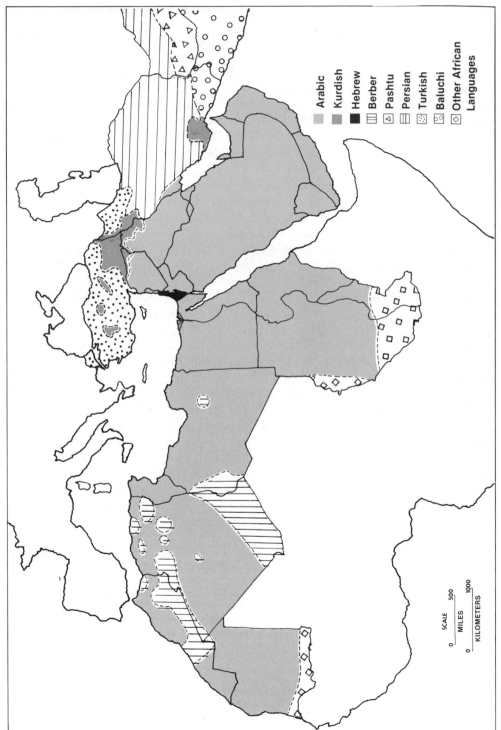

**FIGURE 1-5** Middle Eastern languages.

Legend:
- Arabic
- Kurdish
- Hebrew
- Berber
- Pashtu
- Persian
- Turkish
- Baluchi
- Other African Languages

SCALE
0    500
MILES
0    1000
KILOMETERS

bilingual in Arabic and a Nubian dialect, although use of the Nubian dialects is rapidly becoming limited to domestic contexts.[24]

European languages, especially those of the former colonial powers in certain regions, continue to be important in large parts of the Middle East. Arabic is the national language in all the countries of France's former North African colonies, but the urban educated population is predominantly bilingual in French and in Arabic. Algeria, Tunisia, and Morocco all have adopted official policies of Arabization; yet, after over two decades of independence in Morocco and Tunisia and a slightly lesser period for Algeria, many sections of the government bureaucracy continue to be run primarily in French. The French language remains significant in the schools as well, although Arabization at the elementary and secondary levels is progressing. A network of French educational institutions formally intended for the children of the remaining French still exists, although a number of children from elite North African families also attend these institutions. In the government-run schools French also continues to be important as a secondary language.

To sum up this section, I have tried to indicate enough of the dimensions of complexity in the Middle East to make it clear why expansive generalizations about the region are not always possible. General themes in social anthropology, such as inequality and the interconnection between religious belief and social forms, can be explored in the various societies of the region, but for reasons already discussed, no one part of the region can be taken as a direct microcosm of the others. In what way, then, can this book be said to encompass the Middle East as a whole?

The approach of this book is not encyclopedic, and I shall not attempt to cover equally all the countries of the Middle East. For reasons of historical accident and rapidly shifting political climates for research, American, European, Iranian, Arab, and Turkish anthropologists have been better able to conduct field studies in some areas than in others, just as the historical development of some countries has focused attention on specific issues. Thus many of the anthropological studies of Turkey by both indigenous and foreign researchers have concentrated upon the themes of modernization and nation-building, while those of North Africa have been intensely concerned with various aspects of the continuing impact of the colonial experience. Even if the various countries of the Middle East were equally known through anthropological studies, there would be little point in attempting a direct synthesis of these materials, any more than such an effort for Africa or Latin America would be intellectually rewarding. In general, my procedure will be to develop specific topics on the basis of the best available documentation for a particular country or region and then to sketch as far as possible how such patterns of kinship, political comportment, and the like compare with similar patterns elsewhere in the Middle East. For example, Chapter 4 discusses nomadism, especially through an examination of the Basseri of southern Iran and the *Āl Murra* Bedouin

---

[24] Robert A. Fernea, "Ethnographic Essay," in *Nubians in Egypt: Peaceful People,* eds. Robert A. Fernea and Georg Gerster (Austin and London: University of Texas Press, 1973), pp. 15, 45-46.

of Saudi Arabia. They are chosen not because they represent a "lowest common denominator" typicality for all nomads of the Middle East, but merely because they have recently been the subject of anthropological studies which are sufficiently detailed to form a base for understanding pastoral activities elsewhere and for a discussion of the role of nomads and of tribal societies in the premodern, preindustrial past.

My purpose throughout this book is not simply to convey information, but to convey a manner of thought. The language of social anthropology is not quite so laden with technical jargon as is the language of the other social sciences. This has the handicap in some circles of making our style of inquiry initially appear like a codification of the obvious, but it is often the "obvious" assumptions about cultural conduct and social forms which appear so familiar that they become almost impermeable to analysis. I seek to indicate how the specifically anthropological approach to the study of the Middle East has contributed both to an understanding of the region and to the principal intellectual currents of the discipline.

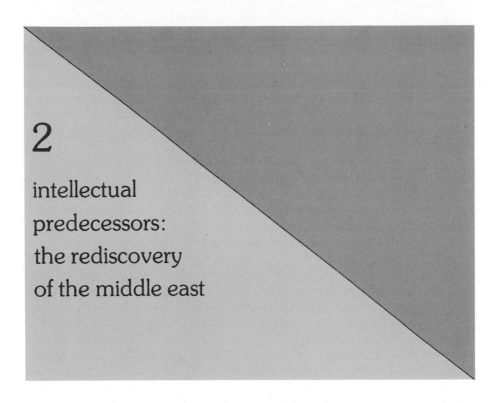

# 2

# intellectual
# predecessors:
# the rediscovery
# of the middle east

Academic chairs in anthropology were created in England and the United States only at the turn of this century. Yet from the beginning of the nineteenth century several styles of inquiry converged which emphasized issues that later became central to our discipline. Standard accounts of the proto-anthropology of the last century correctly emphasize its association with Darwinian theories of evolution and curiosity about primitive peoples, but admittedly these concerns were only marginally pursued in Middle Eastern contexts. Still, the Middle East and a rather diffuse concept of "Oriental" society had a significant impact upon some of the main theses developed by leading sociologists, including Karl Marx, Max Weber, and Emile Durkheim.

The purpose of this chapter is not to hunt for distinguished ancestors who fit contemporary notions of anthropological thought. Instead, through the use of key examples I will indicate some of the principal intellectual currents and geopolitical circumstances that gave impetus to sociologically oriented accounts of the Middle East in the last century. The scholars whose work I discuss share, in varying degrees, three common features with modern social anthropologists: (1) They considered the study of the *contemporary* social order significant to their research, even when their primary goal was the comprehension of remote or "classical" historical periods; (2) they considered it important to describe and comprehend the ordinary activities and taken-for-granted conventions of daily life and sought to do so through direct and prolonged contact; and (3) they consciously made *systematic* observations (especially in the latter half of the century) and sought to make explicit the principles on which their inquiries were based. A significant number of studies of the Middle East in the nineteenth century do not conform to the passionately argued yet curiously ahistorical attempt to portray earlier scholarship provided by Edward Said's *Orientalism*,[1] and it is these studies which this chapter seeks to evaluate.

There were three main reasons for the growing European interest in the Middle East in the nineteenth century. First was a general curiosity about the customs of peoples elsewhere, but particularly those of the Muslim Orient. From the late seventeenth century, the Muslim Orient had been used as a screen against which European fantasies about the primitive or the alien "other" were projected against an often imaginary geography. This is in part reflected in the vast scope of the emerging field of "orientalism," which included everything from Islamic society to the civilizations of India, China, and Japan. This interest was popularly reflected in a number of ways. Moors, Turks, and Persians characteristically appear in operas of the period; artists such as Delacroix romantically depicted what they considered to be the private life of Islam. Successful, if inaccurate, books such as Washington Irving's *Mahomet and His Successors*[2] or more imposing artifacts of intellect such as Ernest Renan's "Islamism and Science" offered a general theory of the "decay" of Muslim civilization in contrast to the vitality of the West.[3] By the mid-nineteenth century, travel to the Middle East, at least to the major cities, was no longer considered hazardous. Novelists such as Thackeray visited the region, and the reading public insatiably followed accounts of such travels.[4] Later in the century this fascination with the Muslim world merged, at least among the British, with the romantic notion of the pure Bedouin nomad as a primitive contemporary with the virtues of a Victorian gentleman. Anachronistically, this strand of attraction to the Middle East might be called the "T. E. Lawrence syndrome."

Such romantic assumptions toward the Islamic Orient were undeniably important in sustaining a scholarly and popular interest in the area, and some travel

[1] See Edward W. Said, *Orientalism* (New York: Pantheon Books, 1978) (best and more accurate on the period prior to the nineteenth century); also Bernard Lewis, "The Study of Islam," *Encounter*, 38, no. 1 (January 1972), 31-41. For a more general essay on the European image of non-Europeans in this period, see Henri Baudet, *Paradise on Earth* (New Haven and London: Yale University Press, 1965), pp. 42-53. Finally, for a convincing essay which breaks with scholarly convention and looks at Islamic civilization as an integral part of the past of the West, see F. E. Peters, "Islam as a Western Civilization," *The Arab World*, 18, no. 3 (May-June 1972), 13-19.

[2] Washington Irving (1783-1859), *Mahomet and His Successors* (New York: Putnam's, 1868). Equally indicative of the kitsch literature concerning the Muslim Orient is Washington Irving's *Legends of the Alhambra* (Philadelphia and London: J. B. Lippincott & Co., 1909).

[3] Renan's essay can be found in his *The Poetry of the Celtic Races and Other Studies*, trans. William G. Hutchinson (London: W. Scott, Ltd., 1896). An essay on the life of Muḥammad can be found in Renan's *Essays in Religious History and Criticism*, trans. O. B. Frothingham (New York: Carleton, 1864), pp. 226-84.

[4] William Makepeace Thackeray (pseud. M. A. Titmarsh), *Notes of a Journey from Cornhill to Grand Cairo* (New York: Wiley and Putnam, 1846).

accounts, such as Charles Doughty's *Travels in Arabia Deserta* (1888),[5] presented valuable and precise ethnographic data, although they were not intended as ethnographies. In the hands of latter-day anthropologists, such accounts have been invaluable in reconstructing the social organization of nomadic tribal societies prior to the effective imposition of modern state controls.

A second reason for attention to the Middle East in this period was a heightened imperial interest in the region. It was considered as both a fertile ground for the enterprises of European financiers and ripe for direct political control. Bonaparte's expedition to Egypt (1798-1801) brought Egypt under French rule for a brief period. Completion of the Suez Canal in 1869 began a period of rapidly growing European interest in the country, which culminated with English occupation in 1882 and the addition of the Sudan (technically an Anglo-Egyptian condominium) shortly thereafter. As for North Africa, Algeria was occupied by France in 1830 and ultimately was legally considered to be an integral part of the metropole; Tunisia was made a protectorate in 1881; Morocco in 1912. If indirect forms of domination are included, such as the presence of British political advisers to the Trucial States of the Arab/Persian Gulf from the early nineteenth century onward to protect imperial lines of communication to India, then the magnitude of European political interest in the region is emphasized even more. In the years following the First World War, direct European control (or control by mandate) over the countries of the Middle East expanded to encompass Libya (Italy), Syria and Lebanon (France), and Palestine and Iraq (England).

Finally, an interest in the Middle East converged with important trends in European scholarship, particularly in the so-called "higher criticism" of the Bible which was then emerging in Germany and later prevailed in other scholarly circles. As Bernard Lewis has written, one reason for this was a Jewish sympathy with Islam. As religious anti-Judaism gave way to a racially expressed anti-Semitism, some Jewish scholars looked to other Semites for comfort. This affinity, Lewis says, was largely imaginary but accounted for part of the interest in Islam.[6] In addition, several prominent scholars trained in ancient and modern Semitic languages became explorers and ethnographers because they saw such research as necessary for the understanding of society in the time of the Old Testament patriarchs.

## BONAPARTE'S EXPEDITION TO EGYPT, 1798-1801

Bonaparte's expedition is often used by historians to symbolize the point at which the Muslim Orient, forced to recognize growing Western hegemony, was compelled to acquire Western technology, especially military, and ultimately was to be pro-

[5] Charles Doughty, *Travels in Arabia Deserta* (New York: Random House, n.d. [orig. 1888]). In terms of literary style, Doughty's *Travels* is probably one of the greatest nineteenth-century travel accounts, although it had little success in the author's lifetime.

[6] Lewis, "Study of Islam," pp. 35-36.

foundly shaken by contact with all aspects of European civilization. Here I am concerned with the inverse process, the European scholarly rediscovery of the Islamic East. (I specify "rediscovery" because at least until the final collapse of Islamic rule in Spain in the fifteenth century, Europeans had recognized the intellectual supremacy of the Muslim world in many fields.) Scattered throughout the ships in Bonaparte's fleet were 150 scientists and Orientalists, scholars whose task was to make as systematic an inventory of Egypt as possible—its geology, rivers, minerals, antiquities, and, of most concern in the present context, the "manners and customs" of its inhabitants. The motivation for the latter was the hope that insight into contemporary society, especially that of the peasants, might provide clues as to the social order of Pharaonic times. The implicit assumption was that peasant society was profoundly conservative and resistant to change. (Parenthetically, the notion that the study of the present is primarily valuable as an indication of the past dies very hard. For example, it still dominates the popular understanding of what anthropologists do.) In any case, the findings of the scholars accompanying Bonaparte were collected in the massive, meticulous, twenty-four volume *Description de l'Egypte* (1820).[7] Even if its ethnographic section was not always as accurate as the sections on geology and natural history, its authors aspired to the same high standards. In the later French colonial conquests in North Africa, an initial byproduct of conquest was the compilation of similar inventories of the new domains. The strength of the surveys of Algeria and Tunisia rests more on an inventory of the physical characteristics of the two territories than in an understanding of their populations. Nevertheless, they indicate in a perfunctory manner the nature of indigenous political activities and institutions.[8] In contrast, the monographs written on Morocco just prior to and in the early years of the protectorate constitute one of the best collections of colonial ethnography to be found anywhere. One reason for the quality of this research in contrast to most of that conducted in Algeria was the conscious decision on the part of the French, at least in principle, to preserve and enhance indigenous institutions. Another clear impetus was the notion that rational, systematic ethnographic inquiry would facilitate the "scientific" implantation of colonial rule. This tendency to regard the exercise of colonial rule as a science was already present at the time of Bonaparte's expedition to Egypt.

Another significant aspect of Bonaparte's invasion of Egypt was the attempt to legitimize the colonial enterprise in the eyes of the conquered population—a

---

[7]*Description de l'Egypte* (Paris: Editions d'Art Albert Guillot, 1966).

[8]Interest in ethnographic inquiry during the colonial era in Algeria was directly linked to political conditions. For example, in periods of sustained local resistance to French rule, there was an increase in ethnographic investigation of political and religious topics. This interest waned when French rule was thought to be secure. For a useful account of changing styles in the ethnography of Algeria, the one country for which a detailed ethnography of ethnographic styles has been made, together with representative texts, see Philippe Lucas and Jean-Claude Vatin, *L'Algérie des Anthropologues* (The Anthropologists' Algeria) (Paris: Maspéro, 1975). Despite this book's occasionally simplistic tendency to correlate styles of inquiry directly with socioeconomic "interests," its basic argument remains plausible.

theme to be developed at greater length in a later chapter. On one of the expedition's ships was an Arabic printing press looted from the Vatican. This was used to print a proclamation, translated into Arabic by an Orientalist, announcing that Bonaparte had come in the name of Islam and would govern in a more Islamic fashion than had the preceding corrupt *Mamlūk* regime. The invading troops were ordered to be scrupulously respectful of mosques. Bonaparte even dressed as a Muslim and prayed in mosques for a time, until the ridicule of his troops forced him to abandon the practice.[9] What is crucial about such actions is that they prefigure later, more systematic, attempts of colonial regimes to legitimate their presence in the eyes of the ruled and whenever possible to win over key elements in indigenous society. Ethnographic investigation was seen as an important contribution to this aspect of the colonial enterprise.

## EXPLORERS AND SCHOLARS

There was a special class of explorers whose works are particularly useful in tracing the rediscovery of the Middle East—those who could speak the languages of the region and who, through long residence in it, could describe its society with reasonable accuracy. One of the best known was the polyglot Sir Richard Burton (1821-1890), who began his career in the Indian Army. After seven years he was forced to resign because of a firsthand report he had made in confidence to a superior regarding the organization and use of male brothels in Karachi. This report created a scandal when one of his rivals caused it to be made public, and the incident forced his resignation. Subsequently he traveled to and wrote extensively on South America, Utah, Central Africa, East Africa, and the Arab world, the last of which specifically concerns this study.

Perhaps the best of Burton's books is his account of a pilgrimage to Mecca in 1853. Like most travelers of the period, he adopted oriental dress, in his case Persian costume and the name of Mirza ᶜAbdallah, an identity he had previously assumed with success in India to conceal his European origin. Although Europeans in the Middle East commonly adopted oriental costume, not all felt compelled to conceal their identity as Europeans. But, then, Burton's attitudes toward "orientals" generally displayed an arrogance and hostility which exceeded even the prevalent Victorian notions of English superiority over other races and nations. Burton's writings emphasize the safety of travel in Egypt, yet he refers to Egyptian society as being somewhere between "barbarism" and "civilization."[10] He offered the following advice on the orient: "The more haughty and offensive [the traveller] is to the people, the more they respect him; a decided advantage to the traveller of

---

[9] Alan Moorehead, *The Blue Nile* (London: Four Square Editions, 1965), pp. 55-133, provides a well-written general account of the French occupation of Egypt.

[10] Sir Richard F. Burton, *A Personal Narrative of a Pilgrimage to al-Madinah & Meccah* (New York: Dover Books, 1964 [orig. 1855]), p. 17.

**FIGURE** 2-1 Sir Richard Burton (1821-1890)
dressed as Mirza CAbdallah. (From Richard F.
Burton, *Personal Narrative of a Pilgrimage to Al-
Madinah & Meccah* [London: Tylston and Edwards,
1893], frontispiece, vol. 2.)

choleric temperament."[11] Elsewhere he rails against what he calls "Asiatic" governments—those that can be dealt with only "by bribe, by bullying, or by bothering
them with a dogged perseverance into attending to you and your concerns."[12]
Given his attitude toward his fellow travelers on the pilgrimage, it is not surprising
that his hostility was often reciprocated.

As fascinating as it is to read Burton's account of his pilgrimage, the book
reveals more of the author than of the nature of Islam or of the Muslim countries
through which he traveled, despite its literary array of erudite footnotes, digressions,

[11] *Ibid.*, p. 15.

[12] *Ibid.*, p. 20. The theme of the inherent corruption and decay of "oriental" governments is a common theme in the literature of the period, although such claims should not be
taken at face value. It runs throughout Alexander Kinglake's *Eothen* (London: Icon Books, 1963
[orig. 1844]), an excellently written account describing the author's travels through the Ottoman domains of eastern Europe to Syria, Palestine, Egypt, and return, in a period when the
plague ravaged the entire region. Although Kinglake spoke virtually no Arabic, he wrote that
Damascus was safer than Oxford and that he could even use the public baths with impunity
without concealing his identity. Kinglake took for granted that as an Englishman he was obliged
to confirm his rank by dealing with local officials through bullying and threats (p. 133).

and incidental geographical and ethnological observations. To his credit, Burton was conscious of this aspect of his narrative style: "I make no apology for the egotistical semblance of the narrative. Those who felt the want of some 'silent friend' to aid them with advice, when it must not be asked, will appreciate what may appear to the uninterested critic mere outpourings of a mind full of self."[13] The very title, *A Personal Narrative,* specifies the nature of the text.

For the purposes of ethnographic (or more precisely protoethnographic) description, there are two nineteenth-century explorers and travelers who are considerably more significant, if less flamboyant, than Sir Richard Burton: John Lewis Burckhardt (1784-1817) and Edward Lane (1801-1876).

Burckhardt was born of a well-to-do Swiss family and became attracted very early in his life to the "discovery" of the Middle East.[14] As a young man he traveled to England to study the Arabic language for two and one-half years at Cambridge. During this time, he prepared himself for what he conceived as the rigors of life in the East by walking barefoot through the English countryside, while living only on vegetables for long periods. In 1809 at the age of twenty-five he left for the Middle East and never returned, for he died there of malaria eight years later.

Burckhardt's books reveal him to be an engaging, if compulsive, scholar who can be relied upon for accuracy. He lived upon a minute stipend sent him by an English group calling itself the Association for Promoting the Discovery of the Interior Parts of Africa.

Throughout his stay in the Middle East, Burckhardt dressed in Turkish fashion, as did the urban elite of the period throughout much of the Middle East. He adopted the name of Shaykh Ibrahim more out of convenience than in an attempt to conceal his true identity. Burckhardt's Arabic was so excellent—both his classical Arabic and several contemporary dialects—that while in Damascus he translated *Robinson Crusoe.* Although recognized as a Christian, he was even accepted as an authority on Islamic law. Among his works are a collection of Arabic proverbs, an account of his travels in Nubia, and his detailed but elegant *Notes on the Bedouins and the Wahábys,* his most ambitious work.[15]

*Notes on the Bedouins* is evenly divided between an ethnographic description of Bedouin society in Arabia and a detailed history of the *Wahhābī* movement, a form of Islamic puritanism which originated in the mid-eighteenth century

[13] Burton, *Personal Narrative,* p. 5.

[14] The biographical details presented here are derived from Katharine Sim, *Desert Traveller: The Life of Jean Louis Burckhardt* (London: Gollancz, 1969).

[15] John Lewis Burckhardt, *Arabic Proverbs; or, the Manners and Customs of the Modern Egyptians* (Totowa, N.J.: Rowman and Littlefield, 1972 [orig. 1830]); *Travels in Nubia* (London: J. Murray, 1822); *Notes on the Bedouins and Wahábys* (London: Henry Colburn and Richard Bentley, 1831). All three books are available in reprint editions. The comments concerning the implications of Burckhardt's modes of description for his assumptions concerning Bedouin social life are derived from an unpublished paper by my student, Kenneth Sandbank, "The Relation of Literary Form to Cognitive Style in the Work of J. L. Burckhardt," typescript, June 1979.

in Arabia and rapidly acquired a political base, reaching its greatest territorial extent during Burckhardt's stay in the Middle East.

The ethnographic section of the *Notes* compares favorably in some respects to recent anthropological studies of pastoral nomads in the Middle East. He describes Bedouin society in a coherent, organized fashion: There are sections on the layout of tents, the segregation of the sexes, dress, etiquette, domestic life and economy, religious practices, tribal organization, marriage, feuds, and warfare. No explicit sociological themes are explored, although an implicit concern with the nature of Bedouin "independence" runs throughout the account. Burckhardt was fascinated by the independence of the Bedouin, their "uncorrupted manners," and their code of honor. His efforts to describe precisely the nature of social life in the desert carry more conviction than Burton's ambiguous but constant reiteration that the Islamic world was beyond the pale of civilization. Admittedly, his point of departure is naturalistic description. He classifies the parts of the tent and the "parts" of tribal organization in virtually the same way a botanist would classify plants. One reason he appears to consider the Bedouin as "uncorrupted" and in contrast to the "debauchery" of townsmen is that stylistically he portrays them as timeless and unchanging. Even towns and the Ka$^c$ba are described primarily by their physical form; many of the "ancient customs" which he describes are also virtually made into part of the physical landscape. In general, Burckhardt makes it clear that the observer is the contemplator and that the Bedouin, for all their initial charm, live a monotonous and unreflective life. Still, his work is not as fully anchored in the "orientalist" assumptions of his period as are other accounts and represents a genuine attempt to portray Bedouin society.

After describing the rules of hospitality, blood revenge, and the autonomy of most Bedouin tribes from the authority of central governments, Burckhardt asks the more general question: How it is possible to have an ordered society such as that of the Bedouin, with a code of law and conventions of conduct but yet have no written codes of law and no formal "legislation"? The form of Burckhardt's question sounds awkward today, but it was one that interested many European political philosophers of the period.[16] Burckhardt's contribution to its discussion was to perceive the relevance of his direct experience with such a society. Segmentation theory in social anthropology (see Chapter 5), which enjoyed considerable popularity from the publication of Evans-Pritchard's *The Nuer* (1940) until the mid-1950s, can in many ways be considered to be a more systematic response to this same question, since societies described as segmentary were said to exist without any formal leaders or governmental apparatus, all conflict within them being regulated by organized violence (feuds) among the groups involved.[17] On the basis of Burckhardt's observations, later social anthropologists have been able to

---

[16] Burckhardt, *Notes,* pp. 378-82.

[17] Burckhardt described in detail the institution of the feud as the Bedouin themselves conceived it. A segmentary diagram even appeared in his account (Vol. 1, pp. 150-51).

construct more theoretically oriented arguments on the nature of political organization in pre-oil Arabia.[18]

The second section of the *Notes* concerns the Wahhābī movement. The ideological goal of this movement was the reform of Islam as it was then practiced. It was especially antagonistic to the popular custom of venerating the shrines of Muslim saints. In their drive to reassert the Quranic doctrine of the equality of all men before God, the Wahhābī movement succeeded even in destroying the tomb of the Prophet Muḥammad. Because the movement politically united the tribes of Arabia, it was considered a threat to the Ottoman Empire and particularly to the Mamlūk regime of Egypt. After repeated attempts to crush the movement, it was finally defeated in 1818 by an army of Muḥammad ᶜAlī, the ruler of Egypt. This occurred shortly after Burckhardt wrote his account. Burckhardt gathered reports of the Wahhābī-s and their doctrines from their representatives and other eye-witnesses. He carefully assesses the implications of the Wahhābī insistence upon settling nomadic groups in order better to control them, their leadership, the exact nature of their doctrines plus the reaction to them by Muslims outside the Arabian peninsula. Like latter-day anthropological descriptions of religious movements, Burckhardt's account of the Wahhābī-s alternates between social history and providing the background material on religious ideologies and social forms necessary to follow his description of specific events.

Edward Lane's *Manners and Customs of the Modern Egyptians* (1836)[19] provides a detailed account of urban Muslim society and thus complements Burckhardt's *Notes*. Lane originally intended to enter the ministry and in this context acquired an enthusiasm for Oriental studies. Later he became an engraver but abandoned the work when it proved too taxing on his health. In 1825, at the age of twenty-four, he set out for Cairo and lived there more or less constantly until 1849. He adopted native clothes—the Turkish dress of Cairo's elite—but never concealed his identity as an Englishman and a Christian. He delicately reminded his Muslim friends that Christ was also seen as a prophet in the Quran. Lane mixed freely with Egyptians and was held in confidence by many of them. Fluency in Arabic, such as he possessed, may not be absolutely necessary for certain types of ethnographic inquiry (such as cultural ecology or certain forms of economic anthropology), but for any account of a society's beliefs, rituals, and social conventions it becomes essential. Anything less than fluency, or at least the anthropologist's ability to convince informants that he is fluent, generally handicaps the gathering of such data.

Lane does not appear to have considered his *Manners and Customs* as his principal work, although it is so considered today. He intended it as a popular book

---

[18]One of the best of such accounts is Henry Rosenfeld, "The Role of the Military in State Formation in Arabia," *Journal of the Royal Anthropological Institute*, 95 (1965), 75-86, 174-94.

[19]Fifth edition (1860) reprinted (New York: Dover Publications, 1973).

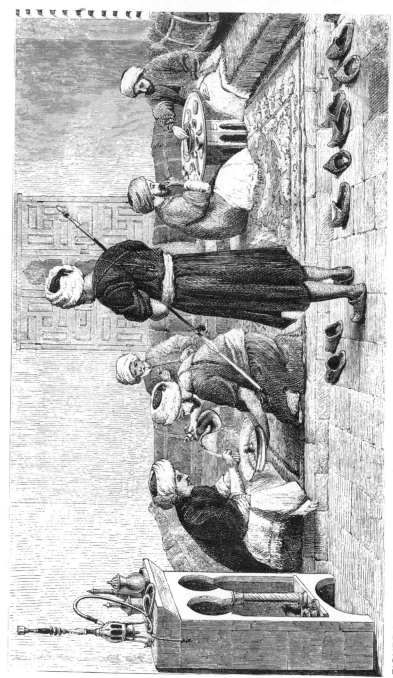

**FIGURE 2-2** Guest room, Cairo, 1830s. (From Edward William Lane, *An Account of the Manners and Customs of the Modern Egyptians* [London: John Murray, 1860], frontispiece.)

to complement an account of the manners and customs of the ancient Egyptians (those of Pharaonic times) that was then in circulation. His other studies included a translation of *A Thousand and One Nights* in a manner more accurate, if less sensational, than that provided by Burton and a massive Arabic-English lexicon which he never lived to complete.

Lane modestly wrote that his intention in *Manners and Customs* was simply to make some of his countrymen "better acquainted with the domiciliated classes of one of the most interesting nations of the world, by drawing a detailed picture of the inhabitants of the largest Arab city." He regarded his book as an accessory to the reading of translations of Arabic literature which was then in vogue.[20]

His descriptions of urban life are elegant in their economy and clarity. They include dress, child rearing, ceremonies associated with birth, marriage, and death, domestic life, the marketplace, government, Islam, and above all the nuances of etiquette and the taken-for-granted conventions of society. As with the writings of Burckhardt, there is no explicit theoretical orientation to Lane's writing, and there is a tendency to view Cairene society as an object to be contemplated and classified. Theoretical concerns become important only in subsequent scholarship such as the work of Robertson Smith.

## WILLIAM ROBERTSON SMITH (1846-1894)

The brilliant, tenaciously cosmopolitan William Robertson Smith is the first of the scholars considered in this chapter to have a specific, conscious theoretical orientation toward the study of Arab society. As Thomas O. Beidelman has written in a

**FIGURE 2-3** Bridal procession in Cairo, 1835. (From Lane, *Manners and Customs*, p. 164.)

[20] *Ibid.*, p. xxiii.

recent appraisal of Smith's work, whatever Smith's shortcomings by today's theoretical perspectives, he "sought to define the essential nature of religious behavior and approached the analysis of social institutions through comparative and historical studies."[21] This explicit goal, and Smith's means of achieving it, remains one of the central concerns of contemporary social anthropology.

Smith's interests are difficult to summarize. He began his scholarly career by acquiring a dazzling reputation as a mathematician but quickly turned to Biblical studies. In 1875 at the age of twenty-nine he was given the extraordinary distinction for a person of his youth of being named to a committee to produce an authorized English translation of the Bible. He also assumed editorship of the *Encyclopaedia Britannica,* where his wide-ranging interests and responsibilities "led him to a personal acquaintance with nearly every important intellectual in Britain and a large number on the Continent . . . men as different as Swinburne and Darwin, Huxley and Kelvin, Spencer and Burne-Jones."[22] So compulsively thorough was he in his editorship that he is said to have personally read every one of the articles submitted.

One of Smith's strongest personal interests was in the "historical" criticism of the Bible. This approach to Biblical study, already prevalent on the Continent, asserted that the texts of the Bible should be treated as any other historical document and analyzed accordingly for authorship and historical authenticity. Like other scholars of his time, Smith found this approach easier to apply to the Quran than to the Bible because of strong opposition from conservative Christians. By all accounts, however, Smith was strong-willed, independent-minded, and had more than a touch of arrogance. His determination to express his views in an uncompromising manner eventually led to dismissal from his professorship at Aberdeen by the General Assembly of the Free Church of Scotland.

Like most Biblical scholars, Smith was fluent in Arabic and other Semitic languages, as well as the principal European languages. To improve his Arabic—he is said to have spoken it better than Burton—he made several voyages to Egypt and North Africa between 1878 and 1890. In 1878-1879 he spent about a year in Cairo, divided between two visits. On one of these visits he managed to make camelback tours of the Arabian peninsula, Palestine, and Syria.[23]

As Beidelman writes, Smith seems to have deeply enjoyed these visits. Like Burton, he traveled in native garb and adopted an oriental name, in this case the Arab one of ᶜAbdallah Effendi. On one brief excursion from Cairo, in fact, he was accompanied by Burton. Smith, with his swarthy looks and dark beard, often managed to pass as an Arab.

[21] T. O. Beidelman, *W. Robertson Smith and the Sociological Study of Religion* (Chicago and London: University of Chicago Press, 1974), p. 29.

[22] *Ibid.,* p. 13.

[23] Smith wrote extensively on his trip to western Arabia. See his "Journey in the Hejaz," in his *Lectures and Essays of William Robertson Smith,* ed. by J. S. Black and G. Chrystal (London: A. & C. Black, 1912), pp. 484-597. This account was first published serially in *The Scotsman* (February-June 1880).

**FIGURE 2-4** W. Robertson Smith as ᶜAbdallah Effendi.
(From J. S. Black and G. Chrystal, *The Life of William Robertson Smith* [London: A. & C. Black, Publishers, 1902].
Courtesy Adam & Charles Black, Publishers.)

Like most Victorians, Smith was profoundly pleased with his Britishness and sometimes shared the excesses and prejudices of his time in thinking about alien peoples. For instance, he wrote:

> It would be a mistake to suppose that genuine religious feeling is at the bottom of everything that justifies itself by taking a religious shape. The prejudices of the Arab have their roots in a conservatism which lies deeper than his belief in Islam. It is, indeed, a great fault of the religion of the Prophet that it lends itself so readily to the prejudices of the race among whom it was first promulgated, and that it has taken under its protection so many barbarous and obsolete ideas, which even Mohammed must have seen to have no religious worth, but which he carried over into his system in order to facilitate the propagation of his reformed doctrines.[24]

Despite these lapses into the conventional stereotyped wisdom of his age, Smith considered the systematic study of contemporary Arab society—at least what he habitually referred to as that of the "pure" Bedouin—as crucial in his attempt to comprehend how men's experiences in society relate to their religious and ethical conceptions.

[24] Smith, *Lectures and Essays*, pp. 491-92.

Smith's two principal books, *Lectures on the Religion of the Semites* (1889) and *Kinship and Marriage in Early Arabia* (1885) are both readily obtainable in paperback reprint editions, so I concentrate here on the principal assumptions contained in them about the study of human society.[25]

First, like many of his contemporaries, Robertson Smith accepted the concept of the evolutionary progress of human society. As T. O. Beidelman stresses, this "evolutionary" perspective was encouraged by the basic Judeo-Christian belief in the ethical and intellectual development of a chosen people that, for Christians, culminated in the message of Christ. Thus societies could be arranged on a sort of ladder, with Victorian England predictably on the highest rung. Smith's studies of Arab—which for him meant Bedouin—kinship were considered in this context to be a key to understanding ancient Semitic society.

Second, Smith saw a close relationship between the stage of development of a social group and the nature of its intellectual, religious, and moral life. He assumed that our perception of nature and the universe is modeled on our experience in society. This idea is adequately developed in his *Lectures* but is even more sharply delineated in a separate study of prophecy in ancient Palestine.[26] Smith argued that each prophet could speak only for his own time and thus had to convey his message in terms that could be understood by members of his own society. The ideas of prophets could be ahead of those prevalent in their own society but not too far. Thus, Smith conceived of the problems of the alienation of people from society and the means by which their ideas could affect social transformations. For example, for a scholar to grasp the message of Ezekiel, the social organization of that prophet's time had to be delineated, together with the cosmology and modes of thought and expression contemporary with it. If Ezekiel's prophetic message was then found to differ from that of Samuel, Smith argued, it is not because of any contradiction in the Bible but because Samuel addressed himself to different groups and situations.

Given Smith's assumption of stages of social development, and their specific relationship to ideologies, his scholarly interest in the Bedouin becomes more apparent. Smith saw Bedouin society as a holdover relatively unchanged from the time of the Old Testament. Through studying the present-day Bedouin and what was known of Bedouin society just prior to and immediately after the time of the Prophet Muḥammad, Smith sought through analogy and comparison to "reconstruct" the state of society as it was in the time of the Patriarchs. Such an ahistorical assumption is no longer acceptable in contemporary social anthropology, but it is important to recognize that it led Smith to evaluate carefully the ideas about kinship and political organization of Arabs both at the time of Muḥammad, on

[25]William Robertson Smith, *Kinship and Marriage in Early Arabia* (Boston: Beacon Press, 1967 [orig. 1885]); *Lectures on the Religion of the Semites* (New York: Schocken Books, 1972 [orig. 1889]). The account of Robertson Smith's ideas is largely derived from Beidelman, *Robertson Smith*.

[26]W. Robertson Smith, *The Prophets of Israel and Their Place in History to the Close of the Eighth Century B.C.* (London: A. & C. Black, 1919 [orig. 1882]).

which extensive information was available through traditional Islamic scholarship, and in the nineteenth century.

Finally, Smith used ethnographic and historical data to support explicitly formulated theoretical assumptions about the nature of Arab social organization and its evolution. Part of his argument concerning the evolution of Arab society is simply wrong. In the second part of *Kinship and Marriage,* for example, he presumes the existence of an earlier, matrilineal system of descent reckoning among the Arabs on the basis of what is today regarded as insufficient evidence. Yet the first section of the book is one of the enduring classics of social anthropology, for it presents the first systematic account of the social structure of the feud and the basic principles of kinship and political organization among the Arab Bedouin. Smith essentially sets forth the fundamental features of what later were to become known as segmentary societies. His argument was a direct inspiration for Evans-Pritchard's later (1940) study of segmentation among the Nuer of the southern Sudan.[27] Similarly, Smith's conviction that symbolic behavior was related to the nature of social groups was the basis upon which Emile Durkheim derived inspiration for his own sociology of knowledge and of symbolic forms.[28]

Smith was also the first to recognize that the genealogies used by the Bedouin to describe their sociopolitical order were not descriptions of concrete, actual relations among themselves but ideological charters for the construction of social groups. Smith realized that ecological necessity and changing political conditions could result in shifts in the composition of groups. To gain political strength, for instance, ambitious chiefs would be anxious to include as wide a net as possible of assumed kinsmen and clients in their following, and Smith was well aware of the means by which weaker groups and individuals could manipulate genealogies so as to establish claims to kinship with more powerful groups.[29]

In Chapter 5, Smith's influence upon the ideas of more recent anthropological concern with segmentation and related concepts, especially in the work of E. E. Evans-Pritchard, Emrys Peters, and Ernest Gellner will be discussed more fully. The critical point to recognize for the present is that studies such as those of Robertson Smith reached a wide audience and provided considerable impetus to the understanding of the Middle East, the Arab world, and Islam. Even when Smith constructed theoretical arguments that are considered faulty in retrospect, he touched upon many of the basic issues of social anthropological inquiry, including the social base of symbolic behavior, the nature of the feud, and the ideological basis of

[27]See T. O. Beidelman's review of the Beacon paperback edition of *Kinship and Marriage, Anthropos,* 63/64 (1968-1969), 592-95. Beidelman, who studied under Evans-Pritchard at Oxford, provides the following further clarification (personal communication, April 1977): "Evans-Pritchard told me that he got his insights on segmentation from Smith and also indicated that he read Smith either before or while at Cairo [where Evans-Pritchard held a teaching post prior to his fieldwork among the Nuer], so that would suggest that the notion was in his head before fieldwork. . . . He certainly had a complete and well-used set of Smith, some of which I now have."

[28]Beidelman, *W. Robertson Smith,* p. 65.

[29]Smith, *Kinship and Marriage,* pp. 5, 7, 42-43, 269.

conceptions of kinship. As with Durkheim, many of his insights remain fresh today. In particular, his theoretical arguments and documentation of them through ethnographic and historical sources were much more boldly conceived than many of the "functionalist" studies that were later to predominate in the study of the Middle East.

## SCHOLARLY INQUIRY AND IMPERIAL INTERESTS

Like the other human sciences, anthropology has become a critically reflexive discipline. By this I mean that its leading practitioners regard an awareness of their implicit theoretical assumptions and how these assumptions are indirectly, yet pervasively, influenced by the intellectual and political setting in which scholarly inquiry is carried out as an integral part of any research. A similar consciousness of implicit scholarly assumptions can be seen to pervade Islamic studies, although without the single-minded focus upon political considerations that pervades much of the anthropological work of this genre.[30] Nineteenth-century scholars were aware of many of the assumptions that pervaded their work, but even when directly concerned with the nature of non-Western political institutions, they remained remarkably silent on the exact consequences of imperial conquest and of European colonial rule.[31] Scholarly investigations by Europeans of "oriental" societies were carried out in the context of impending imperial domination or, in some cases, of actual colonial rule, and this fact must be taken into account, since the direction of scholarly inquiry often merged with the interests of the colonial power. It would be wrong, however, to interpret such a fusion of interests anachronistically by contemporary standards and to regard all such research as politically sinister, as proponents of more simplistic versions of neo-Marxism often argue. Some anthropologists argue that ethnographic inquiry in this century and the last was carried out in the context of European bourgeois society expanding its political, economic, and intellectual domination. This is certainly the case, but the *specific* consequences of such domination for patterns of inquiry still must be demonstrated. In any case, such an assumption in itself hardly invalidates anthropological inquiry. Many ethnographers who participated in colonial rule were quite aware of the context in

---

[30] See Talal Asad, ed., *Anthropology and the Colonial Encounter* (London: Ithaca Press, 1973). Asad's essay in this volume, "Two European Images of Non-European Rule," pp. 103-18, partly concerns Snouck Hurgronje, discussed below. A more thorough study has been made of the basic assumptions of Islamic scholars, again including Snouck Hurgronje, by J. D. G. Waardenburg, *L'Islam dans le Miroir de l'Occident*, 3rd ed. (Paris and The Hague: Mouton & Co., 1969).

[31] One of the few exceptions I know of to this generalization is a small, neglected book by Arnold Van Gennep, better known for his *The Rites of Passage* (Chicago: University of Chicago Press, 1960). Van Gennep's *En Algérie* (Paris: Mercure de France, 1914) devotes several chapters to the means by which French settlers alienated land from native Algerians and the social consequences of these and similar actions of dispossession and political subjugation.

which their work was carried out. A salient example is the French sociologist Jacques Berque, whose father was for many years Director of Native Affairs for the French government in Algeria. Berque himself was raised in Algeria and had a distinguished career in the Moroccan colonial service. Even in the 1930s Berque's writings indicate a subtle awareness of the nature of the colonial situation which he experienced—a theme which in recently years has become much more developed in his work. Of course, Berque, like other scholars, was profoundly affected by the milieu in which his research was conducted, but this fact hardly denies the possibility of competent sociological inquiry.

More plausible than direct correlations between political context and scholarship is the sort of argument put forward by the literary critic Edward Said, among others, that imperial domination and studies of the Islamic "Orient" bear a subtle and abstract relation to each other. They shared in common a general drive to impose "order" upon the non-European world. In one case this order was political and military; in the other it was the attempt to classify, arrange, and codify knowledge of an alien civilization.[32] The two sorts of order and control were often closely related, but they could also operate independently of each other, as has been shown by the radical transformations in the disciplines concerned with Middle Eastern and Islamic studies over the past century and a half.

The nature of traditional Muslim polities and the consequences of colonial rule are important issues and will be dealt with in detail in later chapters. In the present context it is sufficient to demonstrate that the situation of impending or actual colonial rule did much to encourage sociological investigations into the nature of Muslim and Middle Eastern society.

Here I present examples of two styles of research stimulated by imperial interests. The first is the independent scholar who later contributed his skills to solving the problems of colonial administration. This is the Dutch Orientalist Christian Snouck Hurgronje (1857-1936). The other style is exemplified by team research directly tied to colonial control from its inception. This is the French *Mission Scientifique au Maroc* (Scientific Mission to Morocco).

Snouck Hurgronje's lifelong interest was in the study of Islam and he is best known for his intensive studies of Islam and politics in Indonesia, when it was under Dutch colonial rule.[33] Earlier in his career, however, he spent a considerable period of time in the Middle East. As a young student in Holland, he was interested in theology and Old Testament studies but soon shifted his focus to the study of Islam. His thesis topic in 1880 was the origin of the Islamic pilgrimage. In 1881 he obtained an academic post in Leiden at the Institute for Training Administrators for the Dutch Indies, a post he held until 1887. At the same time he devoted himself to the study of the Arabic language. He resolved to travel to Mecca, and in August of 1884 he arrived at Jidda, the principal port of Muslim pilgrims, where he appears to have been courteously received by its religious scholars (ᶜ*ulamā'*).

[32] Said, *Orientalism.*
[33] This section is based largely upon Waardenburg, *L'Islam.*

Although Snouck Hurgronje dressed as a Muslim during his travels in Arabia and adopted a Muslim name, ᶜAbd al-Ghaffār, it appears that he did not conceal his identity as a European to the Muslim scholars and officials with whom he was in contact. He received permission from the Ottoman administration and local Arab notables to continue to Mecca, where he arrived in February of 1885. Unlike most European travelers such as Burton, who visited Mecca only for the brief period of the annual pilgrimage and in disguise, Snouck Hurgronje managed to stay for six months. He had to leave before the pilgrimage itself, which took place on the 17th of September in 1885, because of the indiscretions of a French vice-consul in Damascus that threatened to create a minor scandal for the local officials through whom Snouck Hurgronje had made his arrangements. Nonetheless, it is significant that Snouck Hurgronje was later extended an official invitation to return, although he never did.

In Mecca, both the Turkish officials and the descendants of the Prophet (Ar. pl. *shurafā'*) who were the hereditary rulers there were aware of Snouck's identity. As a sign of the support he obtained from the elite, he managed to take a number of photographs, among which are the first ever obtained of the Kaᶜba, as well as

**FIGURE 2-5** The Kaᶜba, 1884. (From C. Snouck Hurgronje, *Bilder-Atlas zu Mekka* [The Hague: Martinus Nijhoff, 1888] .)

FIGURE 2-6 A Meccan bride, 1884. (From Snouck Hurgronje, *Bilder-Atlas.)*

others of pilgrims, local notables, and even unveiled brides and the women of several of the most distinguished households of the city.[34]

As a result of his stay, Snouck Hurgronje was able to write a detailed account of everyday life in Mecca, with chapters on everything from children's games and rituals surrounding life crises to kinship, trade, religious brotherhoods, political organization, scholarly activities and intellectual life, proverbs, and domestic arrangements.[35] His account of the intellectual activities associated with the princi-

[34] The photographs were published in portfolio form in C. Snouck Hurgronje, *Bilder-Atlas zu Mekka* (The Hague: Martinus Nijhoff, 1888).

[35] C. Snouck Hurgronje, *Mekka in the Later Part of the Nineteenth Century,* trans. J. H. Monahan (Leiden: E. J. Brill and London: Luzac & Co., 1931). This is Volume 2 of a study which originally appeared in 1888-1889. Unlike his early work in the Middle East, Snouck Hurgronje's work in the Dutch East Indies (again as ᶜAbd al-Ghaffār) was directly related to the interests of Dutch colonial rule over its Muslim subjects.

**FIGURE 2-7** Meccan notable with servant, 1880s. (From Snouck Hurgronje, *Bilder-Atlas.*)

pal mosques of Mecca is one of the few treatments of traditional Muslim scholarship which appreciates it for the vigor that such scholarship has managed to maintain until comparatively recent times.

Snouck Hurgronje placed considerable importance upon his ethnographic studies of Mecca. This was in direct contrast to the emerging disciplines of the history of religions and oriental studies, which tended to place greater weight on the evaluation of textual evidence as the basis for comprehending religious traditions. For Snouck Hurgronje, to understand the social reality of any religion, whether in the historical past or in the present, one had to have a thorough understanding of the social context in which that religion was experienced by its believers. This underlying assumption is of course shared by contemporary social anthropologists.

As indicated earlier in this chapter, ethnographic inquiry in the nineteenth and early twentieth centuries was often regarded in colonial contexts as an adjunct to political and military control, especially during periods of "native" unrest. This trend is especially prevalent in the ethnography of North Africa. In Algeria, as I have indicated, the social institutions and beliefs of native Algerians were generally ignored during periods of unquestioned French domination, only to become the subject of intensive analysis during periods of resistance to French rule. The movement against the French led by Amīr ᶜAbd al-Qādir in the 1830s and 1840s was one such occasion; the stiff resistance met by the French in Berber-speaking Kabylia, the last region of Algeria to succumb to French domination in the 1850s, was another. During and shortly after conquest of the region, studies of Kabylia were abundant and created stereotypes about Berbers that were to persist for generations afterward.[36] In the Algerian case similar ethnographic interest was not to be rekindled until the 1950s, in the final, violent years of colonial rule.

It was in Morocco that organized ethnographic inquiry reached its fullest development. The incorporation of Morocco as a protectorate within the *pax gallica* dates only from 1912, but from the late nineteenth century French colonial interests began seriously to contemplate extending their "civilizing mission" to Morocco. The quality of the administrators and scholars first attracted to Morocco is in many ways comparable to the quality of scholars and officials attracted to India within the British Empire. What is certain is that in regions of English influence in the Middle East there is no body of ethnographic study comparable to that which exists for Morocco. French Moroccanists were frequently of high intellectual caliber and heavily influenced by the main sociological currents of their day. Admittedly they were not unaffected by the romantic vision of France as the first imperial power since the Romans to be capable of uniting most of North Africa under one rule. By the late nineteenth and early twentieth centuries, several individual scholars, usually backed by colonial interests or the French government, had begun systematically to describe Morocco.[37]

The collective investigation of the nature of Moroccan society began in 1904 with the founding in Tangier of the *Mission Scientifique au Maroc*. This brought together a group of talented scholars and scholarly diplomats who spoke Arabic and frequently Berber and who were well grounded in current sociology. This group produced extensive monographs on Moroccan history, the workings of the traditional Moroccan legal system and administrative apparatus, the organization of traditional crafts and commerce, Muslim education, religious beliefs and rituals, linguistic texts through which local dialects could be rapidly learned by administrators, tribal divisions, and translations of key legal, religious, and historical

---

[36] So thorough was the ethnography of the region that Emile Durkheim referred to it frequently in his classic *The Division of Labor in Society* (New York: Free Press, 1966 [orig. 1893]).

[37] See, for instance, Edmond Doutté, a lecturer on Islam at the University of Algiers, "Les Morocains et la société Marocaine," *Revue Générale des Sciences,* 14 (1903), 190-208, 258-74, 314-27, 372-87, and Eugène Aubin [pseud. for Eugène Descos, a French diplomatic official], *Morocco of Today* (London: J. M. Dent & Co., 1906; New York: Gordon Press Publishers, 1977 [orig. French, 1904]).

documents.[38] The plan of studies undertaken was conceived in a primarily utilitarian vein. This is clear from the fact that shortly after the beginning of the protectorate, the *Mission Scientifique* formally was attached to the protectorate administration. Later, in the 1920s, it became a part of the *Institut des Hautes Etudes Marocaines* (Institute for Higher Moroccan Studies), an organization whose principal task was to train colonial administrators.

One of the most distinguished members of the original team of scholars was Edouard Michaux-Bellaire, who became director of the *Mission Scientifique* in 1907. After the *Mission* had been in existence for nearly two decades, Michaux-Bellaire described its initial purpose as the sociological "reconstitution" of Morocco's social life not only through the study of books and manuscripts but through the collection of tribal traditions and the study of religious brotherhoods, economic life, and families.

> It was a question of creating . . . so to speak, the catalogue of Morocco, its tribes, its towns, its religious orders, to rediscover through them origins, ramifications, struggles, and alliances, and to follow them in history through different dynasties, to study institutions and customs, in a word, to reconnoiter, so far as possible, the land in which we might be called to act one day, so as to permit us to act in full awareness of the consequences of our actions.[39]

To sum up, this chapter has indicated the convergence of interests which led to the ethnographic discovery of the Middle East in the nineteenth and early twentieth centuries. If at the beginning of this period the Islamic "Orient" served as a projective screen upon which European fantasies about the exotic and unknown could be projected, this was to be replaced by more systematic observations under the impetus of growing colonial and imperial interests and the centrality which the ethnographic study of the region had to key intellectual topics of the period. In later chapters that deal with contemporary anthropological research, some of the themes introduced here will be taken up again in more detail.

---

[38] Their investigations were published in two series of monographs, *Archives Marocaines* and *Villes et Tribus du Maroc,* as well as in several journals. The main journals were *Archives Berbères* (1915-1920), the *Revue du Monde Musulman* (founded in Tangier in 1906), and after 1921, *Hespéris,* which became *Hespéris-Tamuda* shortly after Morocco's independence.

[39] Cited in Abdelkabir Khatibi, *Bilan de la Sociologie au Maroc* (Rabat: Association des Sciences de l'Homme, 1967), p. 10. My translation.

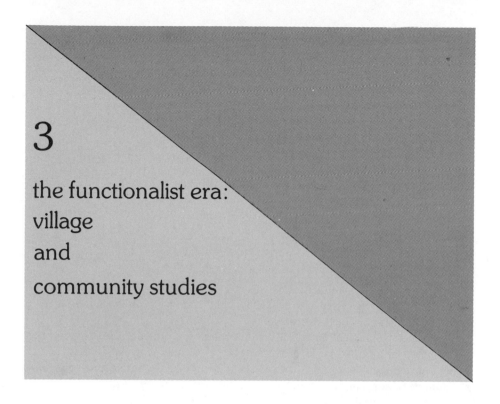

# 3

## the functionalist era: village and community studies

## FUNCTIONALISM AS THEORY AND PRACTICE

This chapter continues the discussion of the intellectual technology by means of which knowledge of Middle Eastern societies has been organized. As a movement dominating social anthropology, functionalism can be traced from its origins in the second decade of the twentieth century through its apogee in the 1930s and eventual decline, but not disappearance, as a theoretical doctrine in the late 1950s. Although it was a dominant trend in English and American anthropology, it never acquired the same firm hold upon German ethnology or the work of French anthropologists and sociologists interested in the non-European world. There also were pockets of anthropologists in the English-speaking world who ignored the functionalist movement, although for the most part such individuals were of an older generation that followed earlier paradigms for scholarly investigation.[1]

The French sociological tradition remained largely uninfluenced by the functionalist movement, although the English and American functionalists often

---

[1] One prominent example is the Finnish anthropologist Edward Westermarck (1862-1939), who taught at the University of London for most of his career (1904-1930). Beginning at the turn of the century, he lived intermittently in Tangier over a period of roughly two decades and produced a number of monographs concerning various aspects of Moroccan rural society. Among his principal publications were *Ritual and Belief in Morocco* (New Hyde Park: University Books, 1968 [orig. 1926]); *Wit and Wisdom of Morocco* (New York: Horace Liveright, Inc., 1931), and *Marriage Ceremonies in Morocco* (London: Macmillan, 1914).

considered Emile Durkheim as providing a theoretical base for their own position. Durkheim's collaborators and successors made extensive use of ethnographic materials and courageously tackled such broad issues as the character of entire civilizations. Marcel Granet's study of China (1922)[2] is the best known of these, although no equivalent study was made for the Islamic world despite Durkheim's own use of Algerian ethnographic data and his interest in complex societies. Likewise, French human geographers took advantage of France's Middle Eastern colonial domain to undertake a number of detailed studies of traditional ecological adaptations, primarily of pastoralists, throughout the region.[3] With the exception of studies of this nature, functionalism pervasively influenced the character of anthropological research in the Middle East as elsewhere in the world.

A by-product of functionalism, however, was the turning of anthropological interest away from the Middle East. The few studies which continued to be undertaken were primarily those which treated villages and tribes as closed social worlds, even when large numbers of villagers regularly sought work in the cities of their countries or overseas and depended upon income from such temporary or permanent migration for their sustenance.

Because functionalism so clearly illustrates how theoretical preconceptions shape what an anthropologist or sociologist "sees" in fieldwork, and is far from being a moribund framework for research, it is particularly interesting to examine its dominant conceptions in detail. As a theory, functionalism emphasizes the explanation of social phenomena on the basis of their interrelation with coexisting events or social forms, rather than in terms of how any of these came to be.

Such an extreme theoretical doctrine requires that societies be treated as closed entities. Hence it appeared to account much better for relatively simple, small-scale societies than for the larger-scale, historically known societies which anthropologists typically encountered in the Middle East. Only by the device of treating Middle Eastern villages and tribes *as if* they were small-scale, relatively isolated societies was it possible to make sense of them in terms of functionalist theory.

The best way of considering functionalism is as a variety of related theoretical perspectives instead of a unified theoretical viewpoint. Yet these perspectives share essential features. One of these is the idea that societies can be considered self-contained organisms, even if they are sometimes so complicated that it is hard to determine just what are their component parts—persons, social roles, or institutions—and the precise "functions" of these parts.

The convenient analogy of the human body to society was occasionally employed by functionalists to illustrate their ideas. In the case of the human body,

---

[2] Marcel Granet, *The Religion of the Chinese People*, trans. Maurice Freedman (Oxford: Basil Blackwell, 1976).

[3] This literature is conveniently summarized in Douglas L. Johnson, *The Nature of Nomadism*, Research Paper 118 (Chicago: University of Chicago, Department of Geography, 1969).

the component parts are dissimilar, but by each performing its complementary task, the organism as a whole is able to survive: The heart pumps blood, the stomach digests food, and the legs transport the body from one place to another. Functionalists argued that societies had similar parts.

The anthropologist A. R. Radcliffe-Brown was an early popularizer of functionalist theory. His own analogy for the study of society was the horse. The articulation of the various parts of a horse, he argued, cannot be explained by study of the origins of the horse and its evolution, but only by the functions performed by each part in the present. In an accurate and biting critique of this approach, E. E. Evans-Pritchard commented that Radcliffe-Brown might be correct in writing of horses, but societies cannot be compared to them.[4] The notion of society is only an observer's abstraction, so that the "parts" do not always fit together. In essence, the anthropological study of social and cultural form necessarily involves the study of these forms in their historical context. Sociological forms are necessarily abstracted from events and situations that to a certain extent are always unique.

In an important sense, all anthropologists are functionalists in that they seek to interrelate various aspects of social action and systems of meaning, or culture. What distinguishes functionalism as an explicit theoretical framework is its emphasis upon describing societies *as if* they were in equilibrium. Only the more extreme of the functionalists completely ignored the data of historical change, but many chose to work in preliterate societies in which accounts of past events independent of immediate social context were unavailable or difficult to obtain. Most functionalists took historical facts into consideration when they could obtain them, but such data fitted only awkwardly into the main theoretical framework. Since functionalist theory has the built-in bias of treating societies as if they were closed systems existing at one historical moment, there was a tendency not to consider the factors that led to the "transition" of a society from one state to another. Historical transformations were instead thought of in layer-cake images, with each slice of time merely superimposed. The limitation of this strategy is that it serves more to contrast the end points of certain processes rather than to focus on the nature of the changes taking place. This is because the "synchronic slices" approach encourages a conception of historical change in terms of discrete, episodic units, rather than as a continuous process. Emphasis was placed upon the description of societies in periods when it was presumed there was little significant change rather than at periods of conflict, revolution, or major transition.[5] An alternate version of the same basic argument regarded social forms as cyclical, in which a tendency to

---

[4] Radcliffe-Brown's "horse" analogy is contained in his *Structure and Function in Primitive Society* (London: Cohen and West, 1952), pp. 184-85; Evans-Pritchard's critique is in his *Social Anthropology and Other Essays* (Glencoe: Free Press, 1964), p. 181.

[5] Abner Cohen's *Arab Border Villages in Israel* (Manchester: Manchester University Press, 1965) is a clear example of such an approach. For a detailed critique of Cohen's study, see Talal Asad, "Anthropological Texts and Ideological Problems: An Analysis of Cohen on Arab Villages in Israel," *Economy and Society*, 4, no. 3 (August 1975), 251-82.

social inequality, for instance, would begin to develop and then be replaced by a movement toward egalitarianism.[6]

Even in the small-scale, relatively isolated societies where the notions of functionalism appeared to work best, there were clear indications of the artificial conventions that functional theory imposed. Such small-scale societies were generally studied in a colonial context but described as they supposedly had existed in the precolonial past, with only passing references being made to the consequences of European conquest and administration. The effects of European incursion upon the central institutions of political authority, kinship, religion, and economics were generally ignored. It was also usually assumed that such societies had been essentially unchanging in form in the period prior to colonial conquest or to sustained contact with the West. In the heyday of functionalism, American anthropologists frequently used the term *base-line* to describe such societies prior to "outside" contact. This term clearly reveals the careless sort of assumption often made about the historical past.

## FUNCTIONALISM IN THE STUDY OF THE MIDDLE EAST

The limitations of the concept of functionalism became particularly clear when the notion was applied to complex, historically known societies. By the 1950s, minor qualifications were being added to the basic arguments of functionalism so that the "functional" description of a society was frequently complemented by historical description. Evans-Pritchard's *The Sanusi of Cyrenaica*[7] is a classic monograph by an anthropologist which embodies the resulting contradiction. Evans-Pritchard's criticisms of extreme forms of functional theory have already been mentioned. My commentary here is based upon the implicit argument of *The Sanusi*.

The goal of the monograph is to describe how an Islamic religious order, the *Sanūsīya*, became in the nineteenth century the predominant religious order to which the transhumant Bedouin tribes of Cyrenaica (Libya) were affiliated. He argues that the *Sanūsīya* was the only order to adapt effectively to the acephalous segmentary social organization of the tribes, in which each individual was presumably an equal of every other and no one occupied a position of full-time leadership,

---

[6]This is one of the elements of the argument presented in Ernest Gellner's *Saints of the Atlas* (Chicago: University of Chicago Press, 1979), a complex study that will be discussed in more detail in a later chapter. See also Paul Stirling, "Cause, Knowledge and Change: Turkish Village Revisited," in John Davis, ed., *Choice and Change: Essays in Honour of Lucy Mair* (New York: Humanities Press, 1974), pp. 191-229. Stirling's original fieldwork in Turkey was conducted at intervals between 1949 and 1952 and is presented in his monograph *Turkish Village* (New York: John Wiley & Sons, Inc., 1965), now unfortunately out of print. In 1971 Stirling was allowed to return to the villages he had studied for the brief period of a week. His "Cause, Knowledge and Change," based on this visit, recognizes the problems of studying change within the compass of a functionalist framework.

[7]Oxford: Clarendon Press, 1949.

so that in the twentieth century, Italian conquest and colonization provided the sustained pressure which was necessary to transform the acephalous segmentary tribal society into a state organization under the leadership of the head of the *Sanūsī* religious order, who subsequently became Libya's first monarch. But a closer examination of this study indicates that the section in which the social structure of Bedouin tribes is described is abstract and totally separated from the much longer straightforward historical account describing the growth of the *Sanūsī* religious brotherhood and the Italian conquest of Libya. Only in two crucial paragraphs (pp. 104-5) does Evans-Pritchard discuss how Bedouin tribal society was presumably transformed from an acephalous segmentary society into a state organization. He speculates that prolonged external pressure forces "segmentary" societies into such transformations but of course provides no detailed description of this process. His historical account is fully intelligible without reference to the abstract description of the segmentary structure of Bedouin society as it presumably was in the precolonial historical past (pp. 29-61). As social history the book is eminently successful, but the ahistorical description of Bedouin social organization is marginal to that success.

Perhaps the most broad-gauged attempt to apply functionalist theory to the Middle East was provided by the physical anthropologist Carleton Coon in *Caravan: The Story of the Middle East,* first published in 1951 and revised several times over the following decade. This book was the first general anthropological introduction to the area and for a time enjoyed a sustained popularity. Yet *Caravan* also glaringly portrays the drawbacks of functionalism. The book's unity is sustained by the metaphor of the mosaic, a device which is useful for conveying some of the bare geographical and ethnographic facts concerning the Middle East and North Africa—modes of livelihood, physical characteristics of the population, religious and linguistic groupings, and political organization. Unfortunately, it is less adequate in explaining the interrelations among these elements or their known historical transformations. In fact, a principal negative virtue of *Caravan* is its clear exemplification of the weakness of functionalist theories in providing meaningful accounts of historically known societies. Thus in his first chapter, "The Picture and Its Pieces," Coon writes that the mosaic pattern of the region becomes clear if the "little pieces of plastic and broken glass" are removed. By plastic and broken glass he means essentially everything that is "modern" or in transition in the Middle East. Coon writes that "a culture in transition is hard to describe and harder to understand; we must find some period in history when the culture was, relatively speaking, at rest."[8]

This assertion means that Coon's method is, for instance, to describe Egyptian society as it presumably was prior to Bonaparte's invasion, Morocco as it existed in the late nineteenth and early twentieth centuries, and Turkey as it was in the nineteenth century and then to assume that these descriptions essentially hold in all key

---

[8]Carleton S. Coon, *Caravan: The Story of the Middle East,* rev. ed. (New York: Holt, Rinehart and Winston, Inc., 1961), p. 8.

respects for much longer periods of time. These are "base times" for Coon, and he assumes that for hundreds of years—from at least the fifteenth to the nineteenth century in most parts of the Middle East—societies were "frozen" in form. Recent historical research has underlined what was already known before the publication of Coon's book: Ahistorical assumptions concerning Middle Eastern societies are profoundly inappropriate. The extraordinary assumption of centuries of cultural "rest" creates a highly artificial and misleading way of looking at any society or civilization and is empirically inapplicable to the civilizational area which he describes. Throughout the period of cultural "rest" that Coon assumes, highly significant transformations were occurring throughout the Middle East. To name only one, in the nineteenth century the Middle East was increasingly being drawn into the world capitalist economy. This was one of the principal factors leading to the instability of central governments in many regions such as Morocco after the 1860s. The resulting instability provided a convenient excuse for European colonial intervention in some instances and the control of vital governmental services such as customs revenues in others. Nor were all transformations of the society related to external factors alone. Much of the impetus for change came from developments "internal" to Middle Eastern societies themselves.

Elsewhere, Coon describes Islam as the "right" religion for the Middle East because it survived as the dominant religion in the area for such an extended period of time. Hence he argues that Islam must be in "equilibrium" with the environment. Here again the "horse" analogy is lurking in the background. A similar argument underlies his explanation of the prohibition upon wine in the Islamic world. Coon suggests that with so much of the area a desert and the Arabs so hospitable, it would be too cumbersome and expensive to carry goatskins of wine through the region.[9] Or consider his more general statement: "The keynote to the Islamic way of life is that it provided a maximum goodness of fit for a swarm of human beings, living in the environment of the Middle East, to a progressively deteriorating landscape."[10] Again, this statement constitutes a massive tautology. It could just as well be adapted to Christianity in Europe or, in the New World, to Aztec human sacrifices. All that needs to be argued is that such practices exist because they fulfill a function.

To return to the specific consideration of the Middle East, Coon's assertion of a "fit" between Islam and the Middle East ignores the fact that the center of gravity of the Muslim population in the world falls somewhere between Pakistan and Iran; in fact, the majority of the world's Muslims live on the Indian subcontinent and in Southeast Asia. Admittedly, Coon's argument also can be adapted to the environmental circumstances of these regions, although again the argument asserts no more than the fact that if things were not the way they are, then they would be different.

The serious theoretical shortcomings of Coon's book did not prevent it from

---

[9] *Ibid.*, p. 347.

[10] *Ibid.*, p. 346.

being a practical and popular introduction to the area, especially at a time when there was no other general text available. Yet there are alternatives to functionalism in the social sciences. General propositions about social organization and culture can be made without turning them into universal "laws." Such universal laws simply do not exist except in a most trivial or acultural sense in human societies.

Coon was exceptional in writing of a civilizational area, for as I have previously indicated, the professional work of anthropologists is primarily upon a much more minute scale. At this reduced scale, whatever the shortcomings of functionalism as sociological theory, it has the decisive practical advantage of providing an organizing guide for anthropological fieldwork. It encourages anthropologists to conceive of societies in their totality—or, to be more modest about the scope of anthropology as actually practiced, it encourages fieldworkers to collect information on kinship, myths, politics, economics, and other aspects of social life and to seek out interrelations between these various activities even when the linkages are not immediately apparent. As a consequence, a substantial number of ethnographies now exist that provide resource materials for purposes other than those for which they were originally intended. It can be argued that the notion of gathering documentation on the "total" social world of individuals, whether they be office workers in an industrial society or villagers who spend a large part of their lives in relation with significant others from the same immediate locale, constitutes a distinctively anthropological technique of viewing culture and society. As a theory, functionalism has limitations which are obvious once they are made explicit, but its organizing concepts have proved to be an enduring *ad hoc* stratagem for effective field research.

Three examples are presented here to indicate the strategies involved in the functionalist study of societies. I have deliberately chosen examples of research toward the end of the functionalist era, the 1950s and early 1960s, and of researchers who have since acknowledged the limitations of their earlier theoretical assumptions. The first two examples concern societies in which irrigation is a main economic feature; the third example involves an agricultural village in southern Lebanon.

There were several converging reasons for the interest in irrigation societies in the 1950s. One was the impact of Karl Wittfogel's *Oriental Despotism*,[11] which argued that irrigation systems, or at least certain forms of them, necessitated the development of hierarchical forms of sociopolitical organization. The thesis attracted the attention of a wide range of archaeologists and social anthropologists, for it provided what was considered to be a testable framework in which the relation between modes of production and social organization could be explored. Another reason was that studies of irrigation societies fit in nicely with the conventions of functional explanation. After all, in a region such as the Middle East, irrigation systems and the scarce resource of water which they distribute are vital to

[11] Karl Wittfogel, *Oriental Despotism: A Comparative Study of Total Power* (New Haven and London: Yale University Press, 1957).

agricultural production and social life. Social institutions are sharply constrained by ecological considerations. It would be a poor use of metaphor, but nonetheless accurate, to point out that functionalist theory itself is a hydraulic theory of the integration of society: A shift in any component invariably brings about shifts in the others.

The first example concerns the *Fadījī* Nubians of Upper (southern) Egypt as they were studied in 1961 by the late Abdul Hamid el-Zein, then an ardent functionalist and later a leading proponent of the structural study of ritual and symbolism.[12]

The people Zein studied were relocated elsewhere in Egypt in 1963 when the construction of the new Aswan dam resulted in the flooding of their old village sites, so that Zein's description is necessarily in the past tense. Prior to the flooding, settlements and fertile land were located in a narrow belt along the Nile, with the settlements framed on both sides of the river by rocky, barren mountains. The region received only one inch of rainfall annually, so that agriculture was entirely dependent upon irrigation. Prior to relocation in 1963, there were earlier pressures upon the availability of land induced by technological change. The first Aswan dam built in 1902 raised the water level in the winter of each year and thus reduced the land locally available for cultivation; the same effect followed later heightenings of the dam in 1912 and 1933. In the low water season of August and September, this low-level land was briefly available for cultivation in addition to the land located at higher elevations. Wheat and beans were the principal crops, although many villagers also owned palm trees and harvested their dates.

In three hundred pages Zein works out the implications of the water wheel for the social life of the *Fadīja.* In the course of his argument, it becomes clear that the *Fadīja* never were self-subsistent agriculturally. In the nineteenth century their village was important as a way station in the slave trade between Cairo and the Sudan, while more recently it was important in the lucrative smuggling between Egypt and the Sudan. In addition, Nubians have for long emigrated to other parts of Egypt—a phenomenon that was already important in the nineteenth century. The remittances these emigrants sent home were necessary for the subsistence of their relatives and families. Significant in this respect, the principal crops of the *Fadīj*a were insufficient for their subsistence, so that many villagers played active roles in the market as merchants and traders as a necessary part of their livelihood.

---

[12] Abdul Hamid M. el-Zein, "Water and Wheel in a Nubian Village." M.A. thesis, American University in Cairo, 1966. A published summary of el-Zein's argument is his "Socioeconomic Implications of the Water Wheel in Adendan, Nubia," in *Contemporary Egyptian Nubia,* ed. Robert A. Fernea (New Haven: Human Relations Area Files, Inc., 1966), Vol. 2, pp. 298-322. For a general account of Nubian society accompanied by an outstanding photographic essay, see Robert A. Fernea and Georg Gerster, *Nubians in Egypt: Peaceful People* (Austin and London: University of Texas Press, 1973). Zein's principal "structural" study of an Islamic community is *The Sacred Meadows: A Structural Analysis of Religious Symbolism in an East African Town* (Evanston, Ill.: Northwestern University Press, 1974). For the life history of an individual Nubian, see John G. Kennedy, *Struggle for Change in a Nubian Community,* Explorations in World Ethnography (Palo Alto: Mayfield Publishing Company, 1977).

But, as Zein specifies, the *Fadīja* nonetheless claimed that their status in the community was linked directly to the ownership of land and water rights.

Zein cites a Nubian proverb to reinforce his theme of the water wheel as a central element in *Fadīji* society: "The water wheel is like a mosque, and those who serve it are like those who serve the mosque." Zein treats membership in the village, status in the local community, and central rituals as if they were all part of a closed system. Thus he emphasizes the land shortage and the ecological constraints that made it impossible for men to build up wealth in animals. He sees education, emigration, and market activities as partial solutions to the chronic land shortage, thus conceiving them as a sort of safety valve so that the system of the village was able to work.

In describing the ownership and operation of the water wheel, Zein emphasizes the functional justification of certain traditional arrangements. Thus the base of a water wheel is hard to site—few locations are suitable for it—and difficult to repair. It must be owned by one man, writes Zein, *because* it is so crucial. The upper parts of the water wheel, including the buckets, are individually owned or rented. In the case of a serious quarrel certain of these upper parts (unlike the base) may be removed and replaced by those belonging to someone else without seriously disrupting the wheel's operation. Through case studies of disputes, Zein indicates how *Fadīji* social institutions prevent conflicts from interfering with their livelihood. Similarly he indicates how patterns of marriage alliances are linked to the ownership of water rights. Co-owners of water rights seek intermarriage between their households in order to solidify their alliances and lessen the problems con-

**FIGURE 3-1** Water wheel, Egyptian Nubia. The wheel is partially covered by branches to retard evaporation. (Courtesy Abdul Hamid M. el-Zein.)

nected with inheritance. The roles played in rituals are also closely associated with such rights. The water wheel thus is a concrete artifact whose study reveals the components and functioning of the supposedly closed social system of the village.

Although Zein's densely packed monograph does not provide a "total" explanation of village life, as functionalist arguments often promise, it manages to provide an intricate description of what he asserts to be a key institutional complex within Nubian life. The ethnographic description of the water wheel, its maintenance and its relation to other aspects of village life provided by Zein constitute what is undoubtedly the best descriptive account of the social organization of irrigation practices available for the Middle East. Less convincing is his overall conceptual framework, in which the components of society at a given moment are considered to be in a closed equilibrium with each other. In the classical functionalist tradition, Zein considers the water wheel and ownership of water rights to be in direct relation to the cultural value of community maintained by the *Fadīja* ("moral" community in Durkheim's terms) and to the acquisition of social honor within the community. Yet Zein is such an exceptionally able ethnographer that his own data suggest that the system of status honor that he described was more complex and less holistic than he claimed. For instance, villagers who could command cash from remittances or from trading activities fail to fit into the nicely established equilibrium of status honor tied to land and water rights which Zein asserts. When returning emigrants invested their money in land, Zein was able to provide an account of their role in the status system. But when the funds were invested in education or new economic activities, his account is more ambiguous and simply treats such forms of status as if they were alien to the local community.

Zein explicitly states that while individuals entered and left the social system and while individual ownership of land and water rights was constantly shifting, the water wheel and the system of allocating rights connected with it persisted. Yet within the monograph Zein acknowledges that the "enduring" system of the allocation of rights which he describes came into its present form only at the turn of the century. As a descriptive convention, Zein's assumption that the water wheel and the social obligations connected with it were a central cohesive force works well so long as his account concerns only those activities directly related to the water wheel. Leaks in the "closed" system show up as soon as other activities of the villagers are considered.

Robert Fernea's *Shaykh and Effendi: Changing Patterns of Authority among the El Shabana of Southern Iraq*[13] is another primarily functionalist monograph on an irrigation society, inspired by the explicit theoretical problem of changing patterns of political authority. At the time of Fernea's fieldwork (1956-1958) in a small town of 3,000 persons 150 miles to the south of Baghdad, Fernea was primarily, if indirectly, interested in the Wittfogel thesis of the relation of irrigation with political authority. Essentially Fernea's approach is to provide a general ecological and social historical description of southern Iraq, with an emphasis

---

[13] Cambridge: Harvard University Press, 1970.

upon the Āl Shabāna tribe. This is followed by an excellent general account of tribal organization. Although the Āl Shabāna tribal structure is characterized as "segmentary" by Fernea, he is a careful ethnographer and realizes that the lineage system by which tribesmen characterize their organization and obligations simply does not correspond to actual groupings.[14] The remainder of the study examines the changing patterns of authority of the tribal leadership under Ottoman rule, the succeeding period of the British mandate, and finally under the independent Iraqi regime. The authority of tribal leaders (*shaykh*-s) was most autonomous under Ottoman rule and in fact was enhanced in the late nineteenth century by the system of land registration implemented by the Ottomans as part of wide-ranging tax reforms. These reforms enabled tribal leaders to register traditionally collective or "tribal" lands in their personal names, thus becoming major landowners and in many cases turning their fellow tribesmen into tenants and sharecroppers. Their authority was more restricted under British rule and, in more recent times, has been even more circumscribed in favor of irrigation engineers and other representatives of the central government. Nonetheless, tribal leaders have managed to maintain considerable political influence as intermediaries between tribesmen and representatives of the central government.

A principal contribution of Fernea's monograph is its clear exposition of present-day tribal organization.[15] Fernea adopts the conventions of functional analysis but, like Zein, does not allow his ethnographic account to be trapped entirely within his theoretical formulations. Fernea clearly depicts the significance of "outside" political forces for comprehending local authority structures, although he is less successful in indicating how individual shaykhs and their followers themselves viewed the successive political transformations which he describes and the way in which perceptions of change affected the action which they took. Attention to such a theme would have avoided at least some of the pitfalls of the layer-cake conception of history, in which social and cultural institutions are seen as unchanging over long, indefinite periods (that is, "premodern," "traditional"). Such ahistorical notions are encouraged by the conventions of functional analysis, an approach that Fernea in fact has abandoned in his more recent writing.[16]

Perhaps the most incisive account of the limitations of the functionalist approach was developed by the British anthropologist Emrys Peters. Peters has worked in two regions in the Middle East. As a student of E. E. Evans-Pritchard, he worked with the Bedouin of Cyrenaica, Libya, shortly after the Second World War. The principal results of that research have been a series of articles exploring the concept of segmentation and the feud (see Chapter 5). His most direct inquiry

---

[14] *Ibid.*, p. 104. The implications of characterizing a society as "segmentary" are discussed in Chapter 5.

[15] *Ibid.*, p. 104.

[16] See especially Robert A. Fernea and James M. Malarkey, "Anthropology of the Middle East and North Africa: A Critical Assessment," in Bernard J. Siegal, Alan R. Beals, and Stephen A. Tyler, eds., *Annual Review of Anthropology*, 4 (Palo Alto: Annual Reviews, Inc., 1975), pp. 193-206.

into the more general issue of functional theory is contained in two articles he wrote on a Shī'ī Muslim village in south Lebanon, where he worked for a year in 1952 and again in 1956. The first analysis was published in 1963, although it had been presented informally at scholarly conferences prior to his return to Lebanon in 1956. A thorough "recantation" of his 1963 article then appeared in 1972.[17]

His earlier analysis is of more than historical interest, for it indicates in detail the social and economic organization of the village. In his first account, published in 1963, Peters used the "equilibrium" assumption to which I earlier referred. Of course, such a notion does not imply that individuals are frozen in place. Peters perceived that at least some individuals were highly mobile but that the *structure* of the society—that is, the orderly arrangement of roles and statuses within it—remained the same. Revolutions against the social order did not bring about the collapse of the social order; rather, they provided opportunities for powerful persons or groups of persons to replace others whose power and influence had diminished.

As Peters writes, there were many characteristics of the village he studied that led him to believe that an equilibrium model of its social structure was appropriate in 1952 and for at least three generations prior to that time. In the first place, the village was territorially discrete, located on a high promontory with a cliff on one side and sharply delineated borders on the others, so that it was set off sharply from the other villages in the region. Its population of eleven hundred people appeared prosperous and largely self-subsistent. There was an abundant rainfall of fifty to sixty inches from November through March, though irrigation was needed for the rest of the year. The luxurious array of crops included tomatoes, eggplant, peppers, beans, peas, carrots, cabbage, apples, oranges, quince, radishes, lettuce, cucumbers, plums, figs, pomegranates, sugar cane, olives, and grapes. Many villagers also had small herds of sheep and goats, although most of the meat consumed in the village was purchased elsewhere.

Another reason that Peters conceived the village to be self-contained was the emphasis which the villagers themselves placed upon landownership as a criterion of social identity. Villagers asserted a special identity with their land and spoke of themselves as being its "sons."

In his 1963 article, Peters accepted the villagers' self-categorization into distinct groups as an adequate model of the actual social structure. Essentially, this division was composed of the "Learned Families," the commercial traders, and a peasant proletariat. The village was predominantly Shī'ī Muslim, although a few Christians were also present. Since nearly all of Peters's analysis concerns the Muslim population, I will concentrate upon it as well. Membership in the three Muslim cate-

---

[17] Emrys L. Peters, "Aspects of Rank and Status among Muslims in a Lebanese Village," in *Mediterranean Countrymen,* ed. Julian Pitt-Rivers (Paris and The Hague: Mouton, 1963), pp. 159-202. This has been reprinted in Volume 2 of Louise E. Sweet, ed., *Peoples and Cultures of the Middle East* (Garden City: Natural History Press, 1970), pp. 76-123. Peters's "recantation" (my term) is contained in his "Shifts in Power in a Lebanese Village,'" in *Rural Politics and Social Change in the Middle East,* eds. Richard Antoun and Iliya Harik (Bloomington and London: Indiana University Press, 1972), pp. 165-97.

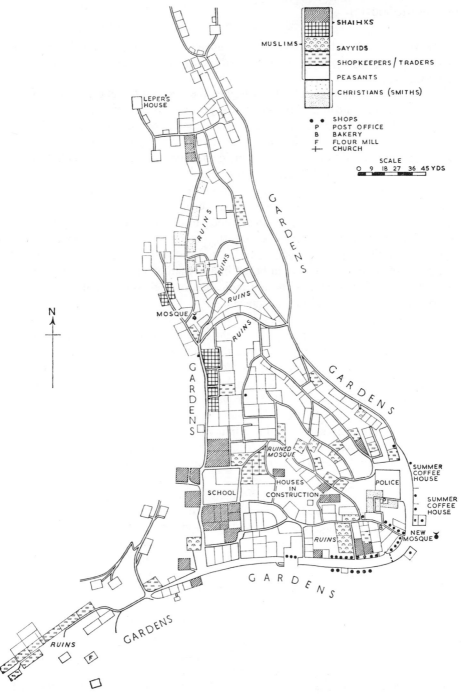

MUSLIMS {
SHAIHKS
SAYYIDS
SHOPKEEPERS/TRADERS
PEASANTS
CHRISTIANS (SMITHS)

•  • SHOPS
P POST OFFICE
B BAKERY
F FLOUR MILL
✝ CHURCH

SCALE
0  9  18  27  36  45 YDS

N

LEPER'S HOUSE

G A R D E N S

RUINS
RUINS
RUINS
RUINS
RUINS

MOSQUE

G A R D E N S

G A R D E N S

RUINED MOSQUE

HOUSES IN CONSTRUCTION

SCHOOL

POLICE

SUMMER COFFEE HOUSE

SUMMER COFFEE HOUSE

NEW MOSQUE

RUINS

G A R D E N S

GARDENS

RUINS

F

**FIGURE 3-2** A village in southern Lebanon, 1950s. (From Emrys L. Peters, "Aspects of Rank and Status among Muslims in a Lebanese Village," in *Mediterranean Countrymen,* ed. Julian Pitt-Rivers [Paris and The Hague: Mouton & Co., 1963], p. 168. Courtesy Emrys L. Peters and Mouton & Co., Publishers.)

gories was primarily related to landownership and use and was reflected in patterns of dress, seating arrangements on social occasions, and other readily visible signs of comportment.

The first group as seen by the villagers, the Learned Families, was composed in part of the descendants of the Prophet's great-grandson ᶜAlī. These were called *sayyid*-s. The remainder of this group were known as *shaykh*-s. They claimed descent from an ancestor who fought alongside the Prophet's grandson at the seventh-century Battle of Karbala, an incident which is crucial to Shīᶜī history. These families were called "Learned" not because they necessarily were educated but because they claimed a superior social and religious status based on descent. Some members of the Learned Families had been to traditional Shīᶜī centers of learning in Iraq. This aristocracy constituted about 20 percent of the population of the village. They intermarried among themselves and with families of similar status in neighboring villages and managed to control local political offices. The Learned Families tended to live in better houses than other villagers, performed no manual labor on their land as another indication of their status, and were said by the villagers to own the majority of the land.

Although the Learned Families claimed a common identity based upon descent, it was possible for persons from the other categories to assimilate to them through persistent effort and the expenditure of wealth in ways approved by the leaders of the Learned Families. Peters provides several specific examples of individuals in the other categories who had become wealthy and powerful and who, through demonstrating proper deference and a willingness to become publicly known as clients of the Learned Families, could put forward a claim to Learned Family status themselves, at least in certain contexts. In his 1972 account, Peters acknowledges that he did not see such social mobility as a force in the realignment of sets of social relationships, but only as a movement of persons within a fixed social system.[18]

The second important group were the commercial traders. These were not so clearly defined as a category, although they cultivated small gardens, tended to wear European clothing, and belonged primarily to two patronymic groups. Together, they constituted another 20 percent of the Muslim population.

The third and largest group was the peasant proletariat, the remainder of the population with the exception of a few Christian households. Peasants worked their own land and served as laborers for the lands of the Learned Families. In his 1963 account of the village, in which he saw status as part of a single, overriding system related to the land, Peters regarded the high rate of migration among the peasant proletariat merely as an indication of pressures upon the land. If persons of peasant origin migrated in large numbers to North and South America, Great Britain, and West Africa, it was simply because of the lack of locally available land, and not because of any other factor. In his later study Peters acknowledged that earlier he had largely neglected the improved access to schools of many

[18] Peters, "Shifts in Power," p. 165.

of these emigrants, the substantial remittances they sent back to the village, and, especially in the case of those who remained in Lebanon, the active influence they maintained in village affairs. Because the villagers insisted to Peters that ownership of land was the key to understanding stratification, he had directed his research strategies primarily toward this topic and assumed that the social structure he so construed was stable over time.

Peters confirmed his earlier conception of a stable social structure through the analysis of two behavioral indices. One was the performance of the annual mourning *(ta^cziya)* plays commemorating the martyrdom of the slaying of Husayn, the Prophet's grandson, by Sunnī Muslims in the year 680. Throughout the regions in which Shī^cī Islam predominates, such reenactments were until recently performed during the first ten days of the Muslim lunar month of Muharram, in some circumstances by professional actors and sometimes by the villagers themselves. In the village studied by Peters, the roles of the Shī^ca, supporters of ^Alī (the Prophet's son-in-law) and descendants of the Prophet, who of course lost the battle and suffered martyrdom, were performed by the Learned Families. The roles of the victorious but treacherous Sunnī Muslims were performed by the peasants, thus dramatically symbolizing what Peters took to be fixed elements of the status of and a symbolic "warning" to the peasants of the anarchy that would prevail if descendants of the Prophet were not allowed their rightful place in the social world.

Peters also considered the fact that despite some signs of discontent, almost everyone in the village exhibited *some* form of deference to the Learned Families, and that in elections for various local offices, the candidates supported by the Learned Families invariably won. Because the Learned Families were a minority, their own votes were insufficient to win an election, but through the manipulation of other village factions, they always managed to win.

Soon after his initial period of fieldwork, Peters saw the architecture of what he had assumed to be a stable system of social structure disintegrate. In 1953, there were municipal elections throughout Lebanon. One of the peculiarities of elections in the Lebanon of this period was that persons could choose to vote where they wished, although most franchised persons chose to vote in their natal villages. This fact in itself renders suspect any account of local politics which considered only the presence of persons in the immediate geographic locale of an electoral region. No village in Lebanon is more than half a day by bus from any other village, so that persons not regularly resident in the village but who had ties with it could easily participate in its elections. In the 1953 elections the candidate supported by the Learned Families was soundly defeated and, moreover, the Learned Families were unable to exert significant political influence from that time on. The winner in the 1953 election was still in office fifteen years later and had been instrumental in bringing a new school to the village, a medical clinic, a paved road, and education for women, among other significant transformations.

The value of the 1972 study by Peters lies in his meticulous account of why his early analysis and implicit theoretical assumptions were invalid. As Peters writes, his principal difficulty was his acceptance of the global social categories used by the villagers themselves. This directed his attention away from certain major economic and status transformations which were then occurring. These were not perceived as patterned regularities by the villagers themselves, but, Peters argues, an understanding of them was essential for an adequate social anthropological account of village structure. The villagers asserted a central unitary value in the ownership of land, *said* that the Learned Families were the major landowners, and accused the Learned Families of coveting the land of the other groups. This obscured for Peters the fact that a large number of Learned Families were poor and, moreover, were handicapped in that their status obliged them not to work their own land. Being hard pressed for funds, they found themselves selling their land to an emerging group of commoners whom Peters calls the "Professionals" in his 1972 article. These were the children of commoners who had attended American missionary schools in the region and who were thus often enabled to acquire further technical and university training. For reasons of their status, the Learned Families were compelled to send their children only to Shī‘ī religious schools, a restriction that the commoners could easily ignore. Hence a number of commoner children became prominent doctors, lawyers, merchants, bureaucrats, and managers in Lebanon and abroad. Likewise, the commercial skills acquired by peasant emigrants familiarized them with modern administrative techniques. These persons had considerable money for investment and put at least part of it in village lands. Yet, while the Learned Families maintained their land in nonmarket crops, the Professional and trader classes were more aware of the possibilities for export crops and invested in such things as apples. By the time the Learned Families became aware of the income to be derived from such crops, the market value had diminished so that much of the initial advantage of investing in them was lost. Nor did the Professionals choose to make the heavy investment necessary to acquire merit in the eyes of the Learned Families.

In many ways, Peters wrote in his 1972 reanalysis, there was a disadvantage to the high rank of the Learned Families. Only a few of them were actually large landowners. Poor *sayyid*-s and *shaykh*-s had to live on loans because it was beneath their dignity to work their own lands. Similarly, though as a group the Learned Families exhibited a high degree of literacy, this was almost exclusively acquired in traditional religious education. This limited their perception of and ability to benefit from modern economic and political opportunities.

Moreover, the social networks and ties of patronage and clientship of the Learned Families showed sharp contrasts to those of the other two groups. The Learned Families tended to marry only among themselves or with persons of similar rank in neighboring villages. The peasant Professionals had weblike connections through marriage and patronage with persons of many different walks of life in Beirut and elsewhere—bankers, politicians, doctors, educators, emigrants, and entrepreneurs—and used these ties to advantage in the acquisition of political influence. The Learned Families were caught up in a narrow web of relations and were pursuing what had become a defunct economic policy of investing their wealth only in land, although the locus of significant economic activities had shifted elsewhere. The Professionals had acquired the training, the connections, and the resources which enabled them to replace the Learned Families as the dominant social group. Furthermore, they were capable of enhancing the welfare of the community as a whole through the effective manipulation of these ties.

The error of Peters's first analysis, as he saw it, had been the attempt to fit all the facts of village life into a single pattern. In his reanalysis, he concluded that the "system" the anthropologist looks for is necessarily open-ended and must be explained at least in part by looking for historical transformations. The key components of status present in any situation must be looked at comparatively in order to be comprehended, both in different social settings and at different historical periods. The system thus described is open-ended, and its components become apparent by the historical analysis of shifts in power. Patterned regularities exist in such open-ended systems, but they are not the elusive and misleading single system presumed by the functionalists. As Peters wrote, the perplexing (for him) results of the 1953 election jolted him into a reconsideration of what he had thought to be a basic, enduring social structure. Through his reanalysis, he perceived that rank as perceived by the villagers operated differentially—that is, to the detriment of some members of the Learned Families and to the advantage of some persons in the other categories and that ownership of land was not of equal significance to all the villagers.

In fairness to Peters, few anthropologists in the 1950s and 1960s realized the full importance of the cultural and social impact of immigration and emigration, education, and exposure to the West and the ensuing feedback upon the political and cultural fate of the region. Even earlier in the century, to take only the countries of North Africa as an example, the presence of large numbers of North African laborers in France led to the development of organized labor movements in the colonies and the coalescence of a nationalist movement. The same was true for the large number of North Africans who fought in France's armies, and a smaller but influential number of North African students who studied in France. More recently, in the 1950s and 1960s, political issues in countries such as Brazil, France, and West Germany related to problems of bicultural education can be traced directly to Middle Eastern immigrant populations. When such workers return to their country of origin, they bring with them changed notions of housing, marriage, family, and society. Their changing tastes in clothing, housing, and other commodities have contributed to the precipitate decline of many traditional crafts such as weaving, rug making, and the like. Whether their experience with the West is one of bitterness and disillusionment or one of partial liberation from some of the constraints of their own society, their lives are profoundly altered. Emigration is significant enough a phenomenon in countries such as Morocco, Algeria, Tunisia, Lebanon, Egypt, and Syria to affect the lives of virtually every town and village. *Immigration* into oil-rich countries such as Libya, Saudi Arabia, and the Gulf states (where immigrants sometimes outnumber local residents) has had a similarly profound impact. Additionally, it has only been in the last two decades that substantial numbers of school-age women have had improved access to higher education in many Middle Eastern countries. The consequences of such change are often delayed, which may be one of the reasons that Peters underestimated its importance in his earlier study, but as he realized in his reanalysis, its cumulative and long-range impact can often be profound.[19]

There are other aspects of Peters's analysis that are explored in later chapters, but for the moment it is critical for its brief indication of certain features of village life in one part of the Middle East and for its unusually straightforward evaluation of the shortcomings of functional analysis and assumptions which imply that villagers, pastoralists, and townsmen live now or lived in the past in closed social worlds. In the ensuing chapters more satisfactory alternatives to such concepts are presented.

[19]*Ibid.*, pp. 174-85.

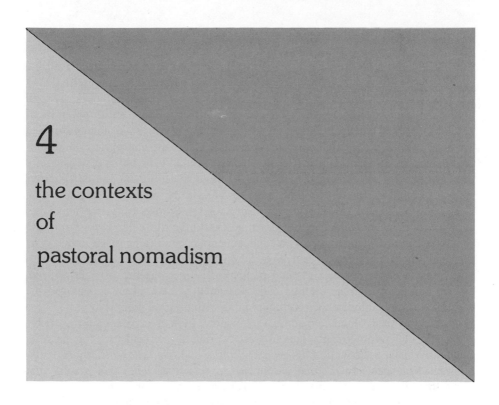

# 4

## the contexts
## of
## pastoral nomadism

As of 1970, pastoral nomads constituted only slightly more than 1 percent of the population of the Middle East, yet such nomadic societies have been more extensively studied by anthropologists than those in village or urban settings. There are major anthropological studies in English of pastoral nomads in Iran, Turkey, Somalia, Israel, Saudi Arabia, the Sudan, and Libya, as well as an extensive literature in professional journals.[1] Until recently, in contrast, the Middle East has been

---

[1] The most significant recent studies include Fredrik Barth, *Nomads of South Persia* (New York: Humanities Press, 1965); Daniel G. Bates, *Nomads and Farmers: A Study of the Yörük of Southeastern Turkey,* Anthropological Papers, 52 (Ann Arbor: University of Michigan Museum of Anthropology, 1973); William Irons, *The Yomut Turkmen: A Study of Social Organization among a Central Asian Turkic-speaking Population,* Anthropological Papers, 58 (Ann Arbor: University of Michigan Museum of Anthropology, 1975); I. M. Lewis, *A Pastoral Democracy: A Study of Pastoralism and Politics among the Northern Somali of the Horn of Africa* (London: Oxford University Press for the International African Institute, 1961); Emanuel Marx, *Bedouin of the Negev* (Manchester: Manchester University Press, 1967); Talal Asad, *The Kababish Arabs: Power, Authority and Consent in a Nomadic Tribe* (London: C. Hurst & Company, 1970); and a series of articles by Emrys Peters on the Bedouin of Cyrenaica (Libya), including "Some Structural Aspects of the Feud among the Camel-Herding Bedouin of Cyrenaica," *Africa,* 37 (1967), 261-82, and "The Tied and the Free: An Account of a Type of Patron-Client Relationship among the Bedouin Pastoralists of Cyrenaica," in *Contributions to Mediterranean Sociology,* ed. J. G. Peristiany (Paris and The Hague: Mouton & Co., 1968), pp. 167-88. The only recent monograph on pastoralism on the Arabian peninsula is Donald Powell Cole, *Nomads of the Nomads: The Al Murrah Bedouin of the Empty Quarter,* Worlds of Man (Chicago: Aldine Publishing Company, 1975). Three useful collections of recent papers are *Perspectives on Nomadism,* eds. William Irons and Neville Dyson-Hudson, International Studies

the only world region for which no equivalent range of studies has been available concerning its major populations, the peasants or settled "tribal" communities.[2]

A partial explanation for the disproportionate emphasis upon pastoral nomadism continues to be the romantic attraction to some anthropologists of nomadic life and virtues. There are also some more important theoretical and practical reasons. First of all, pastoral nomadism offers the appropriate conditions for social groups which conceive their identity primarily in terms of segmentary lineage organization, a subject which raises basic questions on the comparative study of society in the Middle East and elsewhere in the world.[3] A second reason is an anthropological concern with human ecology. Studies of pastoral societies contribute to an understanding of human adaptation to difficult environments and to the constraints which ecological and economic conditions place upon social organization. A third reason is a practical one: Middle Eastern governments have been anxious to settle their pastoral populations for a mixture of political, economic, and humanitarian motives and consequently have often encouraged the work of foreign and indigenous anthropologists with pastoral groups.

Patterns of pastoral nomadism vary widely, even if considered in a strictly ecological dimension. Geographers interested primarily in land use, for instance, frequently make a distinction between *horizontal* and *vertical* nomadism. *Horizontal* nomadism refers to pastoral movements in search of water and pasture that occur throughout the year in roughly similar ecological regions, such as is the case with the camel-herding "noble" tribes of the Arabian peninsula and the Kabābish Arabs of the northern Sudan, who have mixed herds of camels, sheep, and goats. *Vertical* nomadism involves seasonal movement between complementary ecological zones, such as lowland plains for part of the year and mountainous regions for another. This form of pastoralism principally involves the herding of sheep and goats and is frequently combined with agriculture and the use of permanent settlements for part of the year. Among other regions, it is the most common form of pastoralism in Iran, Iraq, and Morocco.

---

in Sociology and Social Anthropology, 13 (Leiden: E. J. Brill, 1972); *The Desert and the Sown: Nomads in Wider Society,* ed. Cynthia Nelson, Research Series, 21 (Berkeley: University of California, Institute of International Studies, 1973), and the Equipe Ecologie et Anthropologie des Sociétés Pastorales, *Pastoral Production and Society* (London and New York: Cambridge University Press, 1978). Finally, Douglas L. Johnson, *The Nature of Nomadism,* Research Paper 118 (Chicago: University of Chicago, Department of Geography, 1969), is a useful geographical study which also contains a thorough bibliography on Middle Eastern pastoralism. The most original and provocative book to appear in recent years on pastoral nomadism and its relation to states and empires, and on the relation between political forms and Bedouin oral literature, is Michael E. Meeker, *Literature and Violence in North Arabia,* Cambridge Studies in Cultural Systems, 3 (New York and London: Cambridge University Press, 1979).

[2]Clifford Geertz, "Studies in Peasant Life: Community and Society," in *Biennial Review of Anthropology, 1961,* ed. Bernard J. Siegal (Stanford: Stanford University Press, 1962), p. 17.

[3]On the significance of studying lineage organization in the context of pastoral societies as opposed to those of towns or villages, see Emrys Peters, "Aspects of Affinity in a Lebanese Maronite Village," in *Mediterranean Family Structures,* ed. J. G. Peristiany, Cambridge Studies in Social Anthropology, 13 (London: Cambridge University Press, 1976), pp. 30-32.

For most anthropological purposes, classifications of pastoral nomadic groups based purely upon ecological considerations or type of seasonal movement are insufficient. Both in recent decades and in earlier historical periods, the political and social relations of pastoral groups with the peasant settlements, towns, and states that are on the periphery of zones of intense pastoral activity have been as important for their livelihood as pastoralism itself. Pastoral nomadism depends upon regular access to settlements for a variety of agricultural products and other goods that can be obtained through trade (or pillage) or, on occasion in the past, by force. Pastoral, agricultural, and trade activities are part of a single economic system articulated by various forms of social and political domination. These forms are complex and the participants do not fall readily into classificatory niches such as nomads, villagers, and townsmen. Both now and in the past, many tribes commonly have had both nomadic and settled components, and political leadership and movements frequently have encompassed groups pursuing combinations of these forms of economic activity.[4]

## PASTORAL NOMADISM:
## THE PAST AND THE PRESENT

Some accounts of pastoral nomadism give the impression that only the political and economic transformations since the eighteenth century have significantly reduced it in scope. Actually, it has probably been the case that nomadic pastoralism has always been part of a larger system including agricultural, settled peasants, and trading urban centers. For no historical period is it possible to think of nomadic pastoralists as an autonomous society. The reasons for the seemingly irreversible decline beginning in the eighteenth century are multiple and vary considerably with region, but among them are the steady expansion of cultivated land to the detriment of lands available for grazing, the declining attractiveness of herds as a capital investment to merchants and other nonpastoralists, the disappearance of significant caravan traffic as alternative investments have become available, and the increasing ineffectiveness of nomads as a military force. Census figures for Iraq indicate the scope of this decline—in 1867 nomads constituted about 35 percent

---

[4]This observation is one of the essential features of Ibn Khaldūn's reflections on tribesmen, peasants, and urban dwellers. See Ibn Khaldūn (d. 1406), *The Muqaddimah,* 2nd ed., trans. Franz Rosenthal, Bollingen Series, 43 (Princeton: Princeton University Press, 1967), pp. 247-310. Among contemporary anthropologists, see Talal Asad, "The Bedouin as a Military Force: Notes on Some Aspects of Power Relations between Nomads and Sedentaries in Historical Perspective," in *Desert and Sown,* ed. Nelson, p. 71; and Philip Carl Salzman, "The Study of 'Complex Society' in the Middle East: A Review Essay," *International Journal of Middle East Studies,* 9, no. 4 (November 1978), 539-57. For a major geographical study emphasizing the importance of studying regions instead of treating communities as if they were social, political, and economic isolates, see Paul Ward English, *City and Village in Iran* (Madison: University of Wisconsin Press, 1966).

of the population as compared with only 2.8 percent, or 300,000, in 1970.[5] The beginning of the pronounced decline of nomadism varies from country to country, but in almost all cases the rate of decline brought about by large-scale economic and political shifts has been rapid.

The major factors involved in the decline of pastoralism are suggested by the case of Egypt, which in the early nineteenth century became the first country in the Middle East to experience a rapid expansion of agricultural production due to increasing involvement in the world capitalist economy and a consolidation of its central government under the reign of Muḥammad ᶜAlī (1769-1848).[6] To increase agricultural production and tax revenues, Muḥammad ᶜAlī sought to settle the Bedouin tribes, and to this end he used a combination of tactics which met with varying success. One was to give land grants to Bedouin tribal leaders (shaykh-s) and to tax this land at a low rate. The drawback to this policy was that many shaykhs preferred to lease their land to peasants rather than induce their own followers to settle. Another technique was to appoint Bedouin leaders to government offices, keeping members of their families as hostages in Cairo to ensure their loyalty. In order to carry out their tasks and to enjoy the wealth which usually was associated with such offices, many of these leaders settled in towns and often built palaces for themselves as an indication of their new status. At the same time, they maintained a firm hold upon fellow tribesmen as their formal representative with the government and persuaded many of them to settle, exacting from them tax revenues and other obligations.

An associated tactic to encourage settlement was to allow Bedouin shaykhs to register uncultivated land in their own names, leaving them to induce their fellow tribesmen by whatever means available to settle and cultivate this land. The process of land registration was confusing enough to illiterate tribesmen (who often thought it to be a prelude to military conscription) so that even when tracts of land were intended for tribes as a whole, tribal leaders found it easy to acquire personal title to such land and progressively to convert their fellow tribesmen into peasants and sharecroppers. A similar process occurred elsewhere in the Middle East, including the former Ottoman provinces of Iraq, Syria, and Palestine.[7]

[5] Peter Beaumont, Gerald H. Blake, and J. Malcolm Wagstaff, *The Middle East: A Geographical Study* (New York: John Wiley & Sons, 1976), p. 187. Cf. p. 124, where the figure is given as 1.1 percent for 1947.

[6] The following account is based upon Gabriel Baer, *Studies in the Social History of Modern Egypt* (Chicago: University of Chicago Press, 1969), pp. 3-16.

[7] The appropriation of lands intended for collectivities by personal title was not confined to attempts to induce nomads to settle. In Syria and Palestine it was common for cultivated lands to be collectively held by villages under a system of land tenure known as *mushāᶜ*. In 1858 the Ottoman administration enacted a major reform involving land registration and intended to eliminate the earlier system of tax farming and its accompanying abuses by making cultivators directly responsible for the tax on their lands. Like many reforms, this one had unintended consequences. It provided an opportunity for unscrupulous village headmen to acquire personal title to the lands of entire villages. See Talal Asad, "Anthropological Texts and Ideological Problems: An Analysis of Cohen on Arab Border Villages in Israel," *Economy and Society*, 4, no. 3 (August 1975), 261.

Although the decline of pastoralism is a long-term phenomenon, many anthropologists recognize a qualitative difference in the sociopolitical context of nomadic groups prior to and after the imposition of sustained and effective central government control. William Irons's study of the Yomut Turkmen of northern Persia is typical of many studies in that he sharply distinguishes between land use patterns and sociopolitical organization before and after the effective imposition of such control in the mid-1930s.[8] Other anthropologists have based their analyses entirely upon earlier sources. Notable among these is Henry Rosenfeld's account of the military and political role of pastoral nomads in northern Arabia in the nineteenth century and prior to the First World War.[9]

Rosenfeld's account is worth considering in detail, for it sharply delineates the inherent tension between the "tribal" social organization and loyalties of pastoral nomadic groups and the principles of leadership and authority associated with state organizations in the premodern period. "Premodern," like "traditional," is a difficult term to define. Here I use the term, as does Rosenfeld, to signify the period prior to significant Western military and economic penetration and its accompanying decisive impact upon political, educational, and other institutions. The terms "premodern" and "traditional" are often useful provided that it is kept in mind that what is "premodern" for a country such as Saudi Arabia (or even a region within a country) occurs historically at a very different time from what is "premodern" for Egypt, the first country in the region to be subject to sustained European intervention.

The specific details of Rosenfeld's argument relate to pastoral groups in northern Arabia, but his main theme is also useful as a starting point for considering the premodern political role of pastoralists in other regions of the Middle East. Rosenfeld argues that the scope of economic and political domination which any social group can exercise is limited by its form of social organization, especially of its military force, and that pastoral nomads are limited militarily because of their "kin-based" social organization. A corollary argument is that pastoral nomadic life contains fewer possibilities for the relatively permanent differentiation by wealth than is possible in settled milieus where, of course, "kin-based" or "tribal" social organization is also found. In the case of pastoral groups, consequently, there is more of a tendency for relationships among individuals to be egalitarian both in ideology and in practice than is the case in oases, villages, and towns. Parenthetically, it is misleading to equate "kin-based" with "tribal" social organization, as do Rosenfeld and many others concerned with pastoral nomads, for reasons which will become clear later in this chapter. For the moment, Rosenfeld's argument is at a level of generality for which a more precise use of terms is not crucial. Essentially, Rosenfeld discusses the different patterns of leadership and social organization among pastoral nomadic groups and the transformations from one form to

[8] For example, Irons, *Yomut Turkmen,* pp. 21-27, 61-81.
[9] "The Social Composition of the Military in the Process of State Formation in the Arabian Desert," *Journal of the Royal Anthropological Institute,* 95 (1965), 75-86, 174-94.

another which occurred in the political context of the nineteenth and early twentieth centuries.

One possibility was for a Bedouin shaykh to possess only a limited form of domination over his fellow tribesmen, relying primarily upon informal persuasion. Ideologically, Bedouin shaykhs were (and still are) considered to be only the first among equals, although in practice they possess a greater control over resources than their followers which enables them to entertain lavishly and to have a web of relations with nontribesmen. To cite Burckhardt's aphorism: "A shaykh's orders are never obeyed but his example is generally followed."[10] Another practical limitation of the control of Bedouin shaykhs over tribesmen was that ecological exigencies required nomadic groups to break up into small units for large parts of the year and to move quickly to take advantage of available rainfall and vegetation. Pastoral groups coalesced into intertribal raiding parties, especially during the winter months when the search for water and pastures was less demanding than in other seasons, but most raids were carried out by small groups which had neither permanent members nor leaders.[11]

Nonetheless, pastoral groups in some circumstances had an advantage over the militia of settlements in certain irregular encounters, in escaping taxation, in disrupting caravan traffic, and in carrying out sporadic raids against outlying oases or agricultural settlements. Often the mere threat of a raid was sufficient to persuade a village, oasis, or weaker pastoral group to pay for protection in cash or kind. Often such payments were known euphemistically as "brotherhood" *(khūwa)* obligations.[12] Even the Ottoman government found it expedient to pay regular subsidies to nomadic leaders to ensure the safe passage of caravans (including those associated with the annual pilgrimage to Mecca) and to ensure the safety of the Damascus-Medina railroad. The railroad was completed in 1908 and destroyed by T. E. Lawrence during the First World War. The extent of such tribute depended upon the rapidly fluctuating strength of particular nomadic groups.

Given the dependence of pastoralists upon the produce and merchandise of settled communities and oases, the dominance of settled communities over nomads was a more common occurrence than was the reverse situation.[13] The possibilities were numerous, but usually pastoral leadership was fragmented or weak. Oases often control access to the only perennial source of water, needed by nomadic groups for the summer months. The leaders of oasis communities commonly sought to create rivalry among nomadic groups through subsidies and other tactics in order

---

[10] John Lewis Burckhardt, *Notes on the Bedouins and Wahábys,* Vol. 1 (London: Henry Colburn and Richard Bentley, 1831), p. 117.

[11] For an interesting reconstruction of "traditional" raiding patterns and an explanation of how such raiding served as a means of redistributing livestock wealth, see Louise E. Sweet, "Camel Raiding of North Arabian Bedouin: A Mechanism of Ecological Adaptation," in *Peoples and Cultures of the Middle East,* Vol. 1, ed. Louise E. Sweet (Garden City, N.Y.: Natural History Press, 1970), pp. 265-89.

[12] Rosenfeld, "Social Composition," pp. 78-79.

[13] Asad, "The Bedouin as a Military Force," p. 62.

**FIGURE 4-1** Ja<sup>c</sup>da camel driver, Ḥaḍramawt, South Arabia. Roads and trucks have profoundly transformed the life of nomadic pastoralists. (From Freya Stark, *Seen in the Hadhramaut* [London: John Murray, Publishers, Ltd., 1939], p. 3. Courtesy of the author and publisher.)

to keep them in a state of dependence. Also common, however, was a situation of uneasy peace between oasis dwellers and nomads, in which pastoral groups exchanged their animals and animal products (and services as transporters of goods and persons) for dates, grains, coffee, salt, cloth, guns, and ammunition and established ties with cultivators that allowed them to forage their animals on harvested fields. Some pastoralists owned date trees and land in these settlements or had settled kinsmen on whom they depended to facilitate their economic transactions.

In some circumstances, as Rosenfeld explains, ambitious Bedouin leaders sought opportunities to acquire firmer control over trade and oases than was possible through their influence as "first among equals" with their fellow tribesmen. Initially, the ruler of an emerging *tribute state* acquired control of oases and settlements with the support of a kin-based militia of fellow tribesmen but gradually replaced these with mercenaries and slaves, whose livelihood depended directly upon their obedience to and support of the ruler. Such a shift in type of authority usually was marked by the settlement of a Bedouin leader in a key town or oasis and a growing identity of his interests with those of leading merchants and a Bedouin elite, as opposed to the interests of the majority of his fellow tribesmen who remained nomadic pastoralists. Nomadic groups and settlements peripheral to such a tribute state received no direct benefit from submission to it and hence sought to break away whenever possible. The militia of the ruler sought regularly through raids or the threat of raids to force such nomadic groups and settlements to accept their protection.

Finally, Rosenfeld describes the features of a rudimentary state organization which he calls *episodic* or *expanding*. In this form of state, kin-based nomadic groups are incorporated but only so long as their interests coincide with those of the ruler of the state and his associates. This occurred when tribal levies were engaged in raiding and military activities directed against external objectives. As soon as such a state ceased to incorporate new settlements or tribes, these levies were not needed and kin-based nomadic groups again sought whenever possible to break away. One example is the *Wahhābī*, or "Unitarian" religious movement in Arabia, associated with Saudi Arabia's ruling dynasty.[14] *Wahhābī* expansion began in the mid-eighteenth century with a raid which involved only seven men and camels, although the movement grew until it encompassed most of the Arabian peninsula by the end of the century. With each successful expedition, more tribesmen and others adhered to the *Wahhābī* state. Participants in successful expeditions were allowed to distribute four-fifths of the booty among themselves, with the remaining fifth going to the central treasury. This division was legitimated by the fact that it was the same practice followed by the Prophet Muḥammad in the early stages of the Islamic movement in seventh-century Arabia. Both in the early phase of the *Wahhābī* movement and after its revival in the late nineteenth century, there were repeated difficulties in securing the loyalty of pastoral nomadic groups. After 1912, for instance, the Saudi dynasty sought with mixed success to settle nomads in about two hundred military and agricultural encampments. These encampments also served as points from which punitive raids could be undertaken against recalcitrant groups.

The basic tension described by Rosenfeld between authority in "tribal" societies and that exercised by the ruler of a state and his entourage continues to prevail to some extent in other contexts. In some of the states of the Arab/Persian Gulf, for instance, a common pattern prior to the 1950s was to have coastal rulers

---

[14] As with many religious movements, the *Wahhābī* movement is known by separate names to its adherents and to outsiders. Adherents know it as "the call to the doctrine of the Oneness of God," after its claim to return to the original principles of Islam as they were in seventh-century Arabia and to eliminate later accretions to Islamic practice. Other Muslims and Westerners know the movement by the name of its founder, Ibn ᶜAbd al-Wahhāb (1703/4-1792), who persuaded the ruler of a small oasis settlement (an ancestor of the present Saudi dynasty) to accept his religious teachings and to undertake a series of military raids to persuade other tribes and settlements to accept them as well. For a compact account, see George Rentz, "Wahhabism and Saudi Arabia," in *The Arabian Peninsula: Society and Politics,* ed. Derek Hopwood, Studies on Modern Asia and Africa, 8 (London: George Allen and Unwin Ltd., 1972), pp. 54-66.

whose interests were closely tied to maritime commerce and who had only a nominal rule over tribal leaders of the interior, both pastoral and settled. The tacitly contractual loyalties of these leaders were maintained through subsidies, political intermarriages, and associated strategies. These tactics continue to be significant in the region, and tribal loyalties are far from being artifacts of the past.[15] The case is the same in Somalia, where nationalist politics prior to independence in 1960 and political activities since then under both democratic and military governments are significantly associated with lineage and clan loyalties, albeit in modified forms.[16]

The decline in pastoral nomadism has rapidly accelerated with the economic and political transformations that have occurred since the end of the Second World War and the influx of oil wealth into several Middle Eastern countries. For example, roughly 40 percent of Saudi Arabia's population was nomadic in the 1950s, as compared with 11 percent in 1970. These figures do not reveal an even more significant shift of many nomadic groups from camel-herding to the raising of sheep and goats and a motorized nomadism in which trucks are used to facilitate seasonal migrations.[17] In Libya, 25 percent of the population was nomadic in 1962 as compared with 3.5 percent in 1970.[18] In some regions, notably those adjoining the Sahara and the Horn of Africa, this trend has been accelerated by the drought and famine which occurred in the early 1970s. Prior to the drought, 75 percent of Somalia's population was nomadic; subsequently, most pastoralists had to be relocated in refugee camps as conditions worsened. The Somali government, like many other governments in the affected zones, responded to the crisis by taking steps to settle the pastoralists permanently and to seek to replace their clan and tribal identities with wider notions of ethnicity and nation.

The range of anthropological studies of contemporary pastoralists indicates that the process of settlement has a variety of consequences for social organization. The Yörük of southeastern Turkey, who began large-scale settlement only after the Second World War, regard sedentarization merely as one of a number of economic strategies. As the economic rewards of pastoralism became increasingly marginal, households and groups shifted to settled life whenever possible, basing the

[15] Few anthropological studies have been made of the Arab/Persian Gulf states, but useful studies by nonanthropologists include J. B. Kelly, "A Prevalence of Furies: Tribes, Politics, and Religion in Oman and Trucial Oman," in *Arabian Peninsula,* ed. Hopwood, pp. 107-41, and Frank Stoakes, "Social and Political Change in the Third World: Some Peculiarities of Oil-Producing Principalities of the Persian Gulf," *ibid.,* pp. 189-215. For the role of tribes in Iran, see Philip C. Salzman, "National Integration of the Tribes in Modern Iran," *Middle East Journal,* 25, no. 3 (Summer 1971), 325-36.

[16] Lewis, *Pastoral Democracy,* pp. 266-95; also I. M. Lewis, "The Politics of the 1969 Somali Coup," *Journal of Modern African Studies,* 10, no. 3 (October 1972), 383-408.

[17] Fredrik Barth, "Nomadism in the Mountain and Plateau Areas of South West Asia," *Problems of the Arid Zone,* UNESCO (1960) [Bobbs-Merrill Reprint A-263], p. 341; Beaumont, Blake, and Wagstaff, *The Middle East,* pp. 187, 321.

[18] *Ibid.,* p. 187; Abdalla Said Bujra, "The Social Implications of Development Policies: A Case Study from Egypt," in *Desert and Sown,* ed. Nelson, p. 156.

decision to settle primarily upon economic considerations. This shift implied significant changes in the distribution of wealth (fixed inequalities of wealth are generally not as pronounced among full nomadic groups), but it did not result in any "massive change in formal institutions or social rules."[19] A similar conclusion was reached by a study of the impact of a government project initiated in the early 1960s to settle the Bedouin of Egypt's western desert, one aspect of which was to encourage participation in an agricultural cooperative movement in order to weaken traditional lineage loyalties. The socialist cooperatives quickly became popular but not for the reasons envisaged by government planners. Nomads regarded the cooperatives as offering an economically advantageous alternative to traditional herding practices, which also permitted the *strengthening* of traditional lineage loyalties and leadership.[20]

In other cases, settlement is resisted even when there are economic advantages to abandoning traditional pastoral activities. This is reported to be the case for some of the camel-herding "noble" tribes of Saudi Arabia, who have opposed settlement because it often involved their mixture with nontribal groups considered their inferiors in the system of social stratification prevalent in the region until recently. Likewise, there was an initial reluctance to shift to the herding of sheep and goats because this was an activity traditionally carried out only by "weaker" (that is, inferior) tribal groups. But because the economic advantages to be gained from such a shift have enabled some of these weaker groups to raise their status, the reluctance of "noble" tribes to adapt themselves to the commercial raising of sheep and goats is rapidly diminishing, only to be replaced by the major ecological problems of lack of water and overgrazing of available pastures.[21]

## SAUDI ARABIAN PASTORALISTS:
## THE ĀL MURRA

So far in this chapter I have provided a general view of the historical, economic, and political contexts in which pastoral nomadism has occurred in the Middle East. The remainder of this chapter involves thicker ethnographic description, primarily of one group of pastoralists, the Āl Murra Bedouin of the eastern deserts of Saudi Arabia. The Āl Murra, numbering around fifteen thousand in 1970, are described in Donald Cole's *Nomads of the Nomads,* which is based upon field research conducted from 1968 to 1970. Cole's monograph is the only modern study of a pastoral group on the Arabian peninsula and for this reason is significant. Cole's

---

[19] Bates, *Nomads and Farmers,* p. 222.

[20] Another reason for the strengthening of traditional leadership and loyalties appears to be the large-scale involvement of the Bedouin in smuggling activities. Livestock is smuggled into Libya, where prices are much higher than in Egypt. Such practices had to be concealed from government officials, at least at a formal level. See Bujra, "Social Implications," p. 150.

[21] Cole, *Nomads,* pp. 144-63; Cole, "The Enmeshment of Nomads in Sa'udi Arabian Society: The Case of Āl Murrah," in *Desert and Sown,* ed. Nelson, pp. 113-28.

study has a further advantage for the purpose of using it as an illustrative case. It accepts most of the conventional anthropological assumptions concerning the social identity and social organization of pastoral nomads and other tribal groups, yet is thorough enough as an ethnography to indicate the shortcomings of these assumptions.

In 1970 there were still 400,000 to 1,000,000 pastoral nomads in Saudi Arabia—the ambiguity of this estimate in itself indicates one of the problems facing development planners even in the richer countries of the Middle East. The Āl Murra have been one of the most "traditional" groups, in part due to the ecological circumstance that part of the grazing lands with which they are traditionally associated is unsuitable for a major shift to the herding of sheep and goats as has been undertaken on a larger scale by other tribes. Likewise, only a few of the Āl Murra had settled permanently as of 1970.[22]

The Āl Murra groups that Cole describes in detail are primarily engaged in subsistence camel-herding, so that their activities are closely tied to ecological conditions. In the course of a year, Cole reports, the Āl Murra range over some 200,000 square miles of Saudi Arabia, occasionally crossing its boundaries to go with

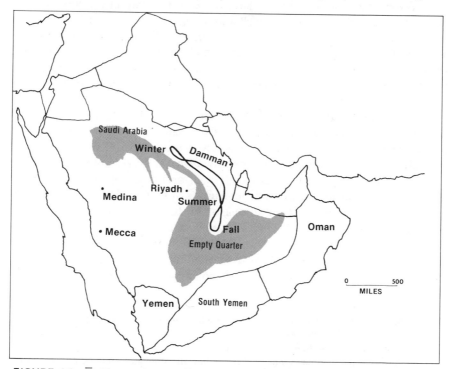

FIGURE 4-2  Āl Murra migrations, early 1970s. (After Donald P. Cole, *Nomads of the Nomads* [Chicago: Aldine Publishing Company, 1975], p. 29. Used by permission.)

[22] Cole, *Nomads,* pp. 24, 161.

their herds into Kuwait, Iraq, and South Yemen. If only their major moves are considered, most tribesmen travel some 1,200 miles yearly with their herds; together with more limited moves from temporary encampments they travel a total of up to 3,000 miles annually in search of pastures and water for their herds.[23] These movements and the rhythm of social life vary considerably with the seasons.

Because of ecological conditions, migratory patterns also differ from year to year. Cole describes the following movements for a year of relatively abundant rainfall. In the fall, which usually lasts from mid-September through December or January,[24] the Āl Murra move some 200 miles to the southwest of their summer camps to the "Empty Quarter," a region particularly associated with the Āl Murra and devoid of permanent settlements. Temperatures are relatively moderate in this season—95°F at noon as compared with up to 120°F in the summer. Tents, the basic household and herding units, are widely dispersed during this season. The 40 tents of the lineage with which Cole lived in 1968, for example, were spread out over 4,000 square miles, with a distance of roughly 15 miles between tents. Every few days, each of these tents was moved in order to take advantage of the sparse vegetation.[25]

During the last days of the fall, the Āl Murra carefully follow reports of where rain has fallen. Annual rainfall varies from 10-100 mm (1/3-4 inches) and occurs in highly irregular patterns. Reports on rainfall are frequently imprecise or conflicting, so such news is carefully sifted and discussed. Now that pickup trucks are used to reconnoiter for water and occasionally to obtain it, the danger of herd loss through lack of water is somewhat reduced, although wrong moves still have serious consequences.

The winter pastures of the Āl Murra are 400 to 600 miles to the north of the general area of their fall encampments. Once rains are reliably reported in the north, the Āl Murra move rapidly, frequently as much as 15-40 miles daily, so that the entire move is accomplished in under two weeks. These moves usually involve a more intense cooperation among tents than occurs during the earlier months. Moves are not formally coordinated, but clusters of tents, called *dār*-s,[26] are formed whose members are often related to each other through affinal ties, or ties through marriage. The Bedouin explain that when such ties of kinship exist among women, visiting and cooperation among them is facilitated because their fathers and brothers are in the other tents, which otherwise they would be unable to visit. According to Cole, the component households of a *dār* do not share herding responsibilities, but

---

[23] *Ibid.*, p. 39.

[24] Seasons are determined by climatic conditions, not by calendar months, so their occurrence varies widely from year to year.

[25] Cole, *Nomads*, pp. 41-43.

[26] *Dār*, like many other terms relating to kinship, residence, and "tribe," has differing meanings throughout the Arab world, so that usage in one locale and context is not necessarily a reliable guide for usage elsewhere. In other contexts in Saudi Arabia, colloquial Arabic dialects elsewhere, and in classical Arabic, *dār*, for example, is translated as "house."

the men commonly gather for the one cooked meal of the day. These camping units also frequently share the expenses of hiring a truck to transport their women and household goods during the move to winter pastures.[27]

Rainfall is relatively abundant in the winter and water can often be collected from the ponds that form in the desert. The water requirements of camels are considerably less in this season than at other periods of the year. Depending on climate, camels can go from four to six weeks without drinking in winter, as opposed to only four days in the summer.[28] Grazing land is also relatively abundant, with access to land being on a first-come, first-served basis, unlike the carefully regulated seasonal rights to land and migratory routes reported for the nomads of south Persia.[29] Because the Āl Murra and neighboring tribes are physically more concentrated during this season than at other times, social life is more intense, with frequent visiting and feasting among the Āl Murra and neighboring tribes. Āl Murra princes (who do not migrate with the tribe) and non-Bedouin dignitaries also visit during this period. Traditionally, winter was also the season of intense, and now banned, intertribal raiding. Pastoralists carefully regulate the breeding of their animals in this period, so that calving takes place when grazing is abundant in the late fall and early winter.

The end of winter is marked by gradually increasing temperatures and the withering of winter vegetation. Since seasons are determined by the climate and not by abstract calendrical notions, spring is not an annual occurrence in the climate of Saudi Arabia. The Bedouin consider spring to occur only in those years when there are fresh pastures for a few weeks in January or February.[30]

From March to June, the Āl Murra return to the area of their summer pastures. Lineages usually camp together during this period around wells which are jointly owned or controlled, although rights to use these wells and the grazing around them are often granted to household groups that do not form a part of that lineage. Camp composition varies from year to year, depending upon ecological conditions and the quality of relations prevailing among specific household units. Grazing land is scarce during this season, herds lose the fat which they may have accumulated in the winter, and the problem of securing adequate water supplies becomes more difficult with the passing months.[31]

So much for an account of the migratory cycle of the Āl Murra. As with other pastoralists, the activities of the Āl Murra and their social organization are closely tied to and constrained by the circumstances of ecology and climate; although, as indicated previously, wider economic and political considerations have

[27] Cole, *Nomads,* pp. 43-46.

[28] *Ibid.,* p. 21.

[29] *Ibid.,* p. 47; Fredrik Barth, "The Land Use Pattern of Migratory Tribes of South Persia," *Norsk Geografisk Tidsskrift,* 17 (1959) [Bobbs-Merrill Reprint A-11], 1-11.

[30] Cole, *Nomads,* pp. 46-51.

[31] *Ibid.,* pp. 51-52.

been of equal or greater significance both now and in the past. Thus for many of the Āl Murra, the work associated with herding constitutes only part of the economic activities in which they are engaged. In addition to the complex patterns of exchange with towns and villages in which some Āl Murra participate as middlemen, many households also receive income from occasional wage labor in towns and oil fields and monthly stipends from participation in the Saudi Reserve National Guard. Politically, of course, the relations of the Āl Murra with other tribes, settlements, and the government significantly affect the availability of pastures, water, and migratory routes.

How do the Āl Murra themselves conceive of their social organization and what constitutes an adequate anthropological description of this organization and the values upon which it is based? Cole's account centers upon the way in which the Āl Murra explain their social identity to themselves and to outsiders. As with many other anthropologists who have studied pastoral groups, Cole does not distinguish clearly between the *ideology* of the social order maintained by the Āl Murra themselves, which emphasizes the equality of all tribesmen and the lack of permanent leadership, and the social anthropological descriptive accounts and analyses of that order. The importance of distinguishing between these two modes of explanation will progressively emerge in this chapter and the next. In any case, the locally held ideology of the social order constitutes an important element of any explanation. As will also emerge, the Āl Murra ideology of their social order has many elements in common with those held by other "tribal" groups in the Middle East; for Cole, the Āl Murra provide an example of *segmentary lineage organization*.

Cole's account of Āl Murra social organization centers upon five distinct units: the tent, or household *(bayt)*; the camping cluster *(dār)*, mentioned earlier; the lineage *(fakhd*, which literally means "thigh"); the clan; and the tribe as a whole. These last two levels of society are both called *gabīla* in Saudi Arabic.

On an abstract level, the Āl Murra consider themselves related through patrilineal descent from a common ancestor. For the Āl Murra, all the basic units of society except the camping cluster *(dār)*, which is ideally built around affinal ties, depend in principle upon the relation of persons to each other through a grid determined through common patrilineal descent. These relations can be conceived in terms of a downward-branching diagram like Figure 4-3. At the top of the diagram is an ancestor common to the entire tribe. The Āl Murra consider this ancestor to be a quasi-mythical "personage who is said to have lived before the beginning of Islam."[32] Clans, of which the Āl Murra presently have seven (not all of which are shown here), also have common patrilineal ancestors who unite all their members. The same thing occurs at the level of lineages, although in this case the common ancestor often is a historical person who was known to elder tribesmen. Of course, such an ideological representation of tribal social organization is not necessarily based upon actual historical persons and is used primarily to explain contemporary

---

[32] *Ibid.,* p. 93. Fig. 4-3 is a simplification of the more complex diagram which appears on p. 92 of Cole's book.

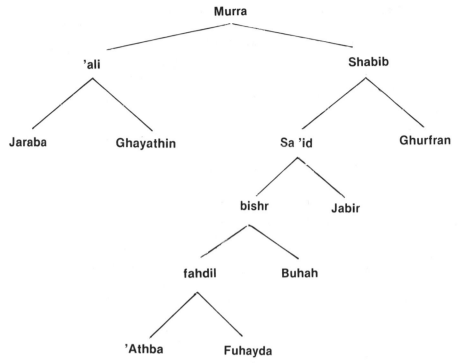

**FIGURE 4-3.** Āl Murra clans. Only the capitalized names are actual clans. The other names serve as connecting links. (After Donald P. Cole, *Nomads.* Courtesy of the author.)

social relationships. Ancestors not needed to provide links between actual groups are quickly "forgotten," just as other linking forebears are "remembered" when realignments in present-day groups require the existence of a common ancestor to give form and legitimacy to their cooperation. The social obligations that the Āl Murra feel are attached to identity (in principle) within this genealogical grid are explained below.

The tent, or household, is the basic social and economic unit among the Āl Murra. There is a range of variation in the composition of tents. A common pattern, for instance, is for an economically viable tent to include an older man and his wife—polygyny, though legally permitted, is relatively rare in practice—their sons and the sons' wives if the sons are married, and their children. The exigencies of herding and domestic life make it difficult for a tent to consist only of a conjugal pair and their children. A moderately prosperous tent often possesses fifty to seventy-five milk camels which must be herded near the tent, twenty to twenty-five pack camels used for carrying the goods of the household and which can graze at greater distances, plus a number of riding camels, giving a total of over one hundred camels. When a household does not have sufficient personnel for herding and the associated tasks, it must hire personnel from other tents or pastoral groups or else entrust some of its animals to other tents.[33] An inability to do so for economic or other reasons jeopardizes the viability of a tent. Another consideration is that the men and women of a tent individually own its animals, although the animals are jointly herded, with the adult males coming to common agreement on pastoral movements. When such agreement cannot be reached, the tents split up. Similarly, if a tent loses large numbers of animals through disease, drought, or other natural disaster and has no adequate supplementary sources of income, it loses its viability as an economic unit and must choose either settlement and agricultural labor or working as subordinates for other pastoralists.

The lineage, the next level of integration of $\overline{\text{Al}}$ Murra society, is a more abstract unit. Cole defines it as "all the people who are descended [patrilineally] from an ancestor who stands about five generations removed from the present adult generations."[34] However, the composition of lineages is more complicated than Cole's definition suggests.

First, let me specify in what ways the lineage is a more abstract social unit than that of the tent. In practical terms, lineages ordinarily camp together only in the summer, usually around wells to which they claim customary rights. Lineages also possess common camel brands, although as stated, ownership of animals is vested in individuals. Such summer encampments are not necessarily exclusive. Tents from other lineages frequently are allowed, just as tents of a lineage may seek to obtain water rights with another group (for example, one with which they have affinal ties) when it is to their advantage.[35]

There are no specially appointed leaders or councils within the lineage, although on occasion it may be represented informally by a mutually agreed-upon spokesman. Most decisions, such as how to defend water rights, are made through an informal consensus.[36] Cole reports that marriages generally occur within lineages, although he provides no clear account of how marriage strategies may vary with status and wealth. In some cases, a marriage contracted with a person of another lineage can give access to needed water and pastures; in other cases, it may cement a useful political alliance. These are important points to consider, for they indicate the inadequacy of assuming that alliances and political obligations are determined primarily by the ideology of patrilineal descent. For instance, the $\overline{\text{Al}}$ Murra told Cole that members of a lineage are jointly responsible for the actions

---

[33]*Ibid.*, pp. 36-39, 69, 90. Throughout his study (for example, p. 96), Cole stresses the egalitarian ideology of the $\overline{\text{Al}}$ Murra, but as he points out on p. 90, poor lineages that are obliged to hire out as herders are considered to be inferior by birth. Such lineages frequently are considered to have as ancestors an Al Murra male and a slave woman rather than a woman of the $\overline{\text{Al}}$ Murra itself. These nuances of genealogical manipulation point to a more complicated ideology of social identity than the simple premise of equality asserted by the $\overline{\text{Al}}$ Murra.

[34]*Ibid.*, p. 85.

[35]*Ibid.*, pp. 85-88.

[36]*Ibid.*, p. 86. Although Cole uses the present tense, it is likely that the statements of his informants refer to conditions in the past, before the effective emergence of Saudi government control.

FIGURE 4-4 Āl Murra herder and younger brother. (From Donald P. Cole, *Nomads.* Courtesy of the author.)

of its members and must seek revenge for an attack upon any of them. Yet in discussing the camping cluster (*dār*), whose membership is *not* determined by agnatic (patrilineal) ties, Cole states that each member of a *dār* has an obligation to defend another "against the attack of even his closest male relative."[37] Such inconsistencies indicate the insufficiency of anthropological analyses which are confined to presenting the ideological claims of members of a given society, although such statements are, of course, important in themselves. For the moment I simply call attention to this problem, for it is discussed in detail in the next chapter.

How an essentially *ideological* claim of this sort can come to resemble the actual norms for action that are followed—that is, how people can come to accept the social obligations associated with such claims—is complex. One crucial requirement lies in the possibility that membership in a lineage can be acquired by means other than birth and subsequently accepted as of "the same" sort of membership as that acquired by birth. There are several reasons why individuals from other Āl Murra lineages and from outside the Āl Murra entirely often seek assimilation. Occasionally an individual breaks with his own lineage because of a serious dispute and seeks to identify with a different lineage. At other times, a man from a lineage poor in camels seeks to marry a woman from a wealthier lineage. Particularly if the wealthier lineage is short of manpower, such an alliance will often be encouraged, provided that the man agrees to live with his wife's lineage instead of his own. Eventually such a man identifies himself primarily with the lineage of his affines rather than his own, although only his grandchildren may "really" be considered

[37]*Ibid.,* p. 63.

part of the lineage. Similarly, a man from a weak lineage may seek to join a more powerful one.[38]

Such shifts in social identity also occur at the level of entire lineages, again indicating the flexibility of claims to patrilineal descent to accommodate contemporary and emerging social realignments. For instance, the lineage with which Cole spent most of his time between 1968 and 1970 was divided into two major groups. One consisted of thirty-five tents whose members were camel pastoralists. The other group was composed of sixteen tents of sheep and goat pastoralists who spent the entire year in northern Arabia. The latter had little to do with the camel pastoralists, and other lineages considered the two groups to be genealogically separate. Shifts of identity are also linked to economic activities and political influence. As has already been indicated, the Āl Murra claim that all lineages and members of the tribe are "equals" does not stand close examination. "Weak" lineages are considered to be genealogically separate from "stronger" ones, although as the economic condition of such groups improves in relation to that of other lineages, over several generations genealogical explanations for their "inferiority" are progressively abandoned by the members of other lineages.[39]

The next two levels of Āl Murra social organization, the clan and the tribe, are both known as gabīla. This entails no confusion, as the Āl Murra rarely think of these "levels" in abstract terms; rather, they refer to the names of specific groups. Thus each of the seven Āl Murra clans contains between four and six lineages. Some clans have princes (amīr-s) associated with them; the others must depend upon the amīr of another clan for assistance in dealing with the government and settling disputes. The clan plays no direct role in the organization of pastoral nomadic activities, but the Āl Murra state that clan identity plays an important role in political disputes. No specific examples are provided by Cole, but the Āl Murra claim that individuals and lineages of a clan "automatically" lend their political support to others in the clan in disputes with outsiders. Clans, in turn, are said to form coalitions with other Āl Murra clans, although these coalitions do not follow the lines suggested by segmentary lineage theory, in which closely related clans should unite against any provocation from a member of a genealogically more distant group.[40]

Finally, the Āl Murra tribe as a whole is a significant political and social unit. The tribe has its own myths, legends, and traditions; marriages are virtually all within it; the tribe has customary (although not formal) identification with certain pasture areas; and, most importantly, no individual in the tribe considers approaching the government on any major matter without the "permission and collaborative support of his tribal leaders."[41]

---

[38]Ibid., p. 88.

[39]Ibid., pp. 89, 90, 93. Cf. p. 102, where Cole contradicts this recognition of the inequality of wealth of lineages by saying that they are all "roughly equal in power and wealth."

[40]Ibid., pp. 91-93, 103.

[41]Ibid., p. 94.

## THE IDEOLOGY OF EQUALITY:
## FURTHER CONSIDERATIONS

The role of the tribal leaders (amirs) emphasizes the difficulty of regarding the Āl Murra as an "egalitarian" society in the past or in contemporary circumstances without exploring the meanings of "egalitarian" in specific contexts. By tribal ideology, Āl Murra amirs are only "first among equals," "slightly differentiated" from other tribesmen.[42] Yet there is substantial evidence of a pronounced inequality, despite the ideological claim to the contrary. A major role of the Āl Murra amirs is to arbitrate disputes among the tribesmen and to serve as intermediaries on all matters of importance with the government. They possess no formal authority in these roles, but their domination over fellow tribesmen is generally unquestioned. To perform these tasks effectively, the amirs and their households do not engage directly in pastoral nomadism or migrate with ordinary tribesmen. They live in tents or houses near the main towns and close to paved roads so that they can maintain effective contact with their tribal clientele and townsmen alike.

The amirs are wealthier than ordinary tribesmen, but a more significant difference is their ability to control or to have access to a wide range of resources that ordinary tribesmen can obtain only with their assistance. Although most amirs are illiterate, their sons and those of their close relatives have attended school. One amir, the paramount leader of the Āl Murra, is also commander of the local unit of the Saudi Reserve National Guard, whose members meet for a few days each month. For this service, each guardsman receives the relatively significant sum of $100 per month. The largest number of guardsmen are selected from the paramount leader's own clan, which again suggests that some Āl Murra are more equal than others.

Another significant indication that the amirs are more than "first among equals" is that the paramount leadership of the Āl Murra has remained within the same lineage since the nineteenth century and has survived a number of major political changes. This ability to maintain political dominance over generations again suggests how misleading it is to regard the Āl Murra ideology of equality and their claim that tribal leadership is achieved through personal effort as practical guides to their social and political organization. To maintain their position, Āl Murra amirs cement close ties with powerful outsiders. Unlike other Āl Murra, the amirs and their close relations contract a significant number of marriages with outsiders and use the relationships established through such marriages for political purposes.

Informally, the tribal leaders are referred to by other Āl Murra as their "eyes" (dual, *caynayn*), a revealing term which stresses the role of the amirs as intermediaries with the government and with outsiders, for in Arabic the term also carries the connotation of "spy" or "informer." Although the Arabic word is not

---

[42]*Ibid.*, p. 96.

as decidedly pejorative as these English glosses may suggest, it does emphasize that tribal leaders owe their positions in part to "outside" interests.[43]

To conclude this chapter, let me more sharply delineate the drawbacks to using the shared ideology of equality among tribesmen as a guide to the relationships which actually prevail by briefly describing the Lūr-s, a sheep- and goatherding tribe in western Iran.[44]

Like the Āl Murra of Saudi Arabia and many other tribal groups, pastoral and nonpastoral, throughout the Middle East, the Lūr-s consider themselves to be political equals. They maintain ideologically that success as a herder is determined by personal qualities and luck. Yet, as their ethnographer indicates, the probabilities are high that the wealthiest 10 percent of the population will be able to maintain or increase their wealth, while the remaining 90 percent will have difficulty in maintaining economic viability. In the sense that the Lūr-s possess "no acknowledged leaders, no officers, and no named ranks," they are equal.[45] However, the majority of the population requires economic patrons from the upper strata of society. The upper strata of society control larger herds, require labor for their herds, and can provide work and salaries for those of the lower strata. Lower strata members have fewer animals, must work for others to make up for their lack of sufficient capital in animals, and are usually obliged to offer the labor of their sons to larger herd owners, so that control over their sons is weakened.[46] Animal mortality figures provide an index to the consistent and marked difference in control of economic and political resources between the upper and lower strata of Lūrī society. The mortality rate for animals owned by the lower 90 percent of the population is 50 percent higher than that for the upper 10 percent.[47]

Lūrī tribesmen claim that as equals they are free to opt out of dependent contractual relationships, as Black points out, but doing so essentially means that they must find another patron, which is not always easy to do. The situation of inequality described by Black may be more extreme than others elsewhere in the Middle East, but it calls into question the adequacy of accounts of tribal society which present the locally maintained ideologies of equality as substitutes for social anthropological description. The inequalities of wealth among the Āl Murra as described by Cole do not appear as great, but the same practical inequality exists: There are dominant individuals in a few lineages who control access to the government over important matters and effectively allocate jobs and other economic benefits. Other tribesmen consistently lack such resources.

[43] *Ibid.*, pp. 95-101, 108-10.

[44] Jacob Black, "Tyranny as a Strategy for Survival in an 'Egalitarian' Society: Luri Facts Versus an Anthropological Mystique," *Man*, n.s., 7, no. 4 (December 1972), 614-34.

[45] *Ibid.*, p. 623.

[46] *Ibid.*, p. 627.

[47] *Ibid.*, p. 631. For an alternative account of the effects of economic processes upon social differentiation and settlement as a consequence both of wealth at one end of the economic spectrum and poverty at the other, see Barth, *Nomads*, pp. 101-11.

This chapter has indicated some of the reasons why there has been a pronounced emphasis by anthropologists on pastoral nomads in their study of the Middle East. I have emphasized shortcomings to considering Bedouin society as essentially "closed" and stressed the need to recognize and study the sustained and necessary ties between pastoralists and nonpastoralists, both in historical and present-day contexts. Ecological conditions place significant constraints upon pastoral nomadic groups and their social and political affairs, but I have indicated reasons why the wider political and social contexts in which pastoral groups exist are of equal if not greater significance.

By providing an extended example of the social organization of a single pastoral group, I have emphasized that ethnographic description necessarily implies a set of theoretical assumptions and have indicated the problems associated with certain types of anthropological explanation. The next chapter examines these issues in more detail and relates them to the more general issue of the cultural nature of social identity.

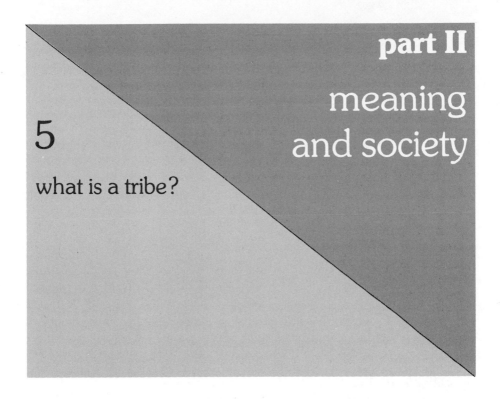

part II

meaning
and society

5

what is a tribe?

## IDEOLOGIES

In current popular usage, the term *ideology* often acquires the connotation of a system of illusory "unreal" beliefs concerning the nature of the social (or economic or political) world. The notion that ideologies are illusory is unfortunate and contrary to how the term is used by most sociologists and social anthropologists, who regard ideologies as significant and irreducible components of any cultural order. Ideologies inform social practice and provide it with meaning. The problem is to specify more precisely what is meant by ideology and its relation to society. The authors of such a classical discussion as *The German Ideology* insisted that ideologies shape and in turn are shaped by the particular social, economic, and historical formations in which they occur.[1] Regardless of the attitude of social theorists today toward contemporary versions of Marxism, the central problem posed by Marx of the relationship between ideology and society continues to inform contemporary social thought. The primary theoretical issue is *how* the relation between

[1] Karl Marx and Frederick Engels, *The German Ideology*, ed. C. J. Arthur (New York: International Publishers, 1970 [orig. 1846]), esp. pp. 46-47. This general principle holds not only for what might be termed social knowledge but also for the underlying assumptions of scientific thought as well, despite the popular notion that "science" is somehow immune from social vicissitudes. See Barry Barnes, *Interests and the Growth of Knowledge* (London and Boston: Routledge & Kegan Paul, 1977).

ideologies and social forms should be described and elaborated, not whether such a relationship exists.

In the past, many sociologists of knowledge have been concerned principally with those ideologies or beliefs that are consciously elaborated and maintained. Such ideologies, especially in the political domain, are of undeniable importance and merit intensive analysis. Yet the term *ideology* encompasses a wider set of notions than formal ideologies alone. Anthropologists and many other social theorists are additionally concerned with what might be called *practical* ideologies, sets of beliefs constituted by largely implicit shared assumptions concerning such basic aspects of the social order as notions of tribe, kinship, family, person, sexuality, nation, religion, and world-view.[2] Most of these notions overlap in various ways and some are more encompassing than others. *World-view,* for instance, is one of the broader concepts and is used by anthropologists to designate shared cultural assumptions concerning the overall nature of the social order. Many of the practical ideologies remain incompletely systematized by those who maintain them, although forms of conduct such as patterns of naming, marriage, residence, and ritual can be used to document them. The fact that many of these ideologies are so "natural" and taken for granted means that in ordinary circumstances they are not consciously or fully articulated. Thus Americans, in looking at their own beliefs and social forms, are not ordinarily prepared to elaborate their shared assumptions concerning family, sexuality, and the like. Or more precisely, to make the anthropologist's task more intriguing, when some "natives" express formal beliefs concerning family, religion, and economic conduct, these beliefs may only obliquely account for the actual, implicit principles which form the basis of their practical ideology. The same is of course true of Middle Eastern and other societies. In dramatic instances, such as the officially Marxist Somali Democratic Republic, tribalism and lineage loyalties have been declared illegal and no longer to exist, yet through mundane but critical indices such as patterns of livestock investments and the lineage composition of governments since the 1969 "revolution," it can readily be demonstrated that lineage loyalties are thriving, although it is illegal to say so publicly in Somalia.[3] How formal and practical ideologies overlap and influence each other is one of the principal themes raised in the discussion of the idea of "tribe" in later chapters of this section.

There are genuinely puzzling problems of analytical strategy and substance which concern the basic problem of the relation of ideologies to society. Notions of tribe, kinship, ethnicity, sexuality, and religion all constitute shared cultural

[2] My "Ideological Change and Regional Cults: Maraboutism and Ties of 'Closeness' in Western Morocco," in *Regional Cults,* ed. Richard P. Werbner, A.S.A. Monograph 16 (New York and London: Academic Press, 1977), pp. 3-28, used the term *part-ideology* instead of *practical ideology.* Out of context, the earlier term could be taken to imply a weakness or inferiority of such ideologies in contrast to those which are formally elaborated; the term *practical ideology* is less likely to be so construed.

[3] I. M. Lewis, "Kim Il-Sung in Somalia: The End of Tribalism?" in *Politics in Leadership: A Comparative Perspective,* eds. William A. Shack and Percy S. Cohen (Oxford: Clarendon Press, 1979), pp. 13-44.

meanings, ways of making sense of the social world and of informing action within it. All patterns of cultural meaning are generated, maintained, and often transformed through social use. If patterns of meaning are generated through social action, why do so many of them (such as notions of family) appear to remain relatively stable over long periods of time, in spite of the massive economic, political, and social transformations of many parts of the Middle East over the last half century? Or is it just that some patterns of meaning appear more stable, perhaps those practical ideologies so taken for granted that they are not fully articulated (and thus not subject to conscious manipulation). A related issue concerns the limits of ambiguity and multiple interpretations of symbolic statements and how such ambiguity often facilitates the accommodation of major social and cultural changes. In the last half century in countries such as Morocco, Iraq, and the Sudan, and only in the last decade or two in countries such as the Yemen and Oman, there have been massive changes in how people make a living, where they live, how they are educated, and what they expect from each other and from the state. The theme of change is pursued in historical as well as contemporary contexts because the scope of some changes in the past has often posed similar problems of the relation of cultural meanings to social forms. Such issues are not only of major interest to social theorists, but they provide persons who live in rapidly changing societies with a means of assessing the significance of their own lived experience.

## THE CONCEPT OF TRIBE

"Tribal" identities at first appear more exotic to Westerners than those based upon kinship, ethnicity, or religion and therefore serve as an apt introduction to a discussion of how ideologies relate to the social order. In part, tribal identities have appeared exotic due to the way in which some anthropologists have chosen to depict such social forms. That is why it is useful to discuss ideas of the "tribe" in writing about the Middle East before considering other bases of social identity. Of course, "tribal" identities do not occur in all Middle Eastern contexts, although there are significant nomadic and settled populations that are tribally organized throughout the entire region, from Morocco to Afghanistan.

The first thing to emphasize is that tribal identity, like other bases of social identity including kinship relationships and even citizenship, is something which natives (and sometimes ethnographers) make. People do things with such social forms; these forms do not exist merely as objects that can be torn from social and cultural contexts by anthropologists to be recorded and classified into typologies.[4] Such patterns of meaning change with historical situations. It makes a great deal of difference whether they occur in the context of strong or weak state organizations or a colonial society.

---

[4] The emphasis upon the practical contexts in which social forms are used follows Pierre Bourdieu, *Outline of a Theory of Practice,* trans. Richard Nice, Cambridge Studies in Social Anthropology, 16 (Cambridge and New York: Cambridge University Press, 1977), pp. 35-36.

There are four principal forms in which people "make" tribal identity in the Middle East. These are: (1) the elaboration and use of explicit "native" ethnopolitical ideologies by the people themselves to explain their sociopolitical organization; (2) concepts used by state authorities for administrative purposes; (3) implicit *practical* notions held by people which are not elaborated into formal ideologies, and (4) anthropological concepts.[5] These various notions of tribe are not entirely parallel. All but the last are actor's notions in the sense that they are implicitly or explicitly held by participants in a society and used as a practical guide to some form of social action. The anthropologist's notion of tribe is primarily for analytical rather than practical purposes, although the sociological "observer," whether native or foreign, also participates in the "observed" society in a special sense and is engaged in the "practice" of theoretical discourse. It should be emphasized that although these various notions of tribe are separable for analytical purposes, in practice they are by no means mutually exclusive and frequently overlap each other. After briefly explaining these notions in more detail, I present two practical examples of them, drawn from Morocco and Libya.

Native, or locally held, ethnopolitical ideologies of tribal identity vary somewhat throughout the Middle East, but they are generally based upon a concept of political identity formed through common patrilineal descent. A major exception is the Tuareg of the Sahara, where "tribal" identity is based instead upon matrilineal descent. Political action in such tribes has generally been explained by anthropologists in terms of *segmentary lineage* theory. People in such tribes sincerely believe that the principles of segmentary ideology explain the essence of their political activity, although as Emanuel Marx points out, this is simply not the case.[6] As I shall indicate in discussing the Moroccan notion of *qbīla* ("tribe"), such ideologies are differentially elaborated by tribesmen, depending upon their social position. Individuals who are socially and politically dominant often elaborate such ideologies in complex ways and use them to solidify political alliances with members of other tribal groups and to enhance their own position vis-à-vis state authorities. Ethnographers working in tribal societies have frequently based their accounts of kinship relations and tribal organization on information provided by such socially and politically dominant individuals, although the notions of tribal identity maintained by ordinary tribesmen often differ significantly from such formal ideologies of the dominant.

[5] The following discussion is based upon Bourdieu, *Outline;* Talal Asad, "Political Inequality in the Kababish Tribe," in *Essays in Sudan Ethnography,* eds. Ian Cunnison and Wendy James (London: C. Hurst & Company, 1972), pp. 126-48; and Dale F. Eickelman, *Moroccan Islam: Tradition and Society in a Pilgrimage Center,* Modern Middle East Series, 1 (Austin and London: University of Texas Press, 1976), pp. 105-21.

[6] Emanuel Marx, "The Tribe as a Unit of Subsistence: Nomadic Pastoralism in the Middle East," *American Anthropologist,* 79, no. 2 (June 1977), 356; Philip Carl Salzman, "Tribal Organization and Subsistence: A Response to Emanuel Marx," and Emanuel Marx, "Back to the Problem of Tribe," *American Anthropologist,* 81, no. 1 (March 1979), 121-25.

The second notion of tribe is based on its use as an administrative device in contexts as varied as the Ottoman empire, Morocco, and other countries prior to and during the period of colonial rule, and a number of independent Middle Eastern countries. Administrative assumptions concerning the nature of tribes are generally based in some degree upon locally maintained conceptions, but modified for political purposes. Thus administrative concepts of tribe frequently assume a corporate identity and fixed territorial boundaries that many "tribes" do not possess and give privileges and authority to tribal leaders that are dependent upon the existence of a state organization and not derived from concepts of leadership as understood by the tribesmen themselves. In cases such as Morocco and the Sudan, the colonial powers formerly promoted "tribal" identities and developed tribal administration to a fine art in an attempt to retard nationalistic movements. In reaction, the postindependence governments of these and other countries have signaled an ideological break with the colonial past by formally abolishing tribes as an administrative device, although such identities continue to be highly significant at the level of practical local administration.

*Practical* notions of tribe, the third analytical category considered here, are those implicitly held by tribesmen as a guide to everyday conduct in their relations between larger social groups. The term *practical* emphasizes that these concepts of identity emerge primarily through social action and not through abstract reflection upon the social order. Such notions are often difficult for anthropologists to elicit, for they are not always formally articulated by tribesmen in ordinary situations and because social alignments based upon these notions frequently shift. Practical notions of tribe and related concepts of social identity implicitly govern crucial areas of activity, including factional alignments over land rights, pastures and other political claims, marriage strategies (themselves a form of political activity), and many aspects of patronage. These notions are explained in detail in the examples which follow later in this chapter.

Finally there are the analytical conceptions of tribe held by anthropologists. A preliminary caution regarding these notions—I emphasize the plural—is in order. In both popular and anthropological usage, the concept of tribe figures in a variety of sociological, evolutionary, and ecological typologies. In some contexts "tribe" is even partially synonymous with "primitive," a usage decidedly out of place in the Middle East.[7] This variety of meanings indicates that careful attention must be paid to the specific way in which the term is used.

The anthropological conceptions are primarily intended to make sociological sense of "tribal" social relations. Like the "native" conceptions outlined above—and "natives," of course, also can be anthropologists—anthropological notions also exist for a purpose, usually that of acquiring a theoretical understanding of the cultural bases of social identity, but they parallel the uses of native ideologies.

---

[7] For a brief review of these usages, see Marx, "The Tribe," 343-44.

Anthropological notions of tribe are not more real than "native" conceptions or superior to them; instead they are intended as a more explicit form of knowledge of social relations.

There is a drawback to providing a general, abstract definition which ignores all of these various overlapping notions of tribe. What an ethnographer "sees" of social forms in any given cultural context depends upon such factors as whether informants attribute the ethnographer with an official capacity, whether the ethnographer is regarded as friendly or hostile or as possessing a greater or lesser degree of understanding of a society. As Pierre Bourdieu points out, ethnographers, whether "native" or from another cultural tradition, are almost inevitably perceived as "learned," so that their questions nearly always elicit the most "learned" representations of society from informants themselves, in accordance with their own conception of learning and of conscious literary tradition. In tribal societies such learned representations generally entail the elaborate use of written or oral traditional (memorized) genealogies. While such ideological representations are important in themselves, they do not take into account the implicit *practical* cultural understandings of society which are so basic that (to paraphrase Bourdieu) they find expression only in silence.[8] The anthropologist's problem is not simply to balance out these various conceptions of tribe in order to arrive at one which is more "real." It is to achieve as adequate an understanding as possible of how persons in a given society conceive of social forms and use this knowledge as a basis for social action.

## A MOROCCAN EXAMPLE: THE BNĪ BATĀW

The Bnī Batāw is a semitranshaumant, Arabic-speaking tribe of roughly ten thousand persons (as of 1960) located on the plains of western Morocco near the foothills of the Middle Atlas mountains.[9] Their livelihood derives from a combination of pastoralism with seasonal agriculture. Each fall they sow fields of wheat and barley on the plains; then they take their herds of sheep and goats to the forested foothills of the mountains where there is sufficient forage for the winter; although there are running disputes with the government's forest guards over the use of these lands. In the past, the Bnī Batāw often moved their herds far into the Berber-speaking highlands, but French colonial restrictions, and now the restrictions of the independent government, substantially limit the timing and extent of these annual moves. In the spring during March or April, depending upon ecological conditions, the Bnī Batāw return with their herds to the plains. Today most of the Bnī Batāw

---

[8] *Outline*, p. 18.
[9] Eickelman, *Moroccan Islam*, pp. 105-21; see also my "Time in a Complex Society: A Moroccan Example," *Ethnology*, 16, no. 1 (January 1977), 39-55.

**FIGURE 5-1** Tents at harvest time among the Bnī Batāw. (Courtesy of the author.)

live in dwellings made of stone and dried mud on the plains and use their tents only in the winter transhumant months. After their fields are harvested in June, the herds are allowed to graze on the stubble in the fields. Water and forage become scarcer as the summer progresses. Eventually they are compelled to move with their herds toward their winter pastures.

How do Bnī Batāw tribesmen conceive of their identity? *Bnī* is an Arabic word literally meaning "sons of." *Batāw* is simply a Berber word meaning "fragment." Bnī Batāw leaders and the government officially consider the tribe to be part of larger tribal "confederations," but those larger groupings exist primarily as administrative entities and as ideological frameworks in which wider political alliances were concluded in the past. There is no historical evidence to indicate that these wider entities ever acted as a collectivity. Within the Bnī Batāw itself, tribesmen speak of their identity in terms of *agnation,* a concept introduced earlier in the discussion of the Āl Murra of Saudi Arabia. But how can tribesmen be "sons of a fragment" or the "sons of" the place names that are used to designate certain subgroupings of the Bnī Batāw? The ideological nature of social identity becomes clear in the answer to this question.

Tribesmen explain their relation to each other and to outsiders such as anthropologists in terms of metaphors. Sometimes the metaphor is based on the parts of a tree—twigs, branches, and the trunk; at other times such parts of the human body as veins and arteries are used.

Ordinarily these metaphors are applied only in a general sense to the three "levels" of the Bnī Batāw. These are known abstractly as the rural local community *(dawwār),* the section *(fakhda),* and the tribe *(qbīla).* Members of such groups claim common descent or, more specifically, "closeness" to each other. Briefly described, the smallest unit of these levels is the *dawwār.* Literally the word means *circle.* Until

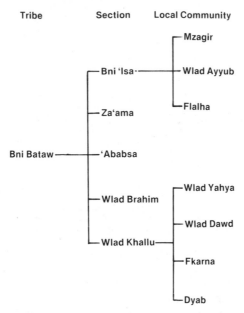

|  Tribe | Section | Local Community |
|--------|---------|-----------------|

```
Tribe            Section        Local Community

                                    ┌─ Mzagir
                   ┌─ Bni 'Isa·─────┼─ Wlad Ayyub
                   │                └─ Flalha
                   ├─ Za'ama
Bni Bataw──────────┼─ 'Ababsa
                   ├─ Wlad Brahim
                   │                ┌─ Wlad Yahya
                   └─ Wlad Khallu───┼─ Wlad Dawd
                                    ├─ Fkarna
                                    └─ Dyab
```

**FIGURE 5-2** Bnī Batāw divisions, early 1970s. (From Dale F. Eickelman, *Moroccan Islam: Tradition and Society in a Pilgrimage Center* [Austin: University of Texas Press, 1976], p. 116. Courtesy of the author and the publisher.)

the 1930s, tribesmen lived in tents throughout the year. Especially when they moved their herds into the highlands controlled by Berber-speaking groups, tribesmen pitched their tents in a circle, herding their animals into the center at night for security. Few groups camp like this any more, since the French effectively managed to limit most intertribal hostilities and raiding. Today tents are more widely spaced during the winter months, just as the permanent dwellings of the Bnī Batāw are located on their agricultural lands, which are individually owned. These dwellings are not clustered into villages. Each local community is composed of 50 to 100 "tents" (*khayma*-s), also frequently called "households" (*dār*-s).

The next level is the section, which is composed usually of three or four local communities. The Bnī Batāw use a number of terms to designate sections, one of which is thigh *(fakhda),* a term also used by the Āl Murra *(fakhd* is the exact term used in the Saudi dialect of Arabic). The Bnī Batāw presently are divided into five such sections.

To understand how tribesmen themselves comprehend their society, the first important thing to notice is that they do not consistently emphasize their relations with each other through patrilineal descent, although this notion is associated with the metaphors of social organization provided by the imagery of blood and the parts of a tree. As one tribesman put it, "We are like the branches of a tree, but each branch is on its own," emphasizing the fact that the claim of common descent does not necessarily determine the lines of faction and political alliance. Actually, in explaining how the metaphors of the parts of trees and the human body relate to their social structure, tribesmen rely heavily on the concept of "closeness" *(qarāba)*. *Qarāba* does not necessarily imply real or assumed kinship, even for tribesmen. Closeness flows along a number of lines besides "blood." It can develop through cooperation with nearby households, mutual herding arrangements, kinship and patronage relations, and other bonds of mutual interest. The notion of "closeness" is an important one and is discussed at length in the following two chapters. On a practical level, moreover, the enumerations of groups and their divisions at any moment never exactly tally. Although all tribesmen conceive of the relations between individuals and groups within the same framework (that is, the metaphor of the tree or of blood), there are regular variations in how these organizing concepts are applied to actual groups.

These variations are particularly clear at the "level" of the rural local community, the most important "level" in terms of everyday activities. Every tent belongs to such a local community. They are not set apart from each other by formal boundaries, only by the tribesmen's shifting understandings of the identity of groups and their composition.

Tribesmen in a rural local community (and most of their wives) claim patrilateral relation to each other (among other ties), but no one can specifically demonstrate how all members of a group are mutually related. When pressed to indicate exact ties, tribesmen generally say that only "older" persons know or that such ties derive from "early" *(bakrī)* times, an unspecified ahistorical past which is used to legitimize present-day social alignments.[10] Tribesmen do not ask each other for exact demonstrations of such ties. What counts is who acts together in a sustained way on various ritual and political occasions. This flexibility is seen in the council *(jmāᶜa)* which each local community has. This is not a formal body but is constituted simply by adult male heads of tents who informally consult on such issues of mutual concern as transhumant movements, quarrels over water and pasture rights, the hiring and payment of a Quranic teacher to reside with them and teach their children the rudiments of the Quran, maintenance of the whitewashed building which serves as a tomb for their marabout, or saint (every local community is identified with one), and similar collective obligations.

Individual tents and groups of tents dissatisfied with belonging to a particular rural local community may seek to break away to join another rural local community or to form their own whenever circumstances permit. Marriage ties, land inherited by a wife, or even the purchase of land from an individual from another rural local community can serve as the basis for such a realignment. Such realignments frequently entail no physical relocation of households since for practical purposes only nearby rural local communities are ordinarily involved. Because of

[10]Eickelman, "Time," pp. 50-52. The discussion of Moroccan tribal organization is further documented in Eickelman, *Moroccan Islam,* pp. 115-21.

these shifts of identity, "official" administrative designations of rural local communities are almost always inaccurate and are considered by tribesmen as a separate category of identity used only in formal contact with local officials.

Since rural local communities are constantly re-forming, one way of determining links is to see the camping arrangements at the annual festival *(mūsim)* of the major marabout of the region, Sīdī Mhammad Sharqī. His shrine and living descendants are located in the nearby town of Boujad. This festival occurs each fall, just before the move to winter pastures. Groups are distinguished both by the placement of tents on these occasions and by the competitive displays of horsemanship and shooting *(tahrīk-s)*, sometimes called powder-plays *(lacb al-barūd)*, in which they engage. The idea of these competitions is for groups to ride in a gallop in a straight line and to fire their guns simultaneously. Heavy betting accompanies these occasions. Participation in these competitions reflects new social alignments, and some realignments are due to disputes over the competitions themselves. Since the marabout's festival is also the one time in the year that tribesmen gather from a large area, such powder-plays in effect constitute public announcements of new social arrangements. As the conception of patrilineal descent is a relative one which changes with actual social arrangements, the groups involved legitimize their new relations to each other by shifting the way in which they represent their ancestors and links with particular marabouts.

The identity of *sections* among the Bnī Batāw is somewhat more stable over time, although these also shift in composition and identity. One reason for their greater stability is their administrative reality. The precolonial, colonial, and independent governments have invested the rights to collective pastures in sections and still allocate many taxes through the administrative apparatus associated with

FIGURE 5-3 Competitive riding at a *mūsim*, Morocco, 1968. (Courtesy of Maurice Grosser.)

sections. Prior to the colonial period, sections also performed significant functions. Each section, for instance, constructed fortified compounds made of mud and stone which were used for collective defense in times of intertribal raiding. Sections also made collective arrangements for grazing rights to pastures controlled by neighboring groups, but there were many other "levels" at which such arrangements could also be made. Individuals from different tribal groups, for instance, could make arrangements among themselves, if they had confidence in each other.

More formal arrangements between relatively stable groups also were common. A common sort were "ritual alliances" *(ṭāṭā)* made between rural local communities and sections of the same and different tribes. In such alliances, groups agreed to refrain from fighting and raiding each other and, at least in principle, to aid each other in the event of threats from third parties. Such alliances generally involved the exchange of herding rights as well. The patterns of such alliances occasionally coincided with "closeness" as reckoned by the formal ideology of patrilineal descent, but such ideology was by no means the primary factor in their formation.

Such ties worked in the following manner. For instance, the Flālḥa (see Fig. 5-2) local community of the Bnī ᶜĪsa section of the Bnī Batāw concluded an alliance with the ᶜAbābsa section of the tribe—the fact that the two groups were considered to be at different "levels" of organization was not considered significant by the Bnī Batāw themselves. They met at the shrine of one of the marabouts in Boujad and swore an alliance.

Each collectivity had multiple alliances of this sort. The Wlād Khallu section had three such alliances with other sections just before the colonial era. One section was part of an Arabic-speaking tribe with adjacent agricultural lands; another involved an Arabic-speaking tribe at some distance from their own; a third alliance was with a Berber-speaking neighboring group, the Ait Bū Ḥaddū.

These alliances were concluded by different ritual means. In one case the groups involved had a communal meal, at the end of which all the men present removed one of their slippers and placed them in a pile, one pile for each of the two groups. Slippers from the two piles were then matched at random. The men whose slippers were paired became companions with a special relation to each other. Whenever one needed permission for pasture rights or other matters, he approached his companion in the other group. In another case, the lactating women of the two contracting groups nursed the children of the opposite group after the men's communal meal, thus creating bonds. In the third case, the councils of the two groups had a communal meal in which the milk from lactating women of the two groups had been mixed in one of the plates, thus creating an enduring tie of milk brotherhood. Once such an alliance was concluded, any violation was considered to invite supernatural (as well as human) retribution.

I have said little of the level of the "tribe" so far, for the simple reason that from the historically known precolonial period, it appears to have existed more as a set of vague "tribal" names which provided a range of potential identities for various groups at different times than as a base for sustained collective action, although coalitions of various sections and rural local communities within the "tribes" frequently occurred. When these coalitions did occur they did not come together along strict lines of closeness of lineal descent. This is demonstrated by the patterns of resistance in which persons from various "sections" and "tribes" associated themselves against the French. Precolonial accounts of disputes in western Morocco also suggest that alliances followed much more flexible lines.

The imposition of colonial government in 1912 had a number of important consequences for tribal organization, especially when the colonial regime had become firmly implanted by the 1920s and 1930s. For one thing, the average size of herds was reduced from what it had been in the precolonial era. Part of the reason was that many townsmen had made substantial investments in livestock, making arrangements with the individual tribesmen in most cases. As alternative investments opened up and became more lucrative, such local investments declined. In addition, the colonial government imposed restrictions upon pastoral movements, reducing the flexibility which was possible in the precolonial era.

An interesting aspect of the French colonial understanding of tribal structure is that it depended more upon the ideology of agnatic relationships than did the Moroccan tribesmen themselves. Segmentary ideology was administratively convenient as an "official" representation of local social structure. How were these administrative understandings translated into practice? Each winter, as I indicated earlier, the Bnī Batāw moved with their herds to the Berber highlands. Yet, for the French, the Berber highlands were under military rule while the lowland plains were under the civil native affairs administration. In the precolonial period, pasture rights could be arranged even between individuals or several tents of different tribal groups when peaceful conditions prevailed. In some circumstances, the host person or group charged a price for such rights; in other cases, only reciprocity at a later date was expected. Of course, disputes occurred frequently, but these only served to emphasize the wide range which such pastoral arrangements could take. The French found this flexibility confusing for administrative purposes, especially when tribesmen crossed administrative boundaries.

Colonial archives for the 1930s indicate that some administrators went so far as to propose a ban on pastoral movements which crossed administrative boundaries, unaware that such radical restrictions would have the consequence of drastically reducing the size of herds and making the survival of the Bnī Batāw precarious. In the end, a compromise was adopted in which movements of herds were authorized but only on a reduced scale and only involving entire sections. The French argued (in line with popular sociological assumptions of the period) that only collective arrangements were "traditional."

French administrative divisions, however, worked more along the lines of a quasi-genealogical framework than Moroccan tribes. For example, let us say that a pastoral dispute broke out between the Bnī Batāw and a group of Berber tribesmen while the Bnī Batāw were with their herds in the Middle Atlas mountains. The French civil official in the town of Boujad who was responsible for the Bnī Batāw was not allowed to communicate directly with his military counterpart twenty miles away who was responsible for the neighboring Berber group. Instead, he was obliged to communicate with his immediate superior in a neighboring town, who in turn communicated with his civilian superior. This administrator, in turn, contacted the ranking military officer responsible for the Middle Atlas region, who in turn communicated with his subordinates. These rigid administrative hierarchies simply had no counterpart in Moroccan tribal organization, although the genealogical grid used by the French to indicate relations among various groups naturally had important consequences since pasture rights and taxes were determined by them, and local strong men had their privileges reinforced by the support they received from the French by appointment as unsalaried officials.

Now what is important about these complex patterns of association and identity? To say that some rural Moroccans are "tribesmen" tells us very little now or in the past about how they conceive of their social identity and comport themselves politically in relation to other groups. Lines of political cleavage follow no preordained pattern but depend upon complex factors of residence, kinship, herding, and land arrangements, among other considerations. Those interests that are most significant often are legitimized by being thought of in the idiom of genealogical grids determined by concepts of patrilineal descent. "Tribal" man, at least in the context just considered, does not respond in a semiautomatic way to the affairs of the various social collectivities to which he belongs. The notion of "closeness" outlined earlier is a more comprehensive one which allows for considerable variation in the forms which social action can take in Morocco.

Of course, the social organization of a Moroccan tribe cannot in itself be taken as "representative" of all Middle Eastern tribes, as I indicated earlier. But the *type* of analysis which I have sketched can serve as a guide to understanding tribes in other contexts. Such analysis involves an account of how persons in a given society explicitly *and* implicitly conceive of the social order and proceed to act on these assumptions. It also involves seeing how these assumptions are modified by and in different historical contexts. Although Middle Eastern countries and regions within them share numerous economic, social, and cultural similarities, they differ in just as many ways. Comparisons of "tribal" societies in these countries based solely upon a single point of resemblance, such as the ways in which ideologies of patrilineal descent are used and manipulated, can be highly misleading because such ideologies in themselves are simply inadequate to describe the political organization of Middle Eastern tribal groups.[11]

[11] Marx, "The Tribe," pp. 356, 359.

## SEGMENTATION IDEOLOGY OR SEGMENTARY THEORY: THE BEDOUIN OF CYRENAICA

One reason for the fascination with segmentary lineage theory as it has been applied to tribal peoples in the Middle East, Black Africa, and elsewhere is the extent to which it assumes that the explicit native ideology of the social order (usually one based on patrilineal descent) and the anthropologist's analytical model of that order were thought to coincide. As I have already indicated, segmentary lineage theory does not account for many crucial features of tribal social and political organization and for this reason is a mistaken way of explaining the working of tribal societies in the Middle East. Yet such theory has played an important role in the social anthropology of the Middle East and elsewhere. When ethnographic accounts developing its assumptions began to be published in the 1940s and 1950s, segmentary lineage theory appeared to provide a framework within which anthropologists could undertake meaningful comparative research.[12]

Figure 5-4 shows the essentials of the idea of segmentation. I am using letters rather than the names of actual groups and numbers to refer to various "levels" of segmentary society so that its abstract features are more discernible. There are three assumptions necessary for segmentary theory to be valid: (1) A society must conceive of its political relationships primarily or exclusively according to a tree of lineal descent (either patrilineal or matrilineal); (2) groups at each "level" of society must be balanced by another group of roughly equal strength; and (3) individuals within such a society must be considered equals.

Political obligations and relationships in such a society become particularly

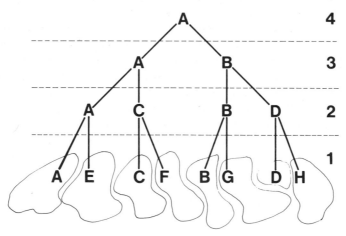

**FIGURE 5-4** The concept of segmentation. (After Dale F. Eickelman, *Moroccan Islam,* p. 207. Courtesy of the author and the publisher.)

[12] See, for instance, M. G. Smith's early review of the use of the concept in "Segmentary Lineage Systems," *Journal of the Royal Anthropological Institute,* 86 (1956), 78.

evident in the case of a feud resulting in homicide. Suppose, for instance, that a dispute occurs between a person from group A and another from group E at level 1. Both disputants presume that they can rely for support upon their fellow group members. If such a dispute involves a person of group A and another of group F, a higher level of escalation occurs. In this case, groups A and E are expected to support the person from group A; groups C and F are expected to support the person from group F. Thus, groups coalesce at level 2. In a dispute involving groups A and H, groups E, C, and F are expected to rally to the support of group A, while B, G, and D are expected to rally to the support of H. Such a conflict involves opposing groups at the more inclusive level 3. Finally, a challenge to the tribe from outside involves the participation of all groups claiming descent from a common ancestor—the tribe as a whole (level 4). This schema of relationships can be expanded indefinitely, although in practice more than four levels are rarely involved. Real names for groups and their levels can, of course, be substituted, such as tent, lineage, clan, and tribe among the Āl Murra of Saudi Arabia and tent, rural local community, section, and tribe among the Bnī Batāw.

The various "higher" levels of segmentation are called *contingent* social forms by anthropologists because they come into being only when a group or individual is threatened. The groups themselves are acephalous, or leaderless, since in principle all members of segmentary societies are considered to be equals, although temporary leaders may emerge at times. Such a society of equals results in what Evans-Pritchard has referred to as "ordered anarchy."[13]

I have already indicated the fascination that this concept of the social order held for anthropologists. It raised a basic question of European social philosophy—how was it possible for individuals to cooperate in society? The seventeenth-century English philosopher Thomas Hobbes had posed the question in the following manner: How could the various wills, passions, and desires of individuals be coordinated so that there would not be a war of all against all? Given his particular image of man and society, his answer was that while all men sought to satisfy their desires to the full, no one could do so in a state of total anarchy. Hence, men possessed a "spark of reason" which enabled them to agree to at least a minimal "sovereign" control over themselves in order to pursue their self-interest. In segmentary societies, the minimum of such control is certainly reached as no permanent "governmental" authority exists, only the contingent social forms of cooperating individuals organized in groups determined by the metaphor of blood relations. The principle of segmentation thus provides the minimal conditions for a society to exist, in which violence and self-help provide the ultimate sanctions. Segmentation theory had the added attraction of providing a key notion by which a wide range of social forms in certain types of societies could be explained.

Interest in the concept of segmentation, although not labeled exactly as such, is evident in such influential sociological studies as *The Division of Labor in Society* (1893), where Durkheim writes of "mechanical" or "segmental" societies in which

[13] *The Nuer* (Oxford: Clarendon Press, 1940), p. 6.

individuals and groups tend to resemble each other to the point that he compares their forms to the rings of an earthworm.[14] Even if cut up, each part is capable of existing on its own. One of his primary examples of such a society was the Kabyle of Algeria,[15] although anthropologists later developed the notion of segmentation in Black Africa as opposed to the regions north of the Sahara.

The most thorough ethnographic application of segmentary lineage theory occurred in the context of Evans-Pritchard's books on the Nuer, the first of which appeared in 1940. As indicated in Chapter 2, it appears likely that Robertson Smith's analysis of Arab kinship had a profound influence on Evans-Pritchard. In conversation he has even indicated that the full potential of segmentary lineage theory first occurred to him after a series of visits he made to the Bedouin of Egypt's western desert in the 1930s.[16]

There is no question that segmentary ideologies provide a "native model of tribal society, but the question remains regarding the extent to which it is an accurate analytical model of the social order of societies so characterized. If the major work of developing the concept of segmentation occurred in the context of Black Africa, the realization of its limitations became most readily apparent in later work in Middle Eastern and other contexts.

Discussions of segmentary ideology in the Middle Eastern context are numerous. The concept is often used in very misleading ways, so that one scholar discussing Iran has written that the notion "somewhat" describes the political comportment of the Iranian elite over long periods of time and another applies the notion loosely to account for political factions among the Moroccan elite, when all that is meant is that political rulers have sought to "divide and rule" in order to maintain their own hegemony. Here I am concerned with the more accurate use of the concept in a tribal setting, and specifically with an important 1967 article by Emrys Peters on the Bedouin of Cyrenaica, which contains a comprehensive critique of segmentation theory.[17]

Peters's account is based upon fieldwork carried out between 1948 and 1950,

[14] Emile Durkheim, *The Division of Labor in Society,* trans. George Simpson (New York: The Free Press, 1933), p. 175.

[15] *Ibid.,* pp. 174-81.

[16] He made this point in speaking with Robert Fernea at Oxford in the early 1960s (Robert Fernea, "Sunrise Semester," CBS-TV, October 10, 1975). Evans-Pritchard taught in Cairo from 1932 to 1934 and made numerous trips to the Bedouin during this period. He later applied the notion of segmentation to the Bedouin of Cyrenaica, Libya, but only in a highly condensed form devoid of specific historical examples. See his *The Sanusi of Cyrenaica* (Oxford: The Clarendon Press, 1949).

[17] Emrys L. Peters, "Some Structural Aspects of the Feud among the Camel-Herding Bedouin of Cyrenaica," *Africa,* 37, no. 3 (July 1967), 261-81. Except where otherwise noted, the following account is based primarily upon Peters's critique. For Peters's more general views on the use of segmentary lineage theory in Middle Eastern contexts, see his "Aspects of Affinity in a Lebanese Maronite Village," in *Mediterranean Family Structures,* ed. J. G. Peristiany, Cambridge Studies in Social Anthropology, 13 (London: Cambridge University Press, 1976). The article has a much wider significance than Peters's title indicates. For an excellent comparative discussion of the feud and its importance for understanding "tribal"

during which time the tribal groups involved still were camel-herding pastoralists. In the first part of the article, Peters explains the social organization of the Bedouin as they themselves see it. Thus, the basic unit of social organization is the camp— that is, groups that herd together. Over 80 percent of the males in these camps, each of which has a population of 200-700, are agnatically related. Acceptance of a common name in such a group implies full political responsibility. Such "tertiary" groups (as they are designated by Peters) are corporate for most purposes. Moreover, each camp has its own wells, ploughland (these groups also cultivate), and pasture. In Fig. 5-4 such groups are represented as level 1, where the irregularly drawn spheres associated with them are meant to indicate the territory possessed by each descent group. The ultimate test of membership in such a tertiary group is conduct during feuds and the payment of blood money. If someone does not participate as expected in such matters, he risks splitting from the group. Bedouin say that homicide within a tertiary group is unthinkable since the group is supposed to respond to the injury of any of its number as "one body." Such homicides occur nonetheless, but Peters points out that the Bedouin do not think of them in terms of murders requiring revenge. The most common result is the voluntary exile of a slayer or his expulsion from the group.

As for homicide between tertiary sections, such as A and E on Fig. 5-4, the payment of blood money or a vengeance slaying is the most probable result. Peters indicates that such collateral tertiary groups are usually neighbors. Although each has a different tract of territory and different wells, social relations between them are fairly intense. A prolonged feud would seriously disrupt such relations, so neighboring groups usually find it expedient to find some way to remain on friendly terms rather than engage in long-term feuds. In most cases, settlement is arranged through an agreement to pay "blood money" *(diya)*. The amount agreed to is rarely paid in full, for, as Peters says, debt, like the feud itself, is a form of social relationship (although the feud is a negative one). As long as the debt is not fully paid, the social relationship endures.

At the next level of segmentary integration (level 2 on Fig. 5-4 and "secondary sections" in Peters's article), homicide characteristically results in a feud. Most such sections occupy different ecological regions. If a feud develops between them, there is no urgent necessity to make peace, unlike the case for neighboring groups on level 1 of the figure. However, feuds which occur between groups at the level of what Peters calls secondary sections also have their etiquette. For instance, feuds were not carried on at the market, although in the case of hostilities, rival groups usually arranged to be present at tribal markets at different times.[18]

---

societies in the Mediterranean, see Jacob Black-Michaud, *Cohesive Force: Feud in the Mediterranean and the Middle East* (New York: St. Martin's Press, 1975). In many ways Black-Michaud's argument develops Peters's insights on the feud. A foreword by Peters presents a summary of his views of the subject.

[18]David Hart describes a situation in the Moroccan Rif prior to colonial rule in which feuds were so endemic that each house took the form of a pillbox in some regions. Since

At level 3 of Fig. 5-4 ("primary" sections for Peters), men of collateral sections often are complete strangers to each other and meet only irregularly. When a homicide occurs, it is unlikely that negotiations will even be undertaken. In this case, reciprocal raiding occurs, often for prolonged periods, but large-scale killing is avoided. Challenges from outside the tribe itself involve the entire tribe, but such hostilities result in wars instead of feuds in which (at least in the nineteenth century) major losses of life occurred. In wars, unlike feuds, there were no conventional restraints upon attacks, at least in principle.

Peters's article elaborates in considerable detail how the Bedouin themselves make use of segmentary ideology to explain their social relationships. In this he makes a valuable contribution, for many accounts of segmentary ideology are highly schematic and present virtually no specific examples of how this ideology is applied by its adherents to specific, historically known situations.[19]

There are a number of ways in which segmentary ideology fails as an analytical model of social action. As Peters indicates, if all secondary sections were engaged in feuding, for instance, pastoral movements would become impossible. Such contradictions present no direct challenge to segmentary ideology for the Bedouin; a number of contingencies are invoked to explain why segmentary ideology does not apply directly to particular situations. Unfortunately, segmentary lineage theorists have similarly tended to invoke contingencies rather than question its viability as a sociological model.

Peters goes into the weakness of segmentary lineage theory in some detail to document his contention that the lineage model is not a sociological one. He sees such theory as possessing four major weaknesses. First, segmentary groups simply do not occur in a balanced opposition to each other. What Peters calls tertiary groups (rural local communities in the context of my Moroccan example) are not balanced against each other. Resources of land and herds are unevenly distributed, as is the population of various groups. There is a great variation in the number of groups which occur at this level of differentiation.

Secondly, when groups combine, they do not do so in terms of the combinations anticipated through an application of segmentary lineage theory. Similarly,

---

women were left out of feuds, special women's markets developed so that households could maintain economic contact with the outside world. Several exclusively women's markets still exist in the region. For an elaborate account of feuds in the Rif using segmentary lineage theory, see David M. Hart, "Clan, Lineage, Local Community and the Feud in a Rifian Tribe [Aith Waryaghar, Morocco]," in *Peoples and Cultures of the Middle East, Volume 2: Life in the Cities, Towns, and Countryside,* ed. Louise E. Sweet (Garden City, N.Y.: The Natural History Press, 1970), pp. 3-75. Another useful study by Hart which historically examines the relation of Moroccan "tribes" to the country as a whole is "The Tribe in Modern Morocco: Two Case Studies," in *Arabs and Berbers: From Tribe to Nation in North Africa,* eds. Ernest Gellner and Charles Micaud (London: Duckworth, 1972), pp. 25-58. For a description of endemic feuding in southern Arabia prior to colonial rule in the 1930s, see H. W. Ingrams, *A Report on the Social Economic, and Political Conditions of the Hadramaut,* Colonial Office, No. 123 (Longon: H.M.S.O., 1936).

[19] For example, see Ernest Gellner, *Saints of the Atlas,* The Nature of Human Society Series (London: Weidenfeld and Nicolson, 1969).

segmentary lineage theory assumes that power is distributed equally throughout the entire tribal political system and does not acknowledge the existence of leaders. As Peters indicates, such leaders exist, although lineage theory has effectively blocked the analysis of patterns of tribal leadership. Moreover, such leadership does not occur along the lines of groups as determined by segmentation theory.

Third, there is considerable disparity in the political resources enjoyed by various groups, as opposed to the rough equality of people and resources presumed by segmentary lineage theory. Groups may appear "equal" as descendants of a pair of brothers from a common father, but such equality in a genealogical sense masks a considerable disparity of political strength and of the actions that a group is willing to take. This point applies equally to the Āl Murra, the example discussed at length in the last chapter.

The fourth objection to segmentary lineage theory is that it says little about ties of kinship created through women. By Bedouin ideology, women and the ties created through them belong to the nonpolitical realm of domestic relations. Yet there are important political and economic links created through marriage ties and other ties through women.[20] The Bedouin (and anthropologists working within segmentation theory) seek to account for such ties through "secondary" rules that do not involve the principles of segmentation. Yet there are important areas of conduct that cannot be explained by such assumptions. As Peters indicates, killing a relative through marriage is as repugnant to the Bedouin of Cyrenaica as killing a close agnate, and there are numerous marriages that occur between neighboring groups. In many circumstances, one's mother's brother may be the only person to whom one can turn to in situations such as access to water rights in years of drought. Similarly, in the payment of blood money, it is not unusual for a mother's brother to contribute even when there is no obligation to do so in terms of segmentation theory.

The Bedouin also have an explanation for such contradictions in terms of segmentation theory. They claim that they marry whenever possible within their own group so as to avoid conflicts of interest between opposing segmentary groups.[21] As Peters indicates, this is simply not the case. By studying the total marriage patterns of Bedouin groups, a different pattern emerges. Bedouin create a significant number of strategic alliances with other groups through highly selective political marriages which taken together give groups access to a range of ecological resources and other aid. Such ties are of more than secondary importance. As Peters writes, throughout his stay in Cyrenaica he never saw groups assembling along the lines expected by segmentary lineage theory. When disputes occurred over wells or ploughlands, agnatically close groups were often absent while genealogically more "distant" groups often were present. A number of men who

---

[20] Pierre Bourdieu, *Outline,* pp. 30-71, is one of the few social anthropologists besides Peters who has realized the full significance of such ties.

[21] See *ibid.,* pp. 33-38 and the discussion in Chapter 6 of this book concerning father's brother's daughter's marriage.

took sides in such disputes were not even kinsmen but were related in other nonkin ways to the main protagonists in such disputes.

These are some of the principal objections to segmentary lineage theory. As an ideology of social relations among many tribal groups in the Middle East, the notion of segmentation has considerable importance. As a sociological model, it is inadequate. I have dealt with it at length only because it has mistakenly led many anthropologists to explain virtually every problem in tribal social relationships in terms of the lineage system.

The issue of whether segmentary lineage theory can usefully explain the workings of tribal society has been important only because such theory has been used uncritically to account for common social elements in the entire region. It also has blocked the development of alternative and more satisfactory ways of accounting for social structure. Some anthropologists have gone so far as to construct elaborate theories accounting for how presumably acephalous and egalitarian tribes in the Middle East coexisted with the inegalitarian social order of the cities and states of the region, at least in the "traditional" past. Unfortunately no clear evidence exists to support such an assumption.[22] Thus Ernest Gellner, one of the main defenders of this point of view, has presumed that the High Atlas region of Morocco on which he based his account of tribal society had "traditional [segmentary] institutions" which until the 1930s "had survived untouched . . . in a kind of sociological ice-box" until his own work in the region in the mid-1950s.[23] Yet significantly, Gellner can provide no specific examples of political action by High Atlas Berbers for the pre-1930s period, and the evidence that he provides for later periods is irrelevant or contradictory to his contention that segmentary theory is valid.[24]

It is possible to make general statements concerning common elements of religious belief, political organization, economic activity, and other fields of activity in the Middle East, but such statements should take the form more of "family resemblances," partial similarities that can meaningfully be compared and contrasted, rather than exact identities asserted by simpler but less accurate theoretical assumptions. This is emphatically the case with Middle Eastern tribes and with the subject of Chapter 6, ideas of kinship and family in the Middle East.

---

[22] On the Bedouin of Cyrenaica, see Peters, "Some Structural Aspects," esp. pp. 269, 280-81.

[23] Ernest Gellner, "Political and Religious Organization of the Berbers of the Central High Atlas," in *Arabs and Berbers*, p. 59.

[24] Detailed analysis of Gellner's use of the concept of segmentation can be found elsewhere. Black-Michaud discusses Gellner throughout his *Cohesive Force*, esp. pp. 269, 280-81, while I have discussed it implicitly in *Moroccan Islam*, pp. 105-21, and explicitly in "Ideological Change and Regional Cults," esp. pp. 23-24. A highly original and detailed critique by a Moroccan sociologist who has worked in the same region as Gellner is Abdellah Hammoudi, "Segmentarity, Social Stratification, Political Power and Sainthood: Reflections on Gellner's Theses," *Economy and Society*, 9, no. 3 (August 1980), 279-303. Another useful discussion of Gellner's thesis is Hildred Geertz's review of *Saints of the Atlas*, which appeared in the *American Journal of Sociology*, 76 (1971), 763-66.

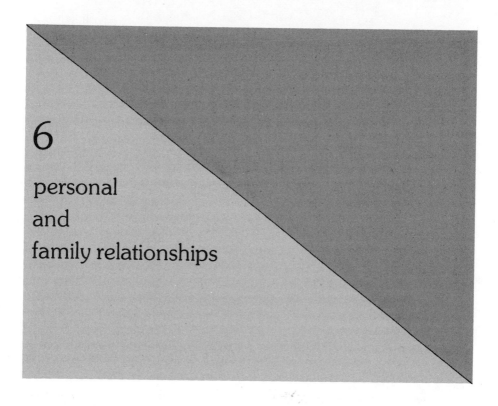

# 6

## personal
## and
## family relationships

### KINSHIP TODAY

Anthropologists today recognize that kinship and family relationships, and cultural ideas concerning them, must be studied in the context of complementary, locally held notions such as patronage, neighborliness, and friendship. This assumption has not always guided ethnographic inquiry and analysis in the past. For instance, a major body of anthropological theory once held that kinship in all societies was concerned with what were essentially biogenetic relationships which could hence be compared cross-culturally. Kinship in such a theoretical perspective is then defined primarily in terms of genealogical criteria instead of other possible bases of interpersonal relationships.

As I see it, there are several rather straightforward arguments that should be made in understanding kinship and family relationships cross-culturally. First, whatever the actual groupings are of people who feel obliged to one another through "family" relationships, these groupings act in cultural terms which have a biogenetic reference. Nonetheless, how people behave toward one another as "kin" and "family" cannot be accounted for entirely in terms of norms of obligation defined in biogenetic terms. Hence anthropologists must elicit what are the shared cultural notions of family and relationship prevalent in any given society rather than presume their content (for example, shared biogenetic substance) in advance.[1]

[1] Among recent studies which take such an approach are David M. Schneider, *American Kinship: A Cultural Account,* Anthropology of Modern Societies Series (Englewood Cliffs, N.J.: Prentice-Hall, Inc., 1968) and his more recent "What Is Kinship All About?" in *Kinship*

Second, in the past, many American and European anthropologists have implicitly and inappropriately imported their own cultural stress on biogenetic "natural" ties when interviewing people in the Middle East and in analyzing their notions of kinship and family. The result has been to overstress genealogical kinship ideologies, which have their main and clearest form for Muslims in the Quranic inheritance code and for all Middle Easterners in the kinship terminological system.[2] Because there are some similarities between the Arabic formulations and American notions, some anthropologists have wittingly or unwittingly extrapolated their own cultural notions much too far into the Middle Eastern data. This has been particularly the case in limiting family ties to blood ties and in assuming that the notions of "clan" and "tribe" have overriding significance in the ordering of behavior and in the determining of choices in moral situations.[3] Such misleading assumptions have in part contributed to the popularity of notions such as segmentary lineage theory, as discussed in Chapter 5. Two related issues are involved here. One concerns how coercive are kinship norms in themselves. The other concerns the independence of kinship norms from other kinds of social obligations.

---

*Studies in the Morgan Centennial Year,* ed. Priscilla Reining (Washington, D.C.: Anthropological Society of Washington, 1972), pp. 32-63. See also Rodney Needham, "Polythetic Classification: Convergence and Consequences," *Man* (N.S.), 10, no. 3 (September 1975), 349-69; and Hildred Geertz and Clifford Geertz, *Kinship in Bali* (Chicago and London: University of Chicago Press, 1975).

[2] The form which kinship terminology takes throughout the Middle East is remarkably consistent and can be indicated briefly. The principal kinship terms for family of origin in formal Arabic are as follows: father *(ab),* mother *(umm),* father's brother *(ᶜamm),* father's sister *(ᶜamma),* mother's brother *(khāl),* mother's sister *(khāla),* brother *(akh),* sister *(ukht),* son *(ibn),* and daughter *(bint).* The principal terms indicating affinal links, or ties through marriage, include husband *(zawj),* wife *(zawja),* and father-in-law *(nasīb); ansibā',* the plural of *nasīb,* designates in-laws in general. There are a few other terms, such as grandson and granddaughter *(hafīd* and *hafīda),* and grandfather and grandmother *(jadd* and *jadda).* The plural of these terms, *ajdād,* is used to designate one's ancestors in general. Terminology such as the above is called *denotative* by anthropologists, because its emphasis is upon specific relatives rather than classes of them. Relatives other than those specified above are generally designated by combinations of these terms. For instance, a father's brother's son is *ibn ᶜamm,* and a wife's father is *abū zawja.* There are other combinations of terms to designate half-siblings, co-wives, and other types of relationships. The exact terminology in colloquial usage varies throughout the Middle East but tends to follow the general pattern described above. For Morocco, see Hildred Geertz, "The Meanings of Family Ties," in *Meaning and Order in Moroccan Society,* Clifford Geertz, Hildred Geertz, and Lawrence Rosen, Cambridge Studies in Cultural Systems (New York: Cambridge University Press, 1979), pp. 356-63; for Egypt, see Hani Fakhouri, *Kafr el-Elow: An Egyptian Village in Transition,* Case Studies in Cultural Anthropology (New York: Holt, Rinehart and Winston, Inc., 1972), pp. 57-61; for South Yemen see R. B. Serjeant, "Kinship Terms in Wadi Hadramaut," *Der Orient in der Forschung* (Wiesbaden: Franz Steiner, 1967), pp. 626-733. Kinship terminology in Turkish and Persian, the two other major languages of the region, follows a similar pattern. See Paul Stirling, *Turkish Village,* The Nature of Human Society (New York: John Wiley & Sons, Inc., 1965), pp. 151-55; Fredrik Barth, *Nomads of South Persia* (New York: Humanities Press, 1965), p. 31.

[3] For an elaboration of this argument in an Algerian context, see Pierre Bourdieu, *Outline of a Theory of Practice,* trans. Richard Nice, Cambridge Studies in Social Anthropology 16 (New York: Cambridge University Press, 1977), pp. 30-71; for a Moroccan example which indi-

Third, the anthropologist or any other person interested in understanding Middle Eastern life should try to follow "native" constructs and logic as thoroughly as possible. Knowledge of the full context in which ideas of family and personal relationships are held is perhaps especially important for an understanding of Middle Eastern societies because kinship forms and the personalization of social relationships permeates even bureaucratic and industrial settings, perhaps in an effort to make such relationships more reliable. It is not unusual to find the key offices of governments of the region constituted in large part by close relations, presumably because kinship ties in some contexts are assumed to be a guarantee of loyalty. This is the case not only in the monarchies of the region, such as Saudi Arabia, Oman, and Morocco, but in other regimes as contrasting as Āyatullāh Khomeini's (and the significant roles of his son and son-in-law) Iran, Syad Barre's Somali Democratic Republic, and Anwar el-Sadat's Egypt. Nor are such actions always regarded as an abuse of political authority.

The study of notions of kinship in the Middle East, like the study of tribes, has been a task often regarded as a distinctly anthropological preserve, although this has not prevented scholars in other fields from making generalizations about the nature of family and group identity without adequate empirical investigation or confirmation. Indeed, such assumptions can intentionally or unintentionally become highly politicized. For instance, Edward Said has taken a distinguished sociologist to task for writing that "co-operation in the Near East is still largely a family affair and little of it is found outside the blood group [sic] or village," on the grounds that it suggests a diminished capacity of Middle Easterners to organize "institutionally, politically [and] culturally."[4] Yet because a large number of personal relationships are cast in the language of family relationships, and such ties pervade government offices, the secret police of some countries, and other key organizations, understanding the elastic uses to which the term *family* is put is especially important in the case of Middle Eastern societies.

As with conceptions of "tribe" in the Middle East, there are no single notions of kinship and family which hold from one end of the region to the other, nor can variations between the kinship systems of the region be used to classify them taxonomically. Cultural notions of personal and kin relationships vary considerably from Rabat to Kabul, from rural to urban settings, and among different educational and socioeconomic categories of society.

---

cates in detail how informants can have genealogical models "suggested" to them by anthropologists, see Hildred Geertz, "The Meanings of Family Ties," pp. 349-56. Emrys Peters, "Aspects of Affinity in a Lebanese Maronite Village," in *Mediterranean Family Structures,* ed. J. G. Peristiany, Cambridge Studies in Social Anthropology 13 (New York: Cambridge University Press, 1976), pp. 27-28, discusses the perils of drawing unwarranted inferences from kinship terminology alone, citing examples from contemporary anthropological literature.

[4]Edward W. Said, *Orientalism* (New York: Pantheon Books, 1978), p. 312. Said's quote is from Morroe Berger, *The Arab World Today* (Garden City, N.Y.: Doubleday Anchor Books, 1964), p. 151.

The best way of recognizing why our own notion of kinship should be used comparatively only as a first-order approximation is to look at concepts drawn from different parts of the Middle East which could be glossed as "kin": These are the notion of *qawm* (Afghanistan), *ḥamūla* (Arabs in Israel), and *qarāba* (Morocco). In Afghanistan, *qawm* refers to a socially united and territorially contiguous group of people who speak of themselves as if they are also linked by agnatic kinship, although such a group actually includes affines, some neighbors, and others. Significantly, the term does *not* apply to persons or households who fail effectively to cooperate with other members of the *qawm,* in spite of close agnatic or affinal ties. A *qawm* is ideally "a territorially and socially integrated group, joined together through ties of kinship, political action, and religious belief and ritual."[5] Although *qawm* can also refer to persons sharing common agnatic descent, it would be incorrect to regard such a usage as primary and its reference to "a territorially and socially integrated group" as secondary. The central feature of the Afghani concept of *qawm* is the active maintenance by its members of a shared notion of relationship. It is this ideological form which is primary, not a "native" recognition of "blood" ties, even if such assumptions are metaphorically important.

The same general point holds for some of the shared notions of identity among Arab villagers in Israel. In a study conducted in 1958-1959, Abner Cohen found that most (but significantly not all) households were identified with a number of patronymic associations called *ḥamūla*-s. The shared identity of the *ḥamūla* was expressed in the idiom of patriliny, although villagers themselves were aware that not all the claimed patrilineal links were historically valid.[6] To emphasize the fact that he was not writing of lineal descent, Cohen used the term *patronymic group* in his book to stress that the shared element of *ḥamūla* identity was the name of a claimed agnatic ancestor. To my knowledge Cohen was the first ethnographer to break with the more conventional assumptions of lineage theory in a Middle Eastern context. In a later publication he referred to the *ḥamūla* by the more appropriate term of *patronymic association* rather than *group* in order to emphasize better the flexibility inherent in the cultural principle of *ḥamūla* and its frequent lack of sharp principles of exclusion in social practice.[7]

For certain specific purposes such as inheritance, a calculation of agnatic relations and affines was made in principle in terms of the tenets of the Quran. However, everyday domestic arrangements and the political alignments of the *ḥamūla*

[5] Robert Leroy Canfield, *Faction and Conversion in a Plural Society: Religious Alignments in the Hindu Kush,* Anthropological Papers, 50 (Ann Arbor: University of Michigan Museum of Anthropology, 1973), pp. 34-35.

[6] Abner Cohen, *Arab Border Villages in Israel* (Manchester: Manchester University Press, 1965), pp. 2-3, 105-29.

[7] Abner Cohen, "The Politics of Marriage in Changing Middle Eastern Stratification Systems," in *Essays in Comparative Social Stratification,* eds. Leonard Plotnicov and Arthur Tuden (Pittsburgh: University of Pittsburgh Press, 1970), pp. 195-209.

were governed by principles of social identity that were not based soley upon ties created through "blood" and marriage, as Cohen's case studies meticulously demonstrate. In practice, _ḥamūla_ identity was based upon a complex web of patrilineal, affinal, and matrilateral ties, neighborliness (most _ḥamūla_ households were located in the same section of the village), and sustained cooperation in political, economic, and ceremonial activities. As political alignments and interests altered, some households even shifted their _ḥamūla_ identity, although such realignments generally occurred only among households not clearly identified with the _ḥamūla_'s core. Nonetheless, when asked to define a _ḥamūla_, villagers did so in terms of common descent, although they privately stated to the ethnographer that such claims could not always be demonstrated. As with other forms of social identity, _ḥamūla_ affiliation in itself did not determine the lines of cooperation and political action, despite the fact of such identity being couched in the idiom of patrilineal descent. Cohen provides numerous examples of cross-_ḥamūla_ ties of friendship, patronage, and common economic and political interests which served equally as bases for unity and cooperation. Ties created through marriage were similarly used. Cohen points out that intra-_ḥamūla_ marriages were relatively common, but that marriages outside the _ḥamūla_ could equally serve as the base for close economic and political cooperation.[8]

A third example, from the "far West" of the Middle East, is the Moroccan concept of "closeness" _(qarāba)_, briefly introduced in its rural/tribal context in Chapter 5.[9] As used by urban and rural Moroccans, "closeness" carries contextual meanings which range imperceptibly from asserted and recognized ties of kinship to participation in factional alliances, ties of patronage and clientship, and common bonds developed through neighborliness. Closeness is constituted by compelling ties of obligations. Often closeness is expressed as a "blood" tie, even when no demonstrable lineal ties exist, because however such ties are valued in practice, they are considered permanent and cannot be broken. Yet in contexts other than those governed by inheritance law, closeness based upon family ties is generally not sharply differentiated from closeness based upon other grounds. Most frequently, persons seek to make the various bases for closeness overlap.

There is evidence that the concept of closeness as used in present-day Morocco is not an accommodation to recent developments. In many respects it

---

[8] See Cohen, _Arab Border Villages,_ pp. 71-93, for his best example of historical changes in the politics of marriage alliances and the elasticity with which normative claims of marriage "rules" are interpreted. Cohen's observations are far from isolated ones. In his study of a provincial urban center in Turkey, Peter Benedict, also reacting against prevailing assumptions of lineage theory and the solidarity of extended families, found that even when there was a compact arrangement of the houses of married sons within a natal courtyard, "many of the households so arranged . . . had virtually nothing to do with their close agnatic neighbors." See Peter Benedict, "Aspects of the Domestic Cycle in a Turkish Provincial Town," in _Mediterranean Family Structures,_ p. 239.

[9] For a more detailed discussion of this concept and its use, see my _Moroccan Islam: Tradition and Society in a Pilgrimage Center,_ Modern Middle East Series, 1 (Austin and London: University of Texas Press, 1976), pp. 95-105, 183-210.

resembles the concept of "group feeling" (ʿaṣabīya) explained centuries earlier by the North African philosopher Ibn Khaldūn (d. 1406). Ibn Khaldūn indicates the multiple bases upon which group feeling can be asserted among both townsmen and tribesmen but ultimately opts for the ideological position that the "natural-ness" of "blood" ties makes them superior to all other modalities as a basis for group feeling.[10] Nonetheless he makes it clear that the underlying cultural con-struct of ʿaṣabīya is not based exclusively or primarily upon socially recognized notions of lineal descent.

## PRACTICAL KINSHIP: MOROCCO

The significance of the shift from talking about kinship to exploring notions such as qawm in Afghanistan, ḥamūla among Arabs in Israel, and qarāba among Moroccans can be stated as follows: Kinship can be considered an *experience-distant* concept. It is one formulated for the purposes of the analytically inclined participant to comprehend a phenomenon or to compare it with others, either typologically or through "family resemblances." On the other hand, *experience-near* concepts are those which individuals use "naturally and effortlessly" to define what they see, feel, think, and imagine and which they "readily understand when similarly applied by others."[11] "Closeness" is such a concept in Morocco.

An illustration of how the notion serves as a guide to practical social relation-ships is provided by the prominent maraboutic (or "saintly") patronymic association in the Moroccan town of Boujad, which had a population of approximately twenty thousand persons in 1973. The town is a local pilgrimage center located on Morocco's western plains, next to the foothills of the Middle Atlas mountains. Roughly a third of Boujad's population claim descent from the marabout Sīdī Mḥammad Sharqī (d. 1601). Collectively these descendants are known as the Sharqāwa—*Sharqāwa* being the plural for Sharqī in Arabic. The town has twenty-six maraboutic shrines of varying importance; twenty-three of which are Sharqāwī shrines. Despite the decline in recent years of popular belief in the efficacy of marabouts as intercessors with the supernatural, the town remains an important regional pilgrimage center and is also the administrative and market center for its rural hinterland.

Because of the advantages of wealth, prestige, and education which derived from the reputation as marabouts of some Sharqāwa in the past, many have managed to maintain prominence in Morocco today as merchants, entrepreneurs, officials, and politicians. Although today Sharqāwī prominence is justified princi-pally on other grounds than maraboutic descent, some Sharqāwa still derive con-

[10] Ibn Khaldūn, *The Muqaddimah,* trans. Franz Rosenthal, Vol. 1, 2nd ed., Bollingen Series 43 (Princeton: Princeton University Press, 1967), pp. 249-310, esp. p. 264.

[11] This distinction is elaborated in Clifford Geertz, "On the Nature of Anthropological Understanding," *American Scientist,* 63, no. 1 (January-February 1975), 47-48.

siderable material and status benefits from the gifts they receive from their largely rural clientele.

What exactly does the claim to Sharqāwī descent mean in Boujad today? The Sharqāwa do not act collectively as a group and never did so consistently in the past. Descent was only one of a number of identities which they shared. In Boujad itself, there are currently eight Sharqāwī patronymic associations. All of these claim descent from sons of Sīdī Mḥammad Sharqī, although none are able to trace their exact genealogical links with him. Nonetheless, this information is said to repose in books and records. Of the eight Sharqāwī patronymic associations represented in Boujad, the members of two of them additionally claim descent from prominent nineteenth-century Sharqāwī marabouts. Each of these patronymic associations is associated with a residential quarter in Boujad. In addition, there are persons who claim Sharqāwī descent elsewhere in Morocco.

One of the two most prominent Sharqāwī patronymic associations in Boujad is that of the ᶜArbāwa. Identification with a patronymic association in itself does not imply an obligation to act in common with other individuals who belong to it, as recent experiences in local electoral politics and disputes over various local issues amply demonstrate. Still, ᶜArbāwī quarter is one of the most tightly knit in Boujad. Approximately 86 percent of its three hundred or so residents (as of 1970) were born in the town itself, as opposed to an average of 54 percent for the town as a whole. A majority of the households in this quarter claim bonds of kinship with each other. In fact, many of them have shared inheritance rights from agricultural estates and other holdings. More importantly, among the descendants of the leading Sharqāwī marabout of the nineteenth century, after whom this quarter is named, are prominent administrators, merchants, politicians, a brother-in-law of the King of Morocco, and even a leading sociologist. There are advantages of prestige in claiming identification with this particular patronymic association.

Ideally the households of a quarter are considered to be bound together by multiple personal ties and by common interests. In fact, a "traditional" residential quarter in Morocco can be defined as the extension of "closeness" *(qarāba)* in physical space. Component households should be able to assume a certain moral unity so that in some respects social space in their quarter can be regarded as an extension of their own households.

Ties of closeness in a patronymic association such as the ᶜArbāwa, especially when many of its component households live near each other, are elaborated and reaffirmed in numerous ways: the exchange of visits, assistance and participation in the ritual activities associated with the births, circumcisions, weddings, and deaths of its members. For closeness to be said to exist in a patronymic association, as in a residential quarter and in a traditional urban setting such as Boujad—the two significantly overlap—the quarter must be capable of collective social action in at least some significant contexts. This usually means that there are one or several men of standing *(kubbār)* with "word" or decisive influence in the patronymic association or quarter who are able to act as spokesmen for the common interest on

**FIGURE 6-1** Tetouan, Morocco. Neighbors in traditional quarters such as this often claim "closeness." (Courtesy of the author.)

critical occasions and to mobilize the heads of households of the collectivity. Ideally, the notions of patronymic association and residential quarter converge. When this overlapping occurs in practice, as in the case of the ᶜArbāwī patronymic association/residential quarter, then mobilization of the collectivity forms a regular part of the fabric of social life.

In many "traditional" spatial settings, neighbors who cooperate effectively with each other will seek to claim to outsiders that they have common descent as a means of enhancing their prestige. Thus the inhabitants of another residential quarter in Boujad, not far from ᶜArbāwī quarter, claim common origin from a nearby tribal group and assert kinship with one another. Although certain households of the quarter are related by ties of kinship and marriage, others are linked solely by occupation, neighborliness, and by other common attributes not related to the attribute of descent. Again, the one feature common to all the quarter's households was their ability on occasions to act successfully as a collectivity.

The quarter in question, Qṣayra ("The Little Fortress"), is so named because it adjoins a fortified, high-walled Sharqāwī quarter and, in fact, looks like a scaled-down version of it. How closeness is demonstrated by residents of the quarter will serve to indicate how notions of "family" and "kinship" must be understood in their Moroccan context. Most residents of the quarter claim that they or their ancestors came from Ait Ṣāliḥ, a tribal grouping to the immediate west of Boujad. Without denying their Ait Ṣāliḥ origin, others prefer to stress their relations with one Ḥajj Bū Bakr, himself reputedly of Ait Ṣāliḥ, who founded the quarter at the turn of the century and whose household serves as the core with which other households claim affinity.

Bū Bakr was a tannery owner and grain merchant when the French arrived in 1913. Not long after this event, he made a fortune through his commercial activities. Soon he converted his fortune into social honor, first by making the pilgrimage to Mecca and thereby acquiring the title of Ḥajj ("Pilgrim"), then by constructing an imposing house for himself, and later by marrying a second wife. As his sons matured and married, he built adjacent houses for them, in the manner of other men of prestige. He also constructed a small mosque for the quarter and made the major contribution toward hiring a Quranic teacher *(fqīh)* to teach in it. He died shortly after the Second World War, but his sons and widows continue to reside in the quarter.

The means vary by which residents of Qṣayra quarter claim "closeness" with Ḥajj Bū Bakr. Most claim closeness by descent and marriage, although in most cases no exact genealogical links can be demonstrated. There are only some thirty dwellings in the quarter, but when I asked residents to enumerate them for me, several were invariably excluded. These turned out to be living units which somehow did not qualify as households—men sleeping in shops; the dwellings of several poor and often childless couples; and all those people excluded from the circle of closeness for some assumed moral defect. These nonhouseholds did not share the visiting patterns of the counted households of the quarter or engage in their multiple reciprocal exchanges.

It is useful to examine the asserted ties of one informant in detail, since they illustrate virtually the entire range of means by which closeness can be claimed. Maᶜṭī (1)[12], a local shopkeeper, at first claimed that Bū Bakr was of his "blood" *(min dammī)*. This he elaborated by claiming that the relation was through his "father's brother" (3), who had married a woman of Ḥajj Bū Bakr's household. In itself this notion is interesting for such a tie would not be considered "blood" in our own concepts.

In another context I had earlier asked Maᶜṭī to tell me whom he considered his kinsmen. I was preparing a "formal" kinship chart, as do many anthropologists, diagramming in an abstract manner his claimed relatives. When I reminded him that previously he had said that his father had no brothers, he replied that, since he was "close" *(qrīb)* to Ḥajj Bū Bakr, then it must be through a half-brother of his grandfather (5). In other words, the knowledge of closeness came first, then its justifi-

[12] The identifying numbers are keyed to Fig. 6-2.

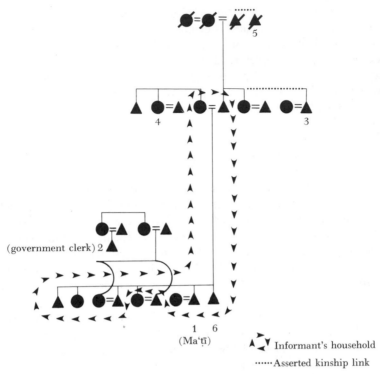

 Informant's household
······Asserted kinship link

**FIGURE 6-2** Kinship ties of Maᶜṭī, Oṣayra quarter. (From Dale F. Eickelman, *Moroccan Islam: Tradition and Society in a Pilgrimage Center* [Austin: University of Texas Press, 1976], p. 101. Courtesy of the author and the publisher.)

cation. He continued that there "probably" was a second link through the marriage of his mother's sister (4), who also lived in the same quarter. Again, this tie could not be demonstrated. Finally, Maᶜṭī said that Bū Bakr's people act *as if (b-ḥāl)* they are related *(qrīb)*; so they must be; and he cited at length the informal visiting patterns which prevailed between their households. No one can remember such genealogical ties clearly, he said; and although—in perfectly comprehensible *Catch-22* reasoning—no one can verify them in any exact way, they must exist. He went on to link himself in a similar manner with a minor, but locally significant, government official (2) also of the quarter founded by Bū Bakr and related to Maᶜṭī through the marriage ties of his brother and sister. The tracing of significant kinship ties through affines and the bilateral reckoning of kin in practical social contexts is a very common feature of Moroccan notions of kinship, the formal emphasis upon the ideology of patrilineal descent notwithstanding.[13]

In the "Little Fortress" quarter, as in the ᶜArbāwī quarter, both "kinship" and involvement in local exchange networks are invoked to justify assertions of

---

[13] Peters, "Aspects of Affinity," p. 32, also emphasizes this point.

closeness. Given the role of the maraboutic Sharqāwa in Boujad's past, one way in which the residents of Qsayra sought locally to enhance their prestige was to build a tomb for one of their claimed ancestors next to some of the Sharqāwī tombs on the outskirts of town. The effort ultimately met stiff opposition from the Sharqāwī and failed, but its near success nonetheless managed to raise the prestige of the quarter's inhabitants in the eyes of most other Boujadis because they successfully managed to act together as a collectivity.[14] Significantly, this process of merging social ties based upon asserted kinship and residential proximity is also characteristic of older residential quarters elsewhere in North Africa and in the shantytowns which have grown up around many of the region's towns and cities.[15]

The overlapping of kinship identities with other forms of identity, including those of residential proximity, is found throughout the Middle East. Fuad Khuri, for instance, has studied the growth of two contrasting suburbs of Beirut, one settled primarily by Maronite Christians, the other by Shīʿī Muslims from southern Lebanon. In both communities, Khuri emphasizes that ties among households were commonly expressed through the idiom of shared patrilineal genealogies, the image of the large extended family (even where particular links were not known with precision), and shared notions concerning a history of common migration and settlement. He further stresses that the use of joint genealogies often shifted with patterns of prestige and influence. Thus when certain individuals and households emerged as prominent, the neighborhood's conception of shared lineages tended also to shift so that the ideology of social relationships tallied with social realities. Moreover, how linkages between persons and groups were expressed remained quite fluid and varied considerably with political and economic circumstances. A prestigious house, with prestige derived from the control of wealth and people, was called a "known" house *(bayt maʿrūf)*, and "lineages" tended to be built up around such houses.[16]

Khuri also found that how asserted kinship ties were elaborated and utilized varied significantly with the religious affiliations of the two communities. In both the Maronite and Shīʿī communities, many extended families were organized into family associations, legal entities which served the collective interests of their members in a variety of ways and which depended upon the entrepreneurial abilities of their organizers. Associations founded by Shīʿī extended families exceeded those founded by Maronites at a ratio of 19 to 2. Khuri attributes this significant difference to the fact that the Maronite church has an effective organizational structure which provides a number of community services, while among the Shīʿa, who lack

[14] For details of the incident, see Dale F. Eickelman, "Is There an Islamic City? The Making of a Quarter in a Moroccan Town," *International Journal of Middle East Studies,* 5, no. 3 (July 1974), 289-93.

[15] See Colette Petonnet, "Espace, Distance et Dimension dans une Société musulmane: A Propos du Bidonville marocain de Douar Doum à Rabat," *L'Homme,* 12 (1972), 47-84.

[16] Fuad I. Khuri, *From Village to Suburb: Order and Change in Greater Beirut* (Chicago and London: University of Chicago Press, 1975), pp. 37-62.

the equivalent of a "church" structure, such community structure depends more exclusively upon family associations.[17]


## PRACTICAL KINSHIP:
## SOME ANALYTICAL CONSIDERATIONS

So far in this chapter I have emphasized the flexibility with which notions of family and interpersonal relationships are conceived and utilized. Because of the many variations in cultural concepts of social identity which occur throughout the Middle East, it is especially important to understand how anthropologists seek to explain and to document these notions. For this purpose, the best available account in my judgment is Hildred Geertz's "The Meanings of Family Ties," based upon extensive field research in the town of Sefrou, Morocco, in the 1960s. Essentially what she does is to describe (1) prior anthropological approaches to the study of Middle Eastern kinship; (2) the living arrangements—the use of space and the "webs" of relationship in which cultural notions of kinship are used to inform and to interpret social action; (3) cultural understandings or "constructs" concerning family; and (4) how marital choices are made and their significance in the study of kinship. Geertz's account has the crucial advantage of thoroughly stating her theoretical assumptions, unlike other outstanding but more specialized studies in which such assumptions and issues of methodology remain largely implicit. The sections in which Geertz describes why she became increasingly uneasy with the earlier anthropological assumptions concerning kinship make her analysis particularly worthwhile.[18]

After a brief review of prior studies of Middle Eastern kinship, with their emphasis upon lineage theory and the so-called "preference rule" for father's brother's daughter (bint ᶜamm) marriage, Geertz situates the study of kinship concepts and ties in the wider context of the complementary notions of friendship and patronage because the lines between these various forms of relationships are not sharply drawn in the Moroccan context. To document the practical contexts in which notions of personal and family relationships are elaborated, Geertz describes in detail the kinship ties and living arrangements of one of the wealthier and more conservative extended families of high status in Sefrou. This extended family is admittedly not typical, but, as Geertz argues, the fact that it is tightly organized and possesses other unique characteristics makes it easier to discern in it "the underlying patterns which inform familial relationships."

The houses of the ᶜAdlūn extended family tend to be clustered in a neighbor-

---

[17]Fuad I. Khuri, "A Profile of Family Association in Two Suburbs of Beirut," in *Mediterranean Family Structures*, p. 93.

[18]Some of the basic theoretical points were published earlier in Clifford Geertz and Hildred Geertz, *Kinship in Bali;* nonetheless, Hildred Geertz's Moroccan work ("Family Ties," pp. 315-91) tends to be presented in a more extensive manner which lends itself more readily to intraregional comparison.

hood or quarter *(darb)* which bears their name. Geertz proceeds to describe in detail how space is used in this quarter and more particularly in one of the oldest, largest, and most distinguished of the ᶜAdlūn houses, called Dār Bū ᶜAlī ("the house of Bū ᶜAlī"). As she points out, many of the larger houses in the older sections of North African cities now tend to be subdivided and tenanted by unrelated poorer families, but in the case of Dār Bū ᶜAlī, eleven related adults, including several married couples (and in the past, their servants), share the same house. Twenty-five other adults living elsewhere are also associated with the household.

As Geertz emphasizes, the notion of "house" deserves particular attention. The house is known by the name of the dominant adult male (or ancestor) associated with it. Such a person is known as the "owner" or "master" of the house *(mūl ad-dār)*. In this case, Bū ᶜAlī was the paternal grandfather of the older residents of the house. The inhabitants of the house, including its women, are collectively known as the "masters" of the house *(mwālīn ad-dār)*. But there is no sharp dividing line between members of the household and other relations. Bū ᶜAlī's claimed descendants are sometimes referred to as "Bū ᶜAlī's people" *(nās Bū ᶜAlī);* ᶜAdlūn refers to the entire extended family, but there is no sharp division made between *nās ᶜAldūn* and *nās Bū ᶜAlī.* The connotations of both these terms and of family *(ᶜāʾila)* are multiple and refer to a number of overlapping categories of kinsmen. Bū ᶜAlī's people *(nās)* are not just a neatly delineated subdivision of the ᶜAdlūn people. The two terms have a variety of connotations, none of which is necessarily primary. The categories cannot be accommodated by lineage theory.

In the past, a number of material circumstances encouraged the daily interaction of quarter residents, especially the women. To a more limited extent this remains the case today. In the past, when there was no piped water—many of the poorer households are still without it—the women of the household had to use a public fountain. The shared fountain, a public bath in the quarter constructed by the ᶜAdlūn family, inheritance laws which tend to subdivide the ownership of houses among relatives who thus share common economic interests, and the use of space such as rooftops (from which women from different houses often can talk with each other as they do their chores) all continue to facilitate interaction among neighbors and kinsmen and frequently to blur the distinction between the two categories.

Geertz's discussion of the web of actual social relationships has a special interest for the anthropological study of kinship because she poses a series of related questions which form comprehensive guides to the study of practical kinship in a number of contexts. As she explicitly acknowledges, her own study is based primarily upon the study of a single high-status urban extended family, an example appropriate for her own particular argument because of its complexity. The issues she poses, however, can be used to make sense of practical kinship in a number of other situations, as I shall suggest by indicating how they can be elaborated and clarified by studies of kinship and domestic organization carried out elsewhere in the Middle East.

Geertz's first issue concerns the size and scope of the daily interacting group of relatives and neighbors, especially women. In the residential quarter described by Geertz, the clustering of houses, the shared water resources, the communal expenses such as the maintenance of a small mosque, and the large number of kinsmen living with each other mean that many relatives have intense daily contact. Of course "relations" means not only persons patrilineally related, but also those related through marriage and matrilaterally. Often through generations of marriage, kinship ties become extremely dense so that people are related to one another in all three ways. Muslims are permitted to marry their first cousins and when such marriages occur the result is to strengthen the multiple ties among relatives. As Geertz explains, "one's cousin is also one's brother-in-law, one's ex-husband has married a woman next door, one's uncle is one's father-in-law, one's husband is a former playmate, and one's child seemingly is shared by everyone."[19] Additionally the feelings and activities of neighbors and relatives in such close physical proximity mean that their behavior is "entirely a matter of open argument

FIGURE 6-3 Returning from market in town, Morocco. Lack of veiling often indicates rural origin or lower social status in North Africa. (Courtesy Paul J. Sanfaçon.)

[19] H. Geertz, "Family Ties," p. 333.

and explicit social pressure."[20] This constant pressure of "publicity," to use Geertz's appropriate term, is an integral part of Moroccan family life and makes privacy and concealment often difficult to obtain.

Of course, residential patterns do not always place relatives in such close physical proximity, but such a pattern is frequent. Khuri's study of two suburbs of Beirut, already discussed, provides an example in historical depth of a pattern

FIGURE 6-4 Woman spinning, southern Iraq. (Courtesy Robert A. Fernea.)

[20]*Ibid.,* p. 334. Such pressures were even more intense in the large households of an earlier generation of the wealthy throughout the Middle East. An Egyptian historian, Afaf Lutfi al-Sayyid Marsot, drawing upon the recollections of her family and friends, writes of her research concerning such houses: "I was given multiple examples of houses where three generations lived together and who with their servants and retainers came to well over sixty inmates— the women could not exactly remember the names of all the retainers so only accounted for the major ones." Polygamy was also prevalent in such circles, although in Egypt at present only 0.05 percent of marriages are polygamous. See her "The Revolutionary Gentlewomen in Egypt," in *Women in the Muslim World,* eds. Lois Beck and Nikki Keddi (Cambridge and London: Harvard University Press, 1978), pp. 263, 275. As with the formal contours of any institution, it would be misleading to regard the social significance of polygamy in one-dimensional terms. Clearly, the institution favors male dominance. In the past, especially when combined with the practice of concubinage, polygamy could be used as a means of sealing political alliances. In other cases, even by contemporary sensibilities, its use could be more benign. For example, a young Moroccan religious scholar was studying at one of the country's mosque-universities just after the inception of the French protectorate in 1912. He was lodged in the house of one of his teachers and took his meals there. In the early 1960s, the wife of his teacher was widowed and left with no adequate means of support. Out of respect and gratitude to both his former teacher and his wife, the former student, now a distinguished *qādī* (religious judge), took the widow as his second wife. Marriage was the only available means by which he could incorporate her into his household and care for her in her later years.

broadly analogous to that described by Geertz, as does Antoun's study of a Jordanian village.[21]

Geertz's second point draws attention to the boundary between informal ("private") and formal ("public") spheres of social action. In the "conservative" setting that she describes, the higher the status of women, the less they are seen in public, although there is considerable variation between generations and according to whether women are young or old and unmarried or married. Age, social status, education and many other complex factors enter into how and when a veil and other covering garments are worn. How these clothes are worn symbolizes the division between the public and the private spheres of action.

In rural settings in North Africa, for instance, women often go unveiled, although they will conceal themselves and act with socially appropriate modesty when strangers are present. In urban settings, women commonly are unveiled before marriage but assume the veil after marriage. The use of the veil can often serve as an indicator of higher social status, although once again there is considerable flexibility as to when and where it will be used. Younger educated women, for instance, are socially freer not to use the veil and to find other means of indicating propriety and status. In comments on the use of veiling in Iran, Michael Fischer suggests that it serves as a "complex moral device" which operates in the domains of modesty where "proper" comportment varies with social space and behavior, status manipulation, and religious-political identity and serves as a marker of the religious group— Muslim, Jew, Bahai, or Zoroastrian. The veil is also at times a powerful political symbol. Fischer's analysis of the component of status manipulation in the use of the veil indicates just how complex this dimension (and the others) can be.

> Not only are veils rough markers of stratification, from villages (in the past and still today often headcloths without chadors) to lower-class urban (veils tied around the waist to allow free use of hands when working) to traditional upper class (full veiling whenever in public); but veils are also markers of intimacy from sons, brothers, husbands (no veils) to close friends and near kin (loose veiling) to the stranger (veiling to the point of covering all but one eye). Modern status, today, is marked by being without veil or with a pastel-colored or transparent veil, or by wearing the veil halfway back on the head so as not to cover all the hair.[22]

Based on their work in western Turkey, Lloyd and Margaret Fallers point out that one of the consequences of the traditional separation of the worlds of men and women outside the domestic realm is that Turkish women have been at least psychologically more independent than their American counterparts. As they participate increasingly in the academic, business, and professional worlds, Margaret

[21] Khuri, *Village to Suburb;* Richard T. Antoun, *Arab Village: A Social Structural Study of a Transjordanian Peasant Community* (Bloomington and London: Indiana University Press, 1972).

[22] Michael M. J. Fischer, "On Changing the Concept and Position of Persian Women," in *Women in the Muslim World,* pp. 207-8.

FIGURE 6-5 Veiling and head covering can communicate a variety of statuses and attitudes. Group of women wearing the traditional San<sup>c</sup>ā' cloak *(sitara)*. (Photograph by Dr. Ronald Lewcock, from *City of San<sup>c</sup>ā'*, ed. James Kirkman [London: World of Islam Festival Publishing Company Ltd., 1976]. Courtesy Middle East Centre, Cambridge.)

Fallers claims that women in Turkey appear to have fewer obstacles to professional advancement than has been the case until recently for American women, although as economic and social circumstances increasingly favor the emergence of single-family households, women somewhat paradoxically again become more dependent upon men.[23]

The third issue in the analysis of practical kinship is the prevalent patterns of hospitality and visiting that prevail among relatives and nonrelatives. In the Moroccan context, there is continuous visiting among relatives and neighbors, and when relatives are neighbors, these patterns of activity are particularly intense. There is also considerable visiting among relatives and close friends at greater distances. As Hildred Geertz indicates, men are considerably more mobile than women, but even their travel patterns are "to a striking degree determined by the location of family connections."[24] These patterns vary considerably according to whether members of the family are urban or rural, wealthy or poor, concentrated in one particular locality, or widely dispersed. Even with the impact of the modern

[23] Lloyd A. and Margaret C. Fallers, "Sex Roles in Edremit," in *Mediterranean Family Structures,* pp. 243-60. The Fallers' study is particularly useful because it presents sketches of a variety of Turkish men and women, thus indicating the nuances of how the division between the public and private spheres shifts according to circumstances of wealth, education, region, generation, and other considerations.

[24] In H. Geertz, "Family Ties," p. 334.

economy and its pressures, at least among the educated middle classes, who occupy modern housing in which it is difficult for relatives to be immediate neighbors (as was traditionally the case), Geertz finds a persistence of strong familial ties expressed in patterns of visiting, a trend largely confirmed by studies conducted elsewhere in the Middle East.[25]

A fourth issue in the analysis of practical kinship is the relative importance of the conjugal family in Middle Eastern settings. In the residential quarter described by Geertz, the conjugal bond is only one of many cross-cutting ties of kinship and affinity, so that household units are not built primarily around the conjugal bond. In an older pattern of polygamous marriages (by Islamic law men are permitted up to four legal wives) which is rapidly diminishing in incidence, affinal links through women were used by wealthier individuals to secure complex political and economic alliances. Still, the overall trend throughout the Middle East is toward separate housing for each nuclear family and the strengthening of the conjugal bond, with the consequences of shifts in the tenor of relationships among members of the family. Mübeccel Kiray argues that a wife's status rises when she lives alone with her husband and children rather than under the same roof with her husband's relatives, although the woman also becomes more dependent on her husband. She shares more in the decision making of the household and in many of the activities of her husband. Extended families remain very important even when such relatives are not living in the same house or immediate neighborhood. Kiray argues that the changes which have occurred with large-scale labor emigration to Europe—a trend now diminishing in importance—and other economic and political shifts have brought about fundamental reinterpretations of family and kinship roles. At the same time, she sees a continued importance in the role of the extended family and in the bonds of obligation and trust which unite family members, facilitate their movement from one region of the country to another, and secure employment.[26]

The complexity of housing patterns and variations in them must be noted. In a study of 140 households in Isfahan, John and Margaret Gulick report that fifty-five compounds, or housing units, were composed of a single nuclear family, but eighteen of these also had other patrilineal and matrilineal relatives present. The rest of the compounds consisted of multiple households in which two or more married couples resided. A particular value of the Gulick study is that it provides almost case-by-case descriptions as to why persons have chosen or were compelled to accept particular residence patterns. Studies conducted elsewhere, including the

---

[25] For an excellent collection of articles which deal with the nature of visiting patterns and their relationship to notions of family and social prestige, see the special issue of the *Anthropological Quarterly*, 12, no. 1 (January 1974), entitled "Visiting Patterns and Social Dynamics in Eastern Mediterranean Communities."

[26] Mübeccel Kiray, "The New Role of Mothers: Changing Intra-familial Relationships in a Small Town in Turkey," in *Mediterranean Family Structures*, pp. 261-71. See also the important article by Alan Dubetsky [Duben] "Kinship, Primordial Ties, and Factory Organization in Turkey: An Anthropological View," *International Journal of Middle East Studies*, 7, no. 3 (July 1976), 433-51.

Egyptian Delta region, similarly emphasize the considerable variations in household composition, many of which are not related directly to issues of tradition or modernity but to changes in the domestic cycle as persons marry, raise children, age, and establish some degree of autonomy by setting up independent households when economically feasible.[27]

A final consideration is the linkage between kinship and patterns of social status, influence, and authority. Hildred Geertz suggests that economic and political achievement in Morocco is "almost entirely an individual matter. An ambitious man may use the help of kinsmen in his climb, and in return may help them, but these exchanges are personally arranged and by no means obligatory."[28] Significant ranges of wealth can be found within a single extended family, and Geertz provides numerous case studies indicating this variation. At the same time, it remains true that the presence of powerful and influential individuals within a single extended family substantially increases the likelihood of the next generation of that family possessing a competitive advantage in retaining their social status. Studies of rural leadership in Morocco suggest that despite the changes from the precolonial regime to colonial domination and later to independence, economic and political advantage has often remained within the same extended families, although not without substantial challenges.[29] The same phenomenon holds for local and national leadership in Saudi Arabia, as the earlier discussion of Cole's study indicated, and elsewhere in the Middle East.

Similarly, how family ties are articulated depends substantially upon the economic situation of the families involved. Maher, in her study of a small town in Morocco's Middle Atlas region, suggests that marriages are much more stable among the urban middle classes than among the less economically affluent in rural areas. When the main inheritance is land, men and women are likely to retain important shared property rights and service obligations with their own kin, and such ties tend to be incompatible with a primary allegiance to the spouse. Marriages in such circumstances are arranged less with a view to conjugal happiness than to serve the temporary interests of those who arrange them, the parents of the spouses and the

[27]John Gulick and Margaret E. Gulick, "Varieties of Domestic Social Organization in the Iranian City of Isfahan," *Annals of the New York Academy of Sciences,* 220 (March 1974), 441-69; Lucie Wood Saunders, "Aspects of Family Organization in an Egyptian Delta Village," *Transactions of the New York Academy of Sciences,* Series II, 30, no. 5 (March 1968), 714-21; Emrys Peters, "Aspects of the Family among the Bedouin of Cyrenaica," *Comparative Family Systems,* ed. M. F. Nimkoff (Boston: Houghton Mifflin, 1965), pp. 121-46. On the continuing importance of the extended family in changing economic circumstances, see especially Henry Rosenfeld, "Social and Economic Factors in Explanation of the Increased Rate of Patrilineal Endogamy in the Arab Village in Israel," in *Mediterranean Family Structures,* pp. 115-36, and Vanessa Maher, "The Extended Family and Lineage Groups in the Maghreb (Morocco)," in *Kinship and Modernization in Mediterranean Society,* ed. J. G. Peristiany (Rome: The Center for Mediterranean Studies and The American Universities Field Staff, Inc., 1976), pp. 47-60.

[28]H. Geertz, "Family Ties," pp. 339-40.

[29]Rémy Leveau, "The Rural Elite as an Element in the Social Stratification of Morocco," in *Commoners, Climbers and Notables,* ed. C. A. O. van Nieuwenhuijze (Leiden: E. J. Brill, 1977), pp. 268-78; Eickelman, *Moroccan Islam,* pp. 211-37.

intermediaries.[30] Maher estimates that for 70 percent of the population of the town she studied, marriages served to maintain the economic and social status quo of the couple. For another 20 percent it meant cultural assimilation to the Arabized and politically dominant group (she studied in a Berber-speaking region); for the remaining 10 percent, the urban elite, women possessed movable capital as opposed to land rights. Marriage with such women was regarded principally as alliances with long-term economic and integrative significance between extended families and hence marriages tended to be more stable. For groups lacking such capital, divorce entailed no significant loss of capital as there was none to lose. This was decidedly not the case for the urban elite.[31] Clearly any study of kinship which neglects the practical domain of economic relationships, as many studies have tended to do in the past, must be treated with some caution.

## MARRIAGE

"Arranging marriages is a highly serious matter, like waging war or making big business deals."[32]

As the above statement suggests, marriage in most Middle Eastern contexts involves not only the personal wishes of the man and woman concerned but the responsibility of many of their respective relatives. In the past, at least among wealthier families, marriages could be said to have been almost entirely the ultimate responsibility of the father or guardian of a boy and girl, although under contemporary circumstances this is no longer the case. Actual marriage practices vary significantly throughout the region, so that studies of particular locales must be consulted for appropriate ethnographic detail. In general, however, the fact remains that marriage choices usually are made by a group of people from the extended families of the conjugal pair, whether the marriage is among Muslims, Christians, or Jews and that marriage notions like those of ideas of family can serve as another indicator of shared assumptions concerning the nature of the social order.[33]

[30] Vanessa Maher, *Women and Property in Morocco,* Cambridge Studies in Social Anthropology, 10 (Cambridge: Cambridge University Press, 1974), p. 157.

[31] *Ibid.,* pp. 191-220.

[32] A Moroccan informant discussing marriage practices with Hildred Geertz, cited in "Family Ties," p. 363.

[33] For an elaboration of the similarities of Muslim and Jewish practices in many domains, see S. D. Goitein, *A Mediterranean Society: The Jewish Communities of the Arab World as Portrayed in the Documents of the Cairo Geniza. Volume III: The Family* (Berkeley and Los Angeles: University of California Press, 1978). Although Goitein is principally concerned with the tenth through the thirteenth centuries, he frequently introduces comparative material from contemporary periods. For particularly useful accounts of marriage negotiations and ceremonies elsewhere in the Middle East, see Hamed Ammar, *Growing Up in an Egyptian Village* (London: Routledge & Kegan Paul Ltd., 1954), pp. 192-201; Paul J. Magnarella, *Tradition and Change in a Turkish Town* (New York: Halstead Press, 1974), pp. 107-30; Richard T. Antoun, *Arab Village: A Social Structural Study of a Transjordanian Peasant Community* (Bloomington:

Since some of the principal examples stressing notions of kinship have come from Morocco, where many of the critical reappraisals of notions of kinship have been conducted, let me provide a further example from that country. Much depends upon the social status and educational background of the couple to be married. Half a century ago in upper-class families, in general the persons to be married had little say in the choices imposed upon them; today, of course, this is no longer the case. In the case of a young man with a living father, his father is expected to take a significant role in the negotiations, and the same is true for a young woman. Now *men,* if questioned, will aver that marriage negotiations are their concern alone, since they claim to have an understanding of the social obligations involved superior to that of women. Women will take a very different view of the process involved and will in fact take quite an active role in the suggestion of marriage partners and in preliminary negotiations.[34]

In the first stages of such discussions, informal go-betweens are often used. These are chosen from among kinsmen and friends thought to be trusted by both parties. For example, a young man might use a trusted school friend to sound out the other family or his own sister or mother. Who is selected to explore such possibilities depends upon the social ties between the parties involved and cannot be predicted from abstract considerations of kinship roles alone. Women's baths and social gatherings involving women exclusively are one place where exploratory talks can take place. After all, as one Moroccan woman explained to me, since Moroccan men presume that women tend to have less "reason" (*[c]qāl*) than men, with *reason* being defined as the ability to act effectively in a wide range of social situations,[35] women are especially useful in such exploratory discussions since anything said by women can be denied by men as not accurately representing their views. Although formally the initiative is supposed to come from the groom's

---

Indiana University Press, 1972), pp. 114-53; and Ladislav Holy, *Neighbours and Kinsmen: A Study of the Barti Peoples of Darfur* (London: C. Hurst, 1974). For valuable older accounts of nineteenth-century marriage practices, see C. Snouck Hurgronje, *Mekka in the Latter Part of the 19th Century* (Leiden: E. J. Brill, 1931) pp. 83-144, and Edward William Lane, *An Account of the Manners and Customs of the Modern Egyptians* (New York: Dover Publications Inc., 1973 [orig. 1836], pp. 155-85.

[34] Daisy Hilse Dwyer, *Images and Self-Images: Male and Female in Morocco* (New York: Columbia University Press, 1978), indicates the complementary images which Moroccan men and women hold of each other, although again Hildred Geertz's "The Meanings of Family Ties" provides the most circumstantial account of marriage negotiations. There are limits in many regions even today, as to how actively women participate in marriage choices. In Turkey, a country with a long tradition of legal reform favoring the equality of women with men, females in small urban centers continue to be "severely segregated" from the age of eleven onward. One Turkish scholar reports that "63 percent of the girls who live in small towns see their husband for the first time on their wedding day, while the proportion for the three large cities and the villages are 16 and 19 percent, respectively." Fatma Mansur Coşar, "Women in Turkish Society," in *Women in the Muslim World*, p. 133.

[35] Note the self-fulfilling cultural definition of *reason*. Since women at least traditionally have been restricted from participating fully in a wide range of public activities, it follows that in comparison with men when they do participate in such activities they do so often less effectively than do men. See Eickelman, *Moroccan Islam*, pp. 130-38.

family, the bride's family often takes the initiative, especially if there have been previous marriages between the two extended families or if the marriage is within the extended family itself, as is the case for father's brother's daughter, or "parallel cousin" marriages, which are permitted in Islamic law.

If the suggestion of a marriage is accepted, then discussions follow concerning the probable date of the wedding and the conditions to be included in the marriage contract (a woman can, for instance, specify that her husband may not take a second wife without granting her a divorce). The subject of the most protracted negotiations is the size of the bridewealth *(ṣdāq)*, or the sum which the groom's family must pay over to the bride's family, part of which goes for the provision of certain furnishings which remain the personal property of the wife. The bride-wealth payment is not usually paid in full but is used as a device to discourage a husband's seeking divorce since in such an event the wife or her family can demand the balance of the agreed sum.

The amounts involved in bridewealth payments have escalated significantly in recent years, and a discussion of how much is involved will indicate why negotiations are taken very seriously. Rosen reports that in the late 1950s the amount involved for a well-to-do family was only a few hundred dollars but had reached as much as $1,000 by 1970.[36] Yet the bridewealth is only a part of the costs involved. Because the ceremonies involved in marriage importantly indicate to the wider public the social standing of the couple, the expenses for gifts and entertainment are often excessive. A 1975 study conducted in Fez estimated that the cost of marriage for a young junior civil servant, including all gifts and the multiple entertainments of guests, came to approximately $14,000. Of this, the groom's family contributed $5,000 and the bride's family the rest. The overall cost was approximately that of the income of the married couple for a period of four years. For the more modest wedding of an ordinary worker, costs were estimated at $1,900, with $1,314 paid by the groom's family and the rest by the bride's. The overall expense equaled the man's estimated income for the first twenty-two months of his marriage. With the cost of marriage so high, many couples prolong their engagement for several years in order to acquire the resources they need in order to afford marriage.[37]

Once the negotiations of financial arrangements are satisfactorily concluded, the fathers of the bride and groom or the relatives acting as their guardians sign a formal agreement before a notary, although there still are marriages in rural areas where the older tradition prevails, at least among families with very modest

---

[36] Lawrence Rosen, "I Divorce Thee," *Transaction,* 7, no. 8 (June 1970), 35. Among the Yörük of southeastern Turkey, one means of coping with the impossible escalation of bride-wealth is by kidnapping, usually done by prearrangement with the couple involved and their trusted relatives. See Daniel G. Bates, *Nomads and Farmers: A Study of the Yörük of Southeastern Turkey,* Anthropological Papers, 52 (Ann Arbor: University of Michigan Museum of Anthropology, 1973), pp. 59-86.

[37] Abdelhaq Cohen, "Le Coût du Mariage à Fès," *Lamalif* (Casablanca), no. 69 (March 1975), 14-16.

resources, of simply concluding agreements in front of reliable witnesses so that the matter, if contested, can later be brought before a court. Either procedure is regarded as legally binding and closely precedes or follows the *khatba*, the public formal request for the woman's hand during a ceremonial dinner at her home.

The engagement, or *khatba*, usually is preceded by a large gift of sugar, publicly delivered, to the woman's household. If the families involved are well-off, this will be delivered with musicians and a number of women from neighboring households joining in. In general, the more socially prominent the families involved, the more public is the delivery of the gift. Families of lesser social prominence and wealth will tend to be more circumspect in the announcement of an engagement. If their gift is not declined, then the engagement feast takes place the following day.

As stated earlier, the actual wedding may be delayed considerably after the formal legal agreement. Not only are financial considerations involved, but in many Middle Eastern cities there is an acute housing shortage, so that many couples postpone living together and having children until suitable accommodations can be found and until they can afford to live together.

Shortly before the actual wedding, the bride's family delivers to the groom's house the various goods purchased with the bridewealth—mattresses, blankets, trays and silverware, cups, clothing, cooking utensils, and so on. For modest families, the procession may be very short and circulate only in the immediate residential quarter. For the weddings of more substantial families, goods are carried on flat-bed trucks and are circulated throughout the town, accompanied by musicians drumming and playing woodwind instruments and clapping and dancing by at least some of the women of the households involved and their neighbors. These occasions are clearly ones of considerable status competition, for they are the means of publicly announcing the social standing of the couple and the prestige of their respective extended families.

On the day of the wedding, a farewell celebration is held at the bride's house. At the groom's house, in the meantime, there is a long evening of feasting and talking. Later, some of the groom's relatives, but not the groom himself, set out to take the bride from her home. There is much weeping and crying as the bride is taken away from her family.

Upon arrival at the groom's house, the bride is ceremonially dressed in wedding clothes—heavy layers of fine brocades and jewels, often rented. The groom finally leaves his guests, lifts his bride's veil, and drinks milk with her and offers her dates. Depending on the region of the country, close relatives and kinsmen may visit the new couple briefly at this stage, or not at all. Wedding gifts are presented at this time, with each gift publicly announced and displayed. The wedding party continues throughout the night, culminating, so to speak, when proof is brought in to the guests of the bride's virginity. In country weddings, this is done by having a hired female dancer place a tray of fruit on her head, over which is placed a handkerchief spotted with the bride's virginal blood. As more Moroccans become exposed to western and urban sensibilities, the practice of insisting upon such direct confirmation of virginity is gradually disappearing. Several days of feasting often follow, during which the bride is expected to feign exhaustion and remain immobile, visited only by her close female friends. Perhaps in part to accustom the bride to her new surroundings—when indeed the bride and groom are not previously related—and to accommodate her to new patterns of domestic authority, the bride will not see her father, brothers, and other male relatives for at least three months.

Moroccans, as well as other Middle Easterners, stress the multiple forces involved in marriage arrangements, of which the feeling of the man and woman for each other is only one factor. The total social networks of the two are more or less directly involved and enter into calculations as to what is a good marriage. Statistics on marriage and divorce are hard to come by because most experts acknowledge that divorces which do not involve property settlements go largely unreported in most Middle Eastern countries. In one village setting in Morocco studied by Vanessa Maher, 49 percent of all marriages ended in divorce and this figure appeared to be relatively constant for those born between 1895 and 1915 and in later generations. Maher's study brought out significant contrasts between marriage stability in the rural setting and in the neighboring town which served as a regional administrative center. Divorce rates were highest in the village—52 percent—as against an average of 38 percent in the town.[38] Maher states that the crucial factor in determining the rate of divorce was the economic and social situation of women. If inheritance was in land instead of liquid assets, if minimal bridewealth was paid, if the bride was young (80 percent of marriages of women under the age of fourteen ended up in divorce), and if each marriage partner retained stronger links with their natal family than that of their spouse—all factors more prevalent in the village as opposed to the town—the divorce was more likely. Another factor is whether a couple has children. Until a woman has children, it is often the case that her primary source of moral—and sometimes financial—support remains her own kin. She can always go back to them if the need arises, and this option is often exercised and remains open even after the couple has children.

## THE IMPORTANCE OF KIN AND FAMILY

Marriage strategies and patterns of kinship obligations reveal underlying notions of personal identity and conceptions of the social self. There has been a tendency in earlier writing on the Middle East to treat kinship rights, practices, and obligations as self-contained objects that can be reduced to fixed rules or normative structures which generate the various practices analyzed by anthropologists. As a conse-

---

[38] Maher, *Women and Property*, pp. 17, 196-98. Maher's comparison of her findings with those of other scholars on pp. 196-97 is particularly useful. For an excellent empirical account, including a discussion of polygamous households, see Gillian Lewando-Hunt, "Conflicts among Bedouin Women," *Royal Anthropological Institute Newsletter*, no. 19 (April 1977), 4-7.

quence, much of the literature on Middle Eastern kinship has for a long time been dominated by an emphasis placed upon the importance of father's brother's daughter marriages and upon the significance of genealogies as a means of determining social and political obligations in a wide range of contexts. The prior attraction of these two topics is worth considering in detail.

Father's brother's daughter *(bint ᶜamm)* marriages are permissible in Islam, as stated earlier, and at least in some social contexts Middle Easterners assert that such unions are preferred, to the point of saying that if a woman and her family choose not to marry a father's brother's son, his consent and that of his family must first be obtained.[39] Proverbs are sometimes cited as evidence for this preference, but proverbs stating contrary opinions toward such unions are equally prevalent. Thus the Moroccan proverb in favor of *bint ᶜamm* marriage, "He who marries the daughter of his father's brother is like him who celebrates his feast with a sheep from his own flock" (that is, one who shows wealth and prestige by having sufficient resources within the family on which to draw) has its contrary in "Keep away from your blood before it defiles you" (in quarrels between the relatives of the spouses).[40] Some anthropologists have sought to document the statistical rate

[39] For example, Antoun, *Arab Village*, p. 74. Donald Powell Cole, *Nomads of the Nomads: The Āl Murrah Bedouin of the Empty Quarter* (Chicago: Aldine Publishing Company, 1975), pp. 71-72, states that the Āl Murra "prefer" *bint ᶜamm* marriages but explicitly states in practice this means that marriages within lineages or with persons of equal status are preferred. Because the topic has held such fascination for anthropologists concerned with the Middle East, it is useful to present a brief listing of the standard articles dealing with the subject. These are as follows: Fredrik Barth, "Father's Brother's Daughter Marriage in Kurdistan," *Southwestern Journal of Anthropology*, 10 (1954), 164-71; Millicent Ayoub, "Parallel Cousin Marriage and Endogamy: A Study in Sociometry," *Southwestern Journal of Anthropology*, 15 (1959), 266-75; Robert Murphy and Leonard Kasdan, "The Structure of Parallel Cousin Marriage," *American Anthropologist*, 61 (1959), 17-29; Raphael Patai, "The Structure of Endogamous Unilineal Descent Groups," *Southwestern Journal of Anthropology*, 21 (1965), 325-50; John Gilbert and Eugene Hammel, "Computer Simulation and Analysis of Problems in Kinship and Social Structure," *American Anthropologist*, 68, no. 1 (February 1966), 71-93; Robert Murphy and Leonard Kasdan, "Agnation and Endogamy: Some Further Considerations," *Southwestern Journal of Anthropology*, 23 (1967), 1-13; Harvey Goldberg, "FBD Marriage and Demography among Tripolitanian Jews in Israel," *Southwestern Journal of Anthropology*, 23 (1967), 177-91; Fuad I. Khuri, "Parallel Cousin Marriage Reconsidered: A Middle Eastern Practice That Nullifies the Effects of Marriage on the Intensity of Family Relationships," *Man* (N.S.), 5, no. 4 (December 1970), 597-618; Jamil Hilal, "Father's Brother's Daughter Marriage in Arab Communities: A Problem for Sociological Explanation," *Mid East Forum*, 46, no. 4 (1972), 73-84; James M. B. Keyser, "The Middle Eastern Case: Is There a Marriage Rule?," *Ethnology*, 13, no. 3 (July 1974), 293-309; and—an article which like Keyser's has a broader perspective—Michael E. Meeker, "Meaning and Society in the Near East: Examples from the Black Sea Turks and the Levantine Arabs," *International Journal of Middle East Studies*, 7, no. 2 (April 1976), 243-70, and no. 3 (July 1976), 383-422. Peters, in "Aspects of Affinity," p. 61, refers to the analysis of "explanations" of *bint ᶜamm* marriage provided by one author as "a veritable thesaurus of errors." By far the best account of the whole issue, despite the author's difficult style of presentation, is contained in Bourdieu's *Outline*, pp. 30-71, which includes a historiographic discussion of why anthropologists got interested in this issue to the exclusion of other issues in the first place.

[40] Cited in Edward Westermarck, *Wit and Wisdom of Morocco* (New York: Horace Liveright, Inc., 1931), p. 72.

of actual occurrence of such marriages, although, as has been indicated in earlier contexts, how certain relatives are designated in social practice is not so straight-forward but depends upon the tenor of existing social relations. Other authors have confined themselves to assuming that such marriages are normative and preferred. For those interested in the statistical incidence of *bint ᶜamm* marriages, they appear to vary from 43 percent in tribal Kurdistan to 2 percent in Lebanon.

In most communities, Richard Antoun estimates that its incidence is approximately 10 to 15 percent of all marriages, although such estimates often are made from incompatible assumptions and should be treated with caution.[41]

The enormous literature on the subject must be consulted to savor fully the nature of the *bint ᶜamm* debate, but examples of several of the issues involved are appropriate here. Keyser, following Patai, indicates that there are four principal reasons advanced by Middle Easterners for the *bint ᶜamm* preference:

1. It preserves the patrimony within the agnatic unit.
2. It strengthens the defensive unit.
3. It confers stability on the household unit.
4. It insures that the status of the partners is equal.[42]

As he summarizes them, the grounds against such propositions are the following. In regard to the first one, women do not inherit equally with male children in Islamic law and in practice often do not inherit at all. Moreover, although such marriages may appear endogamous to Western eyes because in our own system of kinship reckoning such marriages are prohibited, this is not the case in the Islamic Middle East. *Bint ᶜamm* marriages do not fall within an economically defined corporate group. There may be economic gain in such unions, but there may be economic gain in a number of alternative unions as well.[43]

The second argument is related to the notion of kin-vengeance groups, examined in some detail in Chapters 4 and 5. Keyser points out that the proponents of such arguments, notably Barth, have failed to provide specific examples and to indicate that persons who contract such marriages are better off economically and politically than those who do not. As for its conferring greater stability on house-hold units, again evidence is lacking. Maher's evidence on marriage stability indicates that a number of other factors enter into consideration as to whether marriages and households are stable or not.[44] Keyser rather nicely states: "If it is

[41] Richard T. Antoun, "Anthropology," in *The Study of the Middle East,* ed. Leonard Binder (New York: John Wiley & Sons, 1976), pp. 166-68.

[42] Keyser, "The Middle Eastern Case," 293.

[43] Khuri, "Parallel Cousin Marriage," p. 606, points out that in any case, a man's nephews are normatively committed to support him, so that such a marriage is "strategically" unnecessary. Khuri's critique of alternative approaches is interesting, but his own concluding argument that such a union psychologically contributes to harmonious family relationships in that it blends roles that persons learn as children with the responsibilities they have as married adults is as single-stranded and tenuous as the other arguments considered here.

[44] Maher, *Women and Property,* pp. 2, 3, 222-24.

possible for people to like each other only if they know each other, it is also possible for people to hate each other only if they know each other, and marrying within one's own household could be as disruptive and traumatic as not."[45] The final argument concerns the "equal" status of the marriage partners. Equality *(kafā'a)* is a principle enshrined in Islamic law, but whether this principle is defined in economic, social, or other terms is a contested matter. For *bint ᶜamm* marriage to insure equality of status, however the notion is defined, it is necessary to make the further assumption that brothers are always equal, which is decidedly not the case.

The explanations for *bint ᶜamm* marriage preferences, as Keyser points out, often take curious turns, as when a discussion of parallel cousin marriage for the entire Middle East is supported by evidence solely from the Bedouin of the Syrian desert or when kinship ideology is confused with the biology of descent. Keyser's own argument, based upon plausible documentation from field research in Turkey, is that the "preference" for *bint ᶜamm* marriage can best be interpreted as a metaphorical statement which expresses what respective relatives through marriage should ideally be.[46] In reference to the particular issue of *bint ᶜamm* marriage, this is the most plausible argument put forward, for it focuses attention upon the cultural values of family and kin relationships instead of a single, exotic (for non-Muslims) marriage strategy.

The emphasis placed upon genealogies, especially patrilineal genealogies, can be dealt with more summarily as it already has figured significantly in Chapters 4 and 5. Some anthropologists' emphasis upon *bint ᶜamm* marriage has unduly highlighted only certain of the "most remarkable" marriage strategies rather than the entire range of available marriage strategies. Similarly, many anthropologists have taken the importance of genealogies for granted and have analyzed them as static ethnographic artifacts, ignoring how they are used. In my own ethnographic experience, people's use of complex genealogies tends to be correlated closely to wealth and social class. Individuals who have something to gain by imposing their interpretation of genealogies upon the social order tend to do so. It would be considered inappropriate in both tribal and nontribal settings for persons without claims to high social status, as such status is variously defined, to make elaborate claims of descent. Although the anthropological literature is filled with downward-branching diagrams such as Figure 5-4, a number of anthropologists have found that such charts can often be constructions based on the anthropologist's ideas rather than on a meaningful representation of how kinship relationships are conceived by Middle Easterners themselves. Hildred Geertz describes with some amusement her frustration at trying to show informants how to construct logically ordered kinship diagrams. Her findings are better approximated by Figure 6-6, in which informants first thought of a prominent ancestor or living person, then of clusters of indi-

[45] Keyser, "The Middle Eastern Case," 294.
[46] *Ibid.*, 295-96, 307.

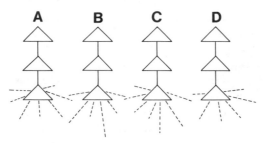

**FIGURE 6-6** A Moroccan conception of "closeness."
(From Dale F. Eickelman, *Moroccan Islam,* p. 208.
Courtesy of the author and the publisher.)

viduals related to each of them.[47] The relationships among the various prominent ancestors were not clearly defined but were spoken of as being of "one family." Such a means of representing notions of kinship may not work everywhere in the Middle East, but it is useful to present an alternative to the earlier analytical frameworks which are proving increasingly unsatisfactory.

In discussing the significance of genealogies, Bourdieu argues that anthropologists have in the past tended to neglect the role of genealogists and the significance of the occasions when a genealogical representation of relationships (as opposed to other representations) is invoked. In drawing up genealogies for analysis, he argues that anthropologists easily forget that genealogies are the product of multiple strategies and thus treat the meaning of kinship relations genealogically defined as a resolved question.[48] Instead, anthropologists should seek to specify the types of situations in which the use of genealogies and relationships defined by them are particularly dominant. Although emphasis is placed upon patrilineal relationships, matrilateral relations can be shown to have equal importance in many social situations, although they have tended to be neglected as they are not "official" genealogical representations of the social order.[49] As Bourdieu illustrates through detailed examples drawn from the Kabyle of Algeria, marriages which are genealogically identical may have different, even opposite, meanings and may be the outcome of very different strategies involving a wide range of symbolic and material interests such as fertility, filiation, residence, inheritance, marriage, and the values of honor and prestige.[50]

A brief practical example from the Morocco of sixty years ago might prove useful. Just after the French gained effective control of one of the southern regions of the country, a new, rather brutal Moroccan *qāʾid,* or tribal administrator, was

[47]This illustration is also found in Eickelman, *Moroccan Islam,* p. 208.

[48]Bourdieu, *Outline,* p. 35.

[49]Maher, *Women and Property,* p. 104.

[50]Bourdieu, *Outline,* pp. 43-52. For a more thorough analysis of Bourdieu's argument and its implications, see Dale F. Eickelman, "The Political Economy of Meaning," *American Ethnologist,* 6, no. 2 (May 1979), 386-93.

put in charge of a region which included a large village in which one of the most respected notables was a pious, aged notary who was regarded almost as a saint by surrounding tribesmen. The *qā'id* soon had a falling-out with the notary and slapped him on the face in public during one of the weekly markets. Soon after, the *qā'id* was told by one of his confidants that a tribal rebellion was in the making because of the slap. So at the next weekly market, the official brought one of his daughters and publicly threw her at the feet of the notary's eldest son (then in his twenties), saying: "She's yours. If you don't take her, she can go kill herself." Confronted with such an act, the notary's son was compelled for the sake of *his* honor to marry the girl. Essentially, her father publicly declared that he repudiated all responsibility for her honor and transferred it to the notary's son; marriage was the only legitimate sort of relation he could have with the girl. (The formalities for a valid Islamic marriage were subsequently resolved.) The offer of his daughter effectively neutralized the offense of the slap.

The marriage turned out to be a success in both personal and political terms. A few years later, a younger son of the notary married his older brother's wife's sister, further strengthening the bonds between the two families. The initial act was a boldly successful political move. The second marriage had a political element, but there were other considerations, including relations between the two brothers, who were at the time living in the same household. Most marriage decisions show a subtle combination of various strategies which cannot be derived from rules or prescriptions, and the anthropologist's principal task is to see the underlying assumptions toward the social order which these strategies reveal, not to reduce their complexity to a single, simplistic "rule," such as *bint ᶜamm* marriage.

A good way to conclude this chapter and to place the legacy of earlier anthropological studies on kinship in the Middle East in perspective is to cite a recent essay by Constance Cronin on kinship among the Iranian elite. Cronin's earlier work concerned Italian immigrants in Australia, so when she began to work in Iran, she did not share the presuppositions that many scholars working principally in the Middle East took for granted concerning what Middle Eastern kinship was all about.[51]

Cronin writes that most of the work on Iranian kinship was a poor carbon copy of the prevalent assumptions concerning Arab kinship, placing undue stress upon the importance of patrilineal genealogies, extended families as corporate units, and rigid marriage rules concerning parallel cousin unions. In speaking both of the "traditional" (Cronin is decidedly uneasy with the term) family and contemporary ones, she says there is no marked discontinuity between past and present. Data which she collected from older informants suggested that they had a bilateral kinship system, despite the fact that patrilineal genealogies were verbally

---

[51] Constance Cronin, "The Effect of Development on the Urban Family," in *The Social Sciences and Problems of Development,* ed. Khodadad Farmanfarmian, Princeton Studies on the Near East (Princeton: Princeton University Program in Near Eastern Studies, 1976), pp. 261-72.

displayed for limited purposes such as responding to questions put by anthropologists. Whenever economically possible, nuclear families lived apart, and close-knit families (in the sense of taking collective actions) were the exception rather than the rule. There were few jointly held investments; important decisions were made household by household without necessarily consulting others in the extended family; patterns of obligations toward relatives were highly flexible and often indistinguishable from those of close friends.

Richard Antoun has written that any scholarly approach which concentrates almost exclusively upon *one* type of kinship tie or social relationship and the "problems" derived from it constitutes a "museum" approach which creates artifacts of kinship exotica.[52] Although it can be argued that his comment unjustly characterizes current trends in museology, I concur with the intention of his comment. Kinship relationships should be treated as something which people make and with which they accomplish things. Such a notion is not exactly startling in its novelty, although meticulous descriptions of how social identities are elaborated and manipulated and which do not treat them as fixed ethnographic objects are still fairly rare. Kinship studies have often been considered to be an arcane anthropological preserve, except when more general writers choose to make sweeping generalizations concerning the importance of family ties in the Middle East. This chapter has suggested a less arcane way of looking at Middle Eastern notions of social identity and how they work.

[52] Antoun, "Anthropology," pp. 166-68.

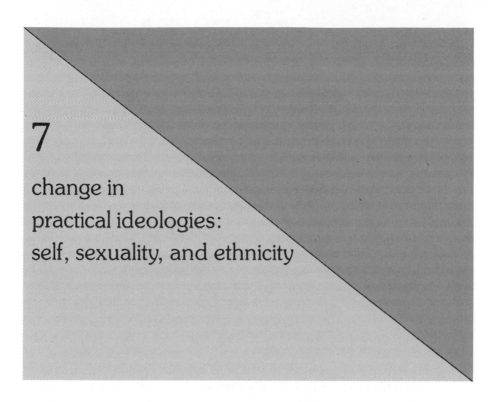

# 7

# change in
# practical ideologies:
# self, sexuality, and ethnicity

The paradox of studying cultural meanings, and the practical contexts in which they are generated, maintained, and transformed, is that the relationship between the two is not always direct or predictable. For one thing, patterns of meaning concerning such concepts as kin, family, person, community, and sect do not occur in isolation but are interconnected with each other in complex ways so that change in any one domain is often irregularly accelerated or impeded. Second, rapid and massive economic and political change affects such notions, but again the influence is often uneven and not fully predictable. In periods of crisis or rapid transformation, new ideologies concerning ideas of lineage, tribe, kinship, sect, religion, and nation are often formulated. As indicated earlier, the mere reference to lineage identities is illegal in Somalia, although such identities can be shown to have a continuing, decisive influence on public and private life; Morocco has abolished tribes as political units and replaced them with "communes," although most communes follow tribal boundaries; other countries have legislated changes in the personal status of men and women which often contrast dramatically with popularly understood rights and expectations. This chapter looks at three of the most sensitive contexts of cultural projections of persons and cultural self: naming, a practice which, because usually not consciously systematized, is a good index of implicit notions of persons and change; sex roles and sexuality, which also are in part regarded as firmly private, immutable, and implicit; and ethnic identities, which have posed special theoretical challenges (discussed later in this chapter) concerning the role of ethnic identities in modern economies.

NAMING

Patterns of naming provide privileged insight into the assumptions concerning cultural ideas of the person, as S. D. Goitein indicates in his ingenious analysis of female names in the Geniza documents. These documents depict the social life of the Jewish (and Muslim) communities of the southern Mediterranean in the tenth through the thirteenth centuries. Goitein's analysis has produced a description of the social life and values of the period which is more thorough than that provided by many contemporary ethnographies. In the Geniza documents, women rarely speak for themselves; many were illiterate and even if not were frequently constrained to speak through male guardians. From inheritance papers, correspondence, and other fragmentary evidence, Goitein nonetheless managed to elicit the implications of naming patterns and what they reveal of attitudes toward self. Names were "living words," the meanings of which were well known to those who bestowed them. Moreover, women were primarily responsible for the names which they gave their daughters, so that the meaning of a name and the frequency of its occurrence are therefore good indicators of what a woman wished for her daughter and, by implication, for herself.[1] The wide variety of names given to women possessed a number of common characteristics. In contrast to the names of men, which often contained references to God or to religious concepts, women's names almost consistently emphasized secular themes. The exceptions were principally confined to upper-class families. Goitein takes the sexual dichotomy in naming patterns to imply a "chasm" between the worldwide Hebrew book culture of the men and the local popular subculture of the women. Additionally, many female names—over 70 percent encountered by Goitein, and an equivalent proportion among Muslim names—suggest ideas of "ruling, overcoming, and victory," such as *Sitt al-Kull* ("She who Rules over Everyone"), *Sitt al-Nās* ("Mistress over Mankind"), *Sitt al-Fakhr* ("Mistress of Glory"), and *Labwa* ("Lioness"). As he argues, such names suggest a self-image of women other than that of frailty, domesticity, or dependence upon men. Indeed, names implying chastity or fertility, attributes regarded by men as praiseworthy, were almost entirely absent, perhaps because such attributes were so taken for granted. Other names implied noble lineage, or a mere welcoming of the newborn, such as *Mūna* ("Wishes Fulfilled"), *Ghunya* ("Gain"), *Yumn* ("Good Luck"), *Saʿāda* ("Long Life"), and *Bāqa* ("Substitute"—for a child who died). Because such names were fairly common, Goitein suspects that they were a protest against the male preference for boys.

In Goitein's studies and in those of other scholars, changing fashions in naming can also be used as documentary indices of shifting religious and national consciousness, another crucial dimension of ideas of self.[2] One such study is

---

[1] S. D. Goitein, *A Mediterranean Society: The Jewish Communities of the Arab World as Portrayed in the Documents of the Cairo Geniza. Volume III: The Family:* (Berkeley and Los Angeles: University of California Press, 1978), p. 314.

[2] Goitein, *Mediterranean Society,* pp. 315-19.

Richard Bulliet's discussion of trends in Turkish naming patterns from the early nineteenth century to the 1950s.[3] For instance, the Turkish names of Mehmet, Ahmet, and Ali are all derived from Arabic and have religious connotations. These names were highly popular prior to the secularizing Ottoman reforms (called the Tanzimat) which were enacted from the 1840s onward. There was a sharp plunge in their popularity until they reached a low in 1885-1889, when the reforming spirit was most intense. Afterward, religious names slowly recovered in popularity, only to reach a new low in 1905-1909, when the Young Turk movement was strong. Later there was a gradual but steady recovery of the incidence of religious names through 1920-1924, after which they maintained a fairly stable level of incidence.

Concurrently, the political circumstances from the rise of the Young Turks in the final years of the Ottoman Empire through the declaration of the Turkish Republic in 1923 were correlated with the replacement of names of Arabic origin with those that were Turkish and secular, reflecting a distinctly Turkish national identity. Such names comprised only 8 percent of the total of the sample in 1910-1914, rose to 65 percent in the decade of 1930-1941, and have declined only slightly in the years since then. Yet, as Bulliet emphasizes, the new trend in the popularity of Turkish secularized names was not at the expense of names with a religious base, suggesting that despite the militantly secularist ideology of the Turkish state promulgated by Atatürk and his successors, a significant component of the population retained its distinctly religious identity. The recent resurgence of Islamic fundamentalism throughout the Muslim world, including Turkey, reaffirms the continuing importance of religious identity.

Another important dimension of naming as a key to the idea of the person in the Middle East is the fact that there is considerably more flexibility as to how persons can be referred to and addressed in Middle Eastern contexts than in our own. In the early years of French rule in Morocco, for instance, when letters of safe conduct and a system of land registration which required the precise legal identity of persons was being put into effect, it was not uncommon for the French to issue papers which referred to individuals by numerous alternative (and equally appropriate) names.[4] For example, a man called Aḥmad could also be known as:

| | |
|---|---|
| Aḥmad wuld Drīss al-Baqqāl | Aḥmad, son of Drīss, the Grocer |
| Aḥmad wuld Drīss wuld Muṣṭafā | Aḥmad, son of Drīss, son of Muṣṭafā |
| Aḥmad "wuld ᶜMsh" | Aḥmad, "son of the man with poor eyesight" (a nickname) |
| Aḥmad al-Tādilī | Aḥmad from Tādla |

[3] Richard W. Bulliet, "First Names and Political Change in Modern Turkey," *International Journal of Middle East Studies,* 9, no. 4 (November 1978), 489-95.

[4] Hildred Geertz, "The Meanings of Family Ties," in *Meaning and Order in Moroccan Society,* Clifford Geertz, Hildred Geertz, and Lawrence Rosen (New York and London: Cambridge University Press, 1979), pp. 341-56.

| | |
|---|---|
| al-Tādilī | the one from Tādla |
| Wuld Drīss | son of Drīss |
| or Aḥmad wuld Drīss ash-Sharqāwī | Aḥmad, son of Drīss, of the Sharqāwī |
| | (patronymic association) |

Only with the spread of the legal registry of births and the necessity, principally for administrative reasons, of identifying persons unambiguously by a single name, has the variety of naming choices been lessened somewhat. Moroccan naming patterns suggest how flexible are the ways in which persons can identify themselves, although there are variations in how these different components are emphasized through the Middle East. Moroccan names can be composed of the following elements: (1) personal names, such as Muḥammad, Aḥmad, and Būzkrī; (2) nicknames (laqab-s), generally relating to some predominant personal identifying feature, such as "the one-eyed," "the colorful," or "the fast one"; (3) names derived from occupation and origin (nisba); (4) patrifiliative names; and (5) "family" names (kunya-s), made obligatory by the government in the 1950s but earlier maintained by wealthy government officials, merchants, marabouts, and descendants of the Prophet (pl. shurfā).[5]

Personal, or "first" names, can be drawn from a range of religious and secular sources. By themselves these names are not always distinctive. In one set of census material, Hildred Geertz found that out of 982 male names, 156 were called Muḥammad.[6] Quite a few names reflect little more than the time of year a child was born. An infant born near the Feast-day of the Prophet (ᶜĪd al-Mīlūd) often is given the name Mīludī. Similarly one born near the Feast of Abraham (ᶜĪd al-Kabīr) will often be known as al-Kabīr. If an earlier child has died, the later child may be given the same name or a name indicating that he or she is a replacement. A child may also be named after an admired person among his immediate relatives who has recently died. Naming a child after a living person is considered an ill omen for the child in Morocco and is therefore not done. There are fashions in naming, and names often acquire a political significance. In earlier generations almost all male names were religiously based (in a pattern reminiscent of that described by Goitein, many female names were not). A name once given is not ordinarily changed, although in some regions such as the Sultanate of Oman a man or woman may change his or her personal name at marriage if the name is thought to be incompatible with that of the proposed spouse. In such contexts, each letter of the alphabet is thought to be correlated with certain values (such as fire and water), some of which are incompatible with others. If the names of a couple intending

---

[5] Part of the following discussion on naming is adapted from Dale F. Eickelman, "Time in a Complex Society: A Moroccan Example," Ethnology 16, no. 1 (January 1977), 48-50. A thorough discussion of names which relates them to the notions of kinship and patronymic association is found in Geertz, "Family Ties," pp. 341-56. This is one of the best discussions of naming available for Middle Eastern contexts. For a discussion of naming ceremonies and the effect of government-imposed civil registries on patterns of naming, see Hamed Ammar, Growing Up in an Egyptian Village (London: Routledge & Kegan Paul Ltd., 1954), pp. 91-93, 97.

[6] Geertz, "Family Ties," p. 342.

marriage lack the proper correspondence, then the name of one of the two is changed.[7]

Nicknames can be acquired for a number of reasons. Usually they refer to a distinctive personal characteristic, or an incident in a person's life which stands out. A Moroccan in one small town was named "Bin Shaqrūn," after a prominent Casablanca merchant of the 1890s, because he used to sell things as a child to other children in his quarter. In a Jordanian village, one man is called *al-Hamshārī*, a Turkish word meaning *countryman,* because his father served in the Ottoman army in the First World War. Upon returning to his village he greeted the first man he saw with: "How are you, *hamshārī*?" using the Turkish term. Another man known for his piety was called *al-Shihādī* ("Testifier" of faith in God), because a male child was born to him at the end of his life.[8] Nicknames easily fall into two categories. Those of persons and groups that convey either neutral or positive images tend to be public and used in the face of the persons involved. Names conveying less desirable invidious personal characteristics, such as *daggār* ("busybody"), can be used as effective means of social control in the contexts of everyday use.[9] There is an inherent ambiguity in many such terms which permits them to be used either pejoratively or simply as signs of intimacy. One Moroccan secondary student is called *al-muqayhir* ("the down-and-out") because, unlike his classmates, he ostentatiously dresses in his oldest clothing. The same nickname might be applied of course to a student who really was in desperate financial circumstances.

Names derived from occupation, origin, and affiliation (for instance with a religious brotherhood) are called *nisba*-s, " a combination morphological, grammatical, and semantic process which consists of transforming a noun into what we would call a relative adjective, but what for Arabs becomes just another sort of noun."[10] Thus the location with which people are identified can become part of their name: al-Marrākshī for a man and al-Marrākshīya for a woman who comes from Marrakesh. Depending on context, the same people can be referred to by the name of a quarter in Marrakesh, or by the name of a tribe in the region or subgroup of it, or by the name of a larger geographical or social entity. For example, in Cairo, Ḥasan al-Marrākshī might be known as Ḥasan the Maghribi ("the Moroccan"); in Morocco itself such a *nisba* would be hardly distinctive, nor would be al-Marrākshī in Marrakesh. *Nisba*-s also can be derived from occupations, such

---

[7]Professor Abdul Hamid M. el-Zein, Temple University, personal communication (June 1979). Ammar, *Growing Up,* pp. 92-93, points out that in Middle Eastern contexts where formal naming ceremonies for children do not exist (such as Palestine in the 1930s) the names of children are sometimes changed in later years from the ones initially given them. This is almost never the case when formal naming ceremonies exist, as occurs seven days after the birth of the child in Egypt and Morocco, among other Middle Eastern countries.

[8]Richard T. Antoun, "On the Significance of Names in an Arab Village," *Ethnology,* 7, no. 2 (April 1968), 159.

[9]*Ibid.,* 164-69.

[10]Clifford Geertz, "On the Nature of Anthropological Understanding," *American Scientist,* 63, no. 1 (January-February 1975), 47-53. For a more extended discussion by the same author of the significance of *nisba*-s in relation to economic roles, see his "Suq: The Bazaar Economy," in *Meaning and Order,* pp. 140-50.

as *al-Khayyāṭī* ("the tailor") and *al-Baqqālī* ("the grocer"); from affiliation with a religious brotherhood, for example, an-Nāṣirī for a member of the Nāṣirīya brotherhood; and from the name of a maraboutic descent group such as ash-Sharqāwī (of the Sharqāwī patronymic association); or ᶜAlāwī from the son-in-law of the Prophet (and thus indicating prophetic descent). The characterization of a person by *nisba* is highly flexible: "Calling a man a Sefroui is like calling him a San Franciscan, it classifies him but it doesn't type him; it places him without portraying him."[11] Combined with other types of naming and situating persons in social contexts, it provides one more means by which notions of self can be specified and expressed.

Patrifiliative names, such as Abū Bakr bin Fu'ād (Abū Bakr, son of Fu'ād), situates persons in the social context of their familial predecessors and elder contemporaries. In ordinary usage, the name of only one ascending generation is indicated, although for clarity or to emphasize particular features of one's genealogy, a string of claimed predecessors may be added, as in Abū Bakr bin Fu'ād bin Drīss, in which the grandfather's name is also added. Occasionally, a mother's name is added as a sort of nickname, especially in the case of plural marriages. Occasionally a matrifiliative link is also indicated, as in Fāṭima bint Zahra (Fāṭima, daughter of Zahra). Children and young adults are commonly referred to only as someone's child, as in Bint Ḥasan (Ḥasan's daughter), until with maturity their own social identity becomes distinct.

Teknonyms, in which people are known after the name of their children, are also common: Abū Nāṣir (Nāṣir's father), Abū ᶜUmār, and Umm Muḥammad (Muḥammad's mother) are examples of this usage. There are variations within and between regions in the use of such names, with their use being more prevalent in the Levant and the Arabian peninsula, for example, than in North Africa. Among some nomadic tribes in Oman, for instance, a man can be given a teknonym based on his daughter's name, although among the settled population of the coast and in the Jabal Akhḍar region, a teknonym is based inevitably upon the name of a son.

One of the principal ideological features of patrifiliative name-chains is that while ideally they can be extended infinitely into the past, in reality they rarely extend further back than two generations. When someone asserts that such a name-chain can be traced over many generations, it usually indicates the assertion of high social status, "noble" antecedents, or descent from the Prophet Muḥammad. Middle Easterners sometimes claim that even elaborate genealogies are "real," which in a certain sense they of course are, although the social base of such claims becomes apparent when it is noted that the most assiduously elaborated genealogical claims are associated with political, religious, and social leadership.[12]

[11] C. Geertz, "On the Nature," 52.

[12] See, for instance, C. C. Stewart, *Islam and Social Order in Mauritania* (Oxford: Clarendon Press, 1973), pp. 62, 134-35, and Abd-al Ghaffar Muhammad Ahmad, *Shaykhs and Followers: Political Struggle in the Rufuᶜa al-Hoi Nazirate in the Sudan* (Khartoum: Khartoum University Press, 1974), pp. 84-92.

Until fairly recent times, the use of family names, or *kunya*-s, was largely confined to members of the elite in many Middle Eastern countries. In Morocco such names became obligatory only in the 1950s and are still known in rural areas and small towns as "government" names. Sometimes family names were chosen for individuals from printed lists of available names, if the person did not suggest one. Some illiterates in fact have to ask other persons to read their "government" names for them, so little are these names a part of ordinary social contexts. Often names that can be thought of as *nisba*-s, such as Sharqāwī, are adopted as family names, and names connoting place of origin and of occupation imperceptibly merge with those of family.

As a basis of social identity, names primarily signify the actual person carrying the name, not abstract groups or genealogical "lines" with an extended temporal reality. The very structure of possible ways of naming a person ensures that the temporal depth is markedly attenuated, as is the notion of the person having a fixed social location. Naming patterns and how they are used thus indicate that there is a considerable flexibility in how persons are identified and can choose to identify themselves. In American and European contexts there is also a certain flexibility: The terms of address used with persons, such as the use of the first name without titles or honorifics, can suggest intimacy or disrespect, according to context and the speaker. The same is true of course in Middle Eastern situations, but the fact remains that the variety of means by which a person can be identified is considerably greater.

## WOMEN, MEN, AND SEXUALITY

Some of the recent writings on women and sex roles in the Middle East assert that these subjects were neglected in earlier studies. Yet Roxann Van Dusen, the author of a comprehensive review of Middle Eastern women's studies, has pointed out that it is not so much that women have been neglected in earlier studies, it is rather that portrayals of them have been unidimensional. For instance, analyses of marriage and domestic life have concentrated principally upon formal roles and procedures. In community studies, women were generally described as "a world apart," or as inhabitants of a "private" sphere of limited "social" significance. In a number of studies, even those concerning family planning and population patterns, there is similarly a significant but incidental coverage of women. Recent literature concentrates explicitly upon such topics as women's economic roles, patterns of friendship and visiting, and the role of women in rituals and in mediating disputes.[13] After criticizing the noncumulative nature of much of the recent research on women and women's roles, Van Dusen suggests that more substantial analytical work can be achieved through intraregional comparisons and, even more importantly, compari-

[13] Roxann A. Van Dusen, "The Study of Women in the Middle East: Some Thoughts," *Middle East Studies Association Bulletin*, 10, no. 2 (May 1976), 2.

sons *among* social strata. Her specific suggestions are to concentrate upon differences of age and generation, patterns of residence (urban and rural), length of time in various locales, and education and its relation to family background. She also suggests the need to conduct comparisons over time and to develop a more critical attitude toward some of the more common themes which run through the past literature on Middle Eastern women: the significance of the public/private dichotomy, male distrust of female sexuality and its implications, women's self-images and patterns of socialization, family interactions, economic roles, and political roles.[14]

Since the appearance of Van Dusen's review, two major collections of essays have appeared which substantially answer these questions and indicate the contribution that the study of women and sex roles can make to the central concerns of social theory.[15] I emphasize the potential contribution of such studies rather than what has been realized to date for the reason that most of the research discussed here has appeared very recently and with few exceptions has been in the form of articles rather than full monographs. For this reason it has been difficult for scholars concerned with such topics as sexuality and the role of women to take substantial account of one another's work. The following discussion is thus necessarily confined to assessing the resources upon which more comprehensive discussions can be elaborated and made to contribute to the main currents of social thought.

Anthropological knowledge has a way of calling into question the most fundamental assumptions concerning "human nature" and the assumption that there are two *gender* roles is no exception. Based on research in Ṣuḥār, a town in the northern coastal region of the Sultanate of Oman, Unni Wikan asserts that in the case of this particular region of Oman there are three and not two genders: man, woman, and *khanīth*. A *khanīth* in Oman is a male transsexual prostitute. Wikan argues that such prostitutes are defined by "a socially acknowledged role pattern whereby a person acts and is classified as if he/she were a person of the opposite sex for a number of crucial purposes."[16] Such a statement in itself suggests a

[14]*Ibid.,* 3-10.

[15]The two collections complement each other. The earlier of the two, Elizabeth Warnock Fernea and Basima Qattan Bezirgan, eds., *Middle Eastern Muslim Women Speak* (Austin and London: University of Texas Press, 1977), is an anthology of writings by and about Middle Eastern Muslim women. The collection is specifically intended as a primary document. Lois Beck and Nikki Keddie, eds., *Women in the Muslim World* (Cambridge and London: Harvard University Press, 1978), is more deliberately analytical. Ayad al-Qazzaz, *Women in the Middle East and North Africa: An Annotated Bibliography,* Modern Middle East Monographs, 2 (Austin: University of Texas Center for Middle Eastern Studies, 1977), contains useful entries. Cynthia Nelson's "Public and Private Politics: Women in the Middle Eastern World," *American Ethnologist,* 1, no. 3 (August 1974), 551-63, contains an excellent review of how the subject of women has been handled in a variety of ethnographic accounts. For an excellent survey of evidence—historical and contemporary—concerning the "informal" political leadership of women, especially in royal circles, see James A. Bill and Carl Leiden, *Politics in the Middle East* (Boston and Toronto: Little, Brown and Company, 1979), pp. 98-111.

[16]Unni Wikan, "Man Becomes Woman: Transsexualism in Oman as a Key to Gender Roles," *Man* (N.S.), 12, no. 2 (August 1977), 304.

variety of role patterns, but not the existence of three genders. In the article, however, Wikan argues that whereas women are always women on the basis of their anatomical features, for men it is their role in the sexual act and not possession of the appropriate sexual organs that is constitutive of gender.[17] She claims that the existence of this "third sex" in the Omani context is a means of protecting the virtue of women, for the "third sex" can act as a safety valve for men's sexual drives.[18] Moreover, Wikan states that members of the Omani "third sex" can redefine their identity simply by marrying and acting as men and can shift back and forth in how they represent their gender in public because each individual in Oman "is his own master"; the world is recognized as imperfect, so that men strive to criticize the actions of others as little as possible unless it directly affects their interests. As several critics of Wikan's argument have pointed out, her discussion rests upon a confusion of cultural definitions of gender and of sex roles. These critics offered alternative explanations which do not invoke claims to the existence of a third gender but instead examine the social roles of male transsexual prostitutes. Wikan's discussion is clearly argued, but many of its key assumptions are flawed. Thus in logically eliminating all possibilities of men's seeking sexual "release" in forms other than male prostitutes, she argues that masturbation is discouraged in part because of the "Islamic fear" of polluting the right hand.[19] (Surely use of the *left* hand could overcome such a "fear"?) And the implicit Quranic injunction against homosexuality contained in the story of Lot (Sura 26, verse 165) surely can also be considered "Islamic" and be used to neutralize the normative base on which this element of Wikan's argument rests. Despite the faulty construction of Wikan's discussion, its presentation and subsequent discussion have served to clarify numerous issues concerning sexuality. The article remains one of the relatively few extensive discussions of the values underlying prostitution in the Middle East (as opposed to its mere incidence) and their relation to notions of person and sexuality.[20]

Apart from Wikan's discussion, most studies concerning sex roles in the Middle East point to the markedly different patterns of socialization of the two sexes. As already indicated, the different types of names which tend to be given to boys and to girls strongly suggest the different attitudes toward the two sexes and their roles in society. Ammar's discussion of childhood socialization in an Egyptian village remains one of the best available accounts and is a significant point of

---

[17]*Ibid.*, 309.

[18]*Ibid.*, 314. For one of the few studies of prostitution in the Middle East (although not one to call gender roles into question), see Samir Khalaf, *Prostitution in a Changing Society: A Sociological Survey of Legal Prostitution in Beirut* (Beirut: Khayats, 1965).

[19]Wikan, "Man Becomes Woman," 315.

[20]The following letters concerning Wikan's argument have been published: Gill Shepherd, "Transsexualism in Oman," *Man* (N.S.), 13, no. 1 (March 1978), 133-34; Robert Brain, "Transsexualism in Oman?" *Man* (N.S.), 13, no. 2 (June 1978), 322-23; Gill Shepherd, G. Feuerstein, and S. al-Marzooq, with a reply by Unni Wikan, "The Omani *Xanith*," *Man* (N.S.), 13, no. 4 (December 1978), 662-71; and Unni Wikan, "The Omani *Xanith*: A Third Gender Role," *Man* (N.S.), 13, no. 3 (September 1978), 473-76.

departure. Boys, he writes, tend to be regarded as a capital investment in peasant settings and a greater contribution to the social prestige of the family. A man with a number of sons is thought to be able to speak with more authority as the sons mature. Consequently, midwives are given more substantial presents on the birth of a boy than that of a girl. Ammar indicates the lesser enthusiasm which greets the birth of a girl, yet points out that normatively it is reprehensible *(makrūh)* formally to evince dissatisfaction at their birth. Villagers are frequently reminded of the pre-Islamic custom of burying female infants alive and of Islam's superiority in this regard as the Quran forbade the practice. Nonetheless, villagers say they regard girls as burdensome and a potential source of shame to the family, so that girls must be carefully protected until their marriage.[21] Ammar lists what villagers consider to be some of the positive attributes of women, such as greater compassion than men are supposed to possess, yet the structure of his account clearly indicates the greater reserve that tends to accompany the birth of women. A practical index of attitudes toward the two sexes might be the infant mortality rates of female as opposed to male infants. The claim is made for Iran that the female infant mortality rate is higher than that for boys.[22] Although Ammar provides detailed statistics concerning overall infant mortality rates—but without regard for sex differences— and such detailed data as the relation between divorce and the number of surviving children, he says only that the family treatment of infants is more protective and more attentive compared with the later period of childhood.[23]

In the village studied by Ammar, girls are shown comparative indulgence in infancy but are expected to reach "sociological adulthood" more rapidly than boys. They soon form separate play groups and are differentially treated throughout their childhood and young adulthood. Perhaps the most striking experience that the two sexes undergo is circumcision, which is practiced on *both* sexes in the Aswan region of Egypt. For boys, this occurs between the ages of three and six and is accompanied by a public communal celebration involving both adult male relatives and friends and a separate meal for women. Girls are circumcised (that is, the internal labia are cut off) at the age of seven or eight, ostensibly "to prevent any suspicion on the bridegroom's part that the bride is not a virgin." While the occasion of male circumcision is regarded as a religious occasion, that of female circumcision is confined to women, and men are not even supposed to evince an interest in it.[24] On reading Ammar's account, it is easy to concur with Paul Vieille's

---

[21] Ammar, *Growing Up,* pp. 94-96.

[22] Paul Vieille, "Iranian Women in Family Alliance and Sexual Politics," in Beck and Keddie, *Women,* p. 452.

[23] Ammar, *Growing Up,* p. 113.

[24] *Ibid.,* pp. 116-18. Despite legislation prohibiting female circumcision in Egypt enacted in 1959, the practice continues in some areas. See Nikki R. Keddie, "Problems in the Study of Middle Eastern Women," *International Journal of Middle East Studies,* 10, no. 2 (May 1979), 240. An even more radical practice—infibulation—occurs despite legislation forbidding it in the Sudan and certain other Middle Eastern countries. Infibulation involves the deliberate mutilation of the female genitalia so as to close off the vaginal opening almost completely. It is an

statement concerning the status of women in Iran that the "progressive devaluation" of women is apparent despite the value placed upon their fertility and their
importance as counters of exchange in "good" marriages.[25] When a girl is married
at the average age of twelve or thirteen, despite the legal requirement that she be
sixteen, as reported by Ammar, or on the average between the ages of thirteen and
fifteen, as the Gulicks report for Isfahan, Iran, clearly she has only a minimal say
in her fate.[26]

As with other topics of key concern in a region so vast as the Middle East, it
is important to consider how such practices fit in with other key social assumptions. Singling out a single attribute of local custom, such as the practice of veiling
(in any case not a specifically Islamic practice despite popular assumptions to the
contrary), often turns out to be relatively unimportant in comparison to overall
patterns of sexual ideology and practice.[27]

The need to examine comprehensively the obligations, rights, and division of
labor of *both* sexes is a main theme of Emrys Peters, who undertook a comparison
of women in four different Middle Eastern settings.[28] Among the Bedouin of
Cyrenaica, he states that there is little separation of the sexes until girls are nubile;
there then follows a pattern of strict control and arranged marriages. After marriage, the formality of male-female interaction decreases somewhat, with men
managing the "external" affairs of the household and women managing the
domestic side. Women generally agree to renounce their inheritance rights at
marriage, but at the same time after marriage acquire a certain amount of political
status. Wives do not own tents, as is the case with other Bedouin societies including

---

excruciatingly painful operation and sometimes has resulted in death. See Rose Oldfield Hayes,
"Female Genital Mutilation, Fertility Control, Women's Roles, and the Patrilineage in Modern
Sudan: A Functional Analysis," *American Ethnologist*, 2, no. 4 (November 1975), 617-33. The
topic is predictably a sensitive one which especially educated Sudanese tend to approach with
caution in public discussion, because of the disapproval which such practices arouse among
both popular and educated circles in countries such as those of North Africa, where equivalent
rites are unknown. It should be noted that such physically painful rites are not entirely confined to women. Although male circumcision occurs in most parts of the Middle East at an early
age, in some parts of North Yemen circumcision occurs only between the ages of twelve and
fifteen. The child is surrounded by a crowd of men and women. A knife is held to his foreskin
while he recites the Muslim creed, "There is no God but God and Muḥammad is his Prophet,"
three times. The foreskin is then cut and thrown into the crowd and then picked up by the
youth, who proudly displays it. He is placed on his mother's shoulders where he continues
to show it off, then he leads a procession of dancers, brandishing a dagger. The boy is humili-
ated for life if he shows any signs of pain or distress. The practice is outlawed, but nonetheless
see the photographs taken of one such ceremony in 1972 in Claudie Fayein, *Yemen* (Paris:
Editions du Seuil, 1975), pp. 34-35. In general, such brutally direct rituals of social identity
are beginning to disappear, in part through government action.

[25] Vieille, "Iranian Women," p. 452.

[26] Ammar, *Growing Up*, p. 183; John Gulick and Margaret E. Gulick, "The Domestic
Social Environment of Women and Girls in Isfahan, Iran," in Beck and Keddie, *Women*, p. 504.

[27] Nikki Keddie and Lois Beck, "Introduction," in Beck and Keddie, *Women*, p. 25.

[28] Emrys L. Peters, "The Status of Women in Four Middle East Communities," in Beck
and Keddie, *Women*, pp. 311-50.

the Āl Murra of Saudi Arabia, but their bridewealth includes a number of furnishings for the tent for which women possess full rights of inheritance.

In the Shīʿī peasant village of south Lebanon studied by Peters, he found that women of higher status (the "Learned Families" discussed in Chapter 3) were veiled their entire lives and confined in their practical activities. In contrast, peasant women wore only head scarves and could move about with relative freedom. Among higher-status families, marriages were carefully arranged within their own circles; among peasants, there was a freer range of choice, and many marriages were love matches. Women inherited, and for peasants the world of men and women often was interchangeable. In contrast to women in Bedouin society, however, peasant women in Lebanon tended to have a low political status.

The two remaining comparisons that Peters makes are with recently settled Bedouin who replaced the Italians as olive farmers in Libya and Maronite Christian women in Lebanon. In the Libyan case, Peters argues that the ethos of sexual segregation was transferred to settled life. But whereas women in the semidesert had freedom of movement within camps, in the settled situation this freedom shrank to the house itself, isolating women and diminishing their status "to the point of degradation."[29] In the case of the Maronites, the impact of male emigration was an important consideration, as women often could assume significant political roles if left to manage households on their own for long periods of time; as with Muslim peasant women in Lebanon, personal and familial compatibility is a serious consideration in marriage and there is a latitude of individual choice.

Peters's observation that the status of the two sexes is strongly correlated with the division of labor is echoed in many writings on the implications of sex roles in the Middle East. For this reason a number of studies have concentrated on the impact of greater educational opportunities for women, legislative reforms, and the effect of changing economic and political conditions upon women's roles and the image of women in society. In countries such as Egypt and Turkey, some women of the middle and upper classes participate in organized movements for the explicit purpose of ameliorating the status of women, and such associations exist today with varying degrees of influence in most of the countries of the Middle East.[30] A notable exception is Saudi Arabia, where among other restrictions women are not allowed to drive, are not allowed to attend university classes with men, and are allowed access to library facilities only at specified and highly limited hours when no men are present.

Legal reforms which have benefited women to varying degrees have been enacted in most Middle Eastern settings, with substantial improvements in the

---

[29] *Ibid.,* p. 343.

[30] See in particular Afaf Lutfi al-Sayyid Marsot, "The Revolutionary Gentlewoman in Egypt," in Beck and Keddie, *Women,* pp. 261-76; Fatma Mansur Coşar, "Women in Turkish Society," *Ibid.,* pp. 124-40; Mangol Bayat-Philipp, "Women and Revolution in Iran, 1905-1911," *Ibid.,* pp. 295-308; and Mark A. Tessler, "Women's Emancipation in Tunisia," *Ibid.,* pp. 141-58.

status of women in countries such as Tunisia, Iran, and Turkey.[31] There are notable omissions in such reforms. Only Turkey, Israel, Tunisia, and the Soviet Union have, for instance, prohibited polygamy altogether, although in other countries, including Iraq and Pakistan, specific legal permission must be obtained for marriages subsequent to the first marriage. In Morocco and Lebanon, women can insert restrictions into marriage contracts against husbands taking second wives.[32] Minimum ages for marriage are in effect in most Middle Eastern countries, and reforms limiting a husband's unrestricted ability to divorce have been enacted in most countries. Laws related to inheritance, on the other hand, have met with greater resistance because of the existence of specific Quranic prescriptions. Of course, legal reforms in themselves do not necessarily change social practice, although they may reflect the changing values of legislators or rulers. In Turkey, which introduced fully secular civil and criminal codes in 1926, marriages in rural areas are often never officially validated by civil courts, and inheritance disputes tend to be settled independently of the formal judicial system.[33] Nonetheless, a recent study indicates a gradually increasing assertiveness by women over the last two decades in using the court system when they are involved in disputes with men. The consequences of legal reforms affecting women have emerged only gradually, but their social impact is now becoming apparent and is tied to the current higher educational level and greater political sophistication of women.[34]

The status of women in revolutionary situations is more difficult to determine. Women in the regions of heavy Muslim population in the Soviet Union appear to be the only ones to enjoy equal legal rights and educational opportunities. Revolutionary countries such as the People's Democratic Republic of South Yemen and liberation movements throughout the Arab world often proclaim the full equality of women with men, but actual practice is virtually impossible to assess.[35] No clear pattern has yet emerged from the Iranian revolution of 1978-1979, but the participation of Iranian women in political life, educational opportunities, and the exercise of legal rights enacted on their behalf by the regime of the last Shah are now being held up to question. During Algeria's struggle for independence, some women participated fully in the revolutionary movement. Because the French rarely searched them, women often were used for carrying bombs and as couriers. Since independence, however, women have continued to be treated as minors, have

---

[31] Two useful surveys of the legal situation of women are Noel Coulson and Doreen Hinchcliffe, "Women and Law in Contemporary Islam," in Beck and Keddie, *Women,* pp. 37-51, and the more comprehensive chapter in the same volume by Elizabeth H. White, "Legal Reform as an Indicator of Women's Status in Muslim Nations," pp. 52-68, which correlates the legal status of women with educational statistics and other data.

[32] Coulson and Hinchcliffe, "Women," p. 30.

[33] *Ibid.,* pp. 44, 47.

[34] June Starr and Jonathan Pool, "The Impact of a Legal Revolution in Rural Turkey," *Law and Society Review,* no. 3 (Summer 1974), 533-60.

[35] Fayein, *Yemen,* p. 184; Fred Halliday, *Arabia Without Sultans* (New York: Vintage Books, 1975), pp. 388-93.

had lesser de facto access to education, and have been discouraged by public policy from competing with men in the labor market.[36]

Access to education is a prerequisite in many ways for a change in women's status throughout the region. In the Middle East as a whole during the 1960s the average percentage of adult women (fifteen and over) who were literate was only 13 percent, ranging from a low of 4 percent for Algeria, Libya, and Morocco to a high of 30 percent for Turkey.[37] Of course, the higher proportion of school-age girls in primary schools as of the early 1970s as opposed to earlier decades indicates the capability and commitment of particular countries to provide for women's education, yet popular resistance to the inclusion of women in mass literacy

**FIGURE 7-1** Education is a major force in changing women's status. Saudi student, Beirut. (Courtesy *Aramco World Magazine,* March-April 1971.)

[36] See the eloquent and scathing account of the status of Algerian women by the Algerian journalist Fadéla M'rabet, excerpted from her *Les Algériennes* and translated in Fernea and Bezirgan, *Women Speak,* pp. 319-58.

[37] Nadia H. Youssef, "The Status and Fertility Patterns of Muslim Women," in Beck and Keddie, *Women,* p. 88.

campaigns (as in Afghanistan) suggests an unwillingness to reconsider the traditional forms of male domination. Enrollment rates vary from 83 percent of school-age girls in primary schools in Tunisia, constituting 55 percent of total enrollment, to the respective figures of 36 percent and 33 percent for Morocco, 50 percent and 29 percent for Iraq, 61 percent and 41 percent for Turkey, 85 percent and 43 percent for Jordan, to less enviable records of 18 percent and 28 percent for oil-rich Saudi Arabia, 21 percent and 33 percent for the Sudan, and 1 percent and 2 percent for the Yemen Arab Republic.[38] In every case there are significant regional disparities, with the percentage of rural women having access to education markedly lower than urban women in every instance and the proportion of women remaining in school after the age of fifteen dropping very rapidly as compared to the proportion of men.

Most studies suggest that the higher the direct involvement of women in non-domestic economic activities, the more open the social roles they can perform. At the same time, recent intensive studies of the economic role of women have documented a greater traditional and nontraditional range of roles that women can occupy than has often previously been reported. Davis reports a total of twenty-two different income-earning activities engaged in by rural Moroccan women. Some of these can result in increased social status; others, such as field labor and prostitution, result in a decrease.[39] Adopting a more global perspective, Maher presents a complex picture of categories of women in Moroccan society and how recent economic transformations have affected their status. These include women of "high bourgeois" origin who have been able to use their status and access to higher education to win a considerable measure of political and social autonomy; "new women," educated women of the "petty bourgeoisie," who have assumed professional roles as teachers, nurses, and secretaries; dependent wives of upwardly mobile petty administrators and teachers, for whom a rise in social status usually means a strict seclusion from men and the organization of activities in time and space so that the social worlds of men and women rarely coincide; "free" women—professional dancers, some divorced women, some wives of migrant workers, and prostitutes—often of rural origin, who trade off their ambiguous status for autonomy from the male tutelage;[40] and women who because of their precarious economic situation—widowed, divorced, kinless, or with husbands unable to work—are forced into factory work and other work considered as socially marginal.[41] Fatima Mernissi's interviews with women working in various craft industries such as

[38] From Table 2.2 in White, "Legal Reform," p. 63.
[39] Susan Schaefer Davis, "Working Women in a Moroccan Village," in Beck and Keddie, *Women*, pp. 416-33. See Davis's companion account of the life history of a village woman, "Zahrah Muhammad," in Fernea and Bezirgan, *Women Speak*, pp. 201-19.
[40] For a poetic view of what such "free" women think of men and marriage, see splendid poems translated by Elizabeth Fernea in "Seven Women's Songs from the Berber Mountains of Morocco," in Fernea and Bezirgan, *Women Speak*, pp. 127-34.
[41] Vanessa Maher, "Women and Social Change in Morocco," in Beck and Keddie, *Women*, pp. 100-123.

weaving textiles and rugs indicate how dependent women are upon men as intermediaries, a situation that only increases their precarious economic position. She concludes that the increasing capitalist penetration of such industries has had the consequence of further degrading women's status.[42] As Maher points out, the progressive impoverishment of the Moroccan countryside with recent economic transformations has had "particularly devasting" consequences for women and children, as a result of their subordination to men and their exclusion from the labor market.[43]

Similar conclusions have been drawn elsewhere in the Middle East: Whether it is the replacement of camels by trucks in nomadic encampments, or more complex economic processes, the most dramatic changes in women's status appear linked to economic transformations.[44] Michael Fischer's analysis of the changing situation of women in Iran might be taken as a general guide for most of the region. He writes that in Iran there has been a conservative ideology which allocates women a subordinate status to men. Until recently this ideology had its base in "small-scale peasant and merchant communities."[45] As this economic-political base has undergone radical transformations, the conservative ideology concerning male-female roles has increasingly been eroded. Changes in state ideology favoring women's suffrage, the admission of women to all levels of education, legal enfranchisement, and access to public employment all have served further to call into question traditional assumptions concerning women's roles.

How the erosion of this conservative ideology will be resolved is a matter open to debate. Economic "modernization" has just as often brought a worsening of women's practical status as an improvement in it. Nonetheless, economic transformations have in almost every instance brought the traditional ideologies concerning male-female relations into question. Even when changes in the status of women appear to move at a glacial pace, women in remote rural areas are increasingly aware of the opportunities available to them and are beginning to question the roles assigned to them in the past or by prevailing conventional ideological assumptions. As one colleague has suggested, the general lack of participation of Muslim women in public life in the past means that when they assume modern professional roles, they experience fewer obstacles to their careers than has been the case until recently for women in the United States.[46] While this observation certainly holds

---

[42] Fatima Mernissi, "The Degrading Effect of Capitalism on Female Labour," *Peuples Méditerranéens/Mediterranean Peoples*, no. 6 (January-March 1978), 41-57. For a similar argument based upon colonial political conditions, see Amal Rassam Vinogradov, "French Colonialism as Reflected in the Male-Female Interaction in Morocco," *Transactions of the New York Academy of Sciences*, ser. 2, 36, no. 2 (February 1974), 192-99.

[43] Maher, "Women," p. 113.

[44] See Dawn Chatty, "Changing Sex Roles in Bedouin Society in Syria and Lebanon," in Beck and Keddie, *Women*, pp. 399-415, and Barbara C. Aswad, "Women, Class, and Power: Examples from the Hatay, Turkey," *Ibid.*, pp. 473-81.

[45] Michael M. J. Fischer, "On Changing the Concept and Position of Persian Women," in Beck and Keddie, *Women*, pp. 189-215.

[46] Elizabeth Fernea, personal communication, 1978. Fernea and Bezirgan's translation of "Excerpts from *The Umm Kulthum Nobody Knows*, as Told by Umm Kulthum," in Fernea

in the case of professionals in countries such as Egypt, no one has demonstrated a "trickle effect" upon the status of women with less extraordinary qualifications or upon their ability to participate in public life in government and commerce.

Change in the status and roles available to women is not a process confined to recent times or to major social upheavals such as the advent of Islam in seventh-century Arabia or nineteenth- and twentieth-century European domination of many parts of the Middle East. Additionally, the ideological conventions concerning women vary considerably in different Middle Eastern societies. To ignore these differences of time, place, and social condition in order to speak of a pervasive "Islamic attitude" concerning sex roles leads to serious distortion.[47] In the West, use of a term such as "the Christian woman" would immediately signal a partisan conception not clearly related to specific historical or social contexts. Yet precisely this sort of transhistorical abstraction is commonly used in writing about women and sex roles in the Middle East, both by outsiders to the region and by those living within it.

One cause for the contributing popularity of such ahistorical abstractions comes from the way that both those advocating maintenance of the status quo and those advocating a rethinking of sex roles, like other significant aspects of social identity and social policy, seek legitimacy for their views. Revolutionaries, modernists, and traditionalists all assert that their positions are identified with the "authentic" message of the Quran and of Islam. Thus, those who wish to emphasize the constraints which Islam places upon women in society emphasize Quranic verses such as the following:

Your women are a tillage for you; so come
    unto your tillage as you wish.
                    (Sura 2, verse 223)

Men are the managers of the affairs of women
    for that God has preferred in bounty
    one of them over another . . .
And those you fear may be rebellious
    admonish; banish them to their couches,
    and beat them.
                    (Sura 4, verse 38)[48]

---

and Bezirgan, *Women Speak,* pp. 135-66, is a poignant account of the famous singer's transformation from a village girl to an international celebrity.

[47] This is a difficulty with Fatima Mernissi's *Beyond the Veil: Male-Female Dynamics in a Modern Muslim Society* (New York: Halstead Press, 1975), which gives summaries of Robertson Smith's speculations concerning women in pre-Islamic Arabia, the Prophet Muhammad's treatment of women in the seventh century, a superficial analysis of the writings of a twelfth-century mystic and scholar, al-Ghazzālī, interviews with fourteen Moroccan women, and an analysis of letters written to a Moroccan radio program to construct an Islamic "ideal type" of male-female relations not clearly related to historical or regional context. Nonetheless, her book is passionately argued and poses some interesting questions.

[48] *The Koran Interpreted,* trans. Arthur J. Arberry (London: George Allen & Unwin, Ltd.; New York: The Macmillan Company, 1955), vol. 1, pp. 59, 105-6. (Courtesy of the publishers.)

Taken in a literal sense, as do many conservative Muslims, such verses can be used to legitimize the effective relegation of women to an inferior status in public life and in relations with men. However, it is equally possible to read these verses in a more liberal sense by emphasizing the contexts in which these verses occur: legal prescriptions which specified the rights of women and frequently improved upon existing customs at the time they were revealed in seventh-century Arabia. The verse following the second of the above quotations, for instance, recommends that if a husband and wife should quarrel, arbiters should be appointed from the kin of each to seek a resolution of the conflict. Moreover, through various judicial and customary interpretations of Islamic doctrine, considerable modifications of doctrine and practice can occur despite the fact that the authors of such changes legitimate them by claiming that no change is involved other than a "return" to pure Islamic principles. Unfortunately, the ideological claim that no change occurs has blocked some analysts from perceiving variations which are often dramatic.

One of the earlier approaches to the study of sex roles in Islamic society was to signal the disparity between what was considered to be the "Great Tradition"—a distillation of what was taken to be Islamic law and Quranic ethics—and locally elaborated practices and traditions as studied by anthropologists throughout the Islamic world. When the study of sex roles and ethics is conceived of in terms of transcultural norms and local comportment, the anthropologist then sees various village practices as "accommodations" of what is taken to be the normative tradition of Islam to the exigencies of village and urban life. The first studies of this kind to appear, notably Antoun's essential 1968 article concerning the "modesty" of Arab village women, performed the valuable service of assembling relevant Quranic citations and aspects of Islamic tradition, of culling appropriate ethnographic sources, and of reporting on his own meticulous Jordanian research.[49] The principal drawback to this approach is the somewhat artificial normative tradition against which local practices are assessed. Muslim intellectuals ranging from Saudi fundamentalists to liberal modernists each construe a particular Islamic tradition and measure contemporary practices and expectations against it. Antoun's attention to translocal norms (as locally understood) and locally accepted practices is useful. Yet by asserting that there is an identifiable Islamic normative "tradition" somehow independent of particular situations and carriers, anthropologists who study the "problem" of accommodation tend to ignore the continuing debate among Muslims as to just what is normative and arbitrarily select one normative construct against which actual practice can be measured.

Another major approach to the study of women in society is what can be called the *structuralist* approach, perhaps best exemplified by the writings of Pierre Bourdieu on the Kabyle Berbers of Algeria. Bourdieu situates his discussion of

---

[49] Richard T. Antoun, "On the Modesty of Women in Arab Muslim Villages: A Study in the Accommodation of Traditions," *American Anthropologist,* 70, no. 4 (August 1968), 671-97; see also Nadia M. Abu-Zahra, " 'On the Modesty of Women in Arab Villages': A Reply," *American Anthropologist,* 72, no. 5 (October 1970), 1079-88, and Antoun's reply, 1088-92.

women in the broader context of issues of honor and a wide range of social relations. As he writes, honor "is the basis of the moral code of an individual who sees himself always through the eyes of others, who has need of others for his existence, because the image he has of himself is indistinguishable from that presented to him by other people."[50] Hence the dynamics of honor necessarily involve those of social exchange in general. When speaking of dishonor in Kabyle society, the formulas employed generally refer to how certain problems appear before others. Social honor in general, he argues, is maintained through a series of challenges and ripostes. Kabyles distinguish between two complementary forms of honor: *nīf* (a term which literally means "nose") and *hurma* ("all that is prohibited under the penalty of committing sin, or is sacred").[51] Bourdieu translates *hurma* as "honor" and *nīf* as "point of honor." Hurma implies both that which is sacred and that which is respectable. The integrity of honor requires a "punctilious and active vigilance" of the point of honor *(nīf)*. At times, matters of points of honor can be manipulated as in a game of two parties seeking to outbid the other, but any challenge to honor deals with the "most fundamental divisions" of Kabyle culture, "those which control the whole mythico-ritual system."[52] Bourdieu proceeds to identify hurma with all that concerns femininity, the "sacred of the left hand," sexuality, food, magic, and privacy, while he identifies *nīf* with the sacred of the right hand, masculinity, all which concerns social and political exchanges, religion, and public life.[53] The propriety of women and the privacy of the family is thus for Bourdieu a crucial component of the broader discussion of the implications of the role of women and sex roles. Indeed, in a complementary essay he links the architecture of the traditional Kabyle house, the practical functions associated with each of its sections and its cultural connotations with a series of dualistic categories (male/female; house/fields and market; day/night; upper/lower; right/left) which make the house a microcosm of "the same oppositions which govern all the universe."[54] Women and sex roles in this view are components of a more comprehensive set of cultural assumptions concerning the world that are shared by persons in a given society.

A broadly analogous approach is the intensive analysis of specific rituals as a means of eliciting attitudes toward sexual differentiation. This type of study is perhaps best exemplified by John Mason's analysis of wedding rituals in a Libyan oasis community. His analysis suggests the confluence of three opposing forces, a principal one being the generalized assumption of female inferiority, in which male honor and the "kinship group requirement of protecting female virtue (via the

---

[50] Pierre Bourdieu, "The Sentiment of Honour in Kabyle Society," in *Honour and Shame: The Values of Mediterranean Society,* ed. J. G. Peristiany, The Nature of Human Society Series (Chicago: The University of Chicago Press, 1966), p. 211.

[51] *Ibid.,* p. 216.

[52] *Ibid.,* pp. 216-17.

[53] See chart, *Ibid.,* p. 222.

[54] Pierre Bourdieu, "The Berber House or the World Reversed," in his *Algeria 1960* (New York: Cambridge University Press, 1979), pp. 133-53 [original French, 1970].

modesty code)" are opposed to women's assumed "ethical incapability of controlling [their] animalistic sexual appetite[s]."[55] As with Bourdieu's structuralist
approach to the study of honor, Mason refers to the changes taking place in Libyan
society and their impact upon sex roles, but these observations do not figure into
his structural analysis as such.

A more comprehensive approach to the study of sexuality and sex roles is
exemplified by the work of Lawrence Rosen. For Rosen, members of a single
society may share "a broad set of cultural assumptions [yet] may nevertheless
possess diverse interpretations of reality."[56] One such set of assumptions concerns
the nature of sexuality and sex roles; although, as he argues, the possession of such
common assumptions does not necessarily imply that both sexes will elaborate their
shared assumptions in quite the same way. After reviewing the essential features of
male and female roles in Morocco—the markedly separate patterns of socialization
for boys and girls, the expectation that women are predominantly confined to
domestic roles, a differential access to resources in which women in general are
economically more insecure—Rosen graphically depicts some of the assumptions
which Moroccans make concerning how men and women differ as persons.

The essential contrast which Rosen draws is between the complementary concepts of *nafs* ("passion, appetite") and *ᶜqāl* ("reason").[57] *Nafs* is possessed by all
living creatures—angels, men, animals, and *jnūn* (sing., *jinn*-s). It is composed of all
the passions and lusts; unchecked it can lead men to do bad and shameful things.
*ᶜQāl* is "reason, rationality, the ability to use our heads in order to keep our passions from getting hold of us and controlling us."[58] Through following God's word
as it is known from the Quran and the teachings of Islam, man can avoid being a
slave to his passions, can distinguish right from wrong, and can live as God intended
man to live. Through discipline and learning, a child learns gradually to control his
passions. Women also possess reason but cannot develop it as fully as men have the
ability to do. "It's just in their nature. Women have very great sexual desires and
that's why a man is always necessary to control them, to keep them from creating
all sorts of disorder. . . . 'A woman by herself is like a Turkish bath without water,'
because she is always hot and without a man she has no way to slake the fire."[59]

As Rosen points out, the notion that women are subordinate to men is an
ideological assumption shared by both sexes, but in practice it is elaborated in
different ways by men and women. Men tend to emphasize the supposedly *natural*

---

[55] John P. Mason, "Sex and Symbol in the Treatment of Women: The Wedding Rite in a
Libyan Oasis Community," *American Ethnologist,* 2, no. 4 (November 1975), 649-61.

[56] Lawrence Rosen, "The Negotiation of Reality: Male-Female Relations in Sefrou,
Morocco," in Beck and Keddie, *Women,* p. 561. See also Amal Rassam Vinogradov, "French
Colonialism."

[57] Rosen, "Negotiation of Reality," pp. 566-68. In the interview cited by Rosen on
which this discussion is based, the notion of soul *(rūh)* is also introduced as a key term but its
significance is not developed.

[58] *Ibid.,* p. 567.

[59] *Ibid.,* p. 568.

differences between the two sexes when they seek to "comprehend their actual ties with women" and how they ought to handle concrete situations regarding them. Women, for their part, tend more to emphasize the *social* relations of the two sexes and "ways in which men can be ignored, outflanked, or outwitted by the arrangement of various social pressures within the household or family."[60] In short, their actions suggest that they regard their subordination as more social than natural. Rosen proceeds then to document how the definition of what is "reality" is negotiated in crucial situations such as marriage negotiations.

The advantage of the analytical approach exemplified by Rosen is that no implicit assumption is made that the "nature" of social reality is fixed and derived from rules. Both the cultural assumptions concerning reality and their articulation in practical social circumstances are regarded as subject to redefinition through changing political and economic circumstances.

Michael Fischer employs a similar approach in the study of Persian women, although he places greater emphasis on the circumstances engendering social and cultural change than does Rosen.[61] Paul Vieille, also concerned with Iran, seeks to depict attitudes concerning sexuality in peasant society and does so by tracing the interrelationships among virginity as a female "capital," fecundity, and the complementarity of the sexes (with women considered to be "incomplete," submissive, and inferior). He writes that in peasant society, "sex is . . . a constant subject of dreaming, of preoccupation, of conversation" and goes so far as to say that Iranian peasant society is "a society centered on sexuality." Yet he proceeds to depict sexual practice as remarkably contrary to the ideal. He writes that the only contact in the course of the sexual act is between the genital organs; caresses are virtually unknown (despite there being no specific religious or cultural prohibitions); there is no communication between spouses regarding the sexual act; and the "avowal of pleasure is inconceivable from woman to man and also from man to woman." Even in married life the woman must refrain from showing her desire; deficiencies such as sterility are almost always attributed to the woman. In sum, and perhaps with hyperbole, Vieille writes: "Comradeship or friendship among men and women is inconceivable and cannot exist; all verbal communication and all physical approaches take on sexual content and are suspect." A woman is "a sexual good at the disposition of a man," yet as Vieille implies, assumptions concerning sexuality suggest a "contradiction" between the level of institutional values, where sex is overrated, and that of actual sexual practice.[62]

Although Vieille's essay makes an attempt to treat sexuality comprehensively by speaking of male-female relations and other forms of sexual gratification, he is not entirely successful. He writes that the laments of popular songs and "the frequency of other forms of sexuality such as masturbation, homosexuality, and

---

[60] *Ibid.*, pp. 569-70. See also Daisy Hilse Dwyer, *Images and Self-Images: Male and Female in Morocco* (New York: Columbia University Press, 1978).

[61] Fischer, "Persian Women," pp. 189-215.

[62] Vieille, "Iranian Women," pp. 461-68.

bestiality" all suggest a masculine dissatisfaction with heterosexual relations despite the lack of "direct indexes" of what men think.[63] Here Vieille reiterates what might be labeled the underlying "hydraulic" theory of sexuality, in which any impediment to heterosexual relations is thought to result directly in the practice of other forms of sexual gratification.

When explicitly stated as above, the deficiencies of "hydraulic" theories of sexuality can easily be recognized. The liberalism of some European countries and parts of the United States has not demonstrably resulted in any shift between homosexual and heterosexual orientations and, if anything, has resulted in a more tolerant attitude toward what Vieille would call "other" forms of sexual gratification. As suggested thus far in this chapter, ideologies of sexuality involve complex dimensions, including notions of domination, authority, intimacy, friendship, economic hegemony, and other essential definitions of, and practical control over, self and social honor.

Nonetheless, or possibly because sexuality in the Middle East as elsewhere is such a crucial component of notions of self, it is difficult to elaborate a more comprehensive discussion of the issue because of the lack of a solid base on which to build. So little reliable discussion has taken place to date in the scholarly literature on the Middle East that Burton's "Terminal Essay" to his translation of *1001 Nights*—an encyclopedic inventory of hearsay and what he considered to be the sexual wonders and extravagances of the "Sotadic Zone" (a region which for him stretched from Tokyo to Tangier, his "Orient")—is astonishingly referred to even today as authoritative in some general books on the region.[64] Most discussions of sexual conduct make cursory references to male and female homosexuality and other forms of sex, as when Snouck Hurgronje wrote of nineteenth-century Mecca that there were many men "who gave themselves up to the vice called after Lot" and their female counterparts as well.[65] The "Orient" writ large was used as a screen against which Western images of its supposed excesses could be projected. Pilgrimages such as that made by André Gide in 1893 to Algeria in search of the "golden fleece" of moral and sexual liberation only served to reinforce the Western notion of the "Orient" as different and exotic, in sexuality as in other spheres.[66]

---

[63] *Ibid.*, p. 468.

[64] *The Book of the Thousand Nights and a Night*, trans. Richard F. Burton (New York: The Heritage Press, 1962 [orig. 1886]), pp. 3653-819. A quotation of Burton's opinion of the Chinese conveys the flavor of his judgments: "The Chinese, as far as we know them . . . are the chosen people of debauchery, and their systematic bestiality with ducks, goats, and other animals is equalled only by their pederasty" (p. 3770). Although to my knowledge he uses the term "systematic bestiality" only once, his catalogue of presumed Middle Eastern amusements is equally hyperbolic.

[65] C. Snouck Hurgronje, *Mekka in the Latter Part of the 19th Century* (Leiden: E. J. Brill, 1931), pp. 51, 106.

[66] For a discussion of Gide's sexual "pilgrimage," see Ernest Gellner, "The Unknown Apollo of Biskra: The Social Base of Algerian Puritanism," *Government and Opposition*, 9 (1974), 279-82.

Such images persist in the travel literature of the present, as when Gavin Maxwell suggests that the marsh Arabs of southern Iraq "are not very selective in their direction of sexual outlet; all is, so to speak, grist to their mill."[67] With sexuality treated superficially as the exotic, it is not surprising that even nineteenth-century ethnographers such as Snouck Hurgronje noted that Middle Easterners, especially educated ones, spoke with circumspection concerning sexual attitudes and beliefs. As ethnography, isolated comments such as those I have cited above only underscore how little is known of sexuality in theory or conduct.[68]

A sketch of what a comprehensive study of sexuality should be and an indication at least of the documentary sources on which it could be built is provided by the Tunisian sociologist, Abdelwahab Bouhdiba. His *La Sexualité en Islam (Sexuality in Islam)* analyzes attitudes toward sexuality in the medieval Islamic world and in the contemporary period both through texts and (by reference to a few relevant colonial and contemporary studies of Tunisia alone) sociological accounts. He insists that although the Islamic community considers itself rightly as a unity, Islam is fundamentally "plastic" in its essence, so that nothing of the ambiguities of existence or of life are "sacrificed," including the serious and playful, collective and individual components of sexuality. For Bouhdiba, one can speak of a Malay Islam, an Arab Islam, and Iranian Islam, a Tunisian Islam, and other Islams, each of which suggests essential comportments and attitudes which cannot be reduced to "folklore."[69] His text is resplendent with suggestions of how the sexual dimension of identity has been elaborated in the context of various expressions of Islamic belief and practice and a multiplicity of social structures.

## ETHNICITY AND CULTURAL IDENTITY

Ethnicity is no less complex a notion than the other aspects of personal and cultural identity so far considered. In a provocative essay written in the late 1960s, Fredrick Barth briefly reviews the drawbacks to defining ethnicity in terms of shared biological features and, as he understands the term, cultural identities and

---

[67]Gavin Maxwell, *People of the Reeds* (New York: Harper & Row, 1957), p. 205. For a more balanced and nonexoticized treatment of the same topic in Morocco, see Maxwell's later *Lords of the Atlas: The Rise and Fall of the House of Glaoua, 1893-1956* (New York: E. P. Dutton & Co., Inc., 1966), pp. 286-87.

[68]A point also argued by Keddie, "Problems in the Study of Women," p. 240. An idea of how interviewing on such delicate subjects can be successfully conducted in Middle Eastern conditions is provided by the frank discussions of sexuality contained in Paul Pascon's and Mekki Bentahar's "Ce Que Disent 296 Jeunes Ruraux," in *Etudes Sociologiques sur le Maroc,* ed. A. Khatibi (Rabat: Bulletin Economique et Social du Maroc, 1971), pp. 147-48 and pp. 211-21, in which the basic technique was collective interviewing.

[69]Abdelwahab Bouhdiba, *La Sexualité en Islam,* Sociologie d'Aujourd'hui (Paris: Presses Universitaires de France, 1975), pp. 127-28. His text is one of the few that includes brief but interesting accounts of concubinage, prostitution, and homosexuality, and references to these topics in medieval Arabic literature.

suggests instead that analytically the crucial elements of any definition of ethnic group are those characteristics "presumptively" determined by origin and background, which actors use "to categorize themselves and others for purposes of interaction."[70]

When Barth's discussion of ethnicity first appeared, it provided a useful corrective to those discussions which either took ethnicity to be a fixed and unchanging element of personal identity or which regarded the notion of culture as composed of set, prescriptive "traits" or rules. However, most modern anthropological notions of culture emphasize how cultural meanings are socially employed, produced, and maintained in social action and interaction. The social production of meaning is a component of such an approach to the study of culture.[71] Barth sought to consider the "*socially* effective" to the exclusion of all considerations of cultural meaning, except insofar as notions of ethnic group identity produced or maintained perceptions of boundaries of groups, as opposed to what he called "cultural stuff," which he saw as merely content filling in social form.[72] As this

**FIGURE** 7-2 Shabak men, northern Iraq. (Courtesy Amal Rassam.)

[70] Fredrick Barth, "Introduction," *Ethnic Groups and Boundaries: The Social Organization of Culture Difference,* ed. Fredrik Barth (Boston: Little, Brown and Company, 1969), pp. 10-14. For an analysis of the persisting use of the "mosaic" model of ethnicity in the Middle East, see Bryan S. Turner, *Marx and the End of Orientalism,* Controversies in Sociology, 7 (London and Boston: George Allan & Unwin, 1978), pp. 39-52.

[71] For an elaboration of this point, see Dale F. Eickelman, "The Political Economy of Meaning," *American Ethnologist,* 6, no. 2 (May 1979), 386-93.

[72] Barth, *Ethnic Groups,* pp. 13, 15.

essay has reiterated in various contexts, the notion of culture as "stuff" is not analytically useful.

As logically elegant as Barth's essay is in some respects, it is limited in theoretical value because it lacks an adequate notion of how social processes are related to the production of cultural conceptions with which people distinguish themselves from "other" ethnic categories and with which they account for, evaluate, and weigh the importance of those distinctions. Instead, Barth focuses upon the organizational forms of social *groups* whose principle of unity is presumed rather than demonstrated to be that of ethnicity rather than alternate or complementary attributes which could form the base of organizational cohesiveness. For example, the essay concerning Fūr cultivators and Baggāra pastoralists in the Sudan explicitly avoids consideration of the historical process of personal shifts of ethnic identity between the two groups. It is explicitly assumed that when persons change the means by which they utilize certain resources, their ethnic identities change as well. Even were this to be the case, little attention is paid to precisely what ethnicity means in the setting of the Fūr and the Baggāra and, indeed, only Fūr views of social identity are provided in any detail.[73]

An analytic framework which presented the principles of ethnic stereotyping (notions concerning the motivations of the members of "other" ethnic groups and what can be expected of them) of both groups and how these notions were maintained in changing historical contexts would have been much more useful.[74] In his own case study in the volume, Barth is concerned with elaborating the economic and productive contexts in which it is useful for Pathans to stress their identities as Pathans and when it is not. By confining his discussion to "traditional" Pathans, and to social groups distinguished by their exploitation of particular ecological "niches," some of the most significant tests of the precise ramifications of ethnicity in contemporary and complex settings are ignored.[75]

The identity of the Shabak of northern Iraq as studied by Amal Rassam (Vinogradov) gives some notion of just how complex ethnic identities can become and why it is misleading to study them as if such identities were part of a fixed ethnic "mosaic."[76] The Shabak are a Muslim Shī'ī sect of about fifteen thousand

[73]Gunnar Haaland, "Economic Determinants in Ethnic Processes," in Barth, *Ethnic Groups,* p. 71.

[74]For an example of a study which incorporates such considerations, see Karen I. Blu, "Varieties of Ethnic Identity: Anglo-Saxons, Blacks, Indians, and Jews in a Southern County," *Ethnicity,* 4 (1977), 263-86.

[75]Fredrik Barth, "Pathan Identity and Its Maintenance," in Barth, *Ethnic Groups,* p. 117.

[76]Amal (Rassam) Vinogradov, "Ethnicity, Cultural Discontinuity and Power Brokers in Northern Iraq: The Case of the Shabak," *American Ethnologist,* 1, no. 1 (February 1974), 207-18; Amal Rassam (Vinogradov), "Al-Tabaʿiyya: Power, Patronage and Marginal Groups in Northern Iraq," in *Patrons and Clients in Mediterranean Societies,* eds. Ernest Gellner and John Waterbury (London: Duckworth, 1977), pp. 157-66. (To avoid bibliographic confusion, it should be noted that studies by Amal Rassam prior to 1976 appeared under the name of Amal Vinogradov.) See also Robert Leroy Canfield's excellent *Faction and Conversion in a Plural*

persons located in some thirty-five villages to the east of Mosul. The area in which they live is fairly delimited, they speak a Kurdish dialect (with most men today bilingual in Arabic), and until recently they worked as sharecroppers on land owned by a group of wealthy Arab families who live in Mosul and who claim descent from the Prophet. In recent land reforms the Shabak have become landowners themselves. They largely marry only among themselves and tend to be secretive toward outsiders with respect to their religious beliefs. In the immediate vicinity of the Shabak are a variety of ethnolinguistic communities: Shī$^c$ī Turkoman tribes in villages along the Tigris, Shī$^c$ī Kurds, Sunni Muslim Arabs in Mosul, Christian villagers (Monophysites, Assyrians, and Nestorians), Jews in both Mosul and in agricultural communities (until 1958), Kurdish-speaking gypsies, and tribally organized Sunni Arabic-speaking Bedouin.[77]

Rassam writes that "the Shabak are completely ignorant of their history and cultural affiliations" yet states that an analysis of what is known of them historically is essential to consider their self-identity and how it is changing. The Shabak claim that their name derives from an Arabic term, *shabaka,* which means "to interweave" or "to tie together," and thus alludes to the fact that they are an amalgam of peoples.[78] Unlike other groups in the Mosul region, the Shabak "claim no common descent and keep no genealogies; neither do they have lineages which provide political leadership." Their social integration is provided almost exclusively by their religious beliefs and practices. As Rassam writes, the very weakness of the Shabak protected them. They made no claims to social honor on the basis of corporate strength, which indeed they did not possess, and they carried no weapons. "Thus, they avoided any involvement in the kaleidoscope of political alliances and feuds that raged around them."[79]

At the same time, the Shabak were in a patron-client relation with their landlords (the *sāda*), a relation that continues today despite the fact that the patrons are now their *former* landlords, as the land has been expropriated and distributed to the tenants. Similarly, there was nothing inevitable about the *sāda,* as the descendants of the Prophet are collectively known, acquiring their favored position. The Ottoman administration in the nineteenth century settled five families of sāda in the Mosul region in order to use their religious prestige and influence to buttress their authority. In return for their cooperation as representatives of the state and

*Society: Religious Alignments in the Hindu Kush.* Anthropological Papers, 50 (Ann Arbor: University of Michigan Museum of Anthropology, 1973). A later series of short papers on the same theme is contained in *Ethnic Processes and Intergroup Relations in Contemporary Afghanistan,* eds. Jon W. Anderson and Richard F. Strand, Afghanistan Council, Occasional Paper 15 (New York: Asia Society, 1978). Anderson's "Introduction and Overview," pp. 1-8, is particularly useful in suggesting the limitations of using the notion of ethnicity in non-Western contexts.

[77] Rassam (Vinogradov), "Ethnicity," 208-9; Rassam (Vinogradov), "Power," p. 157. Data on the Jewish and Christian groups are derived from Rassam, personal communication, 1976.

[78] Rassam (Vinogradov), "Ethnicity," 210.

[79] *Ibid.,* 210.

as intermediaries charged with keeping the population of the region peaceful and politically inactive, the Ottoman government gave the sāda families large tracts of land. As landlords of the Shabak, the sāda gave their peasants a place to stay when they came into Mosul to sell their produce and buy provisions, and "acted throughout as advisors, creditors, and protectors" on their behalf.[80]

Under the conditions of relative insecurity that prevailed under the Ottoman administration, the Shabak had few alternatives to being sharecroppers; a few individuals managed to acquire funds (for example, by working for the British army in Iraq in the 1920s) to buy lands themselves and to become upwardly mobile, one sign of which was to speak Arabic exclusively and to adopt urban life styles. Some even claimed sāda status for themselves, and all sought to downplay their former identity as Shabak. In post-1958 Iraq, with the consequences of land reform and rural education having a major impact on social and cultural identity, Shabak can emigrate to other regions of Iraq or leave their villages to work in nearby factories.[81] As Rassam insists, it is not sufficient to define the Shabak in the context of locally existing ethnic groups and to locate them in time and space: "Equally important is to discover the basis of their differential access to resources, religious, social or economic, and the patterns of their articulation . . . an historical analysis becomes crucial for the proper assessment of the factors involved in the formation of these groups."[82] A sociological comprehension of ethnicity necessitates a historical understanding of how ethnic identities articulate and are manipulated.

The situation depicted for northern Iraq is not dissimilar to the ethnic complexity of neighboring countries, notably Turkey and Iran, both of which contain minority populations which differentiate themselves according to ethnic, religious, and linguistic criteria. Perhaps the most complex country of the region in terms of such identities is Lebanon. The country was on the verge of civil war several times in the 1950s and 1960s prior to the tragic conflagration which began in 1975. Often the fighting is simplistically reported in the foreign press as between "rightists" and "leftists" or between Christians and Muslims. Actually the situation is considerably more complex. By 1975, Lebanon, a country roughly the size of Connecticut but only thirty-five miles wide, had an estimated population of three million, with seventeen officially recognized religious sects. Because Lebanese electoral politics were linked to the strength of the various sects as recorded in the official census, there had been no official census since 1932. Nonetheless, most accounts assume that 30 percent of the population was Maronite Christian, 20 percent Sunni Muslim, 18 percent Shīʿī Muslim, 10 percent Greek Orthodox Christian, 6 percent Greek Catholic, 6 percent Druze, 5 percent Armenian Orthodox (many of whom arrived as refugees from Turkey in the early part of this century), with the remaining 5 percent of the population divided among Armenian Catholics, Protes-

---

[80] *Ibid.*, 211-13; Rassam (Vinogradov), "Power," p. 160.

[81] Rassam (Vinogradov), "Ethnicity," 212-13, 216.

[82] Rassam (Vinogradov), "Power," pp. 157-58.

tants, Jacobites, Syrian Catholics, Syrian Orthodox, Nestorians, Latin Rite Catholics, Jews, and others. An estimated one-third of Lebanon's inhabitants as of 1975 were noncitizens. These included 500,000 Syrians (both Christian and Muslim) and an estimated 300,000 Palestinians (again both Christian and Muslim). Although earlier immigrants to Lebanon, including Armenians and many of the Palestinian refugees who arrived in 1948 were accorded Lebanese citizenship, most of the later arrivals were not. Joseph estimates that 60 to 75 percent of Lebanon's population lives in cities, with over 50 percent of the urban population being in the greater Beirut area.[83] As the fighting in Lebanon's south continues, the refugee population of the capital has increased, further exacerbating the various potential cleavages in Lebanon's society. Furthermore, distances in Lebanon are so short that incidents in one part of the country immediately affect other parts.

Although Lebanon's civil war is characterized as sectarian, this notion must be carefully analyzed. Khuri's enumeration of sectarian differences between a predominantly Maronite region of Beirut and a neighboring Shīʿī one indicate that there are considerable differences of education, occupation, marriage and household patterns, life styles, and other nonreligious identifying features between the various sectarian groups.[84] For example, Christians tended to have contact with European missionaries from the nineteenth century onward and have benefited from educational facilities superior to those available to most Shīʿa. Such educational differences explain in part the marked occupational differentiation between the two confessional groups, with the Shīʿa tending to be concentrated in professions which can be acquired by apprenticeship or which require no specialized training.[85] Although neighborhoods are not distinguishable by class, there has been a marked settlement by sect, but the geographical and social boundaries between Muslim and Christian communities (and various divisions within them) are not always sharp. In general, areas of concentration of one sect tend to serve as a magnet for other persons of the same sect. As Khuri writes—in a study completed prior to the 1975 civil war—"interaction between confessional groups is, by and large, limited to business transactions and to formal occasions: festivals, weddings, and funerals. To interact openly and freely with other confessions requires both knowledge and hypocrisy: knowledge of the etiquette, manners, and cultural sensitivities of the other group; hypocrisy in pretending to appreciate the ways of others while manipulating them."[86]

[83] Suad Joseph, "Muslim-Christian Conflict in Lebanon: A Perspective on the Evolution of Sectarianism," in *Muslim-Christian Conflicts: Economic, Political and Social Origins,* eds. Suad Joseph and Barbara L. K. Pillsbury (Boulder, Colo.: Westview Press, 1978), p. 64. See also Suad Joseph, "Women and the Neighborhood Street in Borj Hammoud, Lebanon," in Beck and Keddie, *Women,* p. 554.

[84] Fuad I. Khuri, *From Village to Suburb: Order and Change in Greater Beirut* (Chicago and London: The University of Chicago Press, 1975).

[85] *Ibid.,* p. 93.

[86] *Ibid.,* p. 57.

Joseph emphasizes in her writings on sectarianism in Lebanon that the boundary markers between various sects have varied historically and that the sects should not, even under present circumstances, be taken as fixed religious and political identities.[87] Her study of Burj Ḥammūd, an independent municipality about 5 kilometers from downtown Beirut, clearly depicts the practical implications of sectarian identity.

Like other parts of Lebanon, population movements in and out of Burj Ḥammūd reflect the political and economic currents affecting the entire country. In 1920, the municipality had a population of 2,000 persons, which increased to 20,000 in 1942 and to about 200,000 in 1973, with a high population turnover. Every one of Lebanon's 17 major confessional groups is represented in its population.[88] Less than 1 percent of its present-day population is composed of the original settlers of the town.

Joseph stresses the importance of the period when various waves of migrants settled in the community, a factor which Khuri also mentions. The first major wave of migrants were the Armenians who came to Lebanon following the massacres in Turkey in 1920. Through the assistance of various Armenian organizations, they bought land in the region and encouraged other migrants to join them. Through the end of the Second World War the Armenians predominated numerically in the region, set up a number of small industries, and built schools, clinics, clubs, and churches. They likewise gained control of the municipal board and have retained that control to the present. Palestinians began arriving in the community after 1948, with the wealthier ones settling directly in the community and the more impoverished ones living in a nearby camp. Following political upheavals in Syria in the 1960s, a large number of Syrians, mostly Sunnī Muslims but also of other Muslim and Christian confessional groups, arrived. Later refugees in the 1970s were largely Shīʿa from Lebanon's south. As a consequence, Joseph estimates that the present population distribution is roughly 40 percent Armenian Christians, 40 percent Shīʿa, and 20 percent Palestinian. Some of the municipality's neighborhoods are mixed in confessional orientation, but in most cases a single group predominates.

Several sorts of bonds emerge from daily interaction. Almost every street constitutes a neighborhood, with households of various confessional groups mixed together. Neighbors tended to share their various goods and to participate in each other's feast days and other special occasions. Women tended to form interconfessional friendship and visiting networks which often served as the basis for maintaining some semblance of security, social control, and unity in the street even in the face of deteriorating political conditions.[89] On the other hand, the sectarian

---

[87] Joseph, "Muslim-Christian Conflict," pp. 64, 85. Also personal communications with the author, 1977.

[88] Joseph, "Neighborhood Street," p. 544.

[89] *Ibid.*, pp. 548-53.

identities and the armed militias maintained by the strongmen of various groups have become increasingly part of the regular fabric of social life. Here the national (and international) repercussions of Lebanese "internal" politics become apparent. In Burj Ḥammūd as elsewhere in the country, each confessional group can call upon its compatriots elsewhere. In fact, many of the Lebanese residents of Burj Ḥammūd did not vote there when elections were held (one of the reasons that the Armenians maintained their local political strength) but in their villages of origin where they were indebted to particular strongmen (*zaᶜīm-s*).

Similarly, groups that might be strong locally but weak nationally coalesce with others. Thus the right-wing Katā'ib party, whose principal base of support is the Maronite Christian community, usually tends to be supported by the Armenians, just as the Palestinians (both Christian and Muslim) tend to be supported by the Shīᶜa of Lebanon's south or refugees from that region. When any one group is threatened, it can call upon compatriots elsewhere to support its conceived interests.[90] These various armed militias are organized almost entirely along confessional lines, as Khuri points out in his comments upon patterns of political leadership in Lebanon. In fact, he goes so far as to say that ideological political parties, such as the Baᶜthists and Communists, appear to appeal primarily to the young, semieducated, and unmarried, many of whom desert these parties after marriage when they have more responsibilities and material interests to protect. Some alliances cross confessional lines, but these usually are among particular leaders.[91] Hence sectarian affiliations and the importance of asserting confessional identity can be more flexible than may at first be apparent.

Several researchers recently have questioned whether the strength of organizational forms along confessional lines is real or apparent and have placed great stress upon the relation of economic realities to political structure and notions of authority. Virtually all accounts of organized violence and political leadership in Lebanon acknowledge that the followings of various strongmen are primarily along sectarian and factional lines. However, Michael Gilsenan, among others, has argued that although sectarian politics of the "Boss Tweed" variety and their associated patron-client relationships were important in an earlier era in Lebanon, fundamental economic transformations have profoundly altered the structure of Lebanese society. One consequence is that despite appearances, there has been a cementing of ties among favor givers (Lebanon's *zaᶜīm-s*) irrespective of sectarian affiliations to the exclusion of all other Lebanese (the favor seekers), in order to keep the favor seekers dependent and to ensure that they continue to think of Lebanon's politics as a spoils system in which only ties to successful strongmen can bring any semblance of security. This "alliance and consolidation at the top" suggests to Gilsenan that class conflict has become the root of current Lebanese political unrest, not locally held ideologies concerning how that society is divided.[92]

[90]*Ibid.*, pp. 552-53.

[91]Khuri, *Village to Suburb*, pp. 200-201.

[92]Michael Gilsenan, "Against Patron-Client Relations," in Gellner and Waterbury, *Patrons and Clients*, p. 182. See also Michael Gilsenan, "Lying, Honor, and Contradiction," in

Amal Rassam's conclusion regarding the ethnic and sectarian divisions of northern Iraq might equally be applied to the situation in Lebanon: "Ethnicity and its attendant patronage system represented an organizational solution through which weak, special-interest groups managed to protect their identities and insure their survival."[93] As this argument stands, it is somewhat circular for what the identity of ethnicity "solved" organizationally were problems of economic and political advantage-seeking. Such identities lost their importance once economic and political circumstances were significantly transformed. The same observation concerning ethnic and sectarian identity and advantage-seeking has been put forward for Lebanon, stating that the major divisions of Lebanese society since the first major capitalist penetration in the nineteenth century have been economic and not religious ones and that such divisions are tied to specific historical circumstances and an intraclass struggle among political leaders.[94] To the extent that such organized factional violence is supported by international political forces, such an argument gains credence. Lebanese political leaders have managed to obtain arms and money from a variety of external political sources, thus prolonging their own tenuous command over their following.

Any consideration of ethnic and factional alliances must look beyond purely local ideological beliefs to understand the particular forms they take. The Kurds are a case in point, and their situation serves in some ways to indicate the difficulties involved in treating ethnic identities as either primordial givens along the lines of Carleton Coon or merely as locally held "apparent" ideologies of identity à la Barth.[95]

Kurdistan is a region which crosses several international boundaries. The majority of Kurds are located in Turkey (7 to 12 million), Iran (4 to 6 million) and Iraq (2 to 3 million), with smaller numbers in the USSR (600,000 to 1 million) and Syria (500,000 to 600,000), and perhaps 400,000 elsewhere.[96] The number of

*Transaction and Meaning: Directions in the Anthropology of Exchange and Symbolic Behavior*, ed. Bruce Kapferer, ASA Studies in Social Anthropology, 1 (Philadelphia: Institute for the Study of Human Issues, 1976), pp. 191-219.

[93] Rassam (Vinogradov), "Ethnicity," 216.

[94] Laurel D. Mailloux, "Peasants and Social Protest: 1975-1976 Lebanese Civil War," in Joseph and Pillsbury, *Muslim-Christian Conflicts*, pp. 101-3.

[95] The Kurds are very poorly known from specifically anthropological studies, as most ethnographers have spent only brief periods of several weeks to two months in Kurdistan and were not familiar with Kurdish or the other languages of the region. With these reservations, the principal studies are E. R. Leach, *Social and Economic Organisation of the Rowanduz Kurds*, London School of Economics, Monographs on Social Anthropology, 3 (London: Percy Lund, Humphries and Co., Ltd., 1940); Fredrik Barth, *Principles of Social Organization in Southern Kurdistan*, Universitetes Ethnografiske Museum Bulletin, 7 (Oslo: University of Oslo, 1953); and Henny Harald Hansen, *The Kurdish Woman's Life: Field Research in a Muslim Society, Iraq*, Nationalmuseets Skrifter, Etnografisk Raekke, 7 (Copenhagen: National Museum, 1961).

[96] Figures derived from "Kurds on the Move," *The Middle East* (London), no. 55 (May 1979), 47-52, which provides a useful summary of the political situation of Kurds today. Similar political ambiguities plague the substantial disparity between the population claims of Egyptian Coptic spokesmen (7 million) and official estimates (2,600,000 as of 1976). See Makram Samaan and Soheir Sukkary, "The Copts and Muslims of Egypt," in Joseph and Pillsbury, *Muslim-Christian Conflicts*, p. 130.

Kurds is itself a significant political issue, with the Kurds themselves suggesting the upper figures and those wishing to diminish their political importance advocating the lower estimates. In Turkey, a recent survey of Kurdish affairs indicates that there has never been official discrimination against Kurds, who have provided prime ministers, millionaires and members of parliament to the country. There is, however, a cultural discrimination: The teaching and writing of Kurdish is banned, and younger Kurds advocating autonomy and independence are carefully watched by the police. There is evidence that the Soviets have encouraged the autonomy of Kurdish Turks (although presumably not of Kurds within the boundaries of the Soviet Union). In Iraq there has been sustained guerrilla warfare against the Baghdad regime, with arms and money supplied in part until 1975 through the Iranian and U.S. governments. One component of the 1978-1979 Iranian revolution was an uprising against garrisoned troops in an effort to gain regional autonomy and official recognition of their cultural and linguistic heritage.[97] Thus, ethnic and sectarian identities are forged and maintained in historically specific economic and political circumstances. As with a range of other attributes of identity, these ideologies have profound practical significance and are actively manipulated, often with requisite cynicism, for reasons of political or economic advantage.

Since ethnic and religious considerations are rarely if ever the sole attribute shared by persons and groups in the Middle East, it is crucial to consider how such social distinctions figure in the overall context of social and personal identity and not to stop at a mosaiclike enumeration of distinctions such as ethnic group, sect, and occupation which indicate their complexity but which provide no clear indication of what they mean in practice. An excellent analysis of such identities in a Moroccan context is provided by two complementary articles by Lawrence Rosen, one concerning the significance of "ethnic" distinctions between Arabs and Berbers, the other concerning Muslims and Jews.[98] Both articles deal with politically volatile aspects of cultural notions of self and community. The essential background is as follows. French colonial administrators, first in Algeria in the nineteenth century and subsequently in Morocco, sought to nurture a notion that "Berber" identity was distinct from that of "Arab and Muslim." It was politically

---

[97]"Kurds on the Move," pp. 47-52.

[98]Lawrence Rosen, "The Social and Conceptual Framework of Arab-Berber Relations in Central Morocco," in *Arabs and Berbers,* eds. Ernest Gellner and Charles Micaud (London: Duckworth, 1972), pp. 155-73; and also his "Muslim-Jewish Relations in a Moroccan City," *International Journal of Middle East Studies,* 3, no. 4 (October 1972), 435-49. For a review of earlier anthropological approaches to the study of North African Jewish communities, see also Rosen's "North African Jewish Studies," *Judaism,* 17, no. 4 (Fall 1968), 422-29. For a critique of Rosen's position concerning Muslim-Jewish relations, see Norman A. Stillman, "The Moroccan Jewish Experience: A Revisionist View," *The Jerusalem Quarterly,* no. 9 (Fall 1978), 111-23. See also Mark A. Tessler, "The Identity of Religious Minorities in Non-secular States: Jews in Tunisia and Morocco and Arabs in Israel," *Comparative Studies in Society and History,* 20, no. 3 (July 1978), 359-73; and Norman A. Stillman's excellent *The Jews of Arab Lands—A History and Source Book* (Philadelphia: The Jewish Publication Society of America, 1979).

useful for the French to emphasize real and imagined differences of "Berbers" (largely residing in mountainous regions and in Morocco's south) from the "Arab" society of the towns and agricultural plains, but this turned out to be politically disastrous in some respects. In 1930 the French issued their famous "Berber proclamation" in Morocco which legally excluded regions designated as Berber from the jurisdiction of Islamic law courts. The proclamation set off violent protests in all of Morocco, but nonetheless the French continued to treat the "Berbers" and "Arabs" as antagonistic to the end of their rule, implemented a number of policies regarding military recruitment, local administration, education ("Berbers" were forbidden to learn Arabic in schools, although most students found the means to do so anyway), which were designed to cultivate a distinctly "Berber" elite. The issue continues in many ways to be a delicate one for the present Moroccan government, many of whose French-educated administrators from the urban milieu, even if skeptical of the ideological justifications of French colonial policy, assimilated its basic assumptions concerning the structural divisions of Moroccan society.[99]

Another major identifying axis in Moroccan society, as with other Middle Eastern societies, is that of Muslim and Jew. The Jewish community in Morocco remains one of the largest in the Middle East outside Israel itself, although significant Jewish minorities remain in other Middle Eastern countries as well.[100] A number of recent studies have suggested major cultural similarities between Moroccan Muslims and Jews. As Rosen writes, the status of Jews in the Middle East has historically differed significantly from the status of Jews in Europe and has in some ways been superior. Through the advent of French colonial rule in Morocco, Jews were scattered throughout the country. Many were in larger towns, where they often, but not always, lived in separate quarters called *mallāh*-s; in many of the smaller centers, regions of Jewish residence were not so sharply set off from their Muslim neighbors.[101] Jews practiced a range of occupations—they were butchers,

---

[99] On the shaping of these French colonial assumptions and their impact upon Moroccan society, see Edmund Burke III's excellent "The Image of the Moroccan State in French Ethnological Literature: A New Look at the Origin of Lyautey's Berber Policy," in Gellner and Micaud, *Arabs and Berbers*, pp. 175-99; Kenneth Brown's "The Impact of the Dahir Berbère in Salé" in the same volume, pp. 201-15; and Charles F. Gallagher, "Language and Identity," in *State and Society in Independent North Africa*, ed. Leon Carl Brown (Washington: The Middle East Institute, 1966), pp. 73-96.

[100] Lawrence Rosen provides the following estimates as of the late 1960s for the Jewish populations of various Arab countries, together with the estimates (in parentheses) of the 1948 populations. "Morocco: 45,000 (225,000); Tunisia: 12,000-14,000 (100,000); Lebanon: 4,000; Syria: 2,500-4,000 (30,000); Iraq: 3,500 (130,000); Algeria: 2,000 (140,000); Egypt: 1,000 (80,000); Yemen: 1,000 (70,000); Libya: nil (35,000). Rosen, "Muslim-Jewish Relations," p. 436, where the sources of these estimates are cited. For Iran, Laurence D. Loeb, *Outcast: Jewish Life in Southern Iran*, Library of Anthropology (New York: Gordon and Breach, 1977), p. 4, provides the contemporary estimate of 85,000, most of whom reside in Tehran. Figures for the late 1970s, if available, would indicate a smaller Jewish community in most cases. For example, Morocco's Jewish population is now estimated to be 25,000.

[101] See Dale F. Eickelman, *Moroccan Islam: Tradition and Society in a Pilgrimage Center*, Modern Middle East Series, 1 (Austin and London: University of Texas Press, 1976), pp. 45-48, 78.

sellers of charcoal, shoemakers, artisans in gold and silver, money-changers, grain traders, cloth merchants, and itinerant traders in rural regions.[102] Various European Jewish organizations made contact with Jews in Middle Eastern countries in the 1880s, and eventually the Europeans set up Jewish schools and community services of various sorts.

As a consequence of these early efforts and the provision of separate schools for Jews with the establishment of the French protectorate in Morocco, the Jews had a competitive edge in commerce, often serving as the local representatives for European commercial interests and as minor functionaries in the protectorate administration. By the 1930s, primary education of a European sort became almost universally available to the Jewish community, while in the same period fewer than 2 percent of Moroccan Muslims had access to such education. After 1948 large numbers of Jews began to emigrate, especially from the smaller communities of the interior. A larger wave of emigration, however, began with Morocco's independence in 1956, with wealthier, educated Jews tending to emigrate to North America (especially French-speaking Quebec) and France and those with fewer skills or connections to Israel.

Even during periods of serious crisis, such as during the Second World War when the Vichy regime sought to deport Morocco's Jewish population and that of Tunisia, North African Jews were protected. Morocco's Sultan reminded the French that formerly Morocco was a sovereign nation and that Moroccan Jews were his subjects and had his full protection. The consequence was that Jews of French citizenship were vulnerable and were subject to deportation but not Moroccan Jewish nationals. The same protection of Jews by the Muslim population occurred in Tunisia, and as late as the 1973 Arab-Israeli war, many Moroccan Muslims took steps to ensure the safety of Jewish households with which they had ties.[103]

Now what does the tenor of Muslim-Jewish relations in Morocco have in common with Arab-Berber relations? Rosen's answer is first to indicate ways by which persons in any society can categorize others, using Alfred Schutz's familiar categories of predecessors, successors, consociates ("persons . . . who actually confront one another in intimate face-to-face relations"), and contemporaries (who do not actually confront one another directly but who have a "structural" relationship through stereotyped and anonymous roles).[104] Various cultures emphasize differ-

---

[102] For a full account of the role of Jews in Morocco's bazaar economy, see Clifford Geertz, "Suq: The Bazaar Economy," in Geertz, Geertz, and Rosen, *Meaning and Order,* pp. 164-72.

[103] See Norman A. Stillman, "Muslims and Jews in Morocco: Perceptions, Images, Stereotypes," in *Proceedings of the Seminar on Muslim-Jewish Relations in North Africa* (New York: World Jewish Congress, 1975), pp. 13-39, especially the comments by Paul Raccah and Moise Ohana on pp. 28-29. See also Lawrence Rosen, "A Moroccan Jewish Community during the Middle Eastern Crisis," *The American Scholar,* 37, no. 3 (Summer 1968), 435-51.

[104] Rosen, "Arab-Berber Relations," p. 167; also his "Muslim-Jewish Relations," pp. 440-41.

ent types of relationships, and Rosen sketches some of the contrasts of Moroccan society, where there is a tendency for persons to seek to turn what Schutz calls ties with contemporaries into ties with consociates—that is, into total social relationships in which relationships with others are rendered stable and more or less predictable through the creation of multiple bonds of obligation. Other patterns predominate in cultures elsewhere, as in Bali where there is a tendency to turn personal relations into those of stereotyped anonymous contemporaries.[105]

Rosen writes that in Moroccan society in general (for "Berbers" as well as "Arabs" and for "Jews" as well as "Muslims"), personal obligations are not prescribed by kinship roles or any other roles. There is a wide, permissible latitude in how bonds, even of kinship, are expressed and a considerable flexibility in how an individual can "actually choose, or contract, particular kinds of relationships with his kinsmen just as, in the absence of strong sanctions to the contrary, he can contract such ties with outsiders. . . . Like ties of kinship, occupation, residence, and so on, inherent ties to other members of a particular ethnic division contribute to but do not wholly typify a given individual."[106]

Within this general framework the meaning of Berber identity becomes more apparent. Berbers are chiefly distinguished from other Moroccans by the fact that they speak a Berber dialect, but even this feature in itself says little of personal identity. Rosen then proceeds to consider patterns of occupation, residence, marriage, urban and rural origin, and other factors to show that distinctions in these

**FIGURE 7-3** Berber men and women, High Atlas region, Morocco. (Courtesy Robert A. Fernea.)

---

[105] See Clifford Geertz, "Person, Time, and Conduct in Bali," in *The Interpretation of Cultures* (New York: Basic Books, 1973), pp. 360-411. This essay was originally published in 1966.

[106] Rosen, "Arab-Berber Relations," p. 158.

areas do not coincide with languages spoken, as well as the modalities of political conduct and ordinary commercial transactions. His analysis bears out his assertion that Berber ethnicity is "only one among a series of factors operative in various situations, and that it serves as only one among a set of social identifiers."[107] It provides a minimalist, baseline identity when nothing else is known of an individual, but even in the mundane activities of buying and selling, Moroccans immediately proceed to seek to make the bonds of obligations with other individuals more multiplex. In hardly any context is identity as Berber or Arab "an all-pervasive typification in terms of which one views and relates to another person."[108]

Muslim and Jewish relations in Morocco must be considered from the same overall basis in which Moroccans culturally typify most interpersonal ties. As is the case in the distinction between Berbers and Arabs, it is not possible to differentiate Jews and Muslims in terms of the economic roles they play. The major distinctions are instead between urban merchants and Jews on the one hand, with the distinctive social roles they play, and persons of rural and Berber-speaking origin on the other, although even this distinction is not a sharp one. Nor are Jewish traders, artisans, and merchants treated differently in the marketplace than other participants.[109] There is, however, an element of differentiation. Rosen argues that Muslims as a group share a "sociological pool" of "prestige resources" in which there is an intense and open competition among persons which ranges from economic transactions to political and marital ties. Jews in Morocco are placed outside this sociological pool according to Rosen in the sense that few marital ties are possible and their participation in politics is indirect and restrained. Relations of Jews with the Muslim community, both Arab and Berber, were more purely those of financial transactions, without the open-ended competitive ramifications engendered by more diffuse relations among Muslims. As with most other social ties in Moroccan society, those between Muslims and Jews were highly personal; in addition, however, they were noncompetitive in all but the economic sense. Thus a traditional role of Jews was to act as economic intermediaries between townsmen and the rural, tribalized population in central Morocco. Rosen writes that Arabs and Berbers (and Jews) did not risk their social independence. Often the resulting ties could even be characterized as those of friendship. Even with the transformation of Muslim-Jewish relationships which occurred with rapid identification of part of the Jewish community with European ways and economic interests in the colonial period, Jews continued to be treated as face-to-face consociates rather than as "stereotyped contemporaries."[110]

Rosen's account of how the meaning of ethnicity should be evaluated and of

[107]*Ibid.,* p. 169.
[108]*Ibid.,* p. 171.
[109] Geertz, "Suq: The Bazaar Economy."
[110] Rosen, "Muslim-Jewish Relations," pp. 444-46.

**FIGURE 7-4** Interior of synagogue, Tunisia, 1972. (Courtesy Nicholas S. Hopkins.)

the relationship of ethnicity to other forms of social identity applies specifically to the Moroccan context, as ethnic (and sectarian) identity makes sense only when more fundamental and general Moroccan notions of collective identity are taken into account. Yet the strength of such an approach to the study of ethnic identity is in many ways independently confirmed elsewhere in the Middle East, notably by anthropological studies of the social and cultural context of "Oriental" Jews in Israel.

Briefly, here are some essential features of Israeli society as related to the situation of "Oriental" Jews, a term which I use here to designate Jews of North African or Middle Eastern origin, who emigrated to Israel or whose parents did so. Roughly half of Israel's Jewish population (about 15 percent of the population is Christian and Muslim) consists of Oriental Jews. Because the majority of such immigrants had little educational background and possessed traditional skills that were of minimal use in Israel, they usually were compelled to become manual laborers and agricultural workers. This reduced status and the strong secularizing influence of Israeli society put severe strains upon them. As an aggregate, such immigrants and their children have considerably less success than their counterparts of European origin; their unemployment rates are significantly higher, the number of cabinet members and members of the Knesset (Parliament) is significantly less than their numbers in Israeli society. The same holds true for the number of Oriental Jews in the upper ranks of the military and in the civil service.[111] Israelis are aware of the aggregate disparities between Oriental and European Jews, but it is clear that they are the result of deliberate discrimination. Yet the perception of these relations among Israeli Jews themselves indicates a significant intercommunal problem. In a public opinion poll taken just after the 1967 Six Day War, 84 percent of Israelis thought that intercommunal relations were good; this figure had dropped to 48 percent by 1971.[112]

What does this situation mean for the perception of ethnic identity among Oriental Jews, especially those of North African origin? As one Israeli anthropologist, Shlomo Deshen, reports, Israel's official immigration policies have been founded upon the notion of the absorption of refugee immigrants and encouraging them to think of themselves principally as Jews.[113] A common pattern has been that immigrants from North Africa at first tend to shed their traditional practices which mark them off from other Jews, but as they face the realities of adjustment in Israel they gradually resume some aspects of their particular identities, such as the publication of folktales and scholastic writings peculiar to their own communities, the support of particular immigrant associations, the production of unleavened bread *(matzot)* in forms unique to each of their communities, political support for candidates concerned principally with the problem of immigrants of North African origin, and maintenance of "local" religious practices such as pilgrimages to Jewish saints (in a manner analogous to the visits to maraboutic shrines among some of North Africa's Muslim population). At the same time, the identities which these immigrants seek to project are not simply reconstitutions of identities which they possessed prior to their arrival in Israel. In fact, many immigrants who previously thought of themselves principally as Moroccan, Yemeni, Iraqi, or southern Tunisian Jews now think of themselves in terms of a new category of ethnic identity, that of Orientals. Deshen concludes that the immigrants "are making a stand for certain elements of their culture which they have retained and want to nurture. They seek to identify themselves also in autonomous subethnic terms, but they want that identification to be within the bonds of their overarching identity

[111] For a discussion of intercommunal relations in Israel in the early 1970s, see Amnon Rubenstein, "Jewish Panthers and Other Problems," *Encounter,* 38, no. 6 (June 1972), 80-85.

[112] *Ibid.*

[113] Shlomo Deshen, "Ethnic Boundaries and Cultural Paradigms: The Case of Southern Tunisian Immigrants in Israel," *Ethos* 4 (1976), 271-94, and Shlomo Deshen and Moshe Shokeid, *The Predicament of Homecoming: Cultural and Social Life of North African Immigrants in Israel,* Symbol, Myth, and Ritual (Ithaca and London: Cornell University Press, 1974). See also Harvey E. Goldberg, "The Mimuna and the Minority Status of Moroccan Jews," *Ethnology,* 17, no. 1 (January 1978), 75-87. See also Shlomo Deshen, "Israeli Judaism: Introduction to the Major Patterns," *International Journal of Middle East Studies,* 9, no. 2 (May 1978), 141-69.

as Israelis."[114] These symbolic transformations of the meaning of ethnicity are comprehensive in terms of the specific historical circumstances in which they operate. Ethnic identities forged in other, earlier contexts in Tunisia, Morocco, and elsewhere are the base from which subsequent transformations of these systems of meaning occur: "The derivation is there, even if continuity is most tenuous and subtle; and often it is quite overt."[115]

Several conclusions can be drawn from the various studies of ethnic and sectarian identities discussed so far. First, ethnic identities, like linguistic, sectarian, national, family, and other forms of social definition can be comprehended only in the context of more general cultural assumptions made in a given society concerning the nature of the social world and social relationships. Sex roles, ethnicity, kinship and the like are all simultaneous components of social identity and cannot meaningfully be analyzed independently of more general shared underlying assumptions. Second, such identities must be analyzed in the specific historical contexts in which they are maintained, transformed, and reproduced, and not as blocklike units in an ahistorical mosaic. The theoretical points of departure of contemporary studies of ethnicity vary widely: from an emphasis primarily upon ethnicity as embedded in a system of social meanings (Rosen and Deshen) to ethnicity and sectarianism as principally a product of global economic and political circumstances (most of the contributors to the Joseph and Pillsbury volume). Nonetheless, the majority of the current studies recognize that research into notions of identity entails attention to both cultural meanings and the practical contexts in which they are produced. Anthropologists like other scholars concerned with social theory are not in a position to produce comprehensive schema for indicating the precise interrelationships between economic and political transformations and the ideologies of society and social identity maintained in them. But they recognize that both of these dimensions must be carefully analyzed and that systems of meaning cannot be treated as if they were unchanging, as they have been treated in the past and have sometimes been presumed to be in "native" ideologies. A final observation might be treated as a corollary to the above. Ethnic distinctions, like those of region, sect, sex, language, and even tribe, are not necessarily being erased, as an earlier generation of analysts once facilely assumed, but provide the base from which newer social distinctions are forged and maintained.[116] Even when there is a popular consensus or a desire among intellectual and political leaders to facilitate the reshaping of identities and responsibilities, be these in muting the importance of ethnic or sectarian identities or transforming the roles of women and men in society, the point of departure from which such transformations are made must be considered

---

[114] Deshen, "Ethnic Boundaries," p. 292.

[115] *Ibid.*, p. 293.

[116] Clifford Geertz, "The Integrative Revolution: Primordial Sentiments and Civil Politics in the New States," in *Old Societies and New States: The Quest for Modernity in Asia and Africa,* ed. Clifford Geertz (New York: The Free Press, 1963), pp. 105-57.

in assessing their direction and tenor.[117] Some governments and political leaders often seek to ease possible tensions that arise from making such group definitions by denying their existence, but it would appear more reasonable to recognize them for what they are and constructively seek to harness them. Shared notions of community by ethnic group or region often can provide the basis of trust and solidarity necessary for effective functioning of and participation in modern industrial society.[118]

[117]This point was made with respect to sex roles by Daisy Hilse Dwyer, "Ideologies of Sexual Inequality and Strategies for Change in Male-Female Relations," *American Ethnologist,* 5, no. 2 (May 1978), 227-40.

[118]See Alan Dubetsky (Duben), "Kinship, Primordial Ties, and Factory Organization in Turkey: An Anthropological View," *International Journal of Middle East Studies,* 7, no. 3 (July 1978), 433-51, and also his "Class and Community in Urban Turkey," in *Commoners, Climbers and Notables,* ed. C. A. O. van Nieuwenhuijze (Leiden: E. J. Brill, 1977), pp. 360-71.

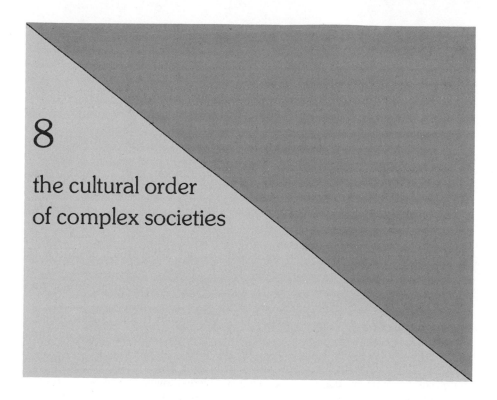

# 8

# the cultural order
# of complex societies

## WORLD VIEW

Institutions such as kinship, community, tribe, responsibility, and trust are subjectively held ideas about social relations shared by members of a society and embodied in rules, customs, symbolic actions such as ritual, and most everyday actions. Such patterns of meaning have been analyzed by some anthropologists as parts of formal systems of classification and symbol systems. For some purposes a formalist approach which is not concerned with social action is entirely legitimate. A complementary approach, emphasized throughout this book, focuses upon how meanings emerge from a social practice.[1] Patterns of meaning are generated in the everyday world of social experience, shape that experience, and in turn are modified by it. This emphasis upon the production of meaning through practice (*praxis* in the vocabulary of some theorists) sets apart most contemporary analyses of *world view* (shared cultural assumptions concerning the nature of the social world) from those earlier studies that were primarily concerned with the "logical fit" among the key symbols of a cultural tradition. Notions of world view overlap with and build upon more specific conceptions such as family, community, ethnicity,

[1] The complementarity of these two approaches is emphasized by Michael Gilsenan, "Lying, Honor, and Contradiction," in *Transaction and Meaning: Directions in the Anthropology of Exchange and Symbolic Behavior,* ed. Bruce Kapferer, ASA Essays in Social Anthropology, 1 (Philadelphia: Institute for the Study of Human Issues, 1976), pp. 191, 214.

and sexuality discussed in Chapters 5 through 7, but differ in that they are more explicitly integrative and comprehensive.

The idea that cultural meanings are socially produced has been introduced in the last few chapters through the discussion of specific topics such as tribe, kinship, the use of genealogies, sex roles, and ethnicity. I have stressed that these specific topics can be comprehended analytically only through the matrix of social definitions of reality through which everyday life and actions become subjectively meaningful to Middle Easterners themselves. The elaboration of concepts of world view in the Middle East, as opposed to how world views (or *cosmologies,* as many English anthropologists use the term) are represented in "primitive" societies, is in the context of historically known societies. The concepts which comprise particular systems of meaning, by being considered Islamic or otherwise universal, are not contained by the frontiers of any particular country, tribal group, or other social division. These concepts change historically in relation to the political and economic circumstances in which they are elaborated; any accounting of them must take account of the patterns in such variations.

As with any sociological study, prior approaches to the understanding of world view or, as it has often been called in the past, "national character," must also be taken into account. In the past, the national character of a particular region was sometimes considered to be virtually unchanging. The attitudes and practices of Egyptian peasants of the twentieth century were thought to be nearly directly similar to those of Pharaonic times.[2] Such portraits of changelessness could be used to justify colonial domination. French colonial ethnographers drew upon those elements of European social thought which emphasized the fixed "primitive mentalities" of certain populations as one means of legitimizing the colonial enterprise. Handbooks prepared for European teachers of Moroccan children emphasized the fixed values and traditions of Moroccans, disregarding the impact of European domination and economic penetration. Such guides advised that "respect" for religious and social beliefs and practices required European teachers to limit what they conveyed to their students, so that education could not be used as a means of transforming what was conceived to be the "traditional" social hierarchy, the status of women, or other sensitive topics.[3] France's "civilizing mission," to use the phrase of the epoch, had its clear limits. Comparable accounts of "Oriental" character were prepared for areas under English colonial domination. As Edward Said and others rightly insist, the "mosaic" representations of Middle Eastern societies that deliberately avoid discussion of the impact of political and economic changes lend

---

[2] Winifred S. Blackman, *The Fellahin of Upper Egypt* (London: Frank Cass & Co. Ltd., 1968 [orig. 1927]); Henry Habib Ayrout, *The Egyptian Peasant* (Boston: Beacon Press, 1968). For a review of earlier studies, see Fouad M. Moughrabi, "The Arabic Basic Personality: A Critical Survey of the Literature," *International Journal of Middle East Studies,* 9, no. 1 (February 1978), 99-112.

[3] An example of such a guide is Louis Brunot, *Premiers Conseils [First Advice]* (Rabat: Ecole du Livre, 1934). Brunot was director of Muslim education in Morocco in the early 1930s.

themselves readily to such assumptions, as do vague assertions concerning the "Arab mind" or "Islamic thought."[4]

Contemporary anthropological discussions of world view are at once more ambitious and more limited in scope. They are more limited in that they do not assume that such representations are shared in quite the same way by all members of a given society, let alone from one end of the Arab and Middle Eastern world to the other. They do not purport to represent all implicit shared understandings, but only those most related to the comprehension of particular patterns of social action—the bazaar economy, kinship, participation in maraboutic ("saintly") cults, friendship, and lying, to mention only the specific examples that will be elaborated in this and later chapters.

The more ambitious aspect of contemporary analyses of world view is that they seek to articulate those taken-for-granted attitudes and values that make everyday social action possible; social conventions that are so deeply rooted that they flow *almost* automatically. As Lloyd Fallers has written, an anthropologist interested in analyzing such basic assumptions must learn to cultivate

> especially the receptive side of communication—the ability to spend most of one's time listening instead of speaking, watching instead of acting; he learns to remember and to record in great detail what he sees and hears. These are difficult disciplines requiring rigorous training for academic intellectuals, who usually would rather talk than listen and who find boring or repulsive what they see as the "trivia" of ordinary life, particularly in their own societies.[5]

Taken together, such "trivia" documents a set of "natural" assumptions concerning the social world. These assumptions, which are felt to be "natural" and not "conventional," are constructed and transformed through social practice and made up of everyday, incompletely systematized common-sense understandings of how the world "really" is.[6] Under ordinary conditions these basic assumptions form the implicit background against which social action is planned and carried out and are so taken for granted that they are not fully articulated by members of a society. Special frames of reference, such as formal religious ideologies, specialized knowledge of commerce and crafts, medicine, political strategies, and the interpretation of dreams, are elaborated against the background of such understandings.

Anthropologists have had different, albeit largely complementary, concerns

[4] See the discussion in Chapter 3 of this book, especially the critique of Carleton S. Coon, *Caravan: The Story of the Middle East*, rev. ed. (New York: Holt, Rinehart and Winston, 1961).

[5] Lloyd A. Fallers, *The Social Anthropology of the Nation-State* (Chicago: Aldine Publishing Company, 1974), p. 8.

[6] The notion of the "natural" attitude toward the social world is developed in Alfred Schutz, *Collected Papers, I: The Problem of Social Reality* (The Hague: Martinus Nijhoff, 1967), and in Clifford Geertz, *The Interpretation of Cultures* (New York: Basic Books, Inc., 1973).

in the elaboration of systems of world view. Some scholars have been particularly concerned with the logico-meaningful relations among the cultural assumptions which comprise particular world views. Others, while not neglecting this task, have paid particular attention to analyzing how such basic assumptions toward the social world are related to changing economic and political conditions. Because such implicit understandings are not fully systematized they cannot be represented as neatly organized "cognitive maps"; there *is* a meaningful fit among the assumptions which comprise particular world views, but the fit is best represented as jagged and uneven. In any case, what we hypothesize about any particular world view is documented by the fragmentary and often inconsistent outward actions and statements of persons in a given society. The ultimate test of an adequate description of world view, therefore, consists of its ability to render intelligible wide varieties of behavior in a given society. Many recent studies have sought to depict such matrices of cultural meaning and to place them in the context of historical and sociopolitical change. An assessment of the basic approaches used in the study of world view serves to tie together the discussion of the preceding three chapters and forms an essential backdrop to the discussion in later chapters of religion, politics, and the economy.

## MOROCCO: GOD'S WILL, REASON, AND OBLIGATION

Several anthropologists have used their various ethnographic studies of Morocco in the 1960s and early 1970s as a basis for exploring complementary aspects of the notions of world view and culture. Most of the resulting publications have also addressed wider issues, so they form a useful point of departure for discussing the theoretical significance of ideas of world view and their importance to the study of the Middle East.

A brief analysis of the relevant sections of my *Moroccan Islam* suggests some of the decisions facing an anthropologist in any discussion of world view. In that study, I sought to indicate the implicit set of cultural assumptions through which Moroccans make sense of the local interpretations of Islam and of transformations in these interpretations, especially over the last century. I worked with the initial assumption, shared for the most part with the participants in the study of Sefrou and its region—Clifford Geertz, Hildred Geertz, Lawrence Rosen, and Paul Rabinow —that Morocco's social structure was best conceived with *persons* as its fundamental units, rather than their attributes or status as members of groups.[7] More-

---

[7]Monographs or book-length essays elaborating such notions include Clifford Geertz, *Islam Observed* (New Haven and London: Yale University Press, 1968); Clifford Geertz, Hildred Geertz, and Lawrence Rosen, *Meaning and Order in Moroccan Society: Three Essays in Cultural Analysis* (New York: Cambridge University Press, 1979); Dale F. Eickelman, *Moroccan Islam: Tradition and Society in a Pilgrimage Center,* Modern Middle East Series, 1 (Austin and London: University of Texas Press, 1976); Paul Rabinow, *Symbolic Domination:*

over, persons are not arranged in layerlike strata or classes but are linked in dyadic bonds of subordination and domination which are characteristically dissolved and re-formed. The relatively stable element in this type of social structure is not the patterns that actual social relations form but the culturally accepted *means* by which persons contract and maintain dyadic bonds and obligations with one another.[8]

How is such an implicit notion of the social order made to appear natural and taken-for-granted to Moroccans themselves?[9] In a chapter entitled "Impermanence and Inequality: The Common-Sense Understanding of the Social Order," I sought to delineate five of the key concepts through which Moroccans comprehend social experience. These five concepts were God's will *(qudrat Allāh)*, reason *(ᶜqāl)*, propriety *(hshūmīya)*, obligation *(haqq)*, and compulsion *(ᶜār)*.[10] The emphasis given to these five concepts rather than others was admittedly arbitrary in the sense that any description of world view is largely shaped by the range of social action that it attempts to render meaningful. Had my study concerned notions of sexuality rather than religious ideologies, for example, then emphasis would have been placed on other sets of Moroccan concepts that in my account were treated only in a subordinate fashion.

There is a problem of boundaries to these concepts in two senses. In the first sense, I deliberately used the term *Moroccan* rather than the name of the particular locale in which I worked, for my experience in research elsewhere in Morocco (and in trying out my formulations on interested Moroccans) suggested that with regional nuances, the same ideas applied elsewhere and in all likelihood did not stop abruptly at the country's frontiers. Indeed, many of the basic Moroccan assumptions concerning the social world are expressed in the form of Islamic ideas that are hardly unique to Morocco or to North Africa.

In the second sense of boundary, the concepts which comprise a world view are not in a fixed relation to one another. They are maintained insofar as they are actualized by individuals and meaningfully explain and render coherent action in the social world. When they cease to do so, they shift in emphasis. This flexibility accounts for their ability to accommodate and accounts for major shifts in the loci

---

*Cultural Form and Historical Change in Morocco* (Chicago and London: The University of Chicago Press, 1975); John Waterbury, *North for the Trade: The Life and Times of a Berber Merchant* (Berkeley and Los Angeles: University of California Press, 1972); and Kenneth L. Brown, *People of Salé: Tradition and Change in a Moroccan City, 1830-1930* (Cambridge, Mass.: Harvard University Press, 1976).

[8]This formulation is derived from a fuller discussion of the notion in my *Moroccan Islam*, p. 90, which contains references to the related work of other scholars.

[9]I specify *implicit* because a number of Moroccan intellectuals write of their own society in terms of the principles of class analysis. For a discussion of the limitations of an uncritical borrowing of the notion of class from European ideological contexts, see A. R. Dubetsky (Duben), "Class and Community in Urban Turkey," in *Commoners, Climbers and Notables,* ed. C. A. O. van Nieuwenhuijze (Leiden: E. J. Brill, 1977), pp. 360-71.

[10]The discussion of these notions is adapted from Eickelman, *Moroccan Islam*, pp. 123-54. (Courtesy of the author and the publisher.)

of economic and political power. Notions such as *God's will* and *reason,* for instance, have rich historical layers of meaning and are used elsewhere in the Muslim world. Both of the terms occur in the Quran and have been the subject of an interesting study of the world view of seventh-century Arabs, as well as an account of changing perceptions of the world in northern Sumatra.[11] The occurrence of these terms in Morocco is not unique, but they appear in a different semantic field, although in ordinary contexts most Moroccans never consider the possibility that these notions could be understood in any way but their own. Indeed, the fact that these implicit notions are tacitly construed by Moroccans as Islamic, as well as human universals, makes the resulting vision of the world all the more reasonable and compelling to them.

Let me briefly sketch how these key notions articulate with each other. God's will is a basic notion for Moroccans. Any expression of future actions or events is almost inevitably prefaced by saying "if God wills" *(in shā' Allāh),* which is also tied to the notion of "that which is written" *(maktūb).* French colonial ethnography glossed this notion as "Islamic fatalism," suggesting a Moroccan passivity and resignation toward the events of this world. This interpretation was congruent with the colonizing power's image of Moroccans but is almost exactly opposite to the way in which Moroccans themselves implicitly use the term. Let us consider the notions of social structure described earlier. For Moroccans, the inequality of men in this world is so matter-of-fact as not to be a matter of speculation. The actual state of affairs in this world at any moment is a manifestation of God's will; being inevitable, it cannot be questioned. An understanding of one's present social situation in terms of God's will legitimizes the momentary—and ephemeral—distribution of social honor as the God-given state of affairs. Men are free to take the world as it is and to determine action on the basis of their empirical observations. God's will attenuates speculation on why *particular* projects succeed or fail and blocks metaphysical speculation on the fate of the individual in this world. The wide-awake, common-sense person is much more concerned with adjusting to circumstances as they arise than with considering how things might have been or should be. Provisionality, the acceptance of God's will, thus focuses attention upon assessing exact differentials of wealth, success, power, and social honor among particular men as a prelude to effective, specific social action, not upon speculation over the general order of the world. A corollary to this notion is that the responsibility of persons for one another is limited. There are abstract, normative obligations incumbent upon each Muslim, but how the obligations which arise from particular ties are valued varies significantly. Here is how one educated Moroccan explained to me the limits of one person's responsibility toward another:

> God created differences among people. . . . Let people do as they want. God
> distinguishes between them. A Muslim's duty is just to show people the path

[11] Toshihiko Izutsu, *God and Man in the Koran* (Tokyo: Keio Institute of Cultural and Linguistic Studies, 1964); and James Siegal, *The Rope of God* (Berkeley and Los Angeles: University of California Press, 1969).

to those who wish to be with God, and that is that. Either they take it or they leave it. The Prophets allow them the choice. There is paradise and there is hell, and God will select who goes to each.[12]

Linked to the notion of God's will is that of *reason,* a notion already introduced in the discussion of sexuality in Chapter 7. In Morocco and elsewhere in the Muslim world, the concept of reason is more explicitly tied to social context than is our own use of the term. Reason in the Moroccan context is primarily the capacity to discern the meanings of the actions of other people and, on the basis of such perceptions, to engage in effective social action. Reason signifies adroitness or cleverness (without the pejorative English connotations of these terms) more than a capacity for dealing with abstract rational phenomena. Its possession assumes a capacity to perceive the empirical ties between persons and to adapt them to one's own interests as best as possible, within the shared code of conduct of society. Reason enables a person to perceive what will pass as acceptable and approved conduct in the management of social obligations to kinsmen, neighbors, merchants, clients, men of influence, and men without.

The word for reason, $^c q\bar{a}l$, comes from an Arabic root which also means "confinement" or "control." It implies an ability of persons to dominate their passions and to act as Muslims. Children are said not to possess reason because they do not yet know the Islamic law and code of conduct. Although Moroccans are highly affectionate toward their children, they say that at birth children are like animals, because only gradually do they acquire the code of conduct and the ability to abide by it that distinguishes them from animals. As children begin to participate in the fast of Ramaḍān and to assume adult patterns of comportment, they are attributed with reason. Similarly, as was pointed out in Chapter 7, reason is popularly considered to be more fully developed in men than in women. This is not due entirely to any innate masculine capacity but to the fact that women's activities are confined primarily to the household and its immediate milieu. Hence a woman's ability to engage in a wide range of social relations and to have full control over expression of her passions is considered to be less than that of a man. Some women are attributed a full capacity for reason, usually when high social class, education, or other circumstances enable them to participate effectively in the wider social world. One Moroccan explained the general difference between the sexes as follows:

A man will think. He sees a quarrel leading to [court]; he knows that the other man has more "pull" with the [court] than he does. He knows how to deal with people bigger and weaker than he is. A woman is light-headed. She doesn't know how to do these things. If she goes to the [government offices], who pays attention to her? Better that she stay at home, where she can teach her daughters to cook and sew. They don't know Islam like men do; they even have tricks to avoid fasting.[13]

[12] Cited in Eickelman, *Moroccan Islam,* p. 128.
[13] *Ibid.,* p. 133.

In the same way that women are collectively considered to be deficient in reason, townsmen often claim that tribesmen are deficient because of their relative lack of skill in dealing with the government and merchants.

The notion of reason is clearly linked to the Islamic code of conduct in the complex symbolism associated with Ramaḍān, the month of fasting. The ability of Muslims to follow the arbitrary pattern of the fast and to refrain (among other restrictions upon appetites) from food and drink from dawn to dusk for one month each year is taken as a key metaphor by which men can discipline their desires in accordance with the arbitrary code of conduct laid down by God. Men's capacity to follow the divine model reaffirms that they are not bound by their passions to live in a totally anarchic world. The five ritual daily prayers also symbolize the divine template for conduct, but Ramaḍān is recognized as a more intensive, sustained discipline of human nature and as an opportunity for the collective exercise of self-control that signals the possession of reason.

*Obligation (ḥaqq)* fits into the same pattern of comprehension of the social world. Men cannot control God's allocation of success and prestige, but they can render the actions of others more predictable by contracting and maintaining bonds of obligation. In the Moroccan context all exchanges, invitations to meals, services as intermediaries, and even offers of rides in a car are seen as obligations which must be reciprocated. Some obligations are minimally prescribed by Islamic law and "the way things are done," such as certain obligations toward kinsmen and communal religious ties. These obligations can be fulfilled within a wide latitude of acceptable conduct. Even exchanges of greetings, with their complex code of gestures and manners, impose obligations, since they publicly assert what one person would like the other, and observers, to think regarding their relations.

If a person repeatedly asks for a service to be rendered but is incapable of reciprocating, then he falls into a client relationship with the other person. The dominant partner in the relationship is said to hold an "obligation over" *(ḥaqq ᶜlā)* or "word" *(kalma)* over the other. The complex web of personally contracted bonds of obligation are always asymmetrical, just as all relationships impose obligations of calculable intensity. Exchanges of obligations can be very finely tuned. There is a carefully nuanced vocabulary for the discussion of gradations in them which depends upon a wide range of such factors as education, wealth, kinship ties, and networks of obligations held or thought to be held over others.

In general, the reasonable individual strives for flexibility in relations in which he is under obligation to others, while at the same time fixing as firmly as possible relations in which he holds obligations "over" other individuals. Since by God's will the social world is viewed as in constant flux, an individual strives to be as free as possible to change the weight of obligations within his personal network, yet to remain within the bounds of propriety *(ḥshūmīya)* or acceptable social conduct.

*Compulsion (ᶜār),* the fifth of the concepts which I sketched in my original presentation, is a special sort of impossible obligation which provides culturally accepted means of mending serious breaks in the web of obligations which bind men together. Essentially, it involves such a profound public effacement of the person or group seeking to oblige another to act in a certain way or to restore ordinary social relations so that refusal to accede risks divine punishment and severe social disapproval. (For examples, see pp. 132-33 and 185-86.)

Taken as a group, all of these five concepts are logically articulated with one another and form a major part of the backdrop against which social relationships are elaborated. There is nothing fixed about these assumptions; some people question them some of the time, but most of the time they are accepted as an adequate and necessary base for daily social conduct and the assessment of the actions of others. These interrelated notions as a group cannot be extended to cover other societies in the Middle East; although, as previously mentioned, some of the concepts figure elsewhere in modified form and in different conceptual contexts.

## NORTH AFRICANS IN ISRAEL

A particularly useful approach toward understanding how basic shared assumptions concerning the social world are modified is through the reanalysis of monographs concerning North African Jewish immigrants in Israel, a topic raised in a different context in Chapter 7. Israeli immigration policy has in many cases sought to "transplant" entire communities of North African Jews, so that villages in North Africa have been reconstituted in Israel and have clearly had to undergo rapid social and environmental change there.

An outstanding example of this genre of study is Moshe Shokeid's *The Dual Heritage.*[14] As opposed to some of Shokeid's later work, in which he is explicitly concerned with changing cultural values, *The Dual Heritage* is concerned primarily with *social* change, so some background is necessary to adapt his study to the present discussion of world view. Shokeid uses the sociological notion of *reference situation,* a complex of values appropriate to a past (or different) situation which continues to be used to discern social order in a novel context. The reference situation for the residents of the Israeli immigrant community he studied was their former village of some 350 persons, located in Morocco's High Atlas mountains to the east of Marrakesh. To specify the nature of what he terms the reference situation, Shokeid attempts to reconstruct the social organization of this community as it once existed.[15]

[14] Moshe Shokeid, *The Dual Heritage: Immigrants from the Atlas Mountains in an Israeli Village* (Manchester: Manchester University Press, 1971). See also Harvey E. Goldberg, *Cave Dwellers and Citrus Growers: A Jewish Community in Libya and Israel* (Cambridge: Cambridge University Press, 1972).

[15] An excellent traditional ethnographic account exists in French for a nearby Jewish community in the 1950s, prior to massive emigration. See Pierre Flamand, *Un Mellah en Pays berbère: Demnate,* Institut des Hautes-Etudes Marocaines, Notes et Documents, 10 (Paris: Librairie Générale de Droit et de Jurisprudence, 1952).

For an anthropologist who has studied contemporary Muslim communities in North Africa, the reanalysis of Shokeid's monograph is fascinating for what it reveals of similarities in shared notions of society between North African Muslim and Jewish communities. The Jewish community studied by Shokeid possessed a myth of how they came to be settled where they were in the High Atlas. He speculates that a quarrel may have led to the splitting apart in the nineteenth century of an earlier village. The event is recalled by the villagers in mythical form: A leading rabbi informed their ancestors not to emigrate to the new location until a fountain was discovered under a tree near the site where they later constructed their synagogue. An analogous type of settlement myth is told by Muslims in various parts of Morocco to account for the location of their villages.[16]

This particular North African Jewish village was surrounded by villages of Berber-speaking Muslims, and the social structure of the Jewish community appears to have significantly resembled that of their Muslim neighbors. Shokeid acknowledges that the memories of the past of the villagers now in Israel are somewhat idealized, so that their recollection of "permanent insecurity" is probably not quite accurate. However, the region was unquestionably insecure at the time of French entry into the area and later, at the announcement in late 1955 of Morocco's imminent independence, there was a threat of renewed disorder which contributed to the departure of most of the community for Israel in 1956.[17]

Shokeid's account of the internal differentiation of the community indicates that in the High Atlas mountains and later in Israel it was divided into patronymic groupings or agnatic clusters, each claiming descent from a common ancestor, a pattern also common to rural and urban Muslims in Morocco.[18] He states that in Morocco these groupings were stratified, with the one possessing the most influential political and economic contacts on the top, skilled itinerant craftsmen next, and the unskilled at the bottom.

On arriving in Israel, the settlers were first assigned to a settlement called *Yashuv*, organized by one of Israel's leading socialist parties. The first settlement did not succeed for a number of reasons. Representatives of several of Israel's religious parties told the Moroccan settlers that their sponsors were antireligious, would compel their daughters to serve in the army where they would lose their virtue, and would not allow their sons to study the Torah. Additionally there were scandals concerning the allocation of wage labor which resulted in demonstrations and some violence. In 1957 a large number of the settlers moved to Romema, another settlement in the Negev, the principal locus of Shokeid's field study.[19]

According to Shokeid's account, the villagers from the three principal patronymic groupings saw themselves as a single cooperating entity upon their

---

[16] Shokeid, *Dual Heritage*, p. 17; for a parallel Muslim settlement myth, see Eickelman, *Moroccan Islam*, pp. 163-68.

[17] Shokeid, *Dual Heritage*, p. 22.

[18] *Ibid.*, pp. 23-28. His use of *patronymic grouping* is essentially equivalent to the term *patronymic association* as used in Chapter 6 of this book.

[19] *Ibid.*, pp. 34-47.

arrival in the Negev. Yet their intention of communal cooperation collapsed when they began to dispute over the allocation of leadership positions. Shokeid argues that the traditional hierarchical stratification of the three patronymic groupings in Morocco broke down in the new situation of the Negev, which was more conducive to egalitarian relations. In fact, by 1958-1959, Israeli settlement officials thought of writing off Romema as a failure and again moving some of the villagers, but by then it was difficult to shift immigrants to new locations.

In reading Shokeid's intricate description of the political maneuvers for land allocations and political office in Romema, I was struck repeatedly by the similarity of his account to those of my own and others describing contemporary local politics in Morocco.[20] The principal alliances were not necessarily along the lines of patronymic groups but along the lines of any available kinship or other form of relationship which could be used as the basis for concerted action.[21] Shokeid acknowledges that kinship relationships in themselves did not necessarily induce cooperation. Only when there were other social links or economic factors or common economic interests did cooperation actually occur.

Perhaps the best indication of the villagers' notion of community is their conception of the committee which was organized to run their agricultural colony *(moshav).* The immigrants' use of Hebrew was admittedly imperfect, but the errors they made appear to have accurately reflected their conceptions. Shokeid explains that the proper way in Hebrew to refer to a member of the *moshav* governing committee was to call him *haveir va'ad,* "a member of the committee." The committee itself was *va'ad.* But the villagers consistently referred to this committee as *va'adim,* "committees," and to each committee member as *va'ad,* "a committee." The implication of this linguistic fact and of other documentation introduced by Shokeid was that each committee member in himself represented a committee. Shokeid's conclusion is that each committee member, instead of drawing his status from the fact that he belonged to the committee, contributed *his* status to the committee. He documents this interpretation through a detailed analysis of how the committee handled the allocation of water during a shortage.[22]

The situation in Romema which Shokeid describes is congruent with the Moroccan notion of social structure in which the basic components of social structure are persons rather than groups and in which the stable cultural element is the means by which persons secure bonds with each other. One of his key examples is an incident in which a member of a lower-status patronymic association kissed the cheek of a higher-status group member on Yom Kippur in a gesture implying "humility and observance of the Jewish moral code." The gesture deprived the higher-status person of the opportunity to demonstrate his superiority through a

[20]*Ibid.,* pp. 62-83; Lawrence Rosen, "Rural Political Process and National Political Structure in Morocco," in *Rural Politics and Social Change in the Middle East,* eds. Richard Antoun and Iliya Harik (Bloomington and London: Indiana University Press, 1972), pp. 214-36; Eickelman, *Moroccan Islam,* pp. 211-37.

[21] Shokeid, *Dual Heritage,* p. 71.

[22]*Ibid.,* pp. 118-29, 143-47.

public display of generosity and forgiveness. In fact, the upper-status man commented that the other man, "who had been his employee in Morocco, was now trying to lord it over him."[23] The entire incident, as with other incidents documented in Shokeid's account, easily makes sense in terms of the notions of obligation (and the constant renegotiation of social status implied by the manipulation of obligations) and the notion of compulsion as they are comprehended in the context of Morocco. Other accounts of immigrant communities of Moroccan origin in Israel, although not intended as analyses of underlying cultural assumptions, also imply similar background values.[24]

Let me suggest what I regard to be an appropriate reinterpretation of Shokeid's analytic framework, made possible by the quality of his ethnographic documentation. Shokeid concentrates upon idealized patterns of social interaction and tends in *The Dual Heritage* not to analyze underlying cultural values. Significantly, although he occasionally refers to past conflict and strife, he gives no elaborate examples of them. By juxtaposing an idealized past to a present in which the lines of conflict do not follow normative statements concerning the unity of patronymic groups, he concludes that the immigrants suffered a "breakdown" of their prior community.[25] I would alternatively argue that Shokeid's account demonstrates a marked continuity of values and of assumptions concerning interpersonal obligations, an interpretation supported by his passing remark in the conclusion that most Romemites were "fairly modern" in their economic comportment (and adaptation to political life in Israel), despite the fact that "on the whole, their value system hardly changed" and that the "new" forms of behavior were legitimized "within the traditional set of norms."[26]

## THE MARKET AS A CULTURAL FORM

A particularly intensive discussion of the economic dimension of cultural values is contained in a recent study of the bazaar (*sūq* in Arabic) economy of a Moroccan town by Clifford Geertz.[27] The strategy of discussing economic activities as opposed to religious or political ones as a means of furthering cultural analysis is particularly appropriate because some economists still treat economic activity as if it were isolable from cultural considerations. Geertz's intention is to sketch the bazaar as a theoretical notion implying certain processes as general as those

[23]*Ibid.*, pp. 152-53.

[24]For example, see Emanuel Marx, *The Social Context of Violent Behaviour: A Social Anthropological Study in an Israeli Immigrant Town* (London and Boston: Routledge & Kegan Paul, 1976), pp. 63-74. What Marx calls "appealing violence" bears significant parallels with the Moroccan notion of *compulsion*.

[25]Shokeid, *Dual Heritage*, p. 62.

[26]*Ibid.*, p. 230.

[27]Clifford Geertz, "Suq: The Bazaar Economy in Sefrou," in Geertz, Geertz, and Rosen, *Meaning and Order*, pp. 123-313.

associated with the ideal type of "industrial" and "primitive" economies. He concurrently treats the bazaar as a concrete institution situated in a particular cultural and historical setting.[28]

As a cross-cultural type, the bazaar economy possesses a number of distinctive characteristics that set it apart from other economic forms. Among them is the prevalence of small-scale enterprises with an intense division of labor, the lack of standardization of products, weights and measures, the preference for partnership agreements over employer-employee ones, the importance of negotiating skills (which predominate over managerial or technical ones), weak or informal government controls, the lack of hierarchical coordination of enterprises, the exploration of economic possibilities in depth with a few selected trading partners rather than a diversity of them, and the personal contract as the main form of legal relationship.[29] The information needed to function effectively in the bazaar is "generally poor, scarce, maldistributed, inefficiently communicated, and intensely valued."[30] The search for information is so important a characteristic of the bazaar that "a great deal of the way in which the bazaar is organized and functions . . . can be interpreted as either an attempt to reduce such ignorance for someone, increase it for someone, or defend someone against it."[31] Consequently the principal prob-

**FIGURE 8-1** Commercial street near market, Sefrou, Morocco. (Courtesy of the author.)

[28] Clifford Geertz, "Suq," p. 124.
[29] *Ibid.*, Table 13, pp. 214-15.
[30] *Ibid.*, p. 124.
[31] *Ibid.*, p. 125.

lem for participants in the bazaar economy "is not balancing options but finding out what they are."[32] Thus ignorance is a known (or known about) characteristic of the bazaar, not just a matter of some participants lacking certain information, and buyers and sellers are aware of this fact. Geertz emphasizes that these various characteristics of the bazaar are not random occurrences but imply each other and together form a coherent system.

Bazaar economies are found in a number of different social historical and cultural settings—Iranian, Moroccan, Chinese, Indonesian, and Mexican, to suggest only a few. Despite their overall similarity in some respects, Geertz's major argument is that there are equally important differences which make it imperative to comprehend each bazaar economy in its particular cultural setting. In the Moroccan case, his argument is that the bazaar is enmeshed in at least three key institutional frameworks. These are detailed in Geertz's presentation, so here it is necessary merely to suggest their wide scope. First is the involvement of the bazaar economy with the "ethniclike" distinctions of *nisba* identity, discussed in Chapter 7, in which a person can be referred to by a number of overlapping attributes of origin, craft, membership in a religious brotherhood, or other characteristics.[33]

Second is the association of the bazaar economy with popular Islam. One aspect of this association is the system of pious endowments *(ḥabus)*. Many urban shops are *ḥabus* properties, whose revenues are used for various religious activities. The Ministry supervising these endowments is one of the town's largest landowners.[34] A principal benefit of these *ḥabus* holdings to the trading community is that the rents for these properties are kept well below market value, largely because of the wishes of the trading community itself. Another aspect of the ties between bazaar and Islam is that the practice of many crafts and trades is associated with participation in certain religious orders, and the fortunes of both appear to have prospered in the period of the late nineteenth and early twentieth centuries when the "region-focusing" bazaar economy in the town studied by Geertz began to crystallize and prosper.

A final consideration spelled out by Geertz was the role of the Jewish community in Sefrou in connecting the regional market of the town with local ones around it. Jews, many of whom were involved in commerce, constituted 40 percent of the Sefrou population toward the turn of the century. In the marketplace, as stated earlier, the activities of Jews were not distinguishable from those of Muslims. Yet there were two distinct roles played by Jewish participants in the trading community. One was to serve as intermediaries in the form of itinerant traders between Berber-speaking tribesmen of the Middle Atlas mountains and the Arab speakers of the plains. The other was for a few of the wealthier Jews both to control the marginal Jewish traders and to serve as sources of financing for the

---

[32] *Ibid.,* see also Fuad I. Khuri, "The Etiquette of Bargaining in the Middle East," *American Anthropologist,* 70, no. 4 (August 1968), 698-706.

[33] Clifford Geertz, "Suq," pp. 140-50.

[34] *Ibid.,* p. 151.

FIGURE 8-2 Itinerant Jewish vendor of clothes and cloth goods (foreground) at market, Tunisia, 1972. (Courtesy Nicholas S. Hopkins.)

bazaar economy, before moving on to the economic opportunities later provided by association with "modern" European commerce in the period of the French protectorate. Geertz merely speculates on why Jews may have filled this intermediary role. He writes that part of the answer may have been their relative political impotence, meaning that their ambitions could be expected to be confined to the economic domain.[35] Geertz's emphasis throughout is upon patterns of "fit" between institutional arrangements and their associated cultural values.

A final, and crucial, element of Geertz's account involves study of the vocabulary used by Moroccans for speaking about and making sense of life in the bazaar. For Geertz, "the flow of words and the flow of values are not two things; they are two aspects of the same thing."[36] Notions of "news," "crowds," "trust," "friendship," "validity," "custom" and "convention," "reason," "understanding," and other key terms are presented and analyzed as a means of invoking the "conceptual world" through which the activities of the bazaar are carried out.

In sketching the principal features of Geertz's approach to the analysis of the Moroccan bazaar as cultural form, little has been said of the social historical context in which such activities take place. On the one hand, his ethnographic presentation documents historical transformations of the political and economic contexts in which the bazaar economy existed as meticulously as oral history and written sources allow. On the other hand, Geertz states that since 1900 "the cultural framework within which the homely business of buying and selling proceeds, the conceptual structure that gives it point and form, has altered but in detail."[37]

[35]*Ibid.*, p. 170.
[36]*Ibid.*, p. 199.
[37]*Ibid.*, p. 139.

FIGURE 8-3 "The flow of words and the flow of values are not two things; they are two aspects of the same thing." Market street, Mutrah, Sultanate of Oman. (Courtesy of the author.)

This may be so, but if indeed the "cultural framework" has remained so constant in the face of significant political and economic changes, then this is an important analytical insight of the nature of cultural values which deserves to be elaborated with the same intensity that Geertz applies to eliciting how the bazaar economy is comprehended and elaborated in the Moroccan context.[38] The silence of Geertz's analysis concerning how systems of cultural ideas change notwithstanding, his study remains a major contribution to comprehending the web of cultural meanings through which trading and associated activities in Morocco are carried out and provides an important complement to his studies of other dimensions of the concept of culture.

## LYING

The studies of world view considered so far in this chapter took the analysis of particular social institutions—Islam as popularly interpreted, community leadership, and the bazaar—as their point of departure. Gilsenan's study of lying *(kizb)* in

---

[38] In "Person, Time, and Conduct in Bali," an essay originally published in 1966 and reprinted in Geertz, *Interpretation of Culture,* p. 408, Geertz wrote that change occurs "rather like an octopus . . . by disjointed movements of this part, then that, and now the other which somehow cumulate to directional change." Octopoid analogies aside, Geertz recognized the problem of cultural change but chose not to give it central analytical importance, as is also the case with the study of the Moroccan bazaar.

Lebanon takes a key cultural concept as his point of departure and indicates how it is tied to and produced by social interaction. He argues that lying is a fundamental element of specific situations and individual actions which serves to restrict the social distribution of knowledge over time. Thus it is woven into the system of power and control present in any society. Its presence creates an uncertainty as to the precise degree of lying or truth present in a given situation.[39] The analogy with the "search for information" described by Geertz for Morocco's bazaar economy and associated institutions is evident.

Gilsenan explains that *kizb* is an everyday word in Lebanon and that from childhood on persons invest a good deal of time in learning the sport of deceiving others. But the practice of *kizb* would be misconstrued if read merely as a negative value or as wordplay. A constant theme in Lebanese society is recognition of an essential tension between "appearance" and "reality." *Kizb* possesses "its own aesthetic of baroque invention and is part of a style, of a wide range of variations on the cultural theme of appearance and reality, and is recognized at once [by Lebanese] for what it is." Here Gilsenan's approach indicates the anthropological rediscovery of how literature and the imagination are linked to cultural constructions of reality.[40]

Lebanese, writes Gilsenan, recognize that access to the true and real are through the Quran and the teachings of Islam, although men recognize that they spend much of their time ignoring it and actively lying. Echoing the phrase of Max Weber, he consequently sets out to document the "elective affinity" between the ideology of lying and social practice in northern Lebanon. He focuses upon the two domains of social honor and religious knowledge. In the domain of social honor, he first describes the social organization of Lebanese villages with the patterns of lords or strongmen (*zaᶜīm*-s) and their followers. The normative code of social honor in Lebanon is public and uncompromising in its simplicity. In normative terms, the line between honor and dishonor is sharply drawn and prescribes direct, violent action in the case of offense. In practice, to preserve a reasonable balance of social order, Gilsenan argues that Lebanese invest considerable effort in creating ambiguities over how situations can be defined. The collective exercise of *kizb* manages to avoid confrontation by preserving the appearance that public honor is satisfied so that social life can go on. Those who persist in defining situations in terms of challenge and response threaten collective interests and consequently tend to be ignored or redefined as hotheads or "mad" so that their definition of events can be disregarded.[41] A parallel situation exists in the domain of religious knowledge, where the perception of who are real men of learning or miracle-producing *shaykh*-s

[39] Gilsenan, "Lying," pp. 191-92.

[40] *Ibid.*, p. 193. This is a topic explored with special intensity in Michael Meeker, *Literature and Violence in North Arabia,* Cambridge Studies in Cultural Systems, 3 (New York: Cambridge University Press, 1979), through the analysis of Bedouin poetry and oral narratives and their relationship to notions of religious and political authority.

[41] Gilsenan, "Lying," pp. 211-12.

depends upon the judgments and attributions made by relevant others as to who *knows,* or can discern the apparent from the true.[42]

Gilsenan's discussion of lying, as with the other elaborations of Middle Eastern world views considered here, looks at complex social situations and the cultural values through which they are constructed. A particularly promising line of argument is his sustained attention to the practical elaboration of social meanings. In addition to evoking the "logical fit" between social action and meaning, he sets himself the ambitious task of at least pointing to the problem of what happens to meaning in circumstances of major political and economic change. He argues that the economic and political bases upon which traditional elaborations of social honor were based have been undercut in recent years. As leaders have managed to purchase more and more land to consolidate their position and tie others to them, families have lost their autonomy, so that competition over honor reflects less and less the realities of power and social structure. "The cars, tractors, and harvesters that [younger men] drive and the guns that they carry belong to others, not to them."[43] The ensuing notion of work becomes more a "false" consciousness which masks a situation that more and more persons consciously recognize. These matters are not just ones of style, Gilsenan concludes, for the "ultimate stake" is the definition of who you are, of self.[44]


## ETIQUETTE

In a practical sense, the best means of advancing discussion of the background conventions and assumptions that make possible the routines of daily life is through the analysis of concrete examples. It has been argued that each culture has at its core a set of common-sense assumptions about reality. These assumptions are usually not regarded as complete, but as sufficient to conduct the ordinary business of life. For this reason, turns of phrase, bodily movements, styles of dress, and patterns of etiquette are all valuable indicators of what these underlying assumptions are.

Within countries as complex as Lebanon, Iran, many of the Arab Gulf states, and Turkey, there is a recognizable diversity of personal and collective interests and beliefs, the commingling of which requires exercise of the virtues of civility, a collective self-restraint, and willingness to coexist with other persons and groups even if they do not share all basic assumptions about the conduct of daily affairs. Moreover, such basic assumptions are not fixed, and fortunately stereotyped metaphors such as "the Arab mind" and "the French mentality" are beginning to disappear from educated usage.

[42]*Ibid.,* pp. 208-9.
[43]*Ibid.,* p. 212.
[44]*Ibid.,* pp. 213-14.

Still, it remains true that there are styles of social conduct indicating such background assumptions specific to particular cultural groups. Anyone who has conducted international negotiations realizes that one of their most difficult components is not what is formally said but the informal nuances of what is *not* said formally that figure significantly into the development of or lack of common trust necessary for satisfactory agreement. Gestures and complexes of beliefs form coherent rhetorical patterns. To take several obvious examples, for Americans (except New Yorkers?), normal conversational distance is about 3-4 feet apart, with closer distances corresponding to greater degrees of intimacy and greater ones suggesting more formality. Deans, business executives, ambassadors, and other high-status persons often have large desks not out of practical necessity but implicitly to modulate distance with visitors. Such functionaries usually also have couches and less formal seating arrangements (and hidden liquor cabinets) which can set an appropriate tone of lesser formality upon occasion and convey this informality by distance and setting. Among most Middle Easterners, by contrast, normal conversational distance is closer than 2-3 feet, a proximity at which many Americans begin to feel uncomfortable. Male friends or even relative strangers on good terms in the Middle East and Mediterranean will frequently hold hands or touch during conversation, without such gestures conveying the sexual intimacy that they are often thought to convey in American contexts. Similarly, notions of time and how long a person can be kept waiting have cultural registers capable of subtle reading and orderly interpretation. Successful negotiators in international contexts tend to develop a flair for empirically comprehending such background assumptions; they may not possess the ability to articulate such assumptions, as is necessary for the anthropological analysis of them, but nonetheless acquire a practical mastery over them and over the delightfully complex problem of how these contrasting codes are practically intermingled.[45]

Older ethnographic accounts such as Lane's *Manners and Customs of the Modern Egyptians* remain valuable for analyzing such assumptions. His discussions of greetings, for example, can be easily reinterpreted so that his model of a rigid social hierarchy determining the forms of Cairene society can be replaced by one which indicates more clearly the niceties of social rank and its public expression.[46]

A more recent study of the etiquette of guest houses (*muḍif*-s) among the marsh dwellers of southern Iraq shows how rules for manners are closely related to social ranking and the Iraqi concept of person.[47] A few wealthy men have their own guest houses, but most are collective ones maintained by each lineage. These guest houses are the center for most male social life. Persons who attend the guest

---

[45] These attitudes toward the practical use of time and space are discussed by Edward T. Hall, *The Silent Language* (New York: Doubleday & Co., 1959).

[46] Edward William Lane, *An Account of the Manners and Customs of the Modern Egyptians* (New York: Dover Publications, Inc., 1973 [orig. 1836]), pp. 198-206.

[47] S. M. Salim, *Marsh Dwellers of the Euphrates Delta*, L.S.E. Monographs on Social Anthropology, 23 (London: The Athlone Press, 1962), pp. 72-80.

**FIGURE 8-4** Men of the "lower classes" (Lane's designation). (From Edward William Lane, *An Account of the Manners and Customs of the Modern Egyptians* [London: John Murray, Publishers, Ltd., 1860], p. 33.)

house are expected to attend fully dressed, with their head rope and outer cloak. One defers speaking before persons of higher status, and jokes and unnecessary laughter must be avoided in their presence. Even in the case of anger and major quarrels, those present are expected to speak clearly and calmly. Salim, the Iraqi ethnographer who has described the etiquette of guest houses, recounts that one day a man who had two quarreling sons ran to the headman of his lineage in the guest house and asked him to intervene. The man had entered with such great haste that he forgot his head rope and was unable to speak clearly. The headman listened to him, then criticized him for speaking in a confused way, adding insultingly, "I thought one of your old wives had run away with a lover." The underlying assumption is that in almost all social situations a respectable man is expected to show reason and self-control.[48]

[48] *Ibid.*, p. 77.

FIGURE 8-5 Tribal guest house *(mudif)*, southern Iraq. (From S. M. Salim, *Marsh Dwellers of the Euphrates Delta* [London: Athlone Press, 1962], plate 5A. Used by permission of the London School of Economics, the publisher, and Dr. S. M. Salim.)

Guest house etiquette in Iraq also clearly reveals relative social ranking. Each person sits in the place which corresponds to his social rank. High-status persons, such as descendants of the Prophet Muḥammad, sit in places of honor, usually set off by carpets and pillows. The senior elder or owner of a guest house shows his respect to an esteemed visitor or stranger by personally leading him to his proper place or ordering tea to be prepared for him as well as the usual coffee. When a man enters a guest house, those assembled show their respect by rising to their feet for those of higher status and merely making the gesture of rising for those of lesser status. Then each person present greets the newcomer, who responds separately to each greeting, rising or making as if to rise as each case merits. Overestimating a person's social status makes a newcomer look ridiculous; underestimating it is tantamount to insult. The whole procedure can be quite complicated, and adult Iraqi males are expected to have mastered these complexities. The search for "information" as described by Clifford Geertz is hence an essential prerequisite for effective social comportment. Questions of rank are not explicitly discussed, but their accurate perception forms a necessary component of social life. If, because of long absence, a man is uncertain as to his relative rank, he will sit at a lower-ranking place and wait for someone to correct him.

**FIGURE 8-6** Guest house etiquette is a key index of notions of person and value. Reception following opening of Quranic school near Nizwa, Sultanate of Oman, 1978. (Courtesy of the author.)

## IRAN: TAᶜĀRUF

Iranian social forms and etiquette provide a final and highly complex indication of how ideology and social institutions fit together and shape social reality. Iran, like other key Middle Eastern countries, has had generations of observers seeking to discern its central values in all-encompassing categories. A recent study sketches a tension for most Iranians between the opposing concepts of *zerangi,* which can be glossed as cleverness, shrewdness, insincerity, cynicism, and a lack of social responsibility, and *ṣafāyi bāṭin,* a term which implies integrity and an inner piety. The first characteristics are regarded ideologically as necessary to deal with an uncertain and treacherous world, in which social relationships outside of a narrow circle are unstable and subject to rapid flux. The second term implies an "inner" self, reserved only for a narrow circle of trusted intimates, which is more pure, constant, and which approaches spiritual ideals. In many of the studies of Iranian "national character" reviewed by Ali Banuazizi, such brief sketches of value tended to become psychological profiles with "universal applicability" to all Persians and as such were untenable.[49] Later studies have sought to indicate how such notions

[49] These early studies are reviewed with appropriate reserve in Ali Banuazizi, "Iranian 'National Character': A Critique of Some Western Perspectives," in *Psychological Dimensions of Near Eastern Studies,* eds. L. Carl Brown and Norman Itzkowitz (Princeton: Darwin Press, 1977), pp. 210-39. The *ṣafāyi bāṭin/zerangī* distinction is developed in M. C. Bateson, J. W. Clinton, J. B. M. Kassarjian, H. Safavi, and M. Soraya, "Ṣafā-yi Bāṭen: A Study of the Interrelations of a Set of Iranian Ideal Character Types," in *Psychological Dimensions,* eds. Brown and Itzkowitz, pp. 257-73.

inform and shape specific patterns of social practice and as such eliminate the assumption of fixity of earlier approaches.

A promising approach to the study of world view in complex societies is to analyze intensively the relation between conventions of social etiquette and social structure. This approach is particularly appropriate for Iran, where the conventions of etiquette *(ta$^c$āruf)* are pervasive. In English, *etiquette* connotes prescribed routine, an unwritten code of honor, and a set of conventions to avoid lowering the dignity of persons or professions. In Iran, according to Beeman, the notion entails a discipline of the inner self in the service of the public self.[50] Only in the most superficial manner can etiquette be "read" as insincerity or the use of empty forms. Indeed, in Iran, knowledge of and use of *ta$^c$āruf* (and of when to disregard its forms as well) appears linked to concepts analogous to *reason* as described for Morocco, in the sense that the possession of the "human refinements" of *ta$^c$āruf* are said to separate men from animals in Iran and those lacking such conduct are thought to be "childlike" regardless of their age or not in possession of their senses.[51] Thus the accurate use of etiquette can also be related to the control over and search for information described by Geertz in the context of the market and Gilsenan in the social implications of lying. The elaborate codes of hospitality found throughout the Arab peninsula, North Africa, and elsewhere in the Middle East can also in part be interpreted in the same manner.

The meaning of etiquette for Beeman is tied to exact stylistic variations employed in different contexts. In almost every case it involves the concealment (or the ability to conceal) true (or "inner") feelings or opinions. Such control is regarded as a highly positive public virtue. Beeman further argues that a careful analysis of the use of *ta$^c$āruf* indicates the shared notion of Iranians that the social order is inegalitarian and without reference to fixed rank or stratification. He argues that in Iran status is relative to specific situations of social interaction and that the weight of social obligations constantly shifts. The control and formal reserve of *ta$^c$āruf* enable persons to avoid overly committing themselves to one course of action or set of assumptions concerning social ranking that might prove difficult to maintain if the relative position of persons should shift at a later date.

James Bill has concisely described how such conventions are related to social forms.[52] He argues that despite the existence of some formal organizations in Iran, notably the state apparatus, the exercise of political power is played out primarily within networks of informal factions, cliques, coteries, and ad hoc collectivities of all sorts. These networks of personal coteries are called *dawra-s*. Each *dawra*—the word literally means "circle"—is an informal group of individuals who meet periodically, usually rotating the place of meeting among its members. These circles may

[50]William O. Beeman, "Status, Style and Strategy in Iranian Interaction," *Anthropological Linguistics*, 18 (1976), 305-22.

[51]*Ibid.*, p. 317.

[52]James A. Bill, "The Plasticity of Informal Politics: The Case of Iran," *The Middle East Journal*, 27, no. 2 (Spring 1973), 131-51.

be formed around any of a number of ties: professional, familial, religious, intellectual, political, or economic. This form of consociation has deep historical roots. Sufi mystics and darvishes, for instance, formed *dawra-s* with their disciples, and many of the groups regularly meet in coffee houses—Bill says there are perhaps 2,000 of them in Tehran alone. Among merchants and craftsmen in the bazaar, membership in *dawra-s* often partially overlaps with that of guild.

One reason for the pervasiveness of such informal organizations is the suppression of formal ones on the part of the prerevolutionary Iranian state and by all appearances the postrevolutionary one. Even when formal political parties exist, most Iranians assume that real access to authority is through informal channels. The existence of personal ties is considered more important than ideological preferences. *Dawra-s* tend to fragment and re-form as the interests of their members change, and most individuals belong to a number of these circles.

From the intimate circles around the Shah in the past and the informal coteries that surround Iran's present leaders to the level of informal village politics, the style of the *dawra* permeates Iranian political life. If a governor visits a village, villagers presume, and with reason, that a request to his driver, secretary, guard, or even his guests constitutes an effective intervention. Iranians expend a great deal of energy in determining how best to approach persons for a given request. Similarly, in the last days of the Shah, members of the foreign press corps were surprised to find announcements as to the Shah's intentions made by persons with no formal capacity but who, in retrospect, were the most reliable sources as to what was going on. The successive postrevolutionary governments have shown a similar lack of clear lines of organization.

The *dawra* makes sense in a setting where the cultural assumption is that "real" power does not flow from institution to institution, as suggested by the formal apparatus of government, but from person to person and groups of persons who effectively manage to impose their authority. The common force that unites the membership of *dawra-s* is a personal one; relationships that are not face-to-face and created out of multiple obligations are not as fully trusted. And as each person belongs to a multitude of *dawra-s,* information is rapidly passed among them.

The underlying conception of asymmetrical interpersonal relationship means that Iranians tend to assume that their survival and success depend upon their ability to cultivate the right personal contacts and to use those contacts to achieve their goals. That attitude in itself does not sharply distinguish Iranians from Americans. Informal "circles," "crowds," and "cliques" exist in every society and are always deeply involved in political ties and administrative functioning. The real difference rests in the degree to which such perceptions and social forms in societies such as Iran are formalized and taken to be normative. "Circles" are culturally recognized or even stressed in Iranian social situations and *also* given sense and legitimacy through connection to, and meaningful association with, fundamental ideas about "natural" social relationships. To draw a parallel between two Middle Eastern contexts, the Iranian term of *nazdīk,* which means "nearness" and which implies reliable close acquaintances, kin, or friends, has much the same contextual meaning as the North African notion of *closeness* introduced earlier in this book.

Another point made by Bill is that the Iranian assumption of the instability of social hierarchies is easily borne out in practice. In Iran's recent past, gardeners, water carriers, stableboys, and the children of drivers have all had excellent opportunities for advancement provided they perform their services close to men of power. There are just as many opportunities for decline, and the scramble for personal power takes these shifts into account. Bill recounts the anecdote of the prominent Iranian who clips obituaries from all the daily newspapers (which contain lists of who attends funerals) in order to fill in and change when necessary a huge chart to figure out the intricate links between the living. When he needs to get something done, he uses the chart to figure out the appropriate persons to contact.[53] Important families and persons at all levels of Iranian society try to spread their members over a number of key positions because of the assumption that all offices and ranks are unstable. Bill even goes so far as to say that Iranian basketball teams are handicapped by how players are selected—personal ties—and the lack of an adequate concept of teamwork, so that "teams" are thought of largely in terms of competing individuals.[54]

In such a social order, the seeming pleasantries of *tacāruf* acquire more significance. *Tacāruf* is a means of avoiding direct, decisive encounters in a political and social world considered with justice to be unstable. Pleasantries, courtesies, politeness, and flattery abound at every level of social encounter just as do uncertainty and doubt. Etiquette buffers opposing views, loosens actual lines of tension, and enables individuals to keep their options open to protect themselves against sudden shifts in political currents. Such styles are not immutable and of course have their limitations. Some forms of bureaucracy and industrial organization require high levels of technical competence and persons are selected on the basis of these professional skills alone, not just personal connections.[55]


CONCLUSION

Throughout this book and in the present chapter I have emphasized the necessity of considering the patterns of meaning and social practice as they are found in each Middle Eastern setting. Nonetheless, the analysis of ideology and social practice in situations as diverse as Morocco, Lebanon, Iraq, Iran, and Israel discussed in this

---

[53] *Ibid.*, 138. I have seen notebooks serving the same purpose kept by Moroccans.

[54] *Ibid.*, 139-40.

[55] Yet as Alan Dubetsky (Duben) demonstrates in "Kinship, Primordial Ties, and Factory Organization in Turkey: An Anthropological View," *International Journal of Middle East Studies,* 7, no. 3 (July 1976), 433-51, such personalistic ties can be highly functional in many modern industrial settings.

chapter suggests important points of "family" resemblance. It also suggests the importance of patterns of social order that would be given the approximate label of "informal" or even "nonstructured" in other contexts. Bill uses the term "plastic." Out of context, such labels can be taken as pejorative. Each of the studies analyzed in this chapter makes sense of such flexible and pragmatic patterns of social action in the context of cultural assumptions concerning the nature of the social world which both informs these actions and serves as guides to them. Finally, an examination of recent accounts of world view and of social identity point to a renewed anthropological interest in how the relation between meaning and social practice changes historically. This is in marked contrast to an earlier generation of anthropological studies and one essential to making sense of events in the Middle East today.

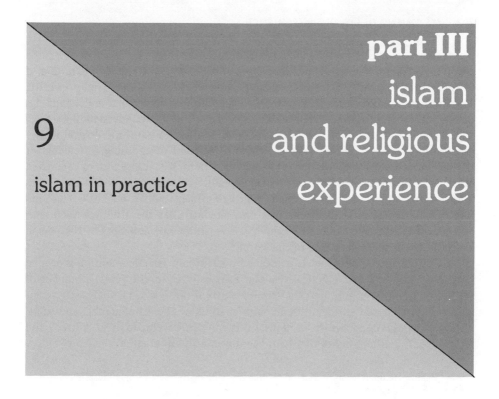

part III
islam
and religious
experience

9

islam in practice

## ISLAM AS A WORLD RELIGION

All major world religions face the problem of how to keep their key traditions vital and meaningful over long historical periods and in diverse contexts. By definition, world religions are not confined to one society or cultural tradition. They transcend specific cultures, including their own culture of origin. The formative ideals and the expression of religious truths at the core of each great religious tradition are considered to be eternal and immutable. Yet for these ideals and truths to maintain their sense of reality in a sociological sense, they must be capable of reformulation and reinterpretation so that they enter meaningfully into local value systems and changing social realities. As with other great religious traditions, Islam is rich and varied in its creativity and expression, so much so that many Muslims, especially those who adhere to certain reformist principles, have difficulty in accounting for the diversity of Islam as it has been expressed over 1,400 years and in the context of varied cultural traditions. As a result, some Muslim and non-Muslim scholars dismiss local practices which they think not to be in accord with "central" truths as non-Islamic or as incorrect understandings of Islam, even though persons who hold such beliefs consider themselves fully to be Muslims. One Muslim intellectual, despite the general richness and sensitivity of his account of the Islamic tradition, has gone so far as to dismiss all "mystical" and popular understandings of Islam not in accord with his own notion of Islamic tradition as being perpetrated by charlatans and "spiritual delinquents" and accepted only by the ignorant.[1] To account for these diversities, anthropologists in the 1940s introduced the notion of "Great" and "Little" traditions. When first applied, the Great Tradition/Little Tradition contrast had the effect of rekindling an interest in popular understandings of religion (among other social institutions) and placing these understandings in the wider context of complex societies; nonetheless, in many anthropological monographs this concept subsequently meant little beyond juxtaposing statements of Islamic principles as elaborated in standard Orientalist texts and by educated Muslims with inventories of local religious practices.[2] The study of "trance" and "possession" states has also suffered from being relegated to the Little Tradition side of the Great/Little divide so that only recently has the study of such rites become more clearly related to comprehensive studies of concepts of the person and to religious understandings of the world.[3]

Critical discussion of what is meant by Islam and Islamic tradition is needed both for analytical and practical reasons. Especially in recent years, a number of studies of Islam have appeared that combine attention to textual analyses, a venerable tradition in the study of Islam, with analysis of the ethnographic and social historical contexts in which notions of Islam are developed, transmitted, and reproduced.[4] Earlier studies of Islam, based primarily upon either the study of key

[1] Fazlur Rahman, *Islam,* 2nd ed. (Chicago: University of Chicago Press, 1979 [orig. 1966, p. 185], p. 153.

[2] See, for example, Harold B. Barclay, *Buurri al Lamaab: A Suburban Village in the Sudan* (Ithaca, N.Y.: Cornell University Press, 1964), pp. 136-210.

[3] See especially Vincent Crapanzano, *The Hamadsha: A Study in Moroccan Ethnopsychiatry* (Berkeley and Los Angeles: University of California Press, 1973); and also his "Introduction," in *Case Histories in Spirit Possession,* eds. Vincent Crapanzano and Vivian Garrison (New York: John Wiley & Sons, Inc., 1976), pp. 1-40.

[4] Clifford Geertz, *Islam Observed* (New Haven and London: Yale University Press, 1968); Ali Merad, *Le Réformisme musulman en Algérie de 1925 à 1940,* Recherches Méditerranéenes, Etudes, 7 (Paris and The Hague: Mouton & Co., 1967); Ernest Gellner, *Saints of the Atlas* (Chicago: University of Chicago Press, 1969); Abdallah Bujra, *The Politics of Stratification: A Study of Political Change in a South Arabian Town* (Oxford: Clarendon Press, 1971); Michael Gilsenan, *Saint and Sufi in Modern Egypt* (Oxford: University Press, 1973); Abdul Hamid M. el-Zein, *The Sacred Meadows: A Structural Analysis of Religious Symbolism in an East African Town* (Evanston: Northwestern University Press, 1974); Dale F. Eickelman, *Moroccan Islam: Tradition and Society in a Pilgrimage Center,* Modern Middle East Series, 1 (Austin and London: University of Texas Press, 1976), "Ideological Change and Regional Cults: Maraboutism and Ties of 'Closeness' in Western Morocco," in *Regional Cults,* ed. Richard P. Werbner, A.S.A. Monographs, 16 (New York and London: Academic Press, 1977), pp. 3-28, "The Art of Memory: Islamic Education and Its Social Reproduction," *Comparative Studies in Society and History,* 20, no. 4 (October 1978), 485-516; Emanuel Marx, "Communal and Individual Pilgrimage: The Region of Saints' Tombs in South Sinai," in *Regional Cults,* ed. Werbner, pp. 29-51; and John P. Mason, *Island of the Blest: Islam in a Libyan Oasis Community* (Athens, Ohio: Ohio University Press, 1977). Perhaps the best single study of the Islamic tradition to date is Marshall G. S. Hodgson's three-volume *The Venture of Islam: Conscience and History in a World Civilization* (Chicago and London: University of Chicago Press, 1974). Hodgson's text is difficult but essential. Two brief review essays concerning his study are useful complementary readings. These are Marilyn Robinson Waldman's review of *Venture,* which appeared in the *Religious Studies Review,* 2, no. 3 (July 1976), 22-35; and Edmund Burke, III, "Islamic History

religious texts or of certain types of religious experience (formal ritual of mysticism, for example), tended to concentrate upon the search for an Islamic "essence." This earlier analytic tradition, which is still vigorous, in part coincided with the ideological premise held by many Muslims that Islamic beliefs and practices are unaffected by historical change.

Recent ethnographic and social historical studies suggest a more complex notion of Islamic tradition than can be extracted primarily from religious texts. As a consequence, the notion of an Islamic "essence" has been difficult to sustain. Although in practice recent studies by anthropologists and social historians of Islam differ widely from each other in analytic assumptions, they suggest that in almost every studied locale there are opposing conceptions of Islam. These opposing (or complementary) conceptions of Islam are distinguished by greater (particularistic) and lesser (universalistic) degrees of compromise with the social order. These opposing conceptions are co-present and in dynamic tension with each other. Some of these ideologies, such as those characteristic of "reformist" Islam and the beliefs of many educated Muslims, tend to be *universalistic* in that they are explicit and more general in their implications. Others, including what can conveniently be labeled as maraboutism in North Africa ("saint cults," to be explained shortly, is a misleading gloss), are *particularistic* in that they are largely implicit and tied to particular social contexts. The co-presence of these alternative universalistic and particularistic ideologies, some of which are not formally elaborated, means that the strength of one or another ideological form cannot be attributed solely to its relation to a specific social context.

In what is perhaps an extreme reaction to the earlier analytic tradition which largely accepted the ideological premise held by many Muslims of the immutability of "true" Islamic belief and practice, an Egyptian Muslim anthropologist has suggested replacing the term *Islam* by *islams*, in order to emphasize better the diversity and vibrancy of the religious tradition which he seeks to interpret and to signal an analytic distance both from the Orientalist seeking of "essence" and from the theological tenets of some Muslims.[5] The intent of this chapter is to incorporate social historical materials with a survey of Islam today, in order to indicate the richness and variety of the Islamic tradition and some of the key components that are constantly refashioned to maintain its vitality and to provide a necessary critical perspective for placing monographs dealing with particular aspects of the Islamic tradition in their appropriate contexts.

as World History: Marshall Hodgson, 'The Venture of Islam,'" *International Journal of Middle East Studies*, 10, no. 2 (May 1979), 241-64. A good general bibliographic survey of the Islamic tradition and sources for its study, despite a weak coverage of sociologically oriented studies, is Charles J. Adams, "Islamic Religious Tradition," in *The Study of the Middle East*, ed. Leonard Binder (New York: John Wiley & Sons, 1976), pp. 29-95.

[5] Abdul Hamid el-Zein, "Beyond Ideology and Theology: The Search for the Anthropology of Islam," *Annual Review of Anthropology*, 6 (1977), 227-54. Despite Zein's many insightful comments, his representations of the analytic assumptions of some of the authors he reviews should not be regarded as substitutes for the original.

Recognizing the lack of a common core of dogma, a problem which Zein accommodates by writing of *islams,* Bryan S. Turner has suggested that in the Islamic case it is better to talk of *orthopraxy,* the "commonality of practice and ritual," rather than of *orthodoxy,* the "commonality of belief."[6] Even this formula has its limitations, despite the growing consensus among many educated Muslims on at least certain elements of practice and belief. Nonetheless, delineation of some basic features of Islam and the five "pillars" of faith serves as a useful point of departure for considering Islam as locally received and understood.


## THE FIVE PILLARS

Islam is the only one of the major world religions to have had a built-in name from its very beginning in seventh-century Arabia. *Islam* (Ar. *Islām*) means "submission," submission to the will of God. Whoever submits is called a *Muslim.* These terms occur repeatedly in the Quran. The word *qur'ān* itself means both "reading" and "recital." It is the word of God revealed to the Prophet Muḥammad by the angel Gabriel. Something is known of how these revelations first came to Muḥammad from verses in the Quran itself. First Muḥammad saw a glorious being stand erect high in the sky toward the horizon; then this being came closer and closer to him. At first Muḥammad thought the being was God Himself, but later he recognized it as Gabriel. No one is sure which part of the Quran was first revealed to Muḥammad. Many Muslims think it is this verse:

> O thou shrouded in thy mantle,
> arise, and warn!
> Thy Lord magnify
> thy robes purify
> and defilement flee!
> Give not, thinking to gain greater
> and be patient unto thy Lord.[7]
> (Sura 74:1-7)

Every word of the Quran is held by Muslims to be the word of God. In fact, Muslims believe that God had earlier communicated His word through other prophets, those recognized by both Jews and Christians. Muslims believe that over time the messages of these earlier prophets became distorted. So Muḥammad was made the "Seal of the Prophets," or the last one, to warn men one final time of their wrong ways and again to provide them with God's word "in clear Arabic."

Any translation from one civilizational tradition to another is treacherous, but a comparison with Christianity is useful here. The Quran should not be seen as

---

[6] Bryan S. Turner, *Weber and Islam: A Critical Study* (London and Boston: Routledge & Kegan Paul, 1974).

[7] *The Koran Interpreted,* tr. Arthur J. Arberry (London: George Allen & Unwin, Ltd.; New York: The Macmillan Company, 1955), Vol. 2, p. 310. (Courtesy of the publishers.)

precisely the equivalent of the Bible. Christians, or anyway most Christians, see the Bible as a record of the prophets and of Christ, but not directly as God's word, as Muslims see the Quran. This is why many Muslims, even those who do not speak Arabic, place such great emphasis upon comprehension of classical Arabic and regard translations of the Quran as mere guides to its meaning rather than substitutes for the original. For Christians (or again, most Christians) it is the person of Christ, the Son of God, that personifies God because Christ is God. In contrast, the Quran insists that Muḥammad is merely the messenger of God. Some Muslims, especially certain mystics, have admittedly considered the person of Muhammad to be a saintlike figure, but most Muslims go no further than to consider Muhammad to be the most perfect of men. In fact, the tomb of Muḥammad was destroyed in the late eighteenth century by zealous *Wahhābī* Muslims intent upon avoiding a personal veneration of the Prophet or of any other figures in Islam.

Clearly the belief in the Quran and the eternal nature of its exact message are important components of the Islamic tradition, but the word of God as embodied in the Quran is made meaningful to Muslims in different ways according to time and place. Problems of revelation and the legitimation of political authority, to take only two major practical examples, are interpreted in various ways throughout the Muslim world.

A Moroccan *qāḍī,* or religious judge, had this to say to me concerning how the Quran should be interpreted:

> How can ordinary men, no matter how much they study, understand by themselves the words of the Quran? Those are high words, the words of God. Instead, you must look at what the Prophet did, the sayings of the Prophet, and the conduct and decisions of the Muslim community in the past. These tell you what is the *sharīᶜa* (the law of Islam or the "straight path").

He then drew two parallel lines on a sheet of paper and explained that conduct within the two lines was permitted by Islam and that all else was not.

Since the Quran cannot be a direct guide to man's conduct, one must turn to what is traditionally done by Muslims. Such a belief is not prevalent everywhere in the Muslim world but is an example of *one* of the ways in which the ideological notion of the immutability of Islamic belief can be maintained yet adjusted to accommodate local traditions. Much of what is considered to be Islamic practice depends upon *consensus (ijmāᶜa)* of morally upright Muslims, especially those considered to be religious scholars, in any part of the Muslim world. The notion of consensus has precise legal connotations in Islam, but here I am primarily concerned with indicating popular conceptions of religious tradition.

Every Muslim considers himself to be part of the *umma,* the community of living Muslims everywhere who are committed to what Hodgson has called the "venture of Islam." The *sharīᶜa,* the straight path of the ritual observances required in principle of Muslims, is only the most visible component of that venture. Muslims differ as to who legitimately succeeded Muḥammad in the leadership of the Muslim world—Sunnī Muslims accept in principle the notion that any Muslim

**FIGURE 9-1** Moroccan *qāḍī.* (Courtesy of the author.)

could be Muḥammad's successor in all matters except prophecy, while the Shīᶜa, principally located in Iran, East Africa, India, southern Iraq, Lebanon, and parts of the Arabian peninsula, feel that succession rightly belongs only to the descendants of Muḥammad through his daughter Fāṭima and his son-in-law ᶜAlī. There are many elaborations and intermediary positions of these principal themes. Despite these differences, Islam is thought of by Muslims as imparting a tone and style to all aspects of their lives—familial customs, sociability, learning, even for some Muslims styles of personal grooming. *Sharīᶜa* can be translated as "law," but it is much more than the concept of law in English usage. Religiously speaking, the *sharīᶜa* governs all aspects of one's conduct as a Muslim.

There are five "pillars" (pl. *arkān*) of Islamic faith incumbent upon most Muslims; I say *most* because some Muslims modify or deny the normative nature of even these pillars because of their own interpretations of Islam. These five pillars are the declaration of faith, the five daily ritual prayers, almsgiving, fasting, and the pilgrimage to Mecca.[8]

---

[8]There are a number of accounts of these obligations. One of the most concise is Gustave E. von Grunebaum, *Muhammadan Festivals* (New York: Henry Schuman, Inc., 1951). Another is contained in a handbook written for English-speaking Muslims, Muhammad Hamidullah, ed., *Introduction to Islam,* enlarged edition, Publications of the Centre Culturel Islamique, Paris, No. 1 (Hyderabad, India: Habib & Co., 1959). The account below of the pilgrimage, the fifth pillar, is based primarily upon von Grunebaum, *Muhammadan Festivals,* pp. 15-49; and the *Aramco World Magazine,* 26, no. 6 (November-December 1974).

The declaration of faith *(shahāda)* is quite simply that there is no god but God and that Muḥammad is His messenger *(rasūl).* Like any living tradition, Islam in practice has varied enormously as it is constantly in the process of becoming. This simple declaration of faith has had the advantage of being so elemental that all Muslims can agree upon it, whatever other differences they may have had for thirteen and a half centuries.

The second pillar of Islam is the *ṣalāt,* or five daily ritual prayers. All Muslims are supposed to cleanse themselves ritually, face Mecca, and pray at dawn, noon, midafternoon, sunset, and dusk. In towns, prayer-callers climb to the top of minarets, even when loudspeakers are prevalent today, and announce each of the prayers. Muslims may pray where they want; the use of mosques is not obligatory, although many believers congregate in mosques at least on Fridays for the midday prayers. The obligatory prayers are fixed in form and content, although personal invocations to God may be added to them upon their completion. The uniformity of these prayers is said by many to symbolize man's equality before God as well as the community's submission to His will.

Almsgiving *(zakāt)* is the third pillar. In some countries at certain periods the *zakāt* has been an obligatory tax upon all Muslims who can afford to pay it. The Quran enjoins the wealthier to set aside at least part of their wealth for the destitute of the Muslim community. Most almsgiving throughout the Middle East remains personal and direct; the donor has a more direct contact with his clients, unlike the anonymous pattern of giving which prevails in our own society.

The fourth pillar of Islam is fasting *(ṣawm),* which occurs each lunar year during the month of Ramaḍān. All adult Muslims who are in good health are expected to fast, and despite the fact that many persons privately may choose not to do so, public fasting is observed almost everywhere. During Ramaḍān, Islam is more consciously brought into daily activities; religious lessons are given nightly on the radio and television and in mosques. It is the month of repentance and purification. Some Muslims, defensive against the West, rationalize the fast by praising its supposed medical virtues in cleansing the vital organs of the body. Yet, as indicated in Chapter 8, its more important meaning is the ability of Muslims to follow the code of conduct fixed by Islam and thus to demonstrate their self-discipline and control over self. The fast carries a variety of more elaborate interpretations, as the Fallerses indicate in their account of the fast in Turkey and Antoun in his account for rural Jordan, but the public manifestation of the community's ability to observe the fast is a key and universal aspect of belief and practice.[9] Eating, drinking, smoking, and sexual intercourse are prohibited between dawn and sunset and, more significantly, Muslims are expected to engage in spiritual self-renewal. At night, in contrast, sociability is in many ways increased; visiting among friends and relatives is intensified, and the practical meaning of what it is to be a Muslim is enhanced for the entire community.

[9] L. A. Fallers, assisted by M. C. Fallers, "Notes on an Advent Ramadan," *Journal of the American Academy of Religion,* 42, no. 1 (March 1974), 35-52; Richard T. Antoun, "The Social Significance of Ramaḍān in an Arab Village," *Muslim World* 58 (1968), 36-42, 95-104.

The fifth pillar is the pilgrimage *(hajj)* to Mecca, obligatory once in a lifetime for every Muslim economically and physically able to do so. Even more than the month of fasting, the pilgrimage is an obligation that removes pilgrims from the constraints of ordinary, particular obligations. From the moment pilgrims set out on the journey, they are removed from ordinary society and become "liminal" in the sense of the term made popular by Victor Turner.[10] Pilgrims agree to dedicate their lives to Islam and must be in a state of ritual consecration to make a valid pilgrimage. Pilgrims may not uproot plants or shed blood—if they do so, they must atone for it by ritual means. Sexual intercourse is also forbidden. As a sign of their consecration, if they die while on pilgrimage, they are thought to enter paradise immediately.

During the pilgrimage, ordinary social relationships with kinsmen, neighbors, and others assume a diminished importance. One's identity as a Muslim and brotherhood in Islam are of paramount significance. Every step of the way becomes highly symbolic of the pilgrim's wider identification with Islam; the web of particularistic social relationships is supposed to be transcended. Ritually speaking, the Kaᶜba is regarded as the symbolic center of the world, however peripheral it might be in terms of the ordinary social and political systems in which pilgrims are otherwise enmeshed.

In recent years, more than a million pilgrims annually have made the voyage. Its timing changes each year, for as with other key Islamic rituals, the time of the

**FIGURE 9-2** Pilgrims often visit the shrines of local marabouts before departing for Mecca. Tunisia, 1973. (Courtesy Nicholas S. Hopkins.)

[10]Victor Turner, "The Center Out There: Pilgrim's Goal," *History of Religions,* 12, no. 3 (1973), 191-230.

pilgrimage is set by the lunar calendar. Pilgrims from nearby countries arrive by bus and even by foot; those from more distant locales arrive by air, with only small numbers now arriving by sea.

In the past, as with equivalent rituals in Europe, the pilgrimage was a long and arduous journey from which many persons never returned. Every step of the way was fraught with danger, but this only enhanced its spiritual richness. A voyage of a year or longer was not uncommon for pilgrims coming from North Africa, so that before they left on the *hajj,* they set their affairs in order in case they should never return. Even in the mid-nineteenth century, when modern sea transport and relative peace and security made the pilgrimage easier, it still had its uncertainties.[11] For many, it was a voyage of intellectual, and even commercial, discovery. Religious scholars at Mecca and along the way had contact with the major intellectual currents elsewhere. Merchants could use the pilgrimage as an occasion to establish bonds which were of use in the conduct of international trade.[12]

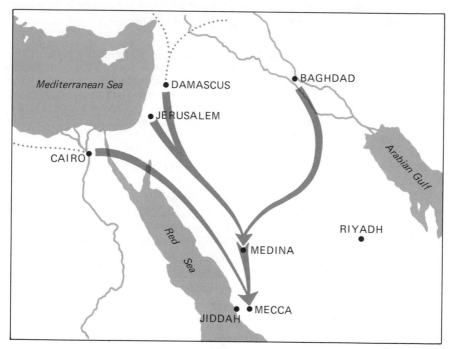

**FIGURE 9-3** Principal traditional caravan routes to Mecca. *(Aramco World Magazine,* November-December 1974.)

[11] See Richard F. Burton, *Personal Narrative of a Pilgrimage to Al-Madinah and Meccah* (New York: Dover Publications, Inc., 1964 [orig. 1893]).

[12] An excellent account of the pilgrimage in the last century and the arrangements made by Meccans to receive pilgrims can be found in C. Snouck Hurgronje, *Mekka in the Latter Part of the 19th Century* (Leiden: E. J. Brill, 1931).

There are many descriptions of both the transformation that the pilgrimage effects upon Muslims and its ritual significance. In most parts of the Muslim world it is a pious act for pilgrims to write an account of their journey for the guidance of others, although it is the unusual pilgrims whose accounts perhaps best reveal the intense meaning that the pilgrimage carries for the community of the faithful.

Malcolm X was one such unusual pilgrim. Given the bitterness of his own racial perceptions in America, his remarks are especially poignant. He remarked on the fact that the tens of thousands of pilgrims "were of all colours, from blue-eyed blondes to black-skinned Africans. But we were all participating in the same ritual, displaying a spirit of unity and brotherhood that my experiences in America had led me to believe could never exist."[13] He went on to say that he observed color patterns in the crowds in the sense that like stayed with like but concluded that "true brotherhood" existed when these patterns existed with no complexes of superiority or inferiority.

For others, the pilgrimage assumed a mystical significance. Even Richard Burton, never a pilgrim to be moved by ordinary emotions, could not refrain from expressing his exaltation upon first arriving, disguised, in Mecca:

> There at last it lay, the bourn of my long and weary Pilgrimage, realising the plans and hopes of many and many a year. The mirage medium of Fancy invested the huge catafalque and its gloomy pall with peculiar charms . . . the view was strange, unique—and how few have looked upon the celebrated shrine! I may truly say that, of all the worshippers who clung weeping to the curtain, or who pressed their beating hearts to the stone, none felt for the moment a deeper emotion than did [I].

Resuming his characteristic orientalist distance, Burton continued:

> It was *as if* the poetical legends of the Arab spoke truth, and that the waving wings of angels, not the sweet breeze of morning, were agitating and swelling the black covering of the shrine. But, to confess humbling truth, theirs was the high feeling of religious enthusiasm, mine was the ecstasy of gratified pride.[14]

There are nine ritual steps to the pilgrimage itself. Here my intent is not to present a structuralist explanation of the significance of these events but merely to suggest some aspects of their symbolic richness.[15] (1) First is the donning of the

---

[13] Malcolm X, with the assistance of Alex Haley, *The Autobiography of Malcolm X* (New York: Grove Press, 1966), pp. 338-39.

[14] Burton, *Personal Narrative*, Vol. 2, pp 160-61. (Emphasis added.)

[15] See in particular the sensitive, beautifully illustrated account of Emel Esin, *Mecca the Blessed, Madinah the Radiant* (London: Elek Books, 1963) which cites copiously from literature concerning Mecca and the pilgrimage. Numbers in the text identifying the stages in the pilgrimage are keyed to Fig. 9-4. See also Muhammad Abdul-Rauf, "Pilgrimage to Mecca," *National Geographic*, 154, no. 5 (November 1978), 581-607.

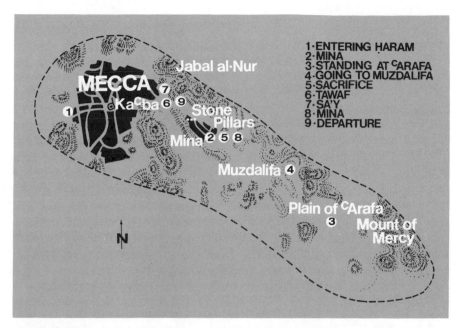

**FIGURE 9-4** Principal steps of the *ḥajj.* (Based upon an illustration in *Aramco World Magazine,* November-December 1974.)

*iḥrām,* a white seamless garment that for many Muslims symbolizes the pilgrims' search for purity and their separation from the ordinary world. This may be donned anywhere along the route but at the latest at fixed points signifying the confines of Mecca. No jewelry or other personal adornment may be worn, nor are pilgrims supposed to engage in disputes. Providing that the pilgrims have declared their intention *(nīya)* of making the pilgrimage, they are ready to enter the *ḥaram,* the sacred enclosure of Mecca itself, thought to have been established by Abraham and confirmed by Muḥammad. Non-Muslims are not allowed within its confines. Then (2) on the eighth day of the lunar month of Dhū l-Ḥijja, the month of the pilgrimage, pilgrims proceed to Mina, a small uninhabited village five miles east of Mecca. There they spend the night meditating and praying.

The next morning, the pilgrims move as a group to the plain of ᶜArafa for the central rite of the pilgrimage, the (3) "standing" before Mount ᶜArafa, the Mount of Mercy. They face Mecca, meditate, and pray. Many spend the entire time standing, from noon to sunset. Some climb almost to the summit of the two-hundred-foot mountain, at the foot of which the Prophet was supposed to have delivered his last sermon.

Just before sunset, a cannon sounds and the pilgrims proceed to (4) Muzdālifa, a few miles back toward Mina. There they worship and sleep under the stars after gathering a number of pebbles for use on the following day. The next morning, before daybreak, they return to Mina, where they throw the pebbles at three whitewashed masonry pillars, especially the one thought to represent Satan, who three times tried to persuade Abraham not to obey God's command to sacrifice his son. The throwing of the pebbles symbolizes the repudiation of evil.

(5) For the Feast of the Sacrifice (*ᶜĪd al-Kabīr*) all pilgrims who can afford to do so buy a sheep or other animal for sacrifice and give away part of it to the poor, although given the quantity of meat sacrificed, most of it is not consumed. This sacrifice has a range of meanings. It commemorates Abraham's willingness to sacrifice his son; it symbolizes the readiness to give up what is dearest to the pilgrim if commanded by God; it offers thanksgiving to God for having communicated with humans and reminds pilgrims to share their blessings with the less fortunate. Muslims throughout the world vicariously share in the elation of the pilgrims by performing their own sacrifices on the same day.

Once pilgrims have offered their sacrifices, they have completed a major part of the pilgrimage. Men shave their heads and women cut off a lock of their hair to symbolize their deconsecration. Pilgrims now are free to bathe and to remove the *iḥrām*, although the prohibition on sexual intercourse remains.

The pilgrims next proceed directly to Mecca and perform (6) the *ṭawāf*, the circling. They circumambulate the Kaᶜba seven times on foot, reciting a prayer on each circuit. This circling is said by some to symbolize the unity of God and man and of heaven with earth and reminds believers of the importance attached to the Kaᶜba by the Patriarch Abraham, his son Ishmael, and Muḥammad. During the circling, many pilgrims try to touch the black stone which is embedded in one corner of the Kaᶜba.

'**FIGURE 9-5** Colonnades of the great mosque, Mecca. (*Aramco World Magazine,* November-December 1974.)

The key ceremonies of the pilgrimage are now completed, and pilgrims have the right to call themselves *ḥājj*-s. Most pilgrims, however, proceed to the "Place of Abraham," where Abraham is supposed to have offered his devotions to God. There pilgrims reenact (7) the "running" *(saᶜy)*, the search for water by Hagar, the wife of Abraham (and Sarah's rival in the Bible). Hagar ran back and forth desperately searching for water for herself and her child until the angel Gabriel appeared, stamped the ground with his heel, and brought forth water from the well of Zamzam for them. Pilgrims drink from this well before starting the running; many return home with bottles of water from the well.

Pilgrims then customarily return for a third and last time (8) to Mina, where they cast their remaining pebbles at each of the three pillars—seven stones at each pillar for each day of the pilgrimage. This also is a time to visit with other pilgrims and to bid farewell to friends. Their final visit is to Mecca again, where pilgrims again circumambulate the Kaᶜba (9) before returning home.

There is a rich tradition of myths associated with each of the steps of the pilgrimage, and these myths have been variously interpreted throughout the Islamic world. The rituals associated with the pilgrimage are interpreted in slightly different ways for Sunnī and Shīᶜī Muslims, at least on a popular level.

## THE SHĪᶜA

Unlike the case for Christianity, there is no formal clergy in the Muslim world and no center of priests who can decide upon what is and is not orthodox. Hence it is misleading to speak of schisms in the Muslim community. There is no formal religious center from which judgments of orthodoxy and heterodoxy can be made. Even with this consideration in mind, Shīᶜa are set apart from Sunnī Muslims in terms both of how they interpret and elaborate the meaning of Islam and in the practical sense of self-differentiation from other Muslims. Nonetheless, the Shīᶜa, like other Muslims, firmly believe in the universality of Islam and the integrity of the Muslim community.

The word *Shīᶜa* itself means "party" or "sect." This label in part reflects the origin of Shīᶜism as a political movement in seventh-century Arabia. ᶜAlī, the son-in-law of the Prophet Muḥammad, was the fourth of his caliphs (*khalīfa*-s), or successors (656-661).[16] ᶜAlī was later assassinated by his opponents, as was Ḥusayn (in 680), the grandson of the Prophet. Both men are considered by Shīᶜa to be martyrs. After ᶜAlī's assassination, the "party" of ᶜAlī in Kufa, in southern Iraq, demanded that succession be restored to ᶜAlī's descendants alone. This legitimist claim continues to be a core belief of the Shīᶜa. One contributing factor to Shīᶜism

---

[16] See Marshall G. S. Hodgson, "How Did the Early Shīᶜa Become Sectarian?," *Journal of the American Oriental Society*, 75, no. 1 (January-March 1955), 1-13, for a subtle account of how what are now accepted as the "basic principles" of Shīᶜī thought and practice emerged. His *Venture of Islam* is also an indispensable reference.

at least in its formative years was the tension between newly conquered non-Arabs and their Arab rulers. From the very beginning Shī<sup>c</sup>ism has been a movement of political opposition and of social discontent and has carried with it the notion that the Shī<sup>c</sup>a are persecuted, although in recent years this component of Shī<sup>c</sup>ī doctrine has had less importance than in the past.

Most Islamic historians have stressed the doctrinal differences between Sunnī and Shī<sup>c</sup>a, an approach which is misleading from an anthropological and social historical perspective because Sunnī Islam is no more a homogeneous entity than is Shī<sup>c</sup>ī Islam. A more promising approach to characterization of the distinctive features of Shī<sup>c</sup>ī Islam is taken in a seminal paper by Leonard Binder.[17] His approach concentrates upon the relation between the practical organization of Shī<sup>c</sup>ī men of learning (called collectively <sup>c</sup>ulamā' as they are among Sunnī Muslims) and certain aspects of Shī<sup>c</sup>ī doctrine that are both theologically propagated and popularly accepted. His overall points are that (1) for doctrinal reasons Shī<sup>c</sup>ī men of learning are accorded greater religious authority than their Sunnī counterparts; (2) for historical reasons, Shī<sup>c</sup>ī men of learning have not been as seriously challenged in their authority as has been the case with Sunnī religious scholars; (3) the Shī<sup>c</sup>ī religious "establishment" is more hierarchically organized and centralized; and (4) Shī<sup>c</sup>ī men of learning have been more effective in maintaining their autonomy from government control and in maintaining a strong popular base for their legitimacy, as the 1978-1979 revolution in Iran vividly demonstrates.[18]

In doctrinal terms, the Shī<sup>c</sup>a hold that the only legitimate successors of Muḥammad were his descendants through his son-in-law <sup>c</sup>Alī and his daughter Fāṭima. Most Shī<sup>c</sup>a believe that there were twelve legitimate Imām-s, or leaders of the Islamic community, including <sup>c</sup>Alī. The twelfth Imām is said to have hidden himself from this world, to return at some later time. Since then, the Imām-s have been hidden, so that it is the responsibility of recognized men of learning to interpret Islamic doctrine and to guide the Muslim community as new situations arise. The Imām-s are thought to have the charismatic qualities of the Prophet, except the gift of prophecy itself. Leading men of learning partake to a certain extent of the charismatic qualities attributed to the Imām-s, a feature almost entirely lacking in at least the formal doctrines of Sunnī Muslims. I stress formal, for at a popular level, neglected until recently by many Islamic historians, other beliefs such as that a mahdī, or "rightly guided one," will return the community of Muslims to its proper course, are often present. The takeover of the Great Mosque at Mecca in November 1979 by a band of armed militants who proclaimed that one of their number was the "hidden" Imām indicates the continuing political potential of such a belief.

Most Shī<sup>c</sup>a stress the practice of taqīya, or "concealment." In the face of

[17]Leonard Binder, "The Proofs of Islam: Religion and Politics in Iran," in Arabic and Islamic Studies in Honor of Hamilton A. R. Gibb, ed. George Makdisi (Leiden: E. J. Brill, 1965), pp. 118-40.

[18]Ibid., p. 121.

persecution, Shī$^c$a are said to be able to dissimulate their real beliefs if the expression of them would result in grave physical danger or threat to the community. Thus $^c$Alī, whose caliphate was contested throughout his lifetime, is alleged to have "concealed" his firm belief in the right of his descendants to be Muḥammad's successors because of such a threat. One practical consequence of this doctrine has been to allow Shī$^c$ism in practice to accommodate a range of complementary beliefs of other religious traditions in the region: Christianity, Manichaeism, and other doctrines.[19] In fact, the practical ties of groups such as the Shabak of northern Iraq to the wider Shī$^c$ī community are virtually nonexistent; they have their own leadership and their need to develop formal doctrine is not as paramount as it is in the case of the predominant "twelver" Shī$^c$a of Iran and elsewhere in Iraq.[20] At a greater extreme, the rituals and formal beliefs of the Alevi (Ar. $^cAl\bar{a}w\bar{\imath}$) Muslims of Turkey, Iran, and Syria (where the current president is an $^cAl\bar{a}w\bar{\imath}$) are such that many of their Sunnī and Shī$^c$ī neighbors do not even accept them as Muslims.[21] Numerous Shī$^c$ī groups exist elsewhere that accept a different number of $Im\bar{a}m$-s and in other ways maintain a separate leadership and sense of practical community.

Binder's second point is that at least in Iran, Shī$^c$ī men of learning had no living $Im\bar{a}m$ to reduce their status. Ayatullah Khomeini's popular support is indicative of the potential strength of such leaders. Elsewhere in the Shī$^c$ī world, as with the $Zaidi$-s in Yemen, the $Ism\bar{a}^c\bar{\imath}li$-s and the Fāṭimite caliphate of medieval Egypt, there were living $Im\bar{a}m$-s. During certain periods in Iran's history, the role of Shī$^c$ī men of learning was strengthened by the government. Because of the lack of formal colonial domination in Iran, the presence of Shī$^c$ī shrines and centers of learning in neighboring Iraq, notably Karbala and Najaf, which serve as places of refuge in times of political crisis, the lack of major religious opposition (such as could be provided by an effective modernist movement), and the lack until quite recently of a large body of intellectuals with Western-style educations has meant that Shī$^c$ī men of learning have had no substantial challenge to their legitimacy other than that of the pre-1978 ruling circles.

Binder's third consideration, the institutional organization of Iran's $^culam\bar{a}'$, fits nicely with Bill's stress upon the significance of patterns of informal associa-

---

[19] See Michael Max Jonathon Fischer, "Zoroastrian Iran between Myth and Praxis," Ph.D. Dissertation in Anthropology submitted to the University of Chicago, August 1973. This unpublished study remains the richest circumstantial account of the parallels and interrelationships among the carriers of the diverse religious traditions of Iran, their relation to social class and political authority.

[20] See Chapter 7 and Amal (Rassam) Vinogradov, "Ethnicity, Cultural Discontinuity and Power Brokers in Northern Iraq: The Case of the Shabak," *American Ethnologist*, 1, no. 1 (February 1974), 207-18.

[21] James A. Bill and Carl Leiden, *Politics in the Middle East* (Boston and Toronto: Little, Brown and Company, 1979), p. 39, are bewildered as to how to "classify" them, for they "maintain a mixture of Christian, Muslim, and pagan beliefs." The authors also report that as of 1973, the $^cAl\bar{a}w\bar{\imath}$-s were formally recognized [by whom?] as part of Lebanon's Shī$^c$ī community. See later in this chapter for a discussion of $^cAl\bar{a}w\bar{\imath}$ beliefs.

tion (see Chapter 8). Strictly speaking, there are no formal patterns of institutional leadership among the Shīᶜa of Iran, but the pervasive informal ones enable Shīᶜī men of learning to mobilize their followers effectively. Perhaps because the patterns of leadership are informal, they are more difficult for hostile governments to control and suppress. There are *mullah*-s, or village preachers, associated with each mosque and a number of other lesser religious figures. At the higher level are scholars called *mujtahid*-s, those who by study and personal piety are capable of making independent judgments and interpreting Islamic tradition. In contemporary Iran, *mujtahid*-s acquire recognition by publishing books outlining their methods and views for public comment. At a level above *mujtahid*-s are scholars called *Āyatullāh*-s, a term which literally means a "sign of God." At the very apex of the hierarchy is a scholar called the "supreme" Āyatullāh, *Āyatullāh al-ᶜUzma,* considered to be the most learned scholar of his age and whose piety is beyond question.[22]   There is no formal "election" of such individuals. At all levels of the hierarchy, success depends in part upon the ability to attract a popular following and to obtain financial support from followers which can be used to support the education of religious students, the upkeep of Shīᶜī shrines, and other religious activities. At higher levels, success depends additionally upon recognition by other men of learning. Binder suggests that recognition as *Āyatullāh al-ᶜUzma* is in practice in the hands of a relatively small group of thirty or forty religious scholars residing at Qum, one of the holy cities of Iran. Many of these leaders are themselves descendants of famous religious scholars of the past, but the succession to leadership still depends largely upon a reputation for religious learning.[23]

Finally, Iran's Shīᶜī religious leadership has managed to retain popular support despite the significant political and economic transformations undergone by at least part of Iran's population.[24] With the exception of the supporters of Iran's former regime, some Westernized intellectuals, and a few Muslims influenced by various reformist movements, traditional Shīᶜī men of learning have managed to retain the support of the peasantry and most of the merchants and craftsmen participating in Iran's bazaar economy. Despite divergences among Shīᶜī leaders, for the most part they have managed to retain the loyalty of "traditional" groups, and to win the support even of a number of students in the "modern" educational sector, as well as the support of what Binder calls somewhat ironically in terms of the 1978-1979 revolution the "uninfluential classes" of Iranian society.[25]

Especially at the popular level Shīᶜism has certain key rituals that dramati-

---

[22] Binder, "Proofs," p. 132.

[23] *Ibid.,* p. 134.

[24] For an analysis of the impact of recent economic reforms upon Iranian society, see Farhad Kazemi and Ervand Abrahamian, "The Nonrevolutionary Peasantry of Modern Iran," *Iranian Studies,* 11 (1978), 259-304. See also the special issues of *MERIP Reports* devoted to the Iranian crisis: 8, no. 6 (July-August 1978), no. 8 (October 1978), and 9, nos. 2-3 (March-April 1979).

[25] Binder, "Proofs," p. 139.

cally indicate the central elements of belief and practice. One of these is the annual mourning *(ta^cziya)* in commemoration of the death of Husayn, the Prophet's grandson, at Karbala, Iraq, in the lunar month of Muharram in A.D. 680. For the Shī^ca, Husayn is the third *Imām*. Muhammad and ^cAlī were the first two. As the late Gustave von Grunebaum wrote: "It would be incorrect to say that Husain stands in the center of Shī^ca dogma, but it is unquestionably true that contemplation of his personality and fate is the emotional mainspring of the believer's religious experience."[26] Shī^ca consider it to be particularly beneficial to be buried next to Husayn's grave in Karbala. For centuries caravans brought the dead to be interred there, and in more recent times an airline specialized in flying remains there has been established.

In the Shī^cī tradition Husayn's death is interpreted as a voluntary sacrifice so that through his suffering, Shī^cī faithful could enter paradise. The popular commemoration of Husayn's martyrdom has been described by Elizabeth Fernea, who was in Karbala in 1957, together with women from a nearby village where she was living.[27] At that time Karbala was a town of thirty thousand people, but with the pilgrims arriving during Muharram its population swelled to over a million, with black tents erected for the pilgrims. Similar ceremonies, although not of course attracting an equivalent influx of pilgrims, occur in various forms in Shī^cī communities in the entire region. From the first of the month, when the commemoration begins, mourning clothes are donned; people refrain from bathing and shaving and adopt a simple diet. Pulpits are placed in the street from which the story of Husayn's martyrdom is recited, often with many added details. Listeners commonly break out in tears. Also during this period, at least through the 1950s, groups of men seeking penance, with their half-naked bodies dyed black or red, toured the streets, pulling out their hair, inflicting sword wounds upon themselves and dragging chains behind them. Not infrequently, fights with non-Shī^ca developed as well as fights between rival neighborhood factions. I use the past tense to describe these activities because both the Iranian and Iraqi governments have at least formally banned the more extreme of these activities, although many continue to be carried out in modified form, especially in more remote areas.

On the 10th of Muharram, a large procession designed as a funerary parade reenacts the last episodes of Husayn's life and his burial. A coffin, a few arms, and Husayn's banner are the only props necessary for the reenactment of the last days of his life.

A number of versions of these mourning plays exist, often keyed to local social and political circumstances.[28] The *ta^cziya* for Husayn consists of some forty

---

[26] von Grunebaum, *Muhammedan Festivals*, p. 87.

[27] Elizabeth Warnock Fernea, *Guests of the Sheik* (Garden City, N.Y.: Doubleday Anchor Books, 1965), pp. 194-208; see also von Grunebaum, *Muhammadan Festivals,* pp. 85-94 (on which portions of the following account of the Muharram festivals are based).

[28] For accounts of the local interpretation and significance of the mourning of Husayn in addition to Fernea's, see Emrys L. Peters, "Aspects of Rank and Status among Muslims in a Lebanese Village," in *Mediterranean Countrymen,* ed. Julian Pitt-Rivers (Paris and The Hague:

FIGURE 9-6 Carrying Ḥusayn's corpse, *taᶜziya* drama, southern Iraq, 1955. (From Sigrid Westphal-Hellbusch and Heinz Westphal, "Die Ma'dan; Kultur und Geschichte der Marschenbewohner im Süd-Iraq," *Forschungen zur Ethnologie und Sozialpsychologie,* Band 4 [Berlin: Duncker & Humblot, 1962], plate 60. Courtesy of the authors and the publisher.)

to fifty loosely connected episodes. Since the audience knows the play in advance, the drama does not rely upon suspense but upon how the particular scenes are constructed. Anachronisms abound in many presentations; in some versions, European Christian ambassadors are made to betray Ḥusayn rather than Sunnī Muslims. Old Testament figures similarly are introduced. The performance is often highly realistic, so realistic in the nineteenth century that condemned criminals often were made to play the part of the slayers of Ḥusayn in case the spectators became so enraged that they attacked the actors themselves. The final scene involves a procession with the martyr's coffin (or in some versions a severed head) to the court of the Sunnī caliph. On the way, Christians, Jews, and Sunnī Muslims are portrayed as bowing before Ḥusayn.

The symbolism of these commemorative plays for Shīᶜa carries the clear message that the sacrificial death of Ḥusayn is linked to their salvation. In one

Mouton & Co., 1963), pp. 195-200, and Chapter 3 of this book. For Iran, see Gus Thaiss, "Religious Symbolism and Social Change: The Drama of Husain," in *Scholars, Saints and Sufis,* ed. Nikki Keddie (Berkeley and Los Angeles: University of California Press, 1972), pp. 349-66. The excessively brief remarks of S. M. Salim, *Marsh Dwellers of the Euphrates Delta,* London School of Economics Monographs on Social Anthropology, 23 (London: The Athlone Press, 1962), pp. 12-13, are also of value. For an overview of *taᶜzīya* performances in various historical and contemporary contexts, see Peter J. Chelkowski, *Taᶜziyeh: Indigenous Avant-Garde Theatre of Iran* (Tehran: NIRT Publications, 1957), and accompanying bibliography.

version of the play, in fact, the angel Gabriel is made to announce to Muḥammad that his grandchild will die, not because he is guilty of any wrongdoing, but so that his blood will be redeemed.[29]

The intensity of such public performances, coupled with the lack until recently of anthropological accounts of popular understandings of Shī$^c$ism, have led to a misunderstanding of many aspects of Shī$^c$ī belief. For instance, the pilgrimage to Mecca is as important to Shī$^c$a as it is to other Muslims, but it is differently interpreted. Most pious Shī$^c$a consider the pilgrimage to Mecca significant at least in part because nearby Medina is the place of burial of the Prophet Muḥammad, one of their recognized *Imām*-s. Pious Shī$^c$a also try to visit the shrines of the other *Imām*-s, located throughout Iran and Iraq, so that structurally the pilgrimage is not of the same importance for them as it is for many Sunnī.

Because the Shī$^c$a tend to be located in regions where their orientation toward Islam is only one of many, and because the tendency of many Western writers has been to consider Sunnī Islam as "orthodox," distorted views of popular Shī$^c$ism still prevail. A personal experience might indicate this attitude. In 1968 I spent a month in Iran. Shortly after my arrival, a Sunnī colleague from a neighboring country warned me that I would most likely encounter Shī$^c$ī hostility, especially in the smaller centers. For example, I was cautioned that the Shī$^c$a would undoubtedly break any glasses or plates after I had used them. I do not speak Farsi, but at the time spoke a reasonably fluent Iraqi Arabic, a dialect known to many Iranians, especially religious scholars. I encountered no hostility and in fact left Tehran for Baghdad by a bus on which most of my fellow travelers were Shī$^c$ī pilgrims on their way to visit the shrines in Iraq. The bus stopped regularly for collective prayers, the pilgrims sang together and shared their food with me. Later I mentioned to a *mujtahid* what I had been told about the breaking of dishes and glasses. He laughed and replied that such objects were too expensive to break each time a nonbeliever was offered hospitality. My direct contact with the Shī$^c$a was brief but sufficient to suggest that in the case of the region of Iran and Iraq, as with the complex religious situation described by Canfield for Afghanistan, each religious group holds strong and often unfavorable sentiments regarding the presumed comportment of the others.[30]

## AN IDEOLOGICAL FRONTIER?: THE ALEVI

The ambiguous situation of the Alevi in eastern Turkey, Syria, and northern Iraq dramatically underscores the difficulty, at least from a sociological perspective, of defining Islam too strictly in terms of a supposed orthodoxy. The Alevis of eastern

[29] von Grunebaum, *Muhammedan Festivals,* p. 90.

[30] See Robert L. Canfield, "What They Do When the Lights Are Out: Myth and Social Order in Afghanistan," paper presented at the ACLS/SSRC Joint Committee on the Near and Middle East Conference on Symbols of Social Differentiation, 25-28 May 1978, Baltimore, Maryland.

Turkey have been the subject of study by Nur Yalman, a Turkish anthropologist who together with other Turkish intellectuals has evinced a renewed interest in the strength of religious traditions in Turkey.[31] From the 1920s until very recently, Turkey's militantly secular leadership has sought in various ways to discourage religious observances. Yalman avers that "Social Darwinism" became the dominant ideology of the Turkish upper classes and a justification for "embracing" Western culture.[32]

This attitude on the part of the elite met with significant popular resistance as many Western-educated Turks have begun to acknowledge in recent years. Some religious orders such as the *Bektāshīya* have had decisive political influence since at least the eighteenth century and were regarded warily by Ottoman officials and later by those of the Turkish state.[33] Many religious orders (*tarīqa-s*) appear to have been driven underground but still enjoy considerable popularity. The rediscovery by Turkey's educated elite of the strength of religious organization and belief also points to the necessity for anthropologists to consider the articulation of divergent religious ideologies or attitudes toward religion within complex national traditions.

The region of Alevi settlement in eastern Turkey is part of a continuum of the shatter-zone of religious groupings described by Rassam for northern Iraq.[34] There are small Christian communities, including Armenians and Assyrians. Most of the population is Muslim, but they are divided between the Sunnī, which Yalman glosses as "orthodox," and Alevi, Bektashi, and Nuseyri. To some extent these divisions coincide with linguistic ones: the Nuseyri speak Arabic, the Bektashi speak Turkish, and the Alevi speak both Turkish and Kurdish. The Sunnī communities are cross-cut by following various of the major legal schools in Islam and various brotherhoods. There is even a community of the *Yazīdī*-s, popularly known as "devil worshippers," in the region.[35]

Many Shīᶜa (and Sunnī) reject the Alevis as non-Muslims. Nonetheless, as the name *Alevi* implies, their beliefs and practices have much to do with the role of ᶜAlī in Islam. Yalman's description mostly concerns a small, bleak peasant village of some sixty-seven houses. As Yalman points out, the first thing a stranger notices

---

[31] Nur Yalman, "Islamic Reform and the Mystic Tradition in Eastern Turkey," *European Journal of Sociology*, 10 (1969), 41-60.

[32] Yalman, "Islamic Reform," 43. See also the important essay by Charles F. Gallagher, "Contemporary Islam: The Straits of Secularism," *AUFS Field Staff Reports*, Southwest Asia Series, 15, no. 3 (1966). See Bernard Lewis, *The Emergence of Modern Turkey* (London: Oxford University Press, 1965); Niyazi Berkes, *The Development of Secularism in Turkey* (Montreal: McGill University Press, 1964); and W. C. Smith's succinct *Islam in Modern History* (New York: New American Library, 1957), pp. 164-208, for standard accounts of religion in modern Turkey.

[33] John Kingsley Birge, *The Bektashi Order of Dervishes* (London: Luzac & Co., 1937), is especially useful in describing the role of this order in consolidating opposition to the government. On the Naqshbandi in another country, see Hamid Algar, "Some Notes on the Naqshbandi Ṭarīqat in Bosnia," *Die Welt des Islams*, 13 (1971), 168-203.

[34] Amal (Rassam) Vinogradov, "Ethnicity," 207-10.

[35] Yalman, "Islamic Reform," 48-49.

about the village is the lack of any building showing a minaret: "There was no call to prayer and no mosque."[36] Additionally, men tended to have mustaches which covered their upper lip in part to symbolize the secrecy of their creed as opposed to the more clipped mustaches of the other sectarian groups.

Alevi ritual practices contrasted markedly with those of the Sunnī of the region. A brief contrast of ritual and belief in terms of the five pillars of Islam indicates the singular nature of their beliefs from a Sunnī perspective. In terms of the declaration of faith, Alevis emphasize the role of cAlī in addition to the oneness of God and the prophecy of Muḥammad. Sunnī Muslims of the prevalent *Ḥanafī* rite of the region pray five times daily, with a total of about forty bowings (*rakca*-s) daily (according to Yalman there are about eight bowings in each of the five prayers). For the Alevis, two bowings *annually* in the presence of their prayer leader are sufficient. Sunnī-s fast the entire month of Ramaḍān; Alevi Musims consider this a fetish. They fast only twelve days of the year in memory of the twelve *Imām*-s. As for the pilgrimage to Mecca, they consider this to be "external pretense." The real pilgrimage is internal and in one's heart.[37] For the Sunnī, or (to use Hodgson's phrase) the *sharīca*-minded Muslims, such interpretations of the Islamic tradition are unacceptable. Yalman delineates other points of contention: *Alevi*-s are reputed not to perform ablutions correctly after sexual intercourse, and their secretive religious organization is regarded with suspicion by their non-Alevi neighbors. All but the most major disputes are resolved in the community itself and are not brought before the formal apparatus of the government. Within the Alevi community the rituals associated with the Feast of Abraham (Ar. *cĪd al-Kabīr)* are known as *Ayin-i Cem.* Outside the community it is known as *mum sondu* ("candle blown out"), a term "associated with the myth of communal sexual intercourse and incest."[38]

This ritual occurs once or twice yearly, when the *Dede,* or spiritual leader of the community, visits it from where he lives in a neighboring town. A key element of the ritual involves members of the community approaching the *Dede* in pairs, hand in hand, kneeling down and walking on all fours, like lambs, to kiss the hem of his coat. They then perform the only obligatory Alevi prayer. This is also the time at which the *Dede* attempts to settle outstanding disputes in the community, and the community sacrifices a ram.

Yalman's article is primarily diagnostic in that it documents Alevi social organization and popular belief and the relations between Alevis and non-Alevis (it might be added that the village described by Yalman had a heavy incidence of labor emigration). He also acknowledges the breakdown of communications between villagers and the Turkish government, especially the ministry responsible for religious affairs, the resilience of religious faith despite all efforts by the earlier

---

[36]*Ibid.,* 50.
[37]*Ibid.,* 51-52.
[38]*Ibid.,* 55.

republican government to discourage religious practices, and the increasingly evident political significance of these popular attitudes toward religion.[39]

## SUFISM

I suggested earlier that "universal" religions such as Islam are prismatic in their richness and involve multiple levels of belief and experience. The pervasive notion of community, the "Five Pillars" of Islam, the respect and authority accorded men of learning, and the *practical* organization of the community of believers (as opposed to normative adherence to the universal community of Islam) vary considerably. This section elaborates the notion introduced earlier of the copresence of alternative, or complementary (depending upon circumstances), notions of Islam. One dimension of Islam is the universalistic one of formal belief and practice, designated by the late Marshall Hodgson as a *sharī*$^c$*a*-minded Islam concerned principally with outward, public credos and behavior (such as normative adherence to the five pillars) and the elaborate body of Islamic scholarship and jurisprudence which has been constructed over the years. Another dimension of the Islamic experience has been glossed as "mysticism," although the notion of mysticism is an elastic one and carries connotations throughout the Islamic world much wider than the intensely personal and often esoteric pursuit of religious truths most commonly associated with the term.[40] In North Africa a key aspect of what is regarded as "mysticism" is *maraboutism*. Marabouts are persons living or dead (dead, that is, only from an outside observer's point of view) thought to have a special relation toward God which makes them particularly well placed to serve as intermediaries with the supernatural and to communicate God's grace *(baraka)* to their clients. Maraboutism is an ideology (usually implicit) and the ritual activities associated with such a belief. Often marabouts are thought to be descendants of the Prophet Muḥammad, of $^c$Umār, the second caliph in Islam (634-644), or of other religious leaders attributed with *baraka*. Tribes and urban neighborhoods often have special ties with particular marabouts or with maraboutic descent groups, such as the Sharqawa of western Morocco.[41] The shrines of such marabouts can be seen throughout North Africa, and the significance of such figures is formally acknowledged in a variety of ways. Throughout North Africa it is common for persons going on the pilgrimage to Mecca first to visit the shrines or sanctuaries of local marabouts and to do so again upon their return (see Fig. 9-2). Such ritual activities suggest an integrated vision among believers of "local" religious practices with those of the "central" rituals such as the pilgrimage. There is in addition an array of

[39] *Ibid.*, 58-60.
[40] Geertz, *Islam Observed*, p. 24.
[41] See Eickelman, *Moroccan Islam;* Brown, *People of Salé.*

religious brotherhoods *(ṭarīqa-s)* and lodges (Ar. *zāwiya;* Per. *khānqah;* Turk. *tekke*) inadequately glossed as associated with "mystic" practices.

Mysticism in Islam is known formally as *taṣawwuf* and in the West as Sufism. A mystic—the ambiguities of this term as signaled above must be kept in mind—is known as a *Ṣūfī.* The word *Ṣūfī* is sometimes said to originate from the Arabic word for wool, referring to the coarse wool garments that early Sufis wore to symbolize their lack of concern for the things of this world. *Ṣūfī* is also thought by some to derive from a word meaning "to be pure." If *sharīᶜa*-minded Islam was primarily concerned with outward, socially perceived behavior and the well-being of the Islamic body politic, then Sufism in the abstract represents more of a concern with the social and spiritual life of the individual (and, as shall be seen, of *specific* social groups).

In the first two centuries of Islam, from the seventh to the ninth centuries, Sufism appears to have remained a largely individual phenomenon, but gradually it developed a mass appeal.[42] The first Sufi gatherings were reputedly informal gatherings, especially among literati, for religious discussions. These gatherings sometimes were associated with the repetition of religious formulas, called *dhikr-s,* but these also could properly be recited in mosques. Hence Sufism was not considered to be a rival growth challenging the formal practices of *sharīᶜa*-minded Islam. (A later development was the addition of elaborate rituals, music, and dancing accompanying the *dhikr,* and *these* practices were regarded by some Muslims as a threat to the integrity of Islam.)

At first, organized Sufism appears particularly to have gained ground among the intellectual elite, constrained by the exigencies of *sharīᶜa*-minded Islam. Despite its stated apolitical objectives, Sufism was regarded from the outset as politically suspect (because of its potential for charismatic leadership), with political authorities sometimes using Sufi organizations for their own purposes or regarding them (often with cause) as being so used by others. The Sufi doctrine of the "inner way," or the "spiritual itinerary" toward greater religious experience, was especially regarded as suspect since by its very nature it claimed a privileged religious insight independent of the community. As a consequence, Sufis began to develop formal disciplines and standard ways of depicting their experiences. Regular stages in spiritual development were articulated in the classical theories of mystical thought, each of which was called a *ṭarīqa,* or "path." The same term also designates Sufi orders or brotherhoods.

In some versions of "classical" Sufi doctrine, the Sufi way consists of seven stages of ascending spiritual insight. Most members of religious orders remain at the lower rungs of these spiritual paths. The upper level is said to be reached when a mystic, in a state of exaltation *(ḥāl),* comprehends the divine attributes. Such per-

---

[42] The best account of the development of Sufi thought is probably Hodgson, *Venture,* I, 359-409; II, 201-54.

sons are considered *walī*-s, or saints, and often were popularly attributed with the ability to perform miracles.

By the eleventh century, particularly in the person of the great scholar and mystic al-Ghazzālī (d. 1111), a synthesis of intellectualized Sufi doctrine and *sharīʿa*-minded Islam was reached. At the level of an educated elite, a beautiful poetry and literature developed around the notions of mysticism, particularly in the principalities of Muslim Spain and in the Persian-speaking regions of the Islamic world.[43]

In many of the accounts of Sufism written by Muslims and by Western scholars concerned primarily with textual analysis there is an unfortunate tendency to consider Sufi doctrine as practiced and elaborated by the educated elite as "pure" Sufism and later, popular developments as a corruption of this purer vision. The result is a distorted view of religious development which led an earlier generation of historians to write of the "decline" of the Muslim world rather than to recognize the multiple levels of religious experience in which the "spiritual" aspects of Sufi practice as interpreted by an elite were balanced by its functions as a socio-political movement intimately tied to other aspects of society.[44] A proliferation of Sufi "paths" developed which were internally differentiated and which appealed to different groups and social classes.

In North Africa, for instance, the *Tijānīya* order had numerous government officials among its adherents.[45] In Turkey the *Bektāshī* order, founded in the thirteenth century, became particularly associated with the Janissaries, a professional military group that played an important part in the maintenance of the Ottoman empire until the early nineteenth century. The influence of this order was such that an estimated 10 to 20 percent of Turkey's adult male population belonged to it just before 1925, when religious brotherhoods were outlawed in Turkey. Other orders were associated with particular crafts or trades. Some of these orders were considered highly respectable; others, such as the Ḥamadsha and the Ḥaddāwa, were associated with the use of drugs, trances, and activities considered marginal to the urban bourgeoisie.[46] Until the 1920s, the strength of these orders was such that the majority of adult urban males and many villagers belonged to a brotherhood in most parts of the Middle East. A popular saying was: "He who does not have a Sufi master as his guide has Satan to guide him."

The organizational backbone of these orders is important to consider. At its

[43] Hodgson, *Venture,* II, 201-54.

[44] Such assumptions of a "decline" as Sufi ideas became popularly received unfortunately permeates most of the Orientalist literature on the subject. See A. J. Arberry, *Sufism: An Account of the Mystics of Islam* (London: George Allen & Unwin Ltd., 1950); W. Montgomery Watt, *Muslim Intellectual: A Study of Al-Ghazzali* (Edinburgh: University Press, 1963), esp. pp. 128-33; Rahman, *Islam.* On this point, see also the analysis of the classic study by the French Orientalist Alfred Bel contained in Eickelman, *Moroccan Islam,* pp. 22-29.

[45] Jamil M. Abun-Nasr, *The Tijaniya: A Sufi Order in the Modern World,* Middle Eastern Monographs, 7 (London: Royal Institute of International Affairs, 1965).

[46] See Vincent Crapanzano, *The Ḥamadsha.*

core was the relation of the Sufi master (Ar. *shaykh;* Per. *pīr*) to his disciple (*murīd* in both languages). In formal doctrine, the disciple was supposed to be under the total authority of the shaykh, like a dead body in the hands of its cleanser. Additionally, local religious lodges were organized in a loose hierarchy ordered by the prestige of their shaykhs. But the larger these organizations grew, the more difficulties they had in controlling their members. Nominally subsidiary lodges were constantly breaking away, with their leaders acting on their own. The dyadic, or two-person, chains of personal authority inherent in the organization of the brotherhoods thus had a built-in weakness. Despite this fact, colonial ethnographers in the nineteenth and early twentieth centuries, especially in North Africa, conceived of the organization of these orders as monolithic "pan-Islamic" conspiracies which could be used by the Ottoman regime and rival colonial powers to weaken colonial rule.[47] In practice, it might be added, the authority of shaykhs over their followers was usually less than total, as is indicated among other things by the fact that many individuals belonged to more than one order and that only a few orders required that their members join no other order.

The proliferation of Sufi "ways" and "saints" or marabouts cannot sufficiently be stressed. Bryan S. Turner has suggested the following contrasts with Christianity as a means of explaining the variety in scope and intensity of religious figures in Islam. In early Christianity, saintship at first was a local and spontaneous phenomenon, but saintship increasingly became tied to the institutional needs of a bureaucraticized church. By the medieval period, saints became officially recognized only after a lengthy process of canonization. There were three implications to this process. First, because of the length of canonization proceedings, persons became saints only after they died. Second, since there were stringent tests of piety required by ecclesiastical authorities, most saints were recruited from monasteries and nunneries. Finally, since trained theologians conducted canonization proceedings, theologians had a much better chance than illiterates for canonization.

In Islam, becoming a marabout stands in marked contrast to the Christian tradition, a principal reason why the term *marabout* is generally preferable to that of saint. First, with no formally recognized body of orthodoxy, the recognition of marabouts is invariably local, although some acquire widespread prominence. Secondly, while Christian saints tend to be orthodox, there is no orthodoxy to which marabouts can adhere. At best they can demonstrate orthopraxy and conform to an established ritual code. Finally, since there are no formal bodies for deciding who are marabouts, the process of labeling them varies widely. Sometimes a person is considered to be a marabout on the basis of descent from religious leaders, as on the basis of performing uncanny acts, outstanding feats of scholarship, or political success.

[47]See the map in Octave Depont and Xavier Coppolani, *Les Confréries religieuses musulmanes* (Algiers: A. Jourdan, 1897), for the most sinister representation of the influence of these orders. The authors were French government specialists on native affairs in Algeria.

There is an "essential looseness," to use Turner's elusive phrase, about Islamic religious organization, which means that it is much more responsive to local social contexts than has often been the case in Christianity.[48] Religious orders and lodges accommodated the local beliefs and customs of their adherents, and this led to their sustained popularity in earlier historical periods. In fact, much of the spread of Islam throughout North Africa after the initial Islamic conquests was due to the actions of these orders and lodges. Some of the leaders of these orders and lodges based their legitimacy upon genealogies of spiritual authority which in form resembled the "teaching licenses" (*ijāza*-s) of men of learning. The source of their teachings could ideally be traced in these chains (*silsila*-s) of authority to the teachings of the Prophet himself. Other lodges claimed genealogical descent from the Prophet Muḥammad. One such leader, the Sudanese Mahdi, Muḥammad Aḥmad (1844-1885), went so far as to model the major activities of his life upon those of the Prophet Muḥammad as a means of convincing followers of his legitimacy.[49]

**FIGURE 9-7** Members of Rifaꞌīya Order parading in Cairo, Muslim New Year, 1965. (From Michael Gilsenan, *Saint and Sufi in Modern Egypt: An Essay in the Sociology of Religion* [London: Oxford University Press, 1973]. Courtesy of the author.)

[48] Turner, *Weber and Islam*, pp. 57-62, 66.

[49] See P. M. Holt, *The Mahdist State in the Sudan, 1881-1898* (Oxford: Clarendon Press, 1958); for discussions of the Sudanese Mahdist movement in the light of later religious developments and a broad spectrum of religious movements in Islam, see John Voll, "Islam: Its Future in the Sudan," *The Muslim World*, 63, no. 4 (1973), 280-96, and his "The Sudanese Mahdi:

The reasons for the general decline of many of these orders by the earlier part of this century have been suggested by Michael Gilsenan. In 1964-1966 he studied one of the new Egyptian religious orders which continues to thrive, the Ḥāmidīya Shādhilīya.[50] This order was established in the first decades of the twentieth century and formally recognized by the government in 1926. In the early 1960s, it had between twelve thousand and sixteen thousand members, concentrated for the most part in Cairo and in the larger towns of the Nile Delta.

Gilsenan's argument for the decline of the other Egyptian orders by the 1920s is the following. In earlier times, the orders provided an "organized associational life" otherwise absent in many Islamic societies. As such, they served the function of being intermediaries between the highborn and the lowborn, rulers and ruled, as well as between persons at the same level of society.[51] As a result of basic changes in Egypt's political economy, the heads of the Sufi orders gradually lost their public and political influence. Professional politicians, landowners, lawyers, and journalists took over some of their functions, and various mutual aid societies were established to fulfill yet others. Additionally, the economic position of most of the orders was undermined as a result of government confiscation of some of the pious endowments (*waqf*-s), and the declining value of others on which they depended. This deprived the leaders of these orders of the resources with which to entertain their followers and to assist them when necessary. Moreover, Sufi teachings and ethics in their conventional form had become less and less responsive to the values of modern society. Many Sufi orders continue to be a major source of emotional gratification for their remaining adherents, but these adherents are now mostly peasants and manual laborers rather than the broader distribution of membership which they often had in the past, and younger Egyptians no longer seek to join most Sufi orders.

Gilsenan observes that the Ḥāmidīya Shādhilīya order was an exception to this general decline. Significantly, its founder, Salāma ibn Ḥasan Salāma (1867-1939), was a minor civil servant and as such was directly familiar with the demands of modern bureaucratic organization. He was largely self-taught but popularly respected for his religious learning and his claim to descent from the Prophet. Salāma was a charismatic figure to his followers: A number of miracle stories circulated concerning him during his lifetime; he was reputed to be capable of confounding the religious scholars opposed to him, was known for his understanding of the "secrets" of Islamic mysticism, and was charitable and generous to his followers.

---

Frontier Fundamentalist," *International Journal of Middle East Studies* 10, no. 2 (May 1979), 145-66. For an account of an Algerian religious figure that is excellent in portraying doctrine, but less so in describing the nature of the shaykh's popularity, see Martin Lings, *A Moslem Saint of the Twentieth Century* (London: George Allen & Unwin Ltd., 1961). A useful study with comparative materials is B. G. Martin, *Muslim Brotherhoods in Nineteenth-Century Africa*, African Studies Series, 18 (Cambridge: Cambridge University Press, 1976).

[50] Gilsenan, *Saint and Sufi.*

[51] *Ibid.*, p. 11.

Organizationally, the Sufi order which Salāma founded was set apart from the others. First, in contrast to the practice in other orders, the founder of the Ḥāmidīya Shādhilīya thoroughly tested his early initiates, so that he had a hard core of subordinates who were thoroughly devoted to him. Salāma demanded that his followers join no other brotherhood. Second, the order was successful in attracting a white-collar following as well as workers and peasants. Its doctrines and firm organization provide a sense of personal worth and security to "middle class" persons blocked in educational advancement (as are many educated Egyptians who hold clerical positions despite university degrees). Gilsenan characterizes most of its adherents as benefiting from, yet not wholly committed to, the new order of Egyptian society. Because of the lack of advancement opportunities, many individuals of humble origin who have had their occupational advancement blocked can find alternative satisfaction, he argues, in the order.[52] It offers the fraternal certitude and security which presumably were once provided by the "traditional" social order, yet is organizationally adapted to the exigencies of modern society.

A corollary organizational feature of the order is that each role in its hierarchy is carefully defined by written charter. Formal reports are required from its branches, and the members of the order are carefully controlled as to the nature of their public displays. While other groups exhibit ecstatic behavior in public, the Ḥāmidīya Shādhilīya is carefully organized and disciplines its members in public and demands exemplary conduct from them. In return, even if a member is transferred from one town to another, the order keeps in touch with him and assists him in adjusting to his new environment. Gilsenan argues that adherence to the primary religious values of the order enables its followers to resolve implicitly the frustrations they find in other aspects of their lives in modern society. Moreover, new branches are authorized by the order's hierarchy only after the order's leaders are convinced that they will be successful. Publicly this increases their prestige. Such administrative efficacy is almost completely lacking in the other orders. The hierarchical control of the Ḥāmidīya Shādhilīya order has enabled it effectively to overcome the problems of schisms and lack of control characteristic of the other orders.

## MARABOUTISM: TOWN AND TRIBE

One factor in the proliferation of Sufi brotherhoods is the contrast between the requirements of formal, community-minded religion as opposed to a more personalized pattern of belief such as that provided by the religious orders. Other factors are the local conceptions of the social order and the popular understanding of religion. A key Quranic notion is that all persons are equal before God, despite the inequalities to be found in this world. Yet the activities of some religious brotherhoods and the often lavish offerings given to marabouts and their descen-

[52]*Ibid.*, pp. 150-51.

dants in North Africa and similar figures elsewhere suggest that some Muslims implicitly act as if they accept a hierarchical conception of the relations between people and the supernatural.

How can the tenet of the equality before God be reconciled with the implicit notion of hierarchy? Analytically, an easy way out is to hold that any doctrine that suggests that all are not equal before God is a magical accretion to Islam. But from the viewpoint of tribesmen who make offerings and sacrifices to marabouts, such intermediaries with God are a part of Islam as they understand it. They regard themselves as Muslims, pure and simple, although they are aware of the disfavor in which such beliefs are held by Muslim scripturalists and reformists. Consequently, clients of marabouts often dissimulate their "local" beliefs in front of such persons, especially in contemporary contexts.

In essence, maraboutism involves the implicit assumption that whatever might be formally stated about Islam, human relations with the supernatural work in almost the same way as do relations among persons themselves. In the Moroccan case, for example, the implicit assumption concerning the social order is that people are related in personally contracted dyadic bonds of inferiority and superiority. In a nearly analogous fashion, marabouts are thought to have a "special" relation toward God and with particular persons or groups. For Moroccans and other North Africans who implicitly accept maraboutism, the main issue is not the existence of marabouts—that is taken for granted—but whether particular marabouts will choose to exercise their powers on one's behalf. They are more likely to do so if a client can claim "closeness" *(qarāba)* to the marabouts or his descendants. Moroccans who hold this belief are aware that there is no place for it in "official" Islam, "the Islam of the radio," as one Moroccan put it.

> Of course the radio says that everything comes directly from God. But just as the king has his ministers, God has his [marabouts]. If you need a paper from the government office, which is better? Do you go straight to the official and ask for it? You might wait a long time and never receive it. Or do you go to someone who knows you and also knows the official? Of course, you go to the friend, who presents the case to the official. Same thing ... if you want something from God.[53]

A range of offerings and sacrifices are made to marabouts and their descendants. Some, such as the sacrifice of bulls or sheep at the annual festival of a marabout are annual obligations which ensure that the social groups involved "remain connected" with the marabout and can count upon his blessings *(baraka)*. Other gifts are given by individuals or groups in exchange for specific requests. These offerings often are contingent. For instance, it is common for women to go to certain shrines asking for the marabout's help in becoming pregnant. They may

---

[53] Cited in Eickelman, *Moroccan Islam*, pp. 161-62. This study contains a more extensive discussion of maraboutism as an element of popular Islamic thought. (Courtesy of the author and publisher.)

FIGURE 9-8 "The radio says that everything comes directly from God. But just as the king has his ministers, God has his [marabouts]." Interior of Sidi Mḥammad Sharqī's shrine, Boujad, Morocco. (Courtesy of the author.)

tear a strip of cloth from their dress and attach it with henna to the door of a shrine as a "reminder" to the marabout. If the request is granted, then a sheep or other promised payment is made. At the larger shrines with attendants or descendants of the marabout acting as custodians, a hostel and even food may be provided for "visitors" (zawwār-s). The Arabic word for pilgrim (ḥajj) is not used to describe such visits; the pilgrimage to Mecca is considered conceptually to be a separate phenomenon. The modest offerings made by women on their own or their placing of "reminders" at such larger shrines is discouraged in favor of more substantial offerings in line with the "rank" of the marabout.

Such offerings are explicitly thought of in North Africa in terms of the ideology of "obligation" (ḥaqq) which informs most other social relationships. As

**FIGURE 9-9** Women often tear strips from their clothing to serve as "reminders" of requests to marabouts. Shrine near Boujad, Morocco. (Courtesy of the author.)

the descendant of one marabout explained: "You must bring a gift to 'open' a matter with God." Offerings and sacrifices create a bond of obligation between the marabout and his client. Just as with other patterns of obligations, those between marabouts and their clients, even if sometimes discussed in terms of the ideology of "blood" relations, are subject to vicissitudes. The reputations of marabouts living and "dead" are as subject to revaluation on the part of the clients as are other concepts of social obligations.

Personal and collective ties with marabouts rest on a similar ideological base, but the collective ties merit particular attention because of the emphasis lavished upon them by anthropologists. Many tribal collectivities are specifically mentioned in popularly known myths, which serve to legitimate the ties between particular maraboutic descent groups and their clients. Such covenants are represented as being maintained through such means as annual sacrifices, the giving of women to prominent leaders of maraboutic patronymic associations, the claim of a common, distant ancestor between marabouts or their descendants and their clients, and the claim of mere physical propinquity in the distant past.[54]

[54]For an example of such a myth, see *ibid.*, pp. 163-68. An analysis of that particular text in the wider context of the relation between oral narratives and Middle Eastern social forms can be found in Michael E. Meeker, *Literature and Violence in North Arabia*, Cambridge Studies in Cultural Systems, 3 (New York: Cambridge University Press, 1979), pp. 214-44.

**FIGURE 9-10** Preparing amulets for sale at a maraboutic shrine, Boujad, Morocco. (Courtesy of the author.)

So pervasive are the basic assumptions concerning the social order upon popular religious conceptions that notions parallel to maraboutism can be found in North African Judaism. Accounts of North African Jewish communities from the 1930s to the 1950s document saints' shrines, local festivals (called *hillūla* instead of *mūsim*), and sacrifices. In fact, many of these communities continued maraboutic practices in modified form after emigration to Israel; in one case, members of the group averred that their saint/marabout had managed to emigrate with them.[55]

The understanding of Islam represented by maraboutic practice is rapidly becoming transformed by changing economic and political conditions. In the past, marabouts in North Africa exercised a wider range of economic, political, and social roles than is today the case. Marabouts and maraboutic descent groups previously served as mediators between tribes and the Sultan's court, secured the safe passage

[55] The primary literature on these practices is principally in French. See Pierre Flamand, *Un Mellah en Pays berbère: Demnate,* Institut des Hautes-Etudes Marocaines, Notes et Documents, 10 (Paris: Librairie Générale de Droit et de Jurisprudence, 1952), pp. 93-122; J. Goulven, *Les Mellahs de Rabat-Salé* (Paris: Librairie Orientaliste Paul Geuthner, 1927), pp. 91-98; and L. Voinot, *Pèlerinages Judéo-musulmans du Maroc* (Paris: Editions Larose, 1948). For Israel, see Shlomo Deshen and Moshe Shokeid, *The Predicament of Homecoming* (Ithaca: Cornell University Press, 1974), esp. pp. 100-105.

FIGURE 9-11 Ḥillūla of Rabbi Yahya, near Rabat. This rare photograph was taken in the early 1920s. (From J. Goulven, *Les Mellahs de Rabat-Salé* [Paris: Librairie Orientaliste Paul Geuthner, 1927], plate 21. Courtesy of the publisher.)

of commerce, and participated in many commercial ventures. At the same time, many marabouts were widely respected as religious scholars. Their popular reputations as miracle workers and politicians in no way diminished the respect that was accorded their religious learning. Marabouts frequently had extensive contact with religious scholars in the principal towns and elsewhere, and in some cases even tutored members of the royal family. Frequently there was a constant tension between royal and maraboutic authority, but the relationship was one of complementarity. Earlier social anthropological studies dealing with the role of marabouts prior to colonial intervention suggested that they placed an interstitial "balancing" role between segmentarily organized tribes in the absence of an effective centralized government. More recent research based upon a more detailed study of social historical documents suggests that this earlier view needs revision. The extent to which maraboutic centers were allied politically with royal authority had previously been underestimated. In addition, far from being in opposition to urban-based religious scholars, many marabouts were respected by them and shared similar notions of Islam, even though popular understandings of their role were often at variance with "formal" Islamic precepts.[56] There was no sharp urban/rural dichotomy of belief and ritual practice but rather a continuum between the two.

The effect of the imposition of colonial rule and its consequent political and

[56]The most comprehensive and elegant case for the opposite point of view is Ernest Gellner's *Saints of the Atlas,* The Nature of Human Society Series (Chicago: University of Chicago Press, 1969). See the discussion of Gellner's argument in Chapter 5 of this book. The argument concerning the tendency of marabouts to benefit from alliances with royal authority is most extensively documented in Abdellah Hammoudi, "Sainteté, Pouvoir et Société: Tamgrout au XVIIe et XVIIIe Siècles," *Annales E.S.C.* (in press).

economic transformations was largely to circumscribe the scope of maraboutic powers. The political and economic roles of marabouts became almost negligible, although many individuals of prestigious maraboutic families were co-opted by the French into positions of local authority. Others, considered notables by the Protectorate administration, managed to use their position to acquire education, property, and the political influence necessary to maintain their elite position. As the kinds of specific actions which marabouts or the descendants can successfully undertake have diminished, so has the importance given to maintaining links with them by various tribal collectivities. The size of offerings has diminished and so has the size of the clientele of particular maraboutic groups. Nonetheless, their importance as a component of Islam as locally received and understood is far from negligible even today. The festivals of major marabouts continue to attract tens of thousands of clients annually. Today's maraboutic clientele tend largely to be rural and tribal, but this circumstance in itself does not seriously reduce their numbers. Despite Morocco's rapid urbanization, over 60 percent of its population continues to be rural, with much of it often benefitting only marginally from participation in modern economic circuits.

Maraboutism is only one of a range of popular religious ideologies that defy firm classification but which form a component of popular religious understandings. In southern Morocco, for instance, resistance to the French as late as 1919 was led by a religious figure from a marginal social group claiming to be a *mahdī*, who continued to attack the French even after more established religious figures had sought accommodation with the colonial power. After the *mahdī* died, the organization which he founded continued its resistance to the French until 1934.[57] The significance of such popular religious leaders has tended to be overlooked in part because of the reluctance of "establishment" religious scholars to recognize the strength of popular religious movements outside their control, the uneasiness of French military intelligence in comprehending such popular beliefs, and the fact that many foreign social anthropologists cannot readily assess the documentation on such leaders, most of which is in Arabic. As social anthropology increasingly becomes a "native" enterprise, significant modifications in how popular religious currents are depicted is certain to take place.

I have concentrated upon Morocco in discussing religious beliefs and "tribes" because in recent years anthropologists there have extensively debated the theoretical implications of how popular religious beliefs are related to the social order. However, earlier seminal studies exist for other regions. One of the first of these was Evans-Pritchard's *The Sanūsīya*.[58] His main thesis is that the Sanūsīya managed to become the most significant religious influence over the tribes of Cyrenaica in Libya because the order's leaders effectively managed to adapt its structure to local tribal conditions, something which no other order managed to do. This may well be

---

[57] Abdellah Hammoudi, "Aspects de la mobilisation populaire à la campagne, vus à travers la biographie d'un mahdi mort en 1919," *Centre de Recherches et d'Etudes sur les Sociétés Méditerranéenes, CNRS* (in press).

[58] E. E. Evans-Pritchard, *The Sanusiya of Cyrenaica* (Oxford: Clarendon Press, 1949).

the case, but several cautions concerning Evans-Pritchard's elegant presentation, briefly introduced in Chapter 3, are necessary. First, he characterizes the tribes of the region as segmentarily organized yet provides no concrete examples of exactly how these segmentary principles worked or how the Sanūsīya lodges were concretely articulated with the tribal structure. He provides a brilliant social history of Sanūsīya resistance to the Italians, their relations with English military authorities, and how they ultimately became highly politicized The details of guerrilla activities against the Italians are fully comprehensible without recourse to his characterization of tribal social structure as segmentary. Surprisingly, Evans-Pritchard deals with the transition from the presumed segmentary structure of the tribes to their integration into a "political form . . . on the model of the European state" in a mere two paragraphs.[59] Such a massive transformation of social form, if accurately depicted, merits more sustained consideration. Later studies of Islam in a tribal milieu, notably Lewis's account of the role of saintly lineages in Somalia from precolonial times to independence, are significantly more successful in suggesting how Islam has adapted to specific political and historical circumstances.[60]

## MEN OF LEARNING (ᶜULAMĀ')

Some studies of Islam in rural and tribal milieus depict a single pattern of religious belief and practice. In the foregoing sections I have presented some of the reasons why it is more accurate to regard belief and practice as prismatic, generating and

---

[59] *Ibid.,* pp. 104-5. See also Peters's analysis of the social structure of the Bedouin of Cyrenaica, discussed (with references) in Chapter 5, and his "From Particularism to Universalism, or the Religion of the Cyrenaica Bedouin," *Bulletin of the British Society for Middle Eastern Studies,* 3, no. 1 (1976), 5-14. For a rich Mauritanian study parallel to Evan-Pritchard's, see C. C. Stewart (with E. K. Stewart), *Islam and Social Order in Mauritania,* Oxford Studies in African Affairs (Oxford: Clarendon Press, 1973). For a study which has the advantage of discussing the contemporary influence of a religious order in a situation where such orders have substantial political and economic influence, see Donald B. Cruise O'Brien, *The Mourides of Senegal* (Oxford: Clarendon Press, 1971), and his *Saints and Politicians: Essays in the Organisation of a Senegalese Peasant Society,* African Studies Series, 15 (London: Cambridge University Press, 1975).

[60] Lewis has three major studies relevant to the role of Islam in Somalia. See I. M. Lewis, "Sufism in Somaliland: A Study in Tribal Islam," *Bulletin of the School of Oriental and African Studies,* 17, no. 3 (1955), 581-602, and 18, no. 1 (1956), 146-60; I. M. Lewis, *A Pastoral Democracy* (London: Oxford University Press, 1961), esp. pp. 196-241, and his "Shaikhs and Warriors in Somaliland," in *African Systems of Thought,* eds. G. Dieterlen and Meyer Fortes (London: Oxford University Press, 1965), pp. 204-223. Another study of Islamic religious leadership in a tribal milieu is Fredrik Barth, *Political Leadership among Swat Pathans,* L.S.E. Monographs on Social Anthropology, 19 (London: The Athlone Press, 1959), esp. pp. 92-103. Extensive critiques of Barth's presentation can be found in Talal Asad, "Market Model, Class Structure and Consent: A Reconsideration of Swat Political Organisation," *Man* (N.S.), 7, no. 1 (March 1972), 74-94, and Akbar S. Ahmed, *Millennium and Charisma among the Pathans,* International Library in Anthropology (London: Routledge & Kegan Paul, 1976). Despite the title of J. C. Wilkinson's *Water and Tribal Settlement in South-East Arabia,* Oxford Research Studies in Geography (Oxford: Clarendon Press, 1977), it is an excellent resource for documenting the relation of the Ibadi religious establishment and popular notions of legitimacy to tribal social structure.

reflecting multiple influences, in both urban and rural contexts. This is why it is misleading to speak of firm divisions among various types of religious leaders—scholars, mystics, *mahdī-s,* and the like. In practice these analytic categories overlap. A scholar can become popularly regarded as a marabout for the quality of his learning and piety, and an unlearned person similarly can acquire a scholarly reputation at least in popular circles. One of the unifying elements in Islam as a religious tradition is the respect for those aspects of belief and ritual which are considered to be fixed and enduring. Thus in religious learning, there is a valued cognitive style, "a set of basic, deeply interiorized master-patterns of language and thought," which places great emphasis upon the accurate memorization and transmission of knowledge which is considered to be fixed.[61] The key exemplar of this cognitive style is memorization of the Quran. Respect for knowledge that is fixed and enduring pervades not only religious knowledge *(ᶜilm)* but the knowledge of secular subjects and skills *(maᶜrifa).* This attitude also produces a particular respect for the exact use of the spoken word and of stocks of set verses from the Quran, proverbs and poetry, and influences much of the popular music, rhetoric, art, and oral literature (both religious and secular) throughout the Muslim Middle East.[62] At least prior to Western economic and colonial penetration, a major source for the inculcation of this style was the mosque-universities at which advanced students learned the Islamic religious tradition and contributed to it. Schools such as the

---

[61] Part of the discussion in this section is based upon Dale F. Eickelman, "The Art of Memory." The quotation defining *cognitive style* is from Pierre Bourdieu, "Systems of Education and Systems of Thought," *International Social Science Journal,* 19 (1967), 343.

[62] One of the few essays concerning the Muslim Middle East that deals extensively with the relation of language and artistic expression to society is Jacque Berque's *Cultural Expression in Arab Society Today,* Modern Middle East Series, 3 (Austin and London: University of Texas Press, 1978). Meeker's *Literature and Violence* is also a seminal study. Even when some modern forms of musical and graphic expression have sought to break away from more traditional art forms, they must generally do so on the basis of popular understandings of creative form, at least if their creators seek a wide audience. The major work on Arabic music (with four volumes of translations of Arabic treatises and two volumes devoted to contemporary modal, rhythmic, and formal structures) is Baron Rudolphe d'Erlanger's six-volume *La Musique Arabe* (Paris: Librairie Orientaliste Paul Geuthner, 1930-1959). For useful monographs and articles on the subject, see Hiromi L. Sakata, "The Concept of Musician in Three Persian-speaking Areas of Afghanistan," Ph.D. Dissertation submitted to the University of Washington, in 1976; Philip D. Schuyler, "A Repertory of Ideas: The Music of the *Rwais,* Berber Professional Musicians from Southwestern Morocco," Ph.D. Dissertation submitted to the University of Washington, in 1979, and his "Berber Professional Musicians in Performance," in *Performance Practice: The Ethnomusicological View,* ed. Gerard Behague (New York: New York University Press, 1980); Karl L. Signell, *Makam: Modal Practices in Turkish Art Music* (Seattle: Asian Music Publications [Series D., no. 4], 1977); Mark Slobin, *Music in the Culture of Northern Afghanistan,* Viking Fund Publications in Anthropology, 54 (Tucson: University of Arizona Press, 1976); and Ella Zonis, *Classical Persian Music: An Introduction* (Cambridge: Harvard University Press, 1973). The forms used in the traditional crafts of carpet-weaving, embroidery, woodcarving, and architecture show similar influences, although with the exception of Berque's and a few other interpretive essays, most literature on crafts and music remains highly descriptive. The transmission of many such crafts—and music is considered a craft as opposed to an art in many parts of the Middle East—has important parallels with the form in which religious knowledge was traditionally transmitted.

Qarawiyīn in Fez, the Yūsufīya in Marrakesh, the Zītūna in Tunis, the Azhar in Cairo, and their equivalents in Mecca and the two Yemens, the Ibāḍī Jabal Akhḍar region of Oman, and Qum in Iran were all well known throughout the Middle East. Beginning with the nineteenth century, the financial base upon which many of these institutions depended was increasingly undermined both by "native" regimes such as Muḥammad ᶜAlī's in Egypt and by colonial regimes such as that of the French in Algeria. Moreover, as European-style schooling, first provided only for specialized military training, rapidly expanded in scope and attracted students from the more privileged social strata and more ambitious poorer ones, Islamic schools were left to students of a modest and often rural origin. Some mosque-universities were "reformed," ostensibly to improve their curricula and standards but also to bring them firmly under government control, but these moves only accelerated their decline. Some mosque-universities continued to thrive until fairly recent dates—those of Morocco until the 1920s and early 1930s, those of the Yemen (Sanᶜāʾ) and the Sultanate of Oman until the middle of this century. Still, the social networks of influence and patronage formed in part through such mosque-universities have remained remarkably intact in many countries and the "cognitive style" conveyed by Islamic education retains a popular legitimacy.

The cultural idea of religious knowledge has remained remarkably constant over time throughout the regions of Islamic influence. Writing specifically of

FIGURE 9-12 Discussing a Quranic commentary, Ghazni, Afghanistan, 1973. (Courtesy Jon Anderson.)

medieval Islamic civilization, Marshall Hodgson states that education was "commonly conceived as the teaching of fixed and memorizable statements and formulas which could be learned *without any process of thinking as such.*"[63] This last phrase raises the crucial issue of the meaning of "understanding" associated with such a concept of knowledge. The supposedly fixed and memorizable statements conveyed by education constitute the religious sciences, the totality of knowledge and technique necessary in principle for a Muslim to lead the fullest possible religious life. These memorizable statements also constitute the most valued knowledge. The paradigm of all such knowledge is the Quran; its "mnemonic domination" *(malaka l-ḥifḏ)* is the starting point for the mastery of the religious sciences. To facilitate the task of memorizing other key texts of grammar and law, many of them are written in rhymed verse.

Because historians and sociologists have tended to take at face value the ideological claim in Islam of the fixed nature of religious knowledge, not much attention has been given to the critical topic of how such knowledge is linked with other aspects of society. In fact, Western scholars and many Muslims who have received a Western-style education merely assume that "stifling dullness" is characteristic of such education.[64] These extreme reactions to Islamic education suggest unfamiliarity with the principles upon which it is based.

Two linked propositions can be made concerning the form of Islamic knowledge. The first is that an intellectual tradition which emphasizes fixity and memory, as is characteristic of many other traditions of religious knowledge, can still be capable of flexibility. In practice there is considerable variation over time and place throughout the Islamic world as to the exact bodies of knowledge to be included in the religious sciences. Once this shifting is recognized, the interesting issue is the circumstances under which redefinitions occur as to what constitutes the proper scope of the religious sciences. The notion of what is meant by "tradition" in Islam, even the "high" tradition of scholarship and learning, may be fixed as to form and style (as the notion of what constitutes "valued" knowledge may be fixed in form and style in any educational system) but not as to content. If the compass of primarily religious studies appears unduly narrow, it was no more so than the curriculum of English public schools in the Victorian era, with their emphasis upon Greek and Latin, or of French lycées with their emphasis until recently upon classical training. As with the graduates of these institutions, former students of mosque-universities have become not only scholars but also politicians, ministers of state, merchants, and financiers who are quite capable of dealing with contemporary

[63] Hodgson, *Venture of Islam,* II, p. 438. (Emphasis added.)

[64] The phrase is from Leon Carl Brown, "The Religious Establishment in Husainid Tunisia," in *Scholars, Saints, and Sufis,* ed. Nikki R. Keddie (Berkeley and Los Angeles: University of California Press, 1972), p. 31. For a similar view expressed by an Egyptian writer (who later studied in France and became Minister of Education), see Taha Hussein, *The Stream of Days,* trans. Hilary Waymont (London: Longman, Green and Co., 1948). This book has been used as a required text in Egyptian primary schools, so it can be assumed that its implicit views concerning religious education have been widely disseminated.

economic and political problems. Hence one must look beyond the mere scope of such learning to understand its significance.

The second proposition is that the cognitive style associated with Islamic education is closely tied to popular understandings of Islam and has important analogues in nonreligious spheres of knowledge. This formal congruence has served to enhance the popular legitimacy of religious knowledge and of its carriers but at the same time has shaped the ways in which changes are perceived. Earlier in this chapter I indicated how a Moroccan religious judge *(qāḍī)* explained to me the notion of Islamic law in its jural sense and as a code for personal conduct. Everything within the two parallel lines which he drew on a sheet of paper were fixed—the content of Islamic law—everything else constituted innovation. Yet not all innovations are negative—they are tolerated so long as they do not explicitly contradict the principles of Islamic law. This formula might not be accepted by all Muslims, but it is one of the several means by which the notion of the fixity of tradition can be maintained while at the same time accommodating political and economic change. Most Muslims do not possess in fact an exact knowledge of the religious sciences but nonetheless share the assumption that religious knowledge is fixed and knowable and that it is known by men of learning.

Secular knowledge encompasses everything not included in the religious sciences, such as knowledge related to commerce and crafts, music and oral poetry. These last have significant parallels in form with the religious sciences and are also presumed to be contained by fixed, memorizable truths. Popular oral poetry takes this shape, just as effective public speech involves both the skillful invocation of Quranic phrases and the more mundane but memorizable stock of knowledge drawn from poetry and proverbs.[65] A further parallel is in the model for the transmission of knowledge. The religious sciences in Morocco and throughout the Islamic world are thought to be transmitted through a quasi-genealogical chain of authority which descends from master or teacher to student to ensure that the knowledge of prior generations is passed on intact. Knowledge of crafts is passed on in an analogous fashion. The measure of "understanding" appropriate to such forms of knowledge is its use, often creative, in wider social contexts than those provided by the milieu of learning itself or by the abstract manipulation of memorized material in "classroom" situations, as is characteristic of some contemporary education in the West.

Any analysis of learning in Islam must convey an idea of how many persons were traditionally educated and who they were, in order to understand the contemporary role of religious learning. The first years of study in Islamic education consisted of memorizing and reciting the Quran; only at later stages did the more advanced students learn to read and write, usually outside the context of the mosque school. In many rural areas that lack adequate "modern" schools, such

---

[65] See Clifford Geertz, "Art as a Cultural System," *Modern Language Notes,* 91 (1976), 1473-99, and John Paul Mason, "Structural Congruities in the Arab Genealogical Form and the Arabesque Motif," *Muslim World,* 64, no. 1 (1975), 21-38.

schools remain the only available form of education. Contemporary literacy is difficult to measure, let alone the literacy rates of earlier periods, but approximate estimates are necessary to indicate the scope of Islamic education. Thus for Morocco for the 1920s and 1930s, it appears reasonable to assume that 4 percent of the adult male rural population was literate, allowing for regional variations, and perhaps 10 to 20 percent of the adult male urban population. My own estimate is that similar figures would prevail for Oman, a country which possessed only three "modern" primary schools as late as 1970 and in which most education was necessarily carried out in mosque-schools.[66]

Religious learning was popularly respected, yet Quranic schools in their traditional settings were characterized by a high rate of attrition. Virtually every urban quarter and rural/tribal community maintained a mosque school, as is still the case, for which a teacher *(faqīh)* was contracted on an annual basis to teach and to perform certain other religious services. Most students attended such schools only long enough to commit to memory a few passages of the Quran; few remained for the long time necessary to memorize the entire Quran.

The formal features of these schools have frequently been described; although the consequences of the form of pedagogical action upon modes of thought have only begun to be critically explored. A typical teacher had between fifteen to twenty students in his charge, ranging widely in age. Printed or manuscript copies of the Quran were not often used, in part because of the lack of printed copies but also because the cultural concept of learning emphasized memorization. Each morning the teacher wrote on a slate the verses to be memorized by the student. The child then spent the rest of the day memorizing these verses and systematically reciting the verses learned earlier. Students were not grouped into "classes" based on age or on progress in memorization.

Two features consistently associated with Islamic education are its rigorous discipline and its lack of explicit explanation of memorized material. Both of these features are congruent with the concept of knowledge as essentially fixed and, of course, with the notion of reason *(ᶜqāl)* as the ability to discipline one's nature, as explained in Chapter 8. The firm discipline of Quranic education was thus just one of many ways in which the respect for the unchanging word of God could be inculcated in students. At least in Morocco, it is popularly believed that any part of a student's body struck in the course of memorizing the Quran will never burn in hell. To indicate the parallel with secular knowledge, the same notion applies to beatings given by a craftsman to his apprentice.

As to the "explanation" of what is memorized, former students of traditional Islamic education have emphasized to me that throughout the long process of

[66] Sources for the Moroccan estimate are provided in Eickelman, "The Art of Memory," 492. Fanny Colonna, *Instituteurs Algériens: 1883-1939* (Paris: Presses de la Fondation Nationale des Sciences Politiques, 1975), p. 30, suggests that around 40 percent of Algeria's male population could read and write just prior to French conquest in the 1830s. Under the French, literacy suffered a precipitous decline because of the systematic destruction of educational institutions.

FIGURE 9-13 Rural families often made financial sacrifices to send their sons to mosque-universities. Moroccan religious student, c. 1946. (Courtesy Bouzekri Draiouiy.)

memorizing the Quran, often six to eight years, they did not ask questions directly concerning its meaning, nor did it occur to them to do so, even when Arabic was not their first language. "Understanding" in the context of such concepts of learning was not measured by any ability to "explain" particular verses explicitly. Such explanation *(tafsīr)* was considered to be a science in itself. Instead, the measure of understanding was implicit and consisted of the ability to use particular Quranic verses in appropriate contexts. Originality was shown by working Quranic references into novel but appropriate contexts, just as knowledge and manipulation of secular oral poetry and proverbs in a parallel fashion were also the signs of good rhetorical style. This notion of style continues to hold in many parts of the Muslim world.

The high rate of attrition from Quranic schools suggests that mnemonic "possession" of the Quran and related texts can be considered to be a form of cultural capital. Aside from small traditional gifts by the parents of the children to their teachers, Quranic education was free. Yet most students were compelled to drop out after a short period in order to contribute to the support of their families or because they failed to receive parental support for the arduous and imperfectly understood process of learning. In practice, memorization of the Quran was

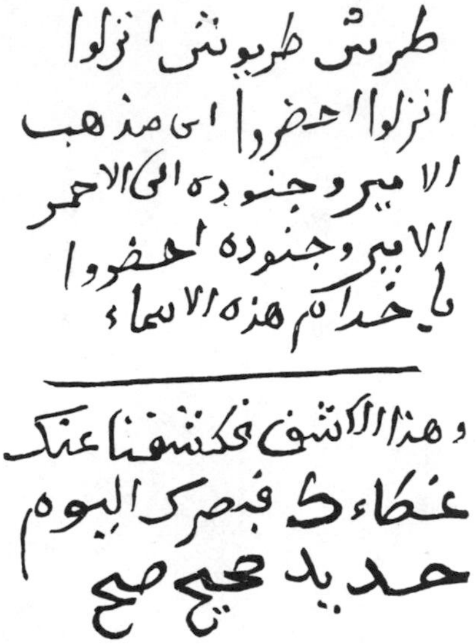

Magic Invocation and Charm.

"Ṭarshun! Ṭaryooshun! Come down!
Come down! Be present! Whither are gone
the prince and his troops? Where are El-Aḥmar
the prince and his troops? Be present
ye servants of these names!"

"And this is the removal. 'And we have removed from thee
thy veil; and thy sight to-day
is piercing.' Correct: correct."

FIGURE 9-14 Even among illiterates, writing is highly respected. Invocation for an amulet. (From Edward William Lane, *An Account of the Manners and Customs of the Modern Egyptians* [London: John Murray, Publishers, Ltd., 1860], p. 269.)

accomplished primarily by the children of relatively prosperous households or by those whose fathers or guardians were already literate. I say "primarily," for education was still a means to social mobility, especially if a student managed to progress despite all obstacles through higher, post-Quranic education. Moreover, the children of the wealthy and powerful had more opportunities to observe gatherings where the proper use of educated rhetorical style was employed than did poorer students. In fact, the biographies of men of learning repeatedly stress the importance of their family milieu in successfully mastering the traditional texts.

The scope of traditional higher education is also significant to consider because of the importance attributed to men of learning in many accounts of the social structure of "traditional" Islamic society. For Morocco in 1931, the year of the first reliable census in at least the French-controlled part of the country, such students constituted a minuscule 0.02 percent of the population.[67] Moreover, since most students left their studies after a few years to become merchants, village teachers, notaries, and the like, the limited number who eventually could claim to be men of learning is readily evident. Mosque-universities in their "traditional" sense (that is, before the al-Azhar reforms of the late nineteenth century and those of Morocco in the 1930s) constituted institutions in the basic sense of a field of activity whose members shared subjectively held ideas and conventions as to how given tasks should be accomplished. In the first place, the use of space in such mosque-universities indicated their lack of separation from the rest of society. Lessons were conducted in the same space used by the wider community for purposes of worship and other gatherings. Onlookers or persons seeking merely to acquire God's blessings by being close to persons discussing religious texts were free to join the lesson circles. Mosque-universities had no sharply defined body of students or faculty, administration, entrance or course examinations, curriculum, or in most cases unified sources of funds. Teachers *(shaykh-s)* did not form a corporate group as they did in medieval Europe, although older and respected *shaykh-s* served as spokesmen for their colleagues on various occasions. In some parts of the Muslim world, shaykhs were formally appointed, but this was just as often not the case. The lack of formal appointment meant that younger scholars had to be especially scrupulous about comporting themselves in ways expected of men of learning and commenting on texts in expected ways in order to demonstrate their claims to be men of learning. Moreover, the formal lesson circles of the mosque-universities often provided virtually no opportunity for students actively to acquire the skills needed to master the rhetorical skills expected of men of learning or to learn the poetry, history, and literature which such men were often expected to learn but which were not formally taught in the public lesson circles of the mosques themselves.

As in any educational system with diffuse, implicit criteria for success, and in which essential skills were not fully embodied in formal learning, the existing elite was favored and certain families often became distinguished for their learning over generations. This was especially so as many of the essential skills needed by educated men were acquired through peer learning and through acquiring the sponsorship of established men of learning. In such activities, students from urban families which already contained men of learning or influence were at a competitive advantage. Students from rural regions were at an initial disadvantage, although once again those from families of rural notables were in a better situation. It was often through peer learning that new interpretations of Islamic tradition, such as the reformist *(Salafīya)* movement of the late nineteenth and early twentieth century first became disseminated. As such learning was strictly informal, it also was extremely difficult for political authorities to monitor. In addition, teaching

---

[67]Sources for these figures are provided in Eickelman, "The Art of Memory," 497.

licenses tended to be perfunctory documents; what counted was sponsorship by influential men of learning and acquiring public recognition, usually from persons not themselves in scholarly circles.

Despite the great respect in which religious learning and men of learning are held in many parts of the Islamic world, the majority of students at traditional mosque-universities rarely ever used such knowledge in more than an iconic fashion, as a marker of participation in the milieu of learning. When in the course of my own research in Morocco I asked former students of such schools why they left their studies rather than remain in the scholarly milieu, most expressed a formal sense of regret, but few considered such "attrition" to be a failure on their part. Instead, most emphasized the opportunities their years at the mosque-university created to secure ties with persons within and outside the community of learning. These ties often were of use later in facilitating commercial, political, and entre- preneurial activities. Most of them stated that their intention in participating in the mosque-university milieu in the first place was to acquire knowledge of the religious sciences. The response was to be expected given the cultural emphasis placed upon such valued knowledge. Acquiring the religious sciences additionally implied participation in social networks with persons drawn from different backgrounds and regions of the country and thus actual or potential access to a wide range of centers of power. No other preparation, except perhaps association with the sultan's entourage, enabled a person to acquire such a wide range of potential associations. Knowledge of the religious sciences was of course a necessary technical prerequisite to performing certain tasks, but these did not begin to exhaust the meaning of education. Acquiring such knowledge also provided the consociational base from which a wide range of extralocal political, economic, and social activities could be undertaken, at least so long as there were no major alternatives to Islamic higher education.

In many contexts throughout the Middle East until recent times, Islamic men of learning were in the heart of political affairs. If a new ruler was to be recognized, the men of learning of each town conveyed or withheld the oath of allegiance of the population to the new sultan. Popular protest often began at the mosque- universities, even though it usually was not initiated by men of learning themselves. Since men of learning tended to be members of the social elite and at the same time appropriated for themselves the symbols of legitimacy provided by religious scholarship, they often represented the will of the population to the government and the intentions of the government to the populace. If the government performed acts which men of learning considered outside the bounds of Islam and if the men of learning were capable of withstanding the ruler's displeasure, the ruler was often compelled to change his course of action. As Albert Hourani has cogently argued, because men of learning had access to rulers, they acted as popular leaders, and be- cause their popular religious legitimacy gave them autonomous authority of their own, rulers needed them and were compelled to listen to them. "But for this reason, [their] modes of action must in normal circumstances be cautious and even ambiguous" so that they do not appear to be either the instruments of authority or the enemies of authority. Hence men of learning usually chose to exercise their influence discreetly in private. Hourani in fact uses the term "patrician politics" to characterize the nature of their influence.[68]

A number of excellent studies by social historians and anthropologists on the role of men of learning in various Muslim communities have recently become available.[69] One of the first of this "new wave" of accounts is Ira Lapidus's study of medieval Damascus from the thirteenth through the early sixteenth centuries.[70] Because most of these studies implicitly suggest the importance of ties of personal dependence in both urban and rural contexts and the importance of *informal* patterns of authority, they suggest key continuities in patterns of authority and legitimacy with many modern situations. In Lapidus's description of medieval Damascus, no special interest group could entirely stand apart from the men of learning or fail to be represented by them. They did not form an organized, collective body and were drawn from heterogeneous origins. Some represented scholarly circles, others important and wealthy families, others major religious brotherhoods appealing to various social groups. The multiple informal roles they played held society together in the sense that this informal body had contact with virtually all elements of society. They had no military power and thus could not defend cities, nor could they always suppress violence. Yet their informal consensus provided the legitimacy and moral authority needed by any ruler to survive or conversely to legitimate popular protest.

In every case where alternatives developed to higher Islamic education, mosque-universities quickly lost their former vitality. Even when families which produced men of learning continued to predominate, it was because of their ability to adapt to new circumstances. In almost every instance, the sons and daughters of such men of learning have been given "modern" education in the light of changing circumstances. However it is still appropriate to say that the popular legitimacy of the form of knowledge conveyed by Islamic education and its carriers remains largely intact, as shown collectively by the sustained prestige accorded to men of learning in Iran and in certain other contexts in the Muslim world.

In the past, the memorizable truths of Islamic learning were passed from

[68] Albert Hourani, "Ottoman Reform and the Politics of Notables," in *The Beginnings of Modernization in the Middle East: The Nineteenth Century*, eds. William R. Polk and Richard L. Chambers (Chicago and London: University of Chicago Press, 1968), pp. 41-68.

[69] Some of the outstanding studies now available are Leon Carl Brown, "The Religious Establishment"; Kenneth L. Brown, "Profile of a Nineteenth-Century Moroccan Scholar," in *Scholars, Saints, and Sufis*, ed. Keddie, pp. 127-48, and his *People of Salé*, pp. 66-99; Edmund Burke, III, "The Moroccan Ulama, 1860-1912: An Introduction," in *Scholars, Saints, and Sufis*, pp. 93-125, and his *Prelude to Protectorate in Morocco*, Studies in Imperialism (Chicago and London: University of Chicago Press, 1976). For medieval Iran, see Richard Bulliet, *The Patricians of Nishapur* (Cambridge: Harvard University Press, 1972) for which the review by Roy P. Mottahedeh in the *Journal of the American Oriental Society*, 95 (1975), 491-95, provides an interesting critique. For Tunisia, see Arnold H. Green, *The Tunisian Ulama, 1873-1915: Social Structure and Response to Ideological Currents* (Leiden: E. J. Brill, 1978).

[70] Ira Lapidus, *Muslim Cities in the Later Middle Ages* (Cambridge: Harvard University Press, 1967).

generation to generation. Since the collapse of most Islamic higher education, this is no longer the case. So far, this collapse of the "technology" of intellectual reproduction has had no pronounced effect, but, as elsewhere, major changes in educational systems take a long time to have a widespread impact. Popular respect for the concept of Islamic knowledge as fixed and memorizable and the cognitive style represented by such education remains largely intact, as does respect for what in many cases may be the last prestigious generation of its carriers.[71]

The shift of religious knowledge from that which is mnemonically possessed to material that can only be consulted in books suggests a major change in the nature of knowledge and its carriers. Ideologically it may still be maintained that religious knowledge is memorizable and immutable, as is certainly the case for the word of God as recorded in the Quran, but the lack of concrete embodiment of this premise in the carriers of such knowledge indicates a major shift. This shift may not be consciously recognized, just as many Muslim intellectuals claim that the imposition of colonial rule in many regions had little impact on the belief and practice of Islam, which from a sociological point of view is decidedly not the case.[72] One of the crucial consequences of this shift is that socially recognized carriers of religious learning are no longer confined to those who have memorized authoritative texts in circumstances equivalent to those of the mosque-universities, with their bias toward favoring members of the elite. Those who can interpret what Islam "really" is are now of more variable social status than was the case when mnemosyne was an essential feature of the legitimacy of knowledge. The carriers of religious knowledge in Islam increasingly are persons capable of claiming a strong Islamic commitment; freed from mnemonic domination, religious knowledge can increasingly be delineated and interpreted in a more abstract and flexible fashion. A long apprenticeship under an established man of learning is no longer a prerequisite to legitimizing one's own religious knowledge.


## REFORM: THE SELF-RENEWAL
## OF ISLAMIC TRADITION

The dates in the title of Albert Hourani's *Arabic Thought in the Liberal Age, 1798-1939* suggest indirectly that the main impetus for reform in Islamic thought was the challenge of Western encroachment upon the area.[73] Egypt was for a long time

---

[71] For contemporary examples of such style translated directly into English, see the speeches contained in the First World Conference on Muslim Education, *Conference Book, 31 March - 8 April 1977* (Mecca and Jeddah: King Abdul Aziz University, 1977).

[72] For a highly intellectualized example of implicit colonial influence, see Sayyid Amir ᶜAli's influential *The Spirit of Islam* (London: Christopher's Ltd., 1922), in which the Prophet Muhammad is portrayed with all the virtues of a Victorian gentleman. The author, a leading Muslim modernist, was a civil servant in colonial India and wrote in English. See also Dale F. Eickelman, "Islam and the Impact of the French Colonial System in Morocco," *Humaniora Islamica*, 2 (1974), 215-35.

[73] Albert Hourani, *Arabic Thought in the Liberal Age, 1798-1939* (London: Oxford University Press, 1967).

the center of such reformist activities. The influence of nineteenth-century intellectuals upon the Islamic body politic was a profound one, and such activities as the "organization" *(niẓām)*—the word *reform* was scrupulously avoided—of the al-Azhar mosque-university had a profound if delayed impact. It was toward the end of the nineteenth century through the 1930s that reformist Islam began to gain popular momentum. In Morocco, the impetus was linked with the impending threat of European penetration. Reformist thought primarily spread in the circles of intellectuals connected with the sultan's court and among educated merchants of the urban bourgeoisie informally linked with the milieu of the mosque-university. It took the form both of the dissemination of the ideas of religious reformers from the Arab "East" such as Jamāl ad-Dīn al-Afghānī (1839-1897) and Muḥammad ᶜAbduh (1849-1905), both of whom attracted disciples throughout the region. Certain religious brotherhoods with modernist tendencies appealed significantly to members of the mercantile and administrative elite.[74]

The concern of this account is primarily with the popular impact of reform or modernist Islam. Ideologically, the essence of the movement was to divest Islam of what the reformers considered to be its particularistic accretions and to return to the essential principles of faith; hence the name of the movement in Arabic, *Salafīya*, which suggests a return to the Islam of the venerable forebears. In Islam it is common for both modernists and conservatives to justify their ideological position by emphasizing that it is a return to essential principles and not an innovation. Clifford Geertz has suggested an association between the crystallization of region-focusing markets in Morocco and the rise of reformist Islam and religious brotherhoods with modernist tendencies. In my own work in western Morocco, the major popular spread of reformist ideas came in the 1930s. The principal carriers of these ideas were urban merchants, many of whom had been associated with mosque-universities. Reformist Islam gave them an ideological base to challenge the domination of a maraboutic family influential in the region which formerly also controlled much of the commercial activity. The Islam which they propagated was one of coherent doctrines based on clearly stated, universalistic grounds, as opposed to the traditional, largely implicit, maraboutic belief system. In many regions, reformist Islam became in part a vehicle for asserting autonomy from the dominant groups of earlier generations and in addition became a prototype for the nationalist movement.[75] Organizationally, it was common in the 1930s for merchants and craftsmen caught up with the reformist movement to set up loosely knit, ephemeral committees to negotiate various matters with the local administration, such as the construction of schools. Reformist Islam had few adherents in this period, but the few tended to be members of influential families. In contrast, marabouts and their supporters were too tied to the particular circumstances of the local communities

[74]K. Brown, "Profile," pp. 135-46. On Afghānī, ᶜAbduh, and their disciples, see Hourani, *Arabic Thought,* pp. 103-92.

[75]Jamil M. Abun-Nasr, "The Salafiyya Movement in Morocco: The Religious Basis of the Moroccan Nationalist Movement," *St. Antony's Papers,* 16 ( 1963), 90-105.

to serve as vehicles for an emerging national consciousness or the practical implementation of a nationalist movement.

The reformist movement in Algeria is one of the best documented in terms of its popular spread. As Ali Merad has written, before the emergence of the reformist movement virtually no Algerian Muslim thought that Islam was anything except maraboutism.[76] Marabouts were the only religious spokesmen for most Algerians and the only alternative to them was a "clergy," subsidized by the French, that was officially authorized to conduct Friday prayers in the mosques of the country. In the Algerian case, an initial impetus for the reform movement was the brief visit of the Egyptian reformer Muḥammad ᶜAbduh to Algeria in September 1903. ᶜAbduh's local contacts, although few, were with Algerians influential in religious circles. The popular impact of the reformist movement accelerated after World War I with the return of Algerians who had fought with the French and who were disillusioned with resuming their former subservient status. Algerians from all parts of the country began to recognize their common situation despite linguistic and regional differences. (Perhaps an unintended byproduct of French rule was to bring "natives" of different regions into more contact with one another.) Distant problems became more familiar, and Algerians began to think actively in terms of a national community. The term "Young Algerian" began to be used, in parallel with the term "Young Turk" for the Ottoman province of Anatolia. The small Algerian cadre of French-trained schoolteachers, doctors, journalists, and attorneys formed the vanguard of this movement, but their direct influence upon other Algerians was limited by their minimal contacts with Algerians who were not so trained and an inability to communicate effectively with this vast majority. Because marabouts and the "official clergy" had supported the French against the Ottoman empire (allied with the Germans) during the war, they rapidly lost popular support. A number of Algerian reformist leaders emerged, of whom ᶜAbd al-Ḥamīd ibn Bādis (ben Badis) (1889-1940) was the key and representative leader. Ibn Badis was from a leading family of Constantine. Immersed in Islamic scholarship, he was influenced by reformist ideas from the Arab East and maintained active ties with Algerians from many walks of life. The high social class of these reformers meant that the French dealt circumspectly with them. Reformists began to visit mosques throughout Algeria, emphasizing in their preachings the unity of Islam, charity, worship, and mutual assistance. While trying to avoid direct confrontation with the marabouts, who were often strongly embedded in local political networks, they challenged the maraboutic claim of communication with the Prophet, their power of intercession and miraculous healing, and magic and sought to convince Algerians that these notions were not part of good Islamic doctrine. By 1933 the French administration had become concerned about the reformists and placed restrictions on them, especially as some of them had become directly involved in the incipient nationalist movement.

[76] Merad, *Réformisme*, p. 58. See also Ernest Gellner, "The Unknown Apollo of Biskra: The Social Base of Algerian Puritanism," *Government and Opposition* (London), 9 (1974), 277-310, which contains an excellent analysis of Merad's work.

Merad makes two major points. First of all, maraboutism was the backdrop against which reformist ideologies in Algeria were forged and elaborated. No matter how many educated Muslims deride the implicit assumptions of maraboutism today, the maraboutic interpretation of Islam was a major force in the 1930s and in many parts of North Africa continues to play a significant role. Secondly, reformism mounted an offensive of educated urban interpretations of Islam, "intelligible and simple," against a tribal and rural religious orientation. Merad argues that consciously or not, urban values impregnated the religious conceptions of the reformist movement and paved the way for "rationalist" conceptions of Islam. He goes so far as to say that without intending to do so, the carriers of reformist Islam managed to secularize Islam by conveying it as doctrines and practices set apart from other aspects of life and to popularize "confused" notions of modernism.[77]

It is possible to argue, as has Wilfred Cantwell Smith, that there has been a tendency in the Islamic world as in the Christian one for religious traditions that once were "coterminous with human life in all its comprehensiveness" to become transformed so that now "the religious seems to be one facet of a person's life alongside many others."[78] Still, it is important to recognize that the reformist movement, by simplifying religion and making it popularly intelligible, also made it a universal vehicle for national and wider anticolonial identities. In fact, it is significant that Muᶜammar al-Qadhdhāfī, the "teacher-leader" of Libya, proclaims himself a devout Muslim, yet his *Green Book,* two pocket-sized tracts concerning social justice and economy, never explicitly mentions Islam. The language of the Arabic version makes clear his reliance upon key themes of Islamic modernism but not upon organized Islam or its men of learning.[79]

The richness of modernist and reformist movements in contemporary Islam is too great to allow a detailed survey here, but another important component of the emerging "essential" Islam of the educated middle classes is a militancy against what they see as any religious compromise or temporizing. In the vocabulary of Ernest Gellner, it can be considered to be a sort of Islamic puritanism.[80] One of the best known of such movements is the Muslim Brotherhood *(al-Ikhwān al-Muslimūn)* of Egypt, founded in 1928. The Muslim Brothers appropriated for themselves the right to challenge organized political authority, and, as a consequence, the movement was forced to go underground several times. Equivalent movements have been created in other Middle Eastern countries and in many cases exercise a strong political influence. This is a movement perhaps more politically committed than other forms of Islamic modernism, although as indicated earlier, other versions of

[77]Merad, *Réformisme,* pp. 437-39.

[78]Wilfred Cantwell Smith, *The Meaning and End of Religion* (New York: The Macmillan Company, 1963), p. 124.

[79]Muammar al-Qadhafi, *The Green Book.* Part One is subtitled "The Solution of the Problem of Democracy: 'The Authority of the People' "; Part Two, "The Solution of the Economic Problem: 'Socialism.' " Neither the Arabic nor the English version contains date or place of publication, perhaps to indicate the document's timelessness. They are available from most Libyan diplomatic missions.

[80]Gellner, "The Unknown Apollo."

Islamic reform (or for that matter Islamic conservatism) also carry strong political implications.[81] The founder of the Muslim Brothers in Egypt, Ḥasan al-Bannā, was born in 1906. His father had been educated at the Azhar, earned his livelihood as a watchmaker, and passed his piety and classical learning on to his son. From the time he entered primary school, Ḥasan al-Bannā was involved in different religious societies and became strongly interested in Sufi teachings. As with other educated youth of the 1920s, he constantly discussed with his associates the state of Islam and the nation and was concerned with the defection of many of the educated from the Islamic way of life. When he founded the Muslim Brotherhood, he was held in personal veneration by many of his followers. Members had to swear complete obedience to the movement, although there were degrees of membership. At the same time, there were punishments for negligent members, so the society had a built-in discipline which set it apart from other religious associations and political movements. Because the organization implicitly made no distinction between the political and social order and called for the purification of society, successive governments saw it as a revolutionary force.[82] The organization was suspected of and actually was involved in considerable political violence.

As for the ideology of the movement, Richard P. Mitchell has characterized it as "the first mass-supported and organized, essentially urban-oriented effort to cope with the plight of Islam in the modern world."[83] Mitchell sees a continuity between earlier reform movements, including the *Wahhābī* movement of eighteenth-century Arabia. Members of the movement see themselves as practical successors to the reformist ideas of earlier leaders such as al-Afghānī. The goals of the Muslim Brotherhood include renewed unity of the Muslim community and an appeal for personal reform as a prelude to making the Islamic community realize its full potential for development in the modern world. Their starting point for this revitalization is Islam and its tradition. Western influences are not excluded but are accommodated only insofar as they can be harnessed to the service of an "integral" Islamic code of behavior. Such ideological notions are very much in line with contemporary Saudi thinking, which is one of the reasons that "integralist" and fundamentalist movements reflecting ideologies similar to the Muslim Brothers appear to receive active financial backing from the Saudi state throughout the Middle East. Saudis evidently see such government as more congenial to their own political and religious interests than other forms of radicalism.[84]

As Mitchell indicates, it is difficult to ascertain with any precision the social

---

[81] Richard P. Mitchell, *The Society of the Muslim Brothers,* Middle Eastern Monographs, 9 (London: Oxford University Press, 1969).

[82] *Ibid.,* p. 312.

[83] *Ibid.,* p. 321.

[84] On the popular bases of contemporary fundamentalist movements and the support which such movements receive from Saudi Arabia and to a lesser extent from Libya, see Detlev H. Khalid, "The Phenomenon of Re-Islamization," *Aussenpolitik* (German Foreign Affairs Review), 29, no. 4 (1978), 433-53. For a Saudi-backed "charter" to design a modern Islamic educational curriculum, see First World Conference on Muslim Education, *Conference Book.*

origins of a quasi-secret organization, but available documentation suggests that despite its large rural membership, the Egyptian brotherhood was dominated by urban activists. These activists were in addition predominantly from the urban middle class. Mitchell attended many of the open meetings of the Brothers between 1953 and 1955 and reports that he saw a fairly regular pattern of attendance: servants, merchants, craftsmen, and a few Azharites but an "overwhelming majority" of students, civil servants, office workers, and professionals in Western dress—in short, "an emergent and self-conscious Muslim middle class" hostile to imperialism and its "internal" agents and interested in conservative reform and the reinstitutionalization of religious life as they conceive it.[85]

In discussing modernist trends in Islam it is easy to convey the impression of highly organized movements with clearly articulated ideologies and political goals. Certainly such movements have been a significant component of modernist tendencies and suggest the continuing capacity of Islam to encompass a variety of social situations. Patterns of financial backing from certain conservative Arab states interested in encouraging political thought which parallels their own interests make such organizations perhaps even more visible.[86] Yet such movements do not exhaust the range of religious expression, which in times of crisis even can cross the boundaries of major world religions.

One such event was the widespread belief in Egypt that the Virgin Mary appeared over a church in a suburb of Cairo from April 2, 1968 until several years later.[87] Thousands of pilgrims flocked daily to the site hoping to see the miracle. As Cynthia Nelson relates, the Virgin commands the respect of both Muslims and Christians in Egypt. Soon after the first apparition, the Coptic Patriarch of Egypt and All Africa announced at a press conference that the Virgin's appearance was real. The government subsequently took formal notice of the event. What is significant about the apparition is the way that it served as a symbol of unity for many Egyptians. Most Egyptians connected the apparition of the Virgin with the Six-Day War of June 1967, "a military defeat that left the country in despair and its people confronting perhaps the severest crisis in their contemporary history."[88] Both Copts and Muslims saw the Virgin as having come to extricate them from their crisis. Copts interpreted her appearance as reaffirming their role in the future of Egypt to the Muslim community. Many educated students and others who had lost their faith, whether Christian or Muslim, interpreted the event either as a ruse of a foreign intelligence agency (the presumably ubiquitous CIA) or alternatively as a warning to restore their faith in the nonvisible and nonrational. Again, the form of the transcendent is tied to the nature of political and social realities.

---

[85] Mitchell, *Muslim Brothers*, pp. 328-31. For a parallel discussion elsewhere of the emergence of a "middle class" interpretation of Islam, see Voll, "Islam: Its Future."

[86] Khalid, "Re-Islamization."

[87] Cynthia Nelson, "Religious Experience, Sacred Symbols, and Social Reality: An Illustration from Egypt," *Humaniora Islamica*, 2 (1974), 253-66. Also see her comments on Jones, "World Views—Their Nature and Their Function," *Current Anthropology*, 13 (1972), 98-102.

[88] Nelson, "Religious Experience," p. 260.

## BEGINNINGS

The flexibility and capacity for self-renewal of Islam are perhaps nowhere more clearly exemplified than in the formation of the early Islamic polity in seventh-century Arabia. In fact, because of the attention lavished on the events of this period by generations of scholars, the origins of Islam are in some respects more fully documented than the beliefs and religious practices of some contemporary Middle Eastern societies. Moreover, much of the key primary literature has been translated into English, so that it is readily accessible to nonspecialists.[89]

In thinking of the great world religions and the polities associated with them, there is a tendency to gloss over their tentative beginnings and to see them as emerging intact in the forms by which they are later characterized. Admittedly the early rise of Islam was spectacular. At the death of Muḥammad in 632, many tribesmen and oasis dwellers on the Arabian peninsula interpreted their pledge of submission to Islam as a personal covenant with Muḥammad from which they were released upon his death. The fact that Muḥammad left no clear successor led further to the temporary disarray of the nascent Islamic state (a "disarray" which incidentally is invaluable analytically for suggesting the popular bases of the strength of Islam). Yet by 634, most of Arabia was firmly within the Islamic polity, and the major conquests had begun. By A.D. 700, all of North Africa and Persia had been

[89] A good place to begin a consideration of this period is with W. Montgomery Watt's two volumes, *Muhammad at Mecca* (Oxford: Clarendon Press, 1953) and *Muhammad at Medina* (Oxford: Clarendon Press, 1956). These volumes are preferable to a later abridgment, *Muhammad: Prophet and Statesman* (London: Oxford University Press, 1961) because they clearly indicate the nature of the sources and how they can be used. Watt's own interpretations should, however, be regarded with caution (for example, he avers that marriage patterns suggest vestiges of a "matriarchate"). Three explicitly anthropological analyses of this period exist. The earliest is Eric Wolf, "The Social Organization of Mecca and the Origins of Islam," *Southwestern Journal of Anthropology*, 7 (Winter 1951), 329-56. Two later accounts are Barbara C. Aswad, "Social and Ecological Aspects in the Formation of Islam," in *Peoples and Cultures of the Middle East*, Vol. 1, ed. Louise E. Sweet (Garden City, N.Y.: Doubleday & Co. for the Natural History Press, 1970), pp. 53-73, and Dale F. Eickelman, "Musaylima: An Approach to the Social Anthropology of Seventh Century Arabia," *Journal of the Economic and Social History of the Orient*, 10 (1967), 17-52. Wolf and Aswad concentrate upon the economic and ecological background to the rise of Islam; Eickelman is concerned primarily with contrasting notions of prophetic authority and their relation to the tribal structure. The "Musaylima" article also lists the primary sources which have been translated into English. Maxime Rodinson's "The Life of Muhammad and the Sociological Problem of the Beginnings of Islam," *Diogenes*, 20 (1957), 28-51, and his "Bilan des Etudes mohammadiennes," *Revue Historique*, 229 (1963), 169-220, provide highly valuable reviews of the sources for the study of seventh-century Arabia and how scholars have used them. See also his *Mohammed*, trans. Anne Carter (New York: Vintage Books 1971 [French original 1961]) which provides an overall study of the period. Most studies of the period rely principally upon Arabic sources or translations of them. However, Patricia Crone and Michael Cook's *Hagarism: The Making of the Islamic World* (Cambridge: Cambridge University Press, 1977), radically (and unevenly in my judgment) reinterprets the origins of Islam by relying upon Byzantine and other non-Arab sources. A major change in scholarly knowledge of this period may emerge as it becomes known archaeologically. Archaeological research now being conducted in Saudi Arabia and the Arab Gulf states promise to transform what is now known of trade and political relations of the pre-Islamic period.

conquered, and in less than a century after the Prophet's death, the Islamic empire had expanded beyond Persia to India (A.D. 713) and west into Spain (A.D. 711).

The argument throughout this chapter has been that ideologies, even prophecies, are communicated in the context of particular economic and social conditions and are profoundly affected by them. A discussion of the rise of Islam, especially in the period from when Muḥammad first revealed himself as a prophet to the years immediately following his death, provides a privileged insight into the relation between ideology and practice because of the abundant documentation of primary sources.

The first thing to note is that Arabia was not a tribal backwater in the sixth and seventh centuries as it has at times been represented. Research in recent years has firmly established that the trade routes crossing the Arabian peninsula were crucial for an expanding long-distance trade and that this commerce was conducted through complex, sophisticated links between nomads and settlers on the peninsula, who in turn had ties with the surrounding great empires. None of the surrounding empires, however, managed to establish firm control over the peninsula itself. Thus the Sassanian (Persian) empire occupied South Arabia around A.D. 570-575 in an effort to safeguard the trade routes but was unable to expand its domination over the rest of the region. The Byzantine empire was more realistic in what might be called the Arab policy. It refrained from any direct military involvement in Arabia, although it encouraged the Abyssinian empire, a Christian ally, to conquer the Yemen in 525 and to conduct a raid (unsuccessful) on Mecca soon after.

In the century before the rise of Islam, Arabia was surrounded by a ring of "buffer" or client states heavily influenced by the ideologies of the dominant powers. Internally, there were Jewish settlements engaged in agriculture and commerce, as well as Christian monks and monasteries. Thus in one of the states allied with the Byzantine empire, Monophysite Christians had success in converting the seminomadic Arab population to their beliefs. Rather than relying solely upon a highly trained priesthood in urban centers, the Monophysites ordained large numbers of priests with little training so that each encampment had a "native" clergy present to perform rites. The ability of the Monophysites to adapt structurally to tribal conditions in Cyrenaica was a key factor in attracting tribal allegiance.[90] In other client states, the rulers bore titles such as king *(malik)*. This is an important consideration, for in the Quran and in other sources for seventh-century Arabia, Muḥammad is made to convey revelations denying that he aspires to be a "king" of the Arabs. Such patterns of leadership were clearly known to Muḥammad's potential supporters, even if not accepted as legitimate by them.

This whole system of buffer states suffered a serious decline in sixth- and seventh-century Arabia, resulting in a major loss of trade. In the late sixth century the Sassanian and Byzantine empires engaged in conflicts with each other. In 628, Khusraw, the Sassanian emperor, died, and in Persia there was a violent internal

---

[90] Henri Charles, *Le Christianisme des Arabes nomades* (Paris: Librairie Orientaliste Paul Geuthner, 1936); Evans-Pritchard, *The Sanusi of Cyrenaica.*

struggle for power. It was during this period that the Muslim conquests began in earnest.

Where did Mecca fit into the political and economic realities of this time? The first permanent settlement at Mecca appears to have been established about A.D. 400. The settlement was much as it is today: barren and arid. There was no agriculture in the immediate region and water was scarce. It is difficult to think of Mecca even in pre-Islamic times except in terms of trade and as a religious center. The town was considered a *haram,* or sacred enclave, even prior to the advent of Islam. The notion of *haram* is a particularly significant one because of the way in which early Islam reformulated the notion and invested it with new implications.[91] The pre-Islamic sanctuary was associated with an elaborate system of sacred months in which surrounding tribes agreed to cease raiding one another during certain periods in order to make a pilgrimage to the *haram.* No blood could be shed within its precincts and tribes could meet there to settle outstanding disputes, agree to the terms by which commerce could pass through their territories, and the like. To violate the rules of the sanctuary was to risk supernatural sanctions and collective retribution from other participants in the *haram.* Mecca was far from being the only sanctuary in Arabia; the distribution of sanctuaries appears to coincide with major nodes in the trade routes of the period. The *Quraysh,* Muhammad's own tribal group, appears to have had a special connection with the sanctuary at Mecca and because of this played an important role in the caravan traffic. Caravans as large as 2,500 camels crossed the peninsula by way of Mecca.

In the immediate period before the advent of Islam, each tribal group appears to have had its own deity, although Mecca's was gaining preeminence. The symbols representing the deity of each tribe participating in the Mecca *haram* were placed in the Ka'ba. The deity particularly associated with Mecca, al-Lāt, seems to have been considered vaguely superior to the others. As Mecca consolidated its religious preeminence in the mid-sixth century (about eighty years before Muhammad's claim to prophecy) the major commercial expansion of Mecca occurred.[92]

The control of the Quraysh over Mecca and the surrounding tribal groups was tenuous, as not all tribes were part of the Meccan religious-commercial system. Leading Meccans proposed to the tribes that in return for a pact of security, they would provide a market for the products of oases under their control in Syria and return the capital and profits to participants. Tribes participating in these arrangements were significantly called *ahl Allāh,* "the people of God." A common name among Muhammad's immediate forebears was 'Abdallah, "servant of God."

As these commercial arrangements became more complex, tension seems to

---

[91]The best source on the significance of the *haram* is R. B. Serjeant, "Haram and Hawtah, The Sacred Enclave in Arabia," in *Mélanges Ṭāhā Ḥusayn,* ed. A. Badawi (Cairo: Dār al-Ma'ārif, 1962), pp. 41-58. See also Eickelman, "Musaylima," 24-26.

[92]M. J. Kister, "Some Reports Concerning Mecca from Jāhiliyya to Islam," *Journal of the Economic and Social History of the Orient,* 15 (1972), 65-92. Despite the modest titles of this and other papers by Kister, his assessment of social and economic conditions in seventh-century Arabia is seminal.

have arisen between "traditional" tribal obligations based upon kinlike egalitarian principles and the consequences of the unequal distribution of commercial wealth. By the early seventh century there were signs of a growing class differentiation with wealth concentrated into a few hands to the exclusion of the poorer clans in Mecca. Certain clans within the Quraysh monopolized the benefits of trade. An oligarchy emerged, with the more powerful clans using mercenaries to enhance their position.

Into this situation came the Prophet Muḥammad. He was born between 570-580, an orphan from the age of six and from a clan whose importance had diminished. The clan head took care of him but died when Muḥammad was eight. From an early age Muḥammad undertook caravan journeys and appears to have acted as a mediator in various commercial disputes, suggesting that his clan must have played an important role in the functioning of the *ḥaram*. He was poor but worked as a camel driver for a rich widow whom he married when he was about twenty-five and she was forty.

For the next fifteen years little is known of Muḥammad. The first revelations came to him in 610. At first Muḥammad was uncertain of the meaning of these visions but soon became convinced that he was God's messenger. The first revelations came to him in short, rhythmic lines, called *saj*[c] verse in Arabic. This is a verse form used also by pre-Islamic *kāhin-s*, or soothsayers, and is the form in which supernatural communication was recognized by pre-Islamic Arabs. Arberry's translation of the Quran seeks to convey the rhythm of the original.

> By the sun and his morning brightness
> and by the moon when she follows him,
> and by the day when it displays him
> and by the night when it enshrouds him!
> (Sura 91:1-4)[93]

There is a short, staccato pattern with an emphasis on every other syllable in the Arabic original. Given the vocal patterns in Arabic, with six vowels in the language and triliteral roots for most words, it is relatively easy to find rhyming sounds.

From 610 to 613 Muḥammad kept the fact of his revelations to the very intimate circle of his wife and close friends. When he finally began to preach, there was initially little opposition to him, but his disciples were not among the rich and powerful. A few were younger men from influential families, others were younger men from weaker families and clans, and others were persons from outside the clan system—persons, in short, with little to gain from the traditional system of alliances.

Muḥammad's early preachings can be summed up by four points which served mostly to "warn" men of their ways rather than to challenge existing political and religious patterns.[94] First was an emphasis on God's goodness and power, which

---

[93] *Koran Interpreted*, trans. Arberry, vol. 2, p. 340. (Courtesy of the publishers.)

[94] These four points follow Watt, *Mecca*, pp. 62-72. The analysis of Muḥammad's early followers is also derived from Watt.

was not so much a criticism of paganism as an articulate expression of the emerging predominant role of the Lord of the Ka$^c$ba. The intent of these verses was not always clear. Coincidental with the first strong opposition to Muḥammad's teachings, he had the so-called "Satanic" verses revealed to him, in which some of the divinities in the Meccan pantheon were accepted as associates with Allah.[95] Muḥammad later retracted these verses, saying that he mistook Satan for the angel Gabriel. A second emphasis of the early revelations is upon a lurid description of Judgment Day and its consequences, evidently to instill in men a notion of responsibility for their acts. Third was the use to which the Quraysh put their wealth, with God encouraging deeds of generosity and works in the service of the community. Finally was an emphasis upon Muḥammad as a "warner." The notion of Muḥammad as prophet of God appears to have gained importance only later.

Thus the first preachings were not very revolutionary. The major themes were to reexamine the bases of Mecca's prosperity and to emphasize the brotherhood of all Meccans. In fact, it is possible to argue that initially Muḥammad thought of himself as sent to his own tribe *(qawm)*, the Quraysh, and only gradually to have realized his wider mission.

In the nine years that Muḥammad preached at Mecca, taunting and harassment of him and his followers increased. Economic warfare ensued between Muḥammad's followers and the Quraysh oligarchy, and Muḥammad began appealing for support to the tribes allied with the sanctuary at Mecca. Finally, the leading clans of Quraysh agreed upon a plan to assassinate Muḥammad.

Warned of this plot, Muḥammad turned to Yathrib (today Medina), a settlement three hundred miles to the north of Mecca. Yathrib was principally an agricultural settlement with its own patterns of internal strife, including tensions between Jewish and non-Jewish clans. Negotiations were conducted with Muḥammad, and in 622 an agreement was drawn up specifying his role as an arbiter *(ḥākim)*.[96] Shortly afterward in the same year, Muḥammad took flight *(hijra)* from Mecca with seventy of his followers and settled in Medina. This is the time from which years are counted in the Muslim lunar calendar.

The fact that there was an explicit agreement concerning Muḥammad's role as arbiter suggests that the members of the Quraysh played similar roles elsewhere in Arabia due to their privileged connection with the sanctuary at Mecca. Muḥammad's claim to prophecy does not figure in the agreement with the Medinans, and very few Medinans appear to have become Muslims at this time.

The transformation in Muḥammad's religious and political authority after his arrival in Medina reveals how his claims to authority were initially understood in the Arabian context. The commonwealth at Medina was called the *umma*, and each group participating in it was specifically enumerated. Initially in 622, being a member of the *umma* did not entail accepting Muḥammad's religious claims. As Muḥammad was only an arbiter, Jews were among those who adhered to the *umma*.

[95] See the Quran, Sura 53, vv. 19-20 and Sura 22, v. 51, and Watt, *Mecca*, pp. 101-9.
[96] R. B. Serjeant, "The Constitution of Medina," *Islamic Quarterly*, 8 (1964), 3-16.

There was only a small core of Muḥammad's followers from Mecca ideologically committed to Islam.

The Quraysh in Medina soon realized that Muḥammad's goals included the reconquest of Mecca; Muslims and their allies began to attack the Meccan caravans. In this period Muḥammad tolerated temporary alignments with his cause. In fact, he needed all the diplomacy for which he was famous during these early years. Tensions rose high as some Medinans feared risking an all-out war with Mecca, especially as trade fell off. Moreover, although some Jewish groups were included in the *umma,* they were hostile to Muḥammad's claims of prophecy. Eventually they were accused of siding with the enemies of the *umma* and were fiercely attacked, with the survivors forced to emigrate and settle elsewhere.

For several years Muḥammad conducted touch-and-go skirmishes with the Meccans; these gradually had their toll and Meccan prestige began to wane. Mecca's leaders accepted Muḥammad's terms for his return to the city in 630. He was generous to most of his former opponents except those who in one form or another had taunted his claims to prophecy. Once Muḥammad assumed control over the Kaᶜba, terms for joining the *umma* became harder. Tribal delegations poured in from all Arabia. To become a member of the *umma,* it was now necessary to accept Islam and to pay a tax called the *zakāt.* There had formerly been a tax paid to Meccans by those tribes desiring to participate in trade alliances, so this development was not without precedent.

Trade patterns centering upon Mecca were temporarily restored, but beginning in 630—some sources suggest after the death of Muḥammad in 632—rival prophetic movements sprang up elsewhere in Arabia. Muslim accounts of these "false prophets" are understandably hostile, but an analysis of the sources suggests the underlying pattern of cultural assumptions by which Arabs initially interpreted Muḥammad's claim to prophecy.

Four major "false prophets" are known through the Muslims sources, including Musaylima, a derogatory epithet meaning "little Muslim."[97] He was from an eastern Arabian tribe called the Banī Ḥanīfa. This tribe had control of a major caravan center called al-Ḥijr, which like Mecca was considered a *haram.* Caravan routes went from there to Mecca and Medina, Oman, South Arabia, and Persia.[98]

Obviously, there is no reason to believe that the content of Musaylima's claimed revelations has been preserved intact by Muslim tradition; he is, in fact, made to appear ridiculous. Of more significance is the fact that his revelations are also in *saj*ᶜ verse, a rhetorical style that marks the early revelations of the Quran and the sayings of pre-Islamic soothsayers. As for differences, the sources suggest a clear distinction between Muḥammad's and Musaylima's conception of authority. Some sources suggest that Musaylima communicated with Muḥammad, suggesting that they settle their differences by dividing their respective spheres of authority, with Musaylima of the Banī Ḥanīfa claiming hegemony over eastern Arabia and

[97]See Eickelman, "Musaylima."

[98]The significance of towns such as al-Ḥijr is one of the issues which may be clarified once the historical archaeology of the Arabian peninsula begins in earnest.

Muḥammad of Quraysh claiming hegemony elsewhere. Muḥammad's reply was to resist any encroachment upon his authority.

Some accounts clearly reveal the cultural expectation that prophets were aligned with particular social groups. Here, as elsewhere, the Muslim chronicles make for lively reading. One account has a tribesman from eastern Arabia asking Musaylima the source of his prophecy. Musaylima replies that it is ar-Rahmān. The tribesman then asks whether ar-Rahmān came to Musaylima in light or in shadow, a distinction which makes sense perhaps in terms of Semitic understandings of prophecy in which God's revelations are in the form of light or in visions and, consequently, were distinguished from those of kāhin-s who worked in darkness and who were thus associated with the pre-Islamic epoch of ignorance (jāhilīya). Musaylima replies that he came in shadows, to which the tribesman responds: "I testify that you are a liar and that Muḥammad is telling the truth. But a liar of [our tribal group] is better for us than a true prophet of [Muḥammad's tribal group] ." Another version of the same account has the tribesman say that a liar of Musaylima's tribal group is better than a liar of Muḥammad's. It should be kept in mind that these accounts derive from Muslim sources, so that such frank recognition of how claims to prophecy actually are understood gives a ring of authenticity to them since they do not always depict the early years of Islam in a reverent way.[99] In any case, prophetic form and the nature of authority appear inextricably linked.

The conception of prophetic authority as exemplified by Muḥammad was not limited in scope to the interests of any particular tribal or ethnic group, whereas the notions of authority of his rivals and their supporters appear to have had such limitations. How Muḥammad's claims to authority were popularly understood was a major problem for the early Islamic community. At the Prophet's death there were no clear plans for the succession, and many tribes considered their covenant of submission to Islam to be at an end. When finally Muḥammad's successor was chosen, the caliph Abū Bakr (632-634), his authority was far from carefully defined. He continued to be a merchant and even had to milk his neighbor's sheep until finally he was allowed money from the communal purse. Fortunately, the Islamic community possessed tacticians capable of using an inferior military force slowly to unify the tribes of the peninsula and bring them back to the Islamic fold.

Perhaps because sociological approaches to the study of religion are often misunderstood, particularly by those committed to the religious tradition which is the subject of consideration, I should state my own commitment to making sense

---

[99] Cited in Ṭabarī (d. 923), *History of Prophets and Kings* (in Arabic), ed. Muḥammad Abu l-Faḍl Ibrāhīm (Cairo: Dār al-Maᶜārif, 1962), p. 1937. (My translation.) After a series of military reverses, another source records the following dry humor of a tribal ally of the Muslims: "Muḥammad used to promise that we should eat the treasures of Chosroes and Caesar and today not one of us can feel safe in going to the privy!" Cited in al-Wāqidī (d. 822), *The Book of Campaigns* (in Arabic), Vol. 2, ed. Marsden Jones (London: Oxford University Press, 1966), p. 675. (My bowdlerized translation.)

of Islam in seventh-century Arabia. For me, a study of Muḥammad's political strategies and marriage alliances, the apparent development both of his prophetic message and how it was understood in seventh-century Arabia, and the growing richness and complexity of the Islamic tradition are made more meaningful when they are viewed with all the critical resources that anthropology and social history allow. The originality and strength of Muḥammad's prophetic message become all the more vivid as one begins to see patterns in the economy, polity, and ideology of the time in which he lived, and how the popular understandings of man and the divine and the implications for human society were reworked and put into practice.

Thus far the economic and political transformations of seventh-century Arabia and the period immediately preceding it have been discussed, although the episode of the "false prophets" has suggested the relation between conceptions of man and the divine and the role of prophecy and the practical importance of these issues. One of the best sources for the nature of pre-Islamic beliefs is the Quran itself, for many of its revelations record the skepticism with which some of Muḥammad's preachings were received and the nature of earlier understandings of the relation between man and the divine. There are other sources as well, but the Quran itself is the best record of the ideological transformations implicit in Muḥammad's prophetic message. Toshihiko Izutsu, a Japanese scholar trained in anthropological linguistics, has written seminal books on the relation of Muḥammad's prophetic message to his sociohistorical context.[100] Despite the forbidding titles of his two studies and the forbidding (but necessary) use of citations from the Arabic original alongside the translated verses, his studies are the best available which show how key Quranic concepts are related to one another and how the message of the Quran brought about fundamental shifts in the meaning of these concepts. To take only one key concept, that of God, Izutsu indicates from Quranic texts how *Allāh* was comprehended in pre-Islamic times. In different verses, Allah is referred to as creator of the world, as giver of rain and life, as the supernatural being who presides over solemn oaths at the Kaᶜba, as a God above all other gods, and as "Lord of the Kaᶜba." The Quran makes clear the pre-Islamic status of these beliefs.

> If you ask them [that is, the pagan Arabs] "Who has created the heavens and the earth, and has imposed law and order upon the sun and the moon?" They will surely answer, "Allāh!" (Sura 39, v. 61)

Other verses can be cited which just as directly confirm the complex of beliefs, not necessarily fully systematic, of pre-Islamic Arabs. An indication of the lack of consistency is in the verses which suggest that Allah is sometimes thought of as the

[100]Toshihiko Izutsu, *God and Man in the Koran: Semantics of the Koranic Weltanschauung,* Studies in the Humanities and Social Relations, 5 (Tokyo: Keio Institute of Cultural and Linguistic Studies, 1964), and his *Ethico-Religious Concepts in the Qur'ān,* McGill Islamic Studies, 1 (Montreal: McGill University Press, 1966).

only God. Thus in one Quranic context pre-Islamic Arabs are made to call upon Allah alone in times of imminent danger such as shipwrecks.

> But when He brings them safe to land, behold, they begin to ascribe partners. (Sura 39, v. 65)[101]

Thus the inconsistency in how Allah's status was regarded is made apparent. Similarly, other verses document the notion that Allah was the God particularly associated with the Ka$^c$ba, a guarantor of two major annual caravans and of the sanctity of the *haram*. Even Izutsu's analysis of how the concept of Allah was reformulated cannot be taken by itself but must be considered in light of the entire complex of assumptions made by pre-Islamic Arabs and later by Muslims about a range of key topics: notions of the person, of relations between man and man, and of relations between man and God. The Islamic vision of religion and society continues to be capable of the effective reformulation of what are regarded to be eternal truths.

---

[101] Izutsu, *God and Man*, pp. 100-105. The English translations of the Quran are Izutsu's.

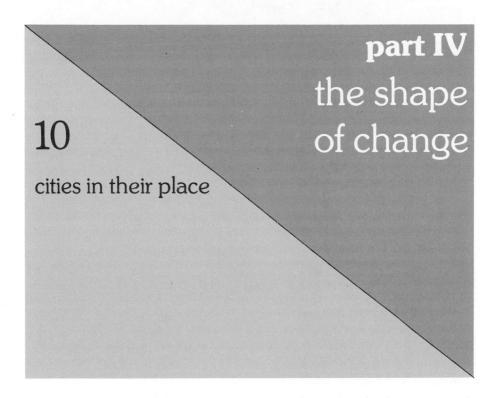

part IV

the shape
of change

10

cities in their place

Cities aren't isolates, but wide-ranging flows of people, authority systems, cultural symbols, capital innovations.[1]

## ISSUES

Anthropologists, social historians, sociologists, and a rapidly disappearing breed of area specialists called "Orientalists" have written substantially on cities in the Middle East. Until recently these discussions have been hampered by two factors. One has been a lack of communication between disciplines. Social scientists, on the one hand, knew their social theory but were less familiar with materials specifically dealing with the Middle East. For their part, Orientalists tended to be so wrapped up in their immediate data that their descriptions rarely posed broader sociological questions. Secondly, scholars concerned with the classical question of the nature of the Islamic city as an ideal type by and large did not seek to articulate their analysis with those scholars concerned with contemporary Middle Eastern cities, the consequences of major economic changes (which of course were not confined only to the last two centuries), migration, and population growth.

Within the last two decades, scholars have sought to join historical with contemporary domains of interest and the insights of "area" scholarship with

[1] Robert McC. Adams, "World Picture, Anthropological Frame," *American Anthropologist,* 79, no. 2 (June 1977), 268.

broader disciplinary trends in sociology and social history.[2] This chapter will assess how the main contours of past and present urban life have been interpreted by anthropologists and scholars in related disciplines. Also it will suggest some of the major social and cultural consequences of the rapid transformation of the urban landscape in the last four or five decades. If there has been a "great divide" until recently between scholars interested in "premodern" Middle Eastern cities and contemporary ones, this is in part because of the lack of adequate social theory to deal with processes and change in values and institutions. Even if such theory is not yet fully developed, anthropologists are now much more aware of the necessity of describing the direction of change and of making full use of social historical materials, as Brown's *People of Salé* and similar studies demonstrate.

One presentational caveat concerning this chapter must be kept in mind. It is short. The reason for this is quite straightforward if a distinction is made between the anthropology *of* cities and anthropology *in* cities. Many studies which are categorized as urban anthropology merely conduct studies of significant anthropological topics in urban milieu. Many such studies have been referred to throughout this book and are reintroduced here only briefly and usually by reference to discussions in earlier chapters. The anthropology of cities, or of urban forms, is more limited in scope. Here is where the integration of studies concerning earlier urban forms and those of the present has been particularly beneficial. This chapter is particularly concerned with the anthropology *of* cities. Of course, the two concerns with cities are not fully separable. The social organization of work in cities and the intensity of their exposure to economic and political currents from elsewhere are such that processes of class formation often appear more pronounced in cities. Hence the topic of class formation and how anthropologists have evaluated it is introduced in this chapter, but discussion of it continues in the wider context of Chapter 11.

In considering cities past and present and their implications for culture and society in general, the magnitude of the growth of the urban population of the

[2] Three outstanding collections of essays have appeared in recent years which effectively serve as guides to the major research. A. H. Hourani and S. M. Stern, eds., *The Islamic City*, Papers on Islamic History, 1 (Oxford: Bruno Cassirer, and Philadelphia: The University of Pennsylvania Press, 1970), concentrates on research concerning the premodern period. Ira M. Lapidus, ed., *Middle Eastern Studies* (Berkeley and Los Angeles: University of California Press, 1969), is now dated by more recent studies by the editor and several of the contributors. L. Carl Brown, ed., *From Madina to Metropolis*, Princeton Studies on the Near East (Princeton: The Darwin Press, 1973), is an excellent collection of copiously illustrated essays. Robert McC. Adams, *The Evolution of Urban Society* (Chicago: Aldine Publishing Company, 1966), comparatively assesses the beginnings of urbanization in early Mesopotamia and Mexico. Michael Bonine has prepared two comprehensive review essays on Middle Eastern urbanization. These are "Urban Studies in the Middle East," *Middle East Studies Association Bulletin*, 10, no. 3 (October 1976), 1-37, and "From Uruk to Casablanca: Perspectives on the Urban Experience of the Middle East," *Journal of Urban History*, 3, no 2 (February 1977), 141-80. An essential analytic review of approaches to the study of urban phenomena is Paul Wheatley, "Levels of Space Awareness in the Traditional Islamic City," *Ekistics*, 42, no. 253 (December 1976), 354-66. For a review of "community studies" in general, not specifically confined to urban milieu, see Erik Cohen, "Recent Anthropological Studies of Middle Eastern Communities and Ethnic Groups," *Annual Review of Anthropology*, 6 (1977), 315-47.

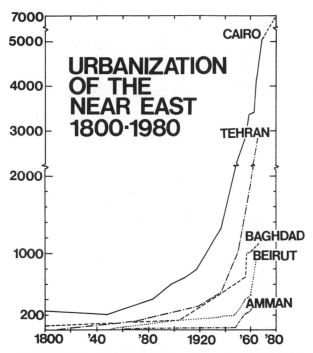

**FIGURE 10-1** Urbanization of the Near East, 1800-1980. (Figures are in thousands. From L. Carl Brown, ed., *From Madina to Metropolis* [Princeton, N. J.: Darwin Press, Inc., 1973], p. 107. Courtesy of L. Carl Brown and The Darwin Press, Inc.)

Middle East in recent years is an important consideration. As with the rest of the Third World, urban growth in the region has occurred at an accelerated pace. In 1900 less than 10 percent of the inhabitants of the Middle East were urban. By mid-century, 25 percent were urban and the projections for 1985 are for 43 percent of North Africa and 47 percent of Southwest Asia's populations to be urban. Moreover, urbanization tends to be overconcentrated in a few centers.[3] Thus in Morocco, which despite an accelerated urbanization remains over 60 percent rural, much of the urban population is concentrated in a narrow strip of land extending 150 km north from Casablanca and 50 km inland.[4] Statistics for Casablanca and Cairo dramatize the rapidity of this growth. At the turn of the century, Casablanca had a population of 20,000. By 1936 it had grown to 260,000, one-third of which was European. By 1963 it had over a million inhabitants despite the fact that the European population had dropped to less than 10 percent and continues to decline.

[3]Peter Beaumont, Gerald H. Blake, and J. Malcolm Wagstaff, *The Middle East: A Geographical Study* (London and New York: John Wiley & Sons, 1976), p. 206.
[4]J. I. Clarke, "Introduction," in *Populations of the Middle East and North Africa,* eds. John I. Clarke and W. B. Fisher (New York: Africana Publishing Company, 1972), p. 31.

THE URBAN HIERARCHY
IN THE SECOND HALF OF THE
TENTH CENTURY

★ Metropolis (miṣr)
■ Provincial capital (qaṣabah)
● District capital (madīnah)
. Other urban centres

1000 miles

**FIGURE 10-2** Urban hierarchy of the Islamic Middle East in the tenth century. (From Paul Wheatley, "Levels of Space Awareness in the Traditional Islamic City," *Ekistics*, 42, no. 253 [December 1976], p. 360. Courtesy of the author and publisher.)

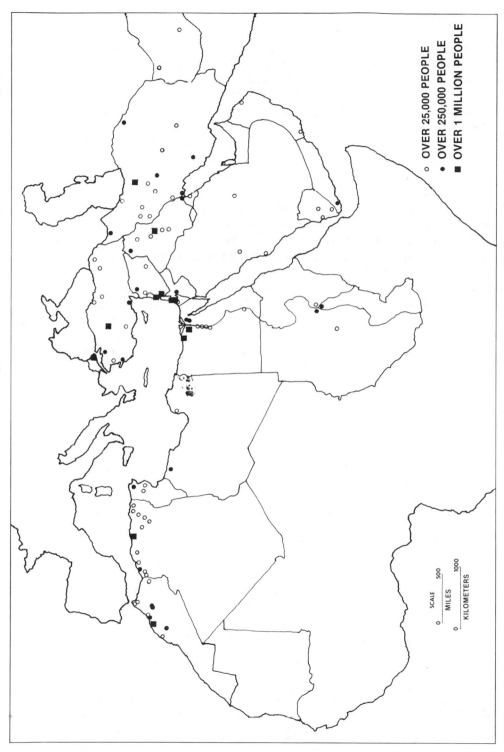

**FIGURE 10-3** The distribution of cities today suggests an overconcentration in a few major centers. (Not all smaller cities are shown on this map.)

○ OVER 25,000 PEOPLE
● OVER 250,000 PEOPLE
■ OVER 1 MILLION PEOPLE

SCALE
0        500
MILES
0              1000
KILOMETERS

In the late 1970s the city's population was nearing the two million mark.[5] Cairo in 1806 had a population of about 250,000. It had 800,000 at the turn of the century, 3.5 million by 1960, and over 5 million in 1970. Since the absorption of refugees from the Suez Canal zone after the June 1967 war and a continuing influx of immigrants from other areas, it will probably have 8 million inhabitants by 1980.[6] Elsewhere the strength of urban growth is equally pronounced, with over half of Lebanon's population concentrated in the capital area and less than one-fourth in villages; Tunis contains over half of the country's population, and the Tel Aviv district has over half of Israel's. Similar overconcentration occurs elsewhere and shows no sign of reversal.[7] The current pace of urban growth is particularly critical. Clifford Geertz, after due cautions concerning comparisons between different historical periods, observes that the period of 1800-1850 is considered one of rapid urban growth in the West, with seven million additional urban inhabitants. In the 1950-1970 period it is safe to estimate that the urban population of the Middle East has nearly doubled and involves a much larger number of persons. Moreover, the urban "leap" in Western Europe and the United States took place in the context of rapid economic development and industrialization. This has not been the case for much of the Middle East. "If seven million over half a century convulsed European social structure," Geertz suggests, the more rapid growth in a shorter period elsewhere "can be expected to raise problems of adjustment which [will] make those of nineteenth century Europe seem like the merest of growing pains."[8]

## THE "ISLAMIC" CITY

Any assessment of "growing pains" or adjustment necessitates an understanding of the social history and patterns of growth of Middle Eastern urban forms. Until recently, most scholars have dealt with the issue in terms of the "Islamic" city, a notion which presumes that Islam prescribes particular urban forms. Only in recent years have advances been made in how this problem is conceived. Social historians and anthropologists concerned with urbanism in the Middle East were handicapped by the form in which the German sociologist Max Weber posed his famous question of comparative urbanism. Why, Weber asked, did a distinct form of urban organization, the *commune,* arise only in medieval Europe and not elsewhere? Weber discerned a distinctly urban, corporate form of social organization in European towns which distinguished them from the larger society of which they

[5] J. Martin, H. Jover, J. Le Coz, G. Murer, and D. Noin, *Géographie du Maroc* (Casablanca: Librairie Nationale, 1967), p. 175.

[6] These figures are derived from Janet Abu-Lughod, "Cairo: Perspective and Prospectus," in *Madina to Metropolis,* ed. Brown, pp. 95-113, esp. p. 106.

[7] Beaumont, Blake, and Wagstaff, *The Middle East,* p. 207.

[8] The analogy and citation are derived from Clifford Geertz, "The Social History of a Moroccan Town," Princeton (March 1971), mimeo. (Used by permission of the author.)

formed a part, but he found no equivalent in the Orient.[9] His discussion of cities elsewhere merely served as a backdrop for what he regarded as the uniqueness of cities in the West. Despite the fact that many traditional cities in the Muslim world were often set apart from their surroundings by towering walls (as were many cities in medieval Europe), in general they possessed little autonomy from the state and no distinctive *formal* organization. Led, or misled, by Weber's formulation of comparative urbanism and similar ones posed by other scholars, some Orientalists sought the equivalent to European communes in the Muslim world but predictably had little success. For instance, the French Orientalist Louis Massignon argued that the so-called guilds of merchants and craftsmen in the Muslim Middle East served much the same purpose as the communes but never produced evidence to support his assertion. As one critic recently commented, despite Massignon's stature as a scholar his work on urban forms abused evidence and constituted no more than a "tissue of fallacies"—strong language in the relatively genteel work of Orientalist scholarship.[10] Other scholars tended to get bogged down in descriptivism, enumerating the features that appeared to characterize particular Islamic cities or "the" Islamic city as an ideal type. Features such as the presence of mosques, marketplaces, public baths, and so on were suggested as essential characteristics of such cities, but exceptions can be found to each of these enumerations. For example, virtually every rural local community in Morocco has a mosque, although not of course as impressive as those of the great urban centers, and many markets in Morocco are unrelated to cities. An enumeration of such features cannot in itself distinguish towns from villages. Other scholars have represented the characteristics of towns as enumerated by Muslim theologians.[11] As the morphology and functioning of cities throughout the Islamic world has become better known, the inadequacies of stereotypic notions of Islamic cites have become increasingly apparent. For instance, Bonine has argued that the gridlike form of medieval Iranian cities is derived primarily from the exigencies of irrigation systems and is not an outgrowth of specifically Islamic influences. Lapidus has reminded scholars that Muslims conquerors more often took over cities from earlier rulers rather than build them anew, and the balance between urban and nonurban populations was not signifi-

[9] Max Weber, *Economy and Society,* eds. Guenther Roth and Claus Wittich (New York: Bedminster Press, 1968), pp. 1212-36, esp. pp. 1226, 1233. For references to the relevant literature concerning the Middle East, see A. H. Hourani, "The Islamic City in the Light of Recent Research," in *The Islamic City,* eds. Hourani and Stern, pp. 9-24; Dale F. Eickelman, "Is There an Islamic City? The Making of a Quarter in a Moroccan Town," *International Journal of Middle East Studies,* 5, no. 3 (June 1974), 274-78; Francisco Benet, "The Ideology of Islamic Urbanism," in *Urbanism and Urbanization,* ed. Nels Anderson (Leiden: E. J. Brill, 1964), pp. 211-26; and Bryan S. Turner, *Weber and Islam: A Critical Study* (London and Boston: Routledge & Kegan Paul, 1974), pp. 93-106.

[10] S. M. Stern, "The Constitution of the Islamic City," in *The Islamic City,* eds. Hourani and Stern, pp. 37, 42.

[11] For example, Gustave E. von Grunebaum, "The Sacred Character of Islamic Cities," in *Mélanges Ṭaha Ḥusain,* ed. A. Badawī (Cairo: Dār al-Maᶜārif, 1962), pp. 25-37.

cantly changed by the Islamic conquests in themselves despite the fact that many Orientalists have characterized Islam misleadingly as an "urban" religion.[12]

Despite the shortcomings of earlier studies, a number of meticulously detailed descriptive monographs concerning "representative" Islamic cities emerged. Thus Le Tourneau's massive work on Fez made the assumption that the city's spatial layout and the economic, political, and social institutions until just prior to French conquest in 1912 were essentially the same as they were for half a millennium.[13] This presumed stasis of urban development encouraged many scholars to think of Islamic cities as analogous to those of Europe in the Middle Ages.

The atemporal assumptions and misplaced analogies of the French tradition concerning the nature of Islamic cities did not prevent the resulting descriptive ethnographies and historical studies from becoming an irreplaceable primary documentation upon which later scholars now rely.

**FIGURE 10-4** Traditional South Arabian architecture. For defensive purposes, there are no windows on lower stories. (From Freya Stark, *Seen in the Hadhramaut* [London: John Murray, Publishers, Ltd., 1939], p. 19. Courtesy of the author and the publisher.)

---

[12] Michael E. Bonine, "The Morphogenesis of Iranian Cities," *Annals of the Association of American Geographers*, 69, no. 2 (June 1979), 208-24; Ira M. Lapidus, "The Evolution of Muslim Urban Society," *Comparative Studies in Society and History*, 15, no. 1 (January 1973), 21-50.

[13] Roger Le Tourneau, *Fès avant le Protectorat*, Institut des Hautes Etudes marocaines, Publications, 45 (Casablanca: Société Marocaine de Librairie et d'Edition, 1949). For an example of a monograph dealing with a modern Moroccan city in the same style, see André Adam's encyclopedic *Casablanca: Essai sur la Transformation de la Société marocaine au Contact de l'Occident* (Paris: Centre National de la Recherche Scientifique, 1972). A comprehensive inventory of French urban studies is contained in Bonine, "Urban Studies."

One of the first breakthroughs in the scholarly impasse of how Islamic cities were studied was the appearance in 1967 of Lapidus's *Muslim Cities*.[14] Essentially, Lapidus changed the form of sociological question asked. Rather than search for social forms that were unique to cities, as suggested by the approach of Weber, Lapidus instead sought to delineate the social forms which were *in* cities and which allowed for the orderly conduct of social life. His emphasis was upon such fundamental social institutions as families and quarters, religious organization, and how the administrative machinery of the state effectively worked. For Lapidus, "Muslim cities are cities by virtue of social processes which are not peculiar to any given culture, but they are Muslim by virtue of the predominance of subcommunities which embodied Muslim beliefs and a Muslim way of life." It is the interaction of the various subcommunities and of the various elites which created the urban community and achieved a "sufficiently good order."[15] There were informal, but crucial, cross-cutting patterns of kinship, religion, politics, and economics. He focuses upon the nature and the comparison of social structures rather than upon cities themselves, firmly breaking with Weber's approach to discussing urban forms.

Lapidus's analysis is in general congruent with the recurrent argument of this book that many of the most significant patterns of constancy and order in Middle Eastern cultures are to be found in what scholars earlier dismissed as "informal" social groupings. There are shared cultural perceptions of how persons relate to each other which do not necessarily manifest themselves in the form of organized groups or classes.

One of the ways in which these underlying cultural notions of the social order are manifested is in their influence upon spatial perceptions and the use of space.[16] This relationship has been a long-standing concern in Middle Eastern studies, but the form in which the issue is discussed has shifted substantially in recent years. For instance, an earlier generation of colonial ethnographers considered the confusing—from a European perspective—maze of narrow, winding streets and blind alleys of traditional North African cities (*madīna*-s) to be a direct spatial projection of the "alogical" disorder of the "indigenous mentality," a notion which unfortunately has not entirely disappeared from the scholarly corpus.[17] There is no generalizing principle which allows a person to get from one place to another on the basis of abstract spatial criteria. In essence, one learns how to get from one point to another

[14] Ira Lapidus, *Muslim Cities in the Later Middle Ages* (Cambridge: Harvard University Press, 1967).

[15] Lapidus, "Evolution," 47-48.

[16] See Wheatley, "Levels of Space Awareness."

[17] *Madīna* in Arabic simply means "town" or "city." In North Africa it has taken on the narrower connotation of the older "native" component of contemporary cities. The quotations are from Louis Brunot, in Georges Hardy, *L'Ame marocaine d'après la littérature française* (Paris; Librairie Emile Larose, 1926), p. 20; for a more recent example of the assumption of urban disorder, see Xavier de Planhol, *The World of Islam* (Ithaca: Cornell University Press, 1959), pp. 14-15 [original French 1957].

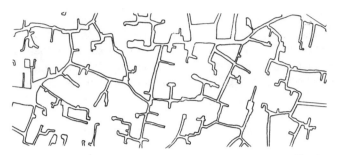

**FIGURE 10-5** The winding streets and blind alleys of traditional North African cities constituted a puzzle for colonial ethnographers. (Courtesy of the author.)

by having gone there before. Even in smaller towns in North Africa, it is not uncommon for persons from one part of town to get lost in unfamiliar sections, and residents will routinely ask "strangers" from elsewhere in their town what they are doing there. Moreover, residential quarters and houses within them are not now and have not been in the past clearly distinguished in any exterior way on the basis of wealth or other criteria, although in southwest Asian cities such as Antioch and Baghdad sectarian groups generally cluster in separate urban quarters.[18] With the exception of Jewish quarters (*mallāḥ*-s) in many towns, such separation is generally lacking in North Africa.

Four discernible patterns of spatial order can be found in most precolonial Middle Eastern cities: the relation of towns to the state, the market *(sūq)* or economic complex, the relation of religious institutions to the town, and the organization of residential and domestic space.[19] These various principles of order overlap. The presence of the central power is often represented by a separate, fortified quarter either within the larger cities or alongside it. In North Africa such a compound is called a *qaṣba*, or fortress. Soldiers or government representatives would be settled in this compound and usually were distinguishable from other towns-folk. A second pattern of order is the complex of economic activity, the traditional patterns of which have been extensively analyzed by Clifford Geertz.[20] There is a

[18] Jacques Weulersse, "Antioche: Essai de Géographie urbaine," *Bulletin d'Etudes Orientales,* 4 (1934), 27-80; John Gulick, "Baghdad: Portrait of a City in Physical and Cultural Change," *AIP Journal,* 33 (July 1967), 246-55.

[19] F. Stambouli and A. Zghal, "Urban Life in Precolonial North Africa," *The British Journal of Sociology,* 27, no. 1 (March 1976), 1-20. The principles of order applied specifically to North Africa may be used in large part elsewhere as well, especially their interesting summary of the "informal" status of elite authority and the general lack of importance of organized groups and classes. See the text and accompanying photographs in James Kirkman, ed. *City of Ṣanʿāʼ* (London: World of Islam Festival Publishing Company, Ltd., 1976).

[20] Clifford Geertz, "Suq: The Bazaar Economy in Sefrou," in Clifford Geertz, Hildred Geertz, and Lawrence Rosen, *Meaning and Order in Moroccan Society: Three Essays in Cultural Analysis* (New York: Cambridge University Press, 1979), also discussed in Chapter 8 of this book.

FIGURE 10-6 Major commercial streets are often partially separated from residential ones. Covered *suq,* Tetouan, Morocco. (Courtesy of the author.)

tendency for commercial and craft activities to be separated from places of residence, so that with the exception of small shops within residential quarters, most mercantile activities and the circulation of people, carts, and animals associated with them are removed from the semiprivate space of residential quarters. There is also a tendency for commercial and artisanal activities to be hierarchically ordered, with the more prestigious closest to the principal mosque and others located on the principal arteries.

The religious institutions cross-cut many of the other notions of order. In larger urban centers such as Tunis and Fez, the principal mosque is the place for the Friday sermon and the rituals associated with major feast days. In the past, it also served as a place of learning and frequently was the focal point for public protest in times of civil unrest. This symbolic centrality of the mosque was frequently replicated by its spatial centrality. In Tunis, the mosque is accessible by major arteries leading to the principal gates of the *madīna,* facilitating access to it from all residential quarters. As earlier discussed, an additional tie between religious institutions and commercial activities is provided by the pious endowments *(waqf; ḥabus),* which rent a number of shops in the commercial sector at below market values.[21] Finally, there are the maraboutic shrines associated with each city or town which even today serve occasionally as focal points of communal activities.

A final principle of order is the division of traditional *madīna-s* into residential quarters, with the households of each quarter claiming multiple personal ties

[21]C. Geertz, "Suq," pp. 151-54.

272 THE SHAPE OF CHANGE

and common interests based on varying combinations of kinship, common origin, ethnicity, patronage and clientship, participation in factional alliances, and spatial propinquity itself. In a small Moroccan town in which I conducted research between 1968-1970, residents divided their town into anything from thirty to forty-three quarters. The fact that there is such a discrepancy in how townsmen evaluate space even in such a small setting indicates that space is not conceived entirely in a fixed way or primarily by abstract physical features. How quarters were evaluated depended on what people knew of the social history of their town, which varied with generation and social position, and formative experiences shared with other persons in the community. The demarcation of quarters cannot always be discerned by physical signs. Many are clustered around impasses, but this is not always the case. For one thing, the social boundaries of many quarters are subject to modification; for another, not all houses are necessarily thought to be part of quarters. Only those clusters of households evaluated as sustaining a particular quality of life are known as quarters.

As previously indicated in Chapter 6, that quality of life is defined by the extension in contiguous physical space of the notion of "closeness" *(qarāba);* component households in a quarter assume that they share a certain moral unity so that in some respects social space in their quarter can be regarded as an extension of their own households. This closeness is symbolized in a number of ways: the exchange of visits on feast days, assistance and participation in the activities connected with births, circumcisions, weddings and funerals of component households, and the like. The heads of household of a quarter share certain minimal collective responsibilities. They often construct and maintain a mosque and hire a Quranic teacher for it. Because of the multiple ties which link the residents of a quarter, respectable women who never venture to the main market can circulate discreetly within their quarter, since the residents all assume a closeness to each other. In Chapter 6, I provided an example of the "formation" of a new quarter due to long-term shifts in social status as perceived by residents of a town. Quarters also decline and lose their cohesiveness. Thus certain quarters took shape in the 1920s and 1930s with the rapid ascendancy of certain rural *Qā'id*-s. Another quarter which emerged in this period was named after a family which had as its "founding" ancestor a merchant who traded in the Berber highlands prior to the arrival of the French in 1912. The descendants of this merchant became prosperous soon after the advent of the colonial era and purchased land on which the French built a major extension of the town in the 1930s. In the nationalist fervor that began in the 1930s and continued for some years after independence, two of the merchant's sons (also merchants themselves) became the leaders of rival political parties. Despite their rivalries, both lived in nearly adjoining houses, and other residents of the quarter continue to stress a variety of ties with the brothers' family. As long as a quarter had men of prominence or "word" capable of acting as their leaders, some sort of claim of common descent or origin, and the ability at least in some contexts to act collectively, it constituted a feature in people's shared conceptual image of the town. As the distribution of power, authority, and prestige shifts, so does the conception of space. Thus despite the apparent "disarray" of such spatial conceptions to outsiders, they follow an articulate cultural logic. Similar conceptions of space appear to prevail elsewhere in the Middle East. To use Kevin Lynch's term, the *imageability* of residential space in the Middle East is not principally in terms of physical landmarks but in shared conceptions of the social order. The cultural bases of these conceptions can be abstractly delineated, but a particular knowledge is needed for orientation in the social space of each town. Gulick's study of Tripoli, Lebanon, clearly indicates that the notion of imageability is more useful when it encompasses not only visual form (which is Lynch's emphasis), but also those which are socioculturally significant in both "modern" and traditional settings.[22] Studies such as Gulick's suggest some of the significant continuities between the social and spatial order discerned for "Islamic" cities and contemporary urban forms.

## COLONIAL CITIES AND THEIR LEGACY

Colonial principles of spatial order are particular instances of the spatial projection of dominant cultural values or, to be more precise, the values of the dominating political power. The colonial cities of French North Africa, especially in Morocco, provide particularly clear examples of the basic principles of colonial urban planning. If India was the colony upon which Great Britain lavished the most elaborate attention, then Morocco was its equivalent for the French. Colonial cities were not just the juxtaposition of the urban forms of the dominating power and the dominated. They were new creations with specific and lasting social consequences.[23] In cities such as Casablanca, commercial and economic interests were so powerful and growth so rapid that colonial authorities were unable to plan effectively for rational growth and development. Elsewhere, however, the French developed almost Cartesian plans which clearly articulated the legitimizing ideology of colonial domination. One of the myths of legitimacy used by the French in Tunisia and Morocco was that they were not a colonial power. "Native" regimes were maintained intact in both countries, and these regimes were "aided" by the authorities of the Protectorate who acted in the name of the Muslim rulers. Technically the French role was one of preserving native institutions. The consequence for urban planning—and in the case of Morocco every town had a developmental plan by the 1930s—was a basic dualism in urban growth. In nearly every case, the "traditional"

[22] Kevin Lynch, *The Image of the City* (Cambridge: The M.I.T. Press, 1960); John Gulick, "Images of an Arab City," *Journal of the American Institute of Planners*, 29, no. 3 (August 1963), 196-97. See also Gulick's *Tripoli: A Modern Arab City*, Harvard Middle Eastern Monographs, 12 (Cambridge: Harvard University Press, 1967).
[23] See Anthony D. King, *Colonial Urban Development: Culture, Social Power and Environment* (London: Routledge & Kegan Paul, 1976).

*madīna* was preserved more or less intact, while a "new" town, meant primarily, but not exclusively, for Europeans, grew up alongside it. In some cases, two "new" towns were created: one for "evolved" natives, another for Europeans. The overall shape of the town of Tunis (Fig. 10-7) suggests how this philosophy was spatially projected. As some Tunisians comment, the overall street plan takes the form of a cross being rammed into the *madīna*, making the colonial imagery even more suggestive. One plan for Tunis, elaborated during the Vichy regime but never carried out, took the notion of colonial planning one step further. The "modern" part of Tunis was divided along one main axis between Christians and Muslims (with a few "neutral" places in between) and along the other axis between bourgeoisie and workers, thus using the principles of religion and class for the spatial ordering of society.[24]

The initial colonial planning for Morocco from the inception of the Protectorate in 1912 until the 1930s was highly coherent and based upon three principles.[25]

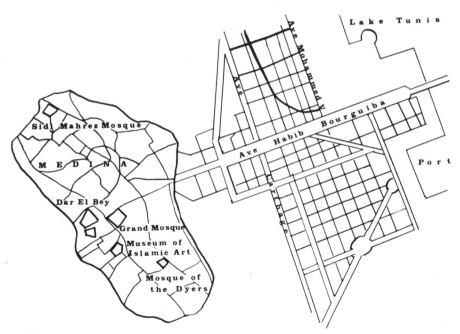

**FIGURE 10-7** "Tunis showing juxtaposition of old and new city, and Bourguiba Avenue as battering ram against old city." (From Brown, ed., *From Madina to Metropolis*, p. 29. Courtesy of L. Carl Brown and The Darwin Press, Inc.)

[24] I am grateful to Ellen C. Micaud (personal communication) for a description of this plan.

[25] Jean Dethier, "Evolution of Concepts of Housing, Urbanism, and Country Planning in a Developing Country: Morocco, 1900-1972," in *From Madina to Metropolis*, ed. Brown, pp. 197-243.

The first was that *madīna*-s were to be separated from European quarters. This division corresponded to what the French saw as the fundamentally "different" mentalities of the Muslims and Europeans. Thus it was argued that most "traditional" Moroccans preferred to be insulated from the outside world so that the vitality of traditional life could be preserved. Although an effort was made to provide the *madīna*-s with improved sewers, water systems, and electricity, the seeds were planted for many *madīna*-s to deteriorate into historic slums, dying a slow death of benign neglect. There were exceptions for cities such as Salé and Tetouan, where many of the traditional bourgeoisie maintained their houses for reasons of prestige, but the overall trend, especially after the economic dislocations of the Second World War, was to abandon such housing to impoverished rural immigrants.

A second principle was for town planning to protect the cultural heritage. Colonial planners enforced strict regulations designed to protect the town as an overall monument, a notion which began to be applied internationally in most countries only by the 1960s. As Dethier suggests, whatever the intentions of the planners, Moroccans often interpreted the decision to retain walls around the *madīna* as a security measure. In fact, some of the older "native" housing developments, one in the phosphate mining center Khouribga and the other in Casablanca, had walls with guards posted at the gates for just such a purpose, although the security was ostensibly for the inhabitants of the developments and not against them.

The final notion was that of constructing the "new" cities according to the most up-to-date principles of planning. The result for many Moroccan towns was the provision of parks and green spaces (admittedly often serving as a buffer between European and Moroccan quarters) and zoning regulations which except for Casablanca adequately managed to control the direction of growth. The state also purchased tracts of land which were then sold under strict controls to prevent speculation. Public buildings were designed and situated so as to contribute to the overall symmetry of towns, and town planners took special care to use distinctive features of local topography. With the exception of the provision of "evolved" native quarters until the late 1940s, such planning was primarily for the benefit of Europeans, as if the political and economic transformations of the colonial regime could leave the indigenous population undisturbed. And in the "evolved" settlements, the proviso that construction had to begin immediately and according to strict (and expensive) specifications ensured that only wealthier Moroccans could take advantage of them. Despite the efforts of colonial authorities to limit emigration from rural areas, so-called "clandestine" housing emerged, especially in the form of the shantytowns, or *bidonvilles,* whose inhabitants were primarily emigrants from rural areas. Such "temporary" housing has become a permanent feature of most large Middle Eastern cities, with local variations such as Cairo's "City of the Dead," where families have taken above-ground tombs for housing. Studies that have been conducted on the value of land in shantytowns indicate that unscrupulous realtors can realize a larger profit from collecting rents from such lands than in building more expensive housing. Because of the illegal nature

FIGURE 10-8 Such "temporary" housing as this has become a permanent feature of many Middle Eastern cities. Bidonville Bni Msik, Casablanca, 1968. (Photograph by D. Papini. Daniel Noin, *La Population rurale du Maroc* [Paris: Presses Universitaires de France, 1970], plate 48. Used by permission of the publisher.)

of such housing, when the land is needed for other purposes the shacks on it technically can be cleared, although actual exercise of such rights involves political risks. Although planners often have thought of shantytowns as a passing phenomenon, the attempts made after the end of the Second World War by the Protectorate government and by Morocco's independent government have never effectively managed to stem their growth. Analogous developments occurred throughout the Middle East; in Turkey fully 13 percent of the urban population live in shantytowns (*geçekondu*-s), and in many towns of the Middle East the figure may be significantly higher.[26]

The planning policies of independent regimes throughout the Middle East unsurprisingly reflect the ideology of dominant groups and the legacy of colonial assumptions concerning urban life. Ellen Micaud has produced what amounts to an ethnography of successive urban plans for post-Independence Tunis. Immediately after Independence in 1956, the Tunisian elite viewed the *madīna* as an obstacle to be surmounted so that the country could have "a capital worthy of the active modernizing image being fashioned on all fronts."[27] After Independence the exodus of all who could afford to leave the *madīna* for other housing rapidly

[26] Alan Duben, "Review of Kemal Karpat, *The Geçekondu: Rural Migration and Urbanization*," *Middle East Studies Association Bulletin*, 12, no. 3 (December 1978), 50.

[27] Ellen C. Micaud, "Urbanization, Urbanism, and the Medina of Tunis," *International Journal of Middle East Studies*, 9, no. 4 (November 1978), 433.

accelerated, thus leaving the *madīna* to rural immigrants and others who had no active say in its future. Commercial and administrative activities had increasingly shifted away from the *madīna* during the colonial period. Finally, the nationalization of pious endowments in 1957 radically changed the economic and legal structure of the *madīna*. At best, some visionary plans called for the neglect of the *madīna* as a sort of natural obstacle which planners sought to avoid. This stage of post-Independence planning can in some ways be considered an implicit acceptance of the colonial devaluation of the *madīna*, in the sense that it was associated with an inferior status and an unvalued past. In the late 1960s with the burgeoning of the tourist industry, there was a shift to regarding the *madīna* as part of the natural heritage, and various plans, some of which were the subject of international competitions, were evolved in an effort to regard it as part of the national tourist business. A final, more realistic phase was begun in 1973 with more modest projects but ones designed to encourage the maintenance of housing within the *madīna* (through legislation to facilitate owner-occupied dwellings) and to provide subsidies for various craft and artisanal activities. Planners began to realize that it was not possible to allow any further deterioration of the *madīna,* given the worsening housing crisis throughout the capital region. Only after two decades of Independence has it been possible to regard the *madīna* as an integral and enduring part of Tunisia's heritage and living present.


## CITIES NOW

The study of cities necessarily involves evaluation of the approaches used by a number of disciplines. Fuad I. Khuri, whose studies on the urbanization of the greater Beirut region have been discussed in earlier contexts, sees Middle Eastern urban studies as falling into three major categories.[28] First is what he calls the survey approach: the compilation of demographic data which indicate something about the age distribution of urban residents as opposed to those of the country, levels of consumption, size and density of urban areas, and other such indices. In the main, he states, such compilations of statistics are part of international efforts to assess the extent of urbanization and the administrative problems associated with it. He writes that although the theoretical contribution of such studies is minimal and their interpretation is often relatively haphazard, such statistics can often highlight problems which require explanation.[29]

A second major approach is the study of particular problems—religious beliefs and practice, child rearing, educational aspirations, and the like—in terms of urban-rural contrasts, sectarian differences, and socioeconomic backgrounds. According to Khuri, the difficulty with most such studies is that they accept uncritically the

---

[28] Fuad I. Khuri, *From Village to Suburb: Order and Change in Greater Beirut* (Chicago and London: University of Chicago Press, 1975), pp. 1-15.

[29] *Ibid.*, p. 2.

validity of the categories used, such as rural and urban. Such studies often do not provide a comprehensive theory of the nature of urban life with which the various characteristics attributed to urban and rural communities or to various socio-economic classes can be systematically linked. He provides as a key example Janet Abu-Lughod's major study of Cairo in which she contrasts the "modern urban" style of life of Cairo as opposed to the "rural." Khuri argues that Abu-Lughod's contrast can be accounted for just as well in both Egyptian and Lebanese contexts by whether people are rich or poor, so that the presumption that the differences are urban and rural is misleading. Rural dwellers can be separated from urban ones on the basis of a set of distinguishing factors or variables, but Khuri questions whether these define the character of either society unless the interconnectedness among the itemized variables is shown.[30] He suggests that other studies (with the exception of Abu-Lughod's meticulous analysis of the demography, socioeconomic characteristics, and social history of every major district of Cairo) have ignored the impressive changes that have modified the "social character" of Middle Eastern cities since the 1930s, and have written, instead, of villages or cities as if they were constants. Khuri sees his own "community" study of two contrasting Beirut suburbs as a third approach which does not assume such constancy. For Khuri, suburbs are communities that are still finding their form and coming into being. His approach to their analysis is to deal "with a wide range of structures, organizations, institutions, customs, socioeconomic differentiation, and political action." Khuri's self-description of his methodological approach is unexceptionable, despite the quality of his analysis, because he downplays his sustained attention to the social history of how these communities came into being. This provides the necessary background against which notions of ethnic and sectarian identity can be evaluated.

In contrast to the Western pattern of specialized suburban communities, many of which serve as dormitories for nearby business and industrial districts, Khuri indicates that there is a tendency for Lebanese suburban communities to be economically independent and self-contained. He concludes that in the communities studied, "Class is the least important instrument of organization. Neither neighborhoods, quarters, or suburbs, nor voluntary associations, societies, clubs, or political constellations are based on class affinities."[31] It is visible in political roles and apartment styles, but there is no American-style association between class and area of residence.

[30] *Ibid.,* pp. 4, 6. Janet L. Abu-Lughod, *Cairo: 1001 Years of the City Victorious,* Princeton Studies on the Near East (Princeton: Princeton University Press, 1971).

[31] Khuri, *Village to Suburb,* p. 217. For markedly contrasting views of the importance of class in Lebanon, see Suad Joseph, "Muslim-Christian Conflict in Lebanon: A Perspective on the Evolution of Sectarianism," in *Muslim-Christian Conflicts: Economic, Political, and Social Origins,* eds. Suad Joseph and Barbara L. K. Pillsbury (Boulder, Colo.: Westview Press, 1978), pp. 63-97; and Michael Gilsenan, "Against Patron-Client Relations," in *Patrons and Clients in Mediterranean Societies,* eds. Ernest Gellner and John Waterbury (London: Duckworth, 1977), pp. 167-83.

Unless Khuri's argument is taken as limited to the relation of class to residential area, his conclusion is markedly controversial in terms of Lebanon, where other analysts have asserted that class factors are decisive and underlie other characteristics such as sectarian loyalties. In fact, Khuri's argument as to the association of class and residential area deserves careful attention because elsewhere in the Middle East spatial differentiation based upon wealth, migrant status, and other key variables has become increasingly common and suggests the increasing importance of class, occupation, and wealth as organizing factors of the social order.[32] In many of the oil-wealthy Gulf states, which have experienced massive building growth since the 1960s, it has been common to construct large blocks of housing designed for particular occupational categories, with regions of villas reserved for engineers, merchants, and other persons of high status, and three-storied walk-up apartment buildings for those of more limited income groups. Such a pattern is also common in older cities. Baghdad has large sectors marked off for particular types of housing—for military officers, civil service employees, and those of particular industries such as oil, railroads, utilities, and banks.[33] Similar patterns prevail throughout North Africa and elsewhere in the Middle East.

Another sort of spatial order is provided by the settlement of migrants in cities, a phenomenon which accelerated at the end of the Second World War and

**FIGURE 10-9** Modern construction in Oman dates almost entirely from the post-1970 era. (Courtesy of the author.)

[32] See Nicholas S. Hopkins, "Traditional Tunis and its Transformations," *Annals of the New York Academy of Sciences,* 220 (1974), 427-40; and Janet Abu-Lughod, "Urban Structure under Decolonization: The Factorial Ecology of Rabat-Sale, Morocco," in *Système urbain et Développement au Maghreb,* eds. Abdelkader Zghal and Amal Rassam (Tunis: Editions CERES-Productions, forthcoming).

[33] On Kuwait, see Saba George Shiber, "Kuwait: A Case Study," in *From Madina to Metropolis,* ed. Brown, pp. 168-93. On Baghdad, see Gulick, "Baghdad."

has continued unabated ever since. Abu-Lughod has presented a portrait of a "typical" migrant to Cairo in the late 1950s. He was a young male, who spent his first days in the city with a relative or friend from his village of origin. When he found more permanent lodging, it usually was in a neighborhood or subsection of the town occupied by other migrants from the same region. A similar pattern prevails today. Such migrants often formed benevolent associations to look after some of their common interests. To help them to adjust to city life, migrants have a network of primary personal associations "far beyond" what is deemed possible in the West to help them adjust, enmeshing "not hundreds but thousands of individuals."[34] A similar pattern of settlement and the use of personal networks to adapt to new situations prevails elsewhere in the Middle East.[35]

Not all recent settlements of migrants consist of shantytowns; often individuals move out of them when their financial circumstances allow. For modest civil servants, employees of factories, bus conductors, and persons of similar occupation, this means renting or buying a house in a neighborhood such as Casablanca's ᶜAyn Shuq (Aïn Chok). This is a neighborhood about half an hour to the east from the center of town by municipal bus, named after one of the first post-World War II housing developments constructed for Moroccans by the French. It is close to what in 1979 was still the periphery of a rapidly expanding Casablanca. The original development consists of carefully laid out rectangular streets; only the principal streets can be used by automobiles. Shops, a bath, and a mosque are located along these main internal streets; impasses lead off them, and the whole complex is accessible from the outside by only a few streets, so that the overall spatial principles of a traditional *madīna* are replicated. The visual impression of its inhabitants suggests that they are older, retired persons or elderly soldiers, including many of those initially granted rights to housing in the development. Because rents for government developments are lower than commercial ones, such rights are jealously protected. In fact, with Morocco's current housing crisis, rights to such housing are often seconded to others at higher prices.

The original project is now dwarfed by the adjoining housing which is privately constructed. Principal shops are located along a major highway and boulevard which determine the limits of the quarter. These are almost the only streets which have trees along them. The remaining sides of the quarter are bounded by empty lands owned in part by the government. Large primary and secondary schools and an orphanage adjoin the quarter. Every morning thousands of schoolchildren cross paths through the garbage-strewn empty spaces to these various

[34] Janet Abu-Lughod, "Migrant Adjustment to City Life: The Egyptian Case," in *Arab Society in Transition,* eds. Saad Eddin Ibrahim and Nicholas S. Hopkins (Cairo: The American University in Cairo, 1977 [orig. 1970], pp. 395, 402.

[35] See Khuri, *From Village to Suburb;* Colette Petonnet, "Espace, Distance et Dimension dans une Société musulmane: A Propos du Bidonville marocain de Douar Doum à Rabat," *L'Homme,* 12 (1972), 47-84; Alan Dubetsky (Duben), "Class and Community in Urban Turkey," in *Commoners, Climbers and Notables,* ed. C. A. O. Van Nieuwenhuijze (Leiden: E. J. Brill, 1977), pp. 360-71; John Waterbury, *North for the Trade: The Life and Times of a Berber Merchant* (Berkeley and Los Angeles: University of California Press, 1972), pp. 37-88.

schools, some for boys and girls together, others with separate education. Most of these schools are of recent construction, in a desperate effort to keep up with population growth in which over half the population is under the age of eighteen. Because schools can be a symbol of progress and improvement, it is important to indicate how they are experienced by the children of the quarter. So much time is spent by the under-eighteen population in school or in school-related defined activities that the relation of the school to other aspects of society is decidedly crucial. The school buildings are modestly but adequately designed, with a high wall cutting them off from the outside, adequate lighting on sunny days, and small internal courtyards. In the late 1970s there was no problem of ventilation as virtually every window was broken during a series of student demonstrations against the growing inadequacies of an educational system unable to cope with rapid expansion. Even the fewer than 10 percent of the entering school students who eventually obtain diplomas cannot be assured of gainful employment. School furniture is broken or defective; blackboards and books are few. For the teachers who take an interest in them, students show a marked enthusiasm. For the others, especially when official visitors are present to evaluate teaching performance, students deliberately show inattention or indifference. More than twenty years after Morocco's independence, many of the teachers in the secondary cycle continue to be foreigners, some from France and other European countries, including Eastern Europe, and a few from Eastern Arab countries. Almost none of the

**FIGURE 10-10** Fewer than 10 percent of entering secondary school students eventually obtain diplomas. Secondary school in ᶜAyn Shuq, Casablanca. (Courtesy of the author.)

European teachers makes any effort to learn Arabic, to converse with their Moroccan colleagues outside of formal meetings, or to meet with their students outside of classroom situations. The moment school is over, they leave for other parts of Casablanca, much like many teachers in America's inner cities. Only the younger Moroccan teachers live in the quarter itself, unless they have a family or relatives elsewhere in Casablanca. Almost all of these teachers meet informally with their students to discuss their progress and offer them advice.

As for the quarter itself, few of its streets are paved. The streets are laid out in rectangular fashion and houses are provided with sewers, electricity, and water, all indicating the essentials of urban facilities even if no other amenities are provided. Only a few of the larger stores on the periphery of the quarter are well stocked. Most stores sell in small quantities, carry only basic commodities and sell at higher prices to their clients in exchange for extended credit. Several garages have been converted into mosques without minarets. Houses are mostly two-storied, but the houses of the entire quarter, with their gaudy façades of pink, light blue, green, yellow, and orange indicate that most inhabitants gradually constructed their own properties. The interiors of many houses show that originally they were single-storied with open courtyards. As owners acquire the funds, they add on, a room or a story at a time. Many owners rent part of their houses to other families or to single civil servants such as teachers in order to pay for additional construction. Casablanca has rent control laws as do many other cities in the Middle East, but in practice they work effectively only for long-term tenants.

There are virtually no factories near the quarter, and many inhabitants are underemployed or support numbers of persons not in the labor force. Outside of school hours, the streets are crowded with children playing; radios blare throughout the daytime, and in the early evening they are joined by the noise of television sets. There are some cars parked on the streets and a much larger number of scooters, but most residents depend upon public buses. Bus rides to elsewhere in the city are long and often uncomfortable, but the lower rent and cost of housing in a peripheral, popular quarter outweigh such inconvenience.

Most of the quarter's residents are by origin from elsewhere in Morocco, but there are no evident patterns of settlement. Neighbors are civil and cooperate with each other but usually at a fairly minimum level. The structure of ownership and the feeling of many residents that they belong to the quarter only until they find more substantial housing militates against more permanent bonds. Teenagers and young adults—both men and women in the case of Casablanca—are attracted more by the bright lights and amusements of promenading in Casablanca's center or sitting in its cafés, where they are freer than in their own quarter to meet friends. There are virtually no cafés, cinemas, or recreational facilities beyond the streets and vacant land on the quarter's edge. In all, the quarter shows only minimally the forms of solidarity which develop in older, more established *madīnas* or even in the city's *bidonvilles,* where residents are perhaps compelled to cooperate more with each other.

## CITIES AND SOCIAL CLASS

One of the few substantial attempts to relate the impact of shifts in world economic currents upon the social order of a Middle Eastern city is Kenneth L. Brown's *People of Salé*. Brown makes the important point, confirmed by numerous other studies, that status and social relations were not determined by any fixed characteristics. Attributes such as Arab or Berber identity, religious learning, patrilineal descent, and membership in occupational groups and religious brotherhoods constituted "cultural categories, not concrete, isolated social aggregations or classes." Social relations were instead "characterized by a pattern of shifting coalitions, of networks of patrons and clients" based upon common interests that were "sometimes strengthened (but not determined) by descent, marriage, or friendship."[36] His description of the elite of the city is likewise congruent with descriptions of other Middle Eastern contexts. They were persons "who dominated cross-cutting social networks" and who were less leaders of "powerful extended families" than "men who controlled clientele groups held together by mutual interests, not ties of consanguity."[37]

The long-range consequences of capitalist and colonial penetration, Brown argues, were to create a situation in which a few entrepreneurs amassed considerable wealth while the majority of small merchants, artisans, and peasants became increasingly impoverished and social mobility became more difficult. Stated in the abstract this theme of the growth of class relationships instead of vertical ones of patron-client and other ties recurs in contemporary anthropological and social historical literature. Brown's almost unique contribution is twofold. First, he analyzes in detail and over long historical periods the consequences for particular crafts and mercantile activities of these economic and political changes; most other studies merely juxtapose before and after contexts without assessing the interplay between market forces and social relations. Second, he argues that the "local patterns of relationships," which he meticulously describes, remain largely intact and to date have not led to a "class-based social structure."[38] Thus, even with the growing differentiation of persons along lines of wealth, individuals perceived their "interests" in a multiplicity of settings and manipulated an intricate range of identities and loyalties.

If the growing importance of economic differentiation was apparent in the critical period dealt with by Brown through the 1930s, it has become much more so in the accelerated social change of the post-World War Two era. For this

---

[36] Kenneth L. Brown, *People of Salé: Tradition and Change in a Moroccan City, 1850-1950* (Cambridge: Harvard University Press, 1976), p. 6. For one of the earliest accounts recognizing the impact of colonial penetration upon social relations, see Charles Le Coeur, *Le Rite et l'Outil* (Paris: Presses Universitaires de France, 1969 [orig. 1939]), pp. 59-131. I am grateful to Nicholas S. Hopkins for first referring me to this neglected study.

[37] Brown, *People of Salé*, pp. 56, 60.

[38] *Ibid.*, p. 224.

more recent period, Alan Duben's (Dubetsky's) 1970-1971 research in a *mahalle* (neighborhood) of thirty thousand persons which he calls Aktepe, located on the outskirts of Istanbul, is one of the more intensive studies available. Aktepe's population is heterogeneous in origin, ranging from the "religiously conservative" Black Sea Sunnī-s to Alevi-s from east and east-central Anatolia. Duben is concerned with understanding the interplay between older notions of consociation, which he glosses as "the moral community which is Islam," and "the organization of individuals according to social class."[39]

Aktepe is divided into two principal quarters. One is occupied by people of Black Sea origin ("Laz" territory, after the principal ethnic characterization of the Black Sea region). The other consists predominantly of persons of eastern Anatolian origin. It is known as "Kurdish" territory, although not all persons from this region are Kurds. A few persons from other regions are interspersed in these two quarters. This regional/ethnic distinction is also taken as a religious one. The Kurds (Alevi-s) live in the lower part of the neighborhood. There are no mosques there and during Ramaḍān a number of residents appear not to be keeping the fast. In contrast, the upper Sunnī ("Laz") part of the neighborhood has two mosques. Although administratively united, Duben characterizes the upper and lower quarters of Aktepe as "two rather different moral communities" in terms of the "objective facts" of regional ties, marriage patterns, and "different religious belief systems." In the sense that a "moral community is a self-conscious social unit," the residents of the two quarters belong to different social worlds; in this sense their differences are comparable to those of the two suburban Lebanese communities described by Khuri in *From Village to Suburb*.[40]

The pattern of migrants settling in Aktepe is much the same as that described by Abu-Lughod for Cairo. Persons from the same village or general region settle together. In the case of Aktepe, a common pattern is for persons first of all to construct single-story makeshift homes and later to move into four- and five-floor modern apartment buildings nearby. There is an evident differentiation of wealth and occupation, as a few laborers have formed their own small workshops or as others become successful as entrepreneurs in real estate or in commerce. Most residents of the quarter remain laborers, either in the small workshops and factories within Aktepe itself or in the large industrial zone which adjoins it.

Duben views classes "as conflict groups determined by their relation to the means of production." He argues that it is more useful to consider classes merely as one type of conflict group, together with others such as "status groups, sects, or regional groupings."[41] There is an unequal distribution of wealth and power among Aktepe's residents, as elsewhere in Turkey, but for Duben the nature of significant groupings within this inegalitarian framework remains to be classified empirically; he does not regard the formation of social classes as a self-evident

---

[39] Dubetsky, "Class and Community," p. 360.

[40] *Ibid.*, p. 362.

[41] *Ibid.*, p. 364.

**FIGURE 10-11** Workers in small factories and workshops are thought to work better when they are all from the same region of origin. Aktepe, Turkey. (Courtesy Alan Duben.)

phenomenon nor the existence of other forms of conflict groups as a "false" consciousness. All such groupings which are significant to the members of a particular society and which serve as a guide to social action must be taken into consideration. For Duben, any use of terms such as *class* must take into account both the social and historical institutions of the society being studied and economic and social forces from outside the area.[42] In fact, he reviews recent work on the consequences of industrialization in non-Western contexts which suggest that increasing social differentiation, including the separation of kinship ties from those of work, is not a necessary concomitant of industrial development. In the Turkish case, he points out that in many of the small factories and workshops of Aktepe, workers are hired according to the patron's assessment of a worker's reliability and trustworthiness *(dürüstlük)*. Such relationships of trust are particularly developed among persons with a common religious identity. Patrons and workers are linked by a complex of social obligations which extend beyond the workplace. Some of the larger workplaces even provide mosques on their premises. These complex bonds of social obligations ensure the workers' loyalty. The principle of recruiting workers with such common bonds is also followed by larger industries such as textile factories. Only when a high level of skill is necessary are technical factors given predominance. Duben's argument is that these "traditional" social alignments structure the workplace and contribute to its effective functioning. In short, the more important grouping for patrons and workers is community instead of class, and bonds of class solidarity are not inevitably a consequence of increasing economic differentiation. Neighborhood improvement associations among both the

[42]*Ibid.*, pp. 364-65.

Alevi "Kurds" and the Sunnī "Laz" populations pay for the support of various community facilities, including primary schools, dispensaries, and (for the Sunnī population) a mosque, and the wealthier members of the two communities are the leaders in these associations.[43]

Nonetheless, Duben acknowledges the development of a "politically conscious" labor movement and the growth of class consciousness among some Turks. He concludes that such consciousness has become increasingly important, particularly in Turkey's larger industries and among workers returning from Europe; but that in Aktepe, where most individuals work in smaller factories and workshops, a sense of distinct class has developed most clearly only among the patrons. Their wealth and mobility enables them to meet other persons in similar positions elsewhere in the city, and many are becoming distinguished by a distinctive style of dress and manners. In Duben's argument, class differentiation is becoming more significant, but a comprehension of *how* it shapes Turkish notions of society and identity necessitates comprehending other forms of social cohesion as well and not postulating that class consciousness alone will shape the future.[44]

Another valuable argument concerning the significance of class relationships in an urban context is provided by the work of Nicholas S. Hopkins in Testour, Tunisia, a town about fifty miles southwest of Tunis with approximately ten thousand persons in the mid-1970s.[45] The town is an active craft and marketing center in the middle of a fertile region with an economy of extensive agriculture based on wheat, barley, and olives as well as irrigated orchards and gardens. Much of the land and many of the flocks in the region are owned by townsmen. In Hopkins's study as in others concerned with the concept of class, constant reference is necessarily made to the national and international economic and political context; although Hopkins stresses the advantage which anthropologists possess in being able to ascertain empirically the significance of the notion of class. Hopkins, like Duben, stresses the importance of the differential access which members of society have to the mode of production, the emergence of two (and sometimes more) groups based on this differential access, and the political opposition associated with them. This "contradictory relationship" does not mean that humans are lined up like manikins on the dominating or dominated sides of the class line or that notions of class can automatically be derived from the mode of production. The "life experience" of individuals, the "degree of consciousness" of class, and observations of behavior (which can be an indirect index of class) are all equally important and must be taken into account. Individuals must possess the ideologi-

---

[43] *Ibid.*, p. 367. See also his "Kinship, Primordial Ties, and Factory Organization in Turkey: An Anthropological View," *International Journal of Middle East Studies,* 7, no. 3 (July 1976), 433-51.

[44] Dubetsky, "Class and Community," pp. 368-69.

[45] Nicholas S. Hopkins, "The Emergence of Class in a Tunisian Town," *International Journal of Middle East Studies,* 8, no. 4 (October 1977), 453-91, and his "The Articulation of the Modes of Production: Tailoring in Tunisia," *American Ethnologist,* 5, no. 3 (August 1978), 468-83.

cal forms in which to express class consciousness, and Hopkins sensitively portrays just what the nature of these forms is and their relation to the mode of production in one Tunisian context.[46]

Hopkins suggests that the most important factors in the emergence of class consciousness in the Testour context are the improvement of communications and the mechanization of agriculture which have made a market orientation possible and that change in productive forces is linked with changes in other aspects of society.[47]

In earlier, especially precolonial, times, the work force was mobilized from within the family and extended kin, with the occasional use of various sharing arrangements. This earlier system of production was correlated with a complex evaluative process involving wealth, religious status, and the honorable behavior of family members, and links within the society tended to be vertical, patron-client ones. Land was concentrated in the hands of town notables. With the shift to mechanized agriculture beginning with the colonial period, there has been a shift to agricultural wage labor along with the emergence of horizontal social links in which many persons recognize their common interests with other persons in society. This has particularly been the case for landowners and for agricultural workers. Employers for the most part tend to be Testouris. They live in the center of town, share a number of activities together, including control of some of the key local shrines, and think of themselves as a group. The agricultural laborers tend to be migrants from poorer regions of Tunisia who live in adobe houses on the periphery of the town itself. Their tenure in the houses is insecure. Employers speak of the lack of confidence *(thıqa)* they have in their workers, claiming that the workers are bad Muslims and even practice witchcraft. The laborers, for their part, have to some extent organized (as have the employers) to defend their common interests, such as gaining more secure title to their houses and obtaining better working conditions.

Hopkins clearly points out that the class system which he is describing does not embrace the entire population. There are still a number of independent small farmers who own and work their land, and a number of people in transport, crafts, and mercantile activities who are not enveloped by the class system. In his intensive study of tailoring, for instance, Hopkins has described an aggregate shift in the mode of production from an artisanal to a manufacturing mode of production. Many tailors accept piecework at unfavorable rates but do so because of a value system in which independence or the appearance of it is highly valued. A cooperative might secure them a higher return for their labor, but the tailors would have to give up some of their independence. Because of their value system workers tend "to think in terms of individual advancement rather than collective experience." As a result, tailors do not realize the commonality of their interests. Hopkins concludes that they are not fully integrated into the capitalist mode of production, but that

[46] Hopkins, "Emergence of Class," p. 454.
[47] *Ibid.,* p. 455.

once they are, then there might be a "full emergence of class relations."[48] Hopkins goes beyond Duben in suggesting that class relationships will eventually diminish the importance of all other forms of relationship, and that certain "value systems" impede some persons and categories of occupations from realizing where their economic interests lie. Both of their analyses stress the importance of considering how class relations articulate with other forms of social solidarity and identity.

In discussions of the emergence of class relationships, the importance of the distinction between the anthropology *of* cities and the anthropology *in* cities becomes paramount. The emergence of class relationships is a process which affects entire economies and regions and cannot be confined to a discussion of urban milieus. Certain transformations may appear more pronounced in urban contexts but cannot be explained within those contexts alone.

[48] Hopkins, "Tailoring," p. 481.

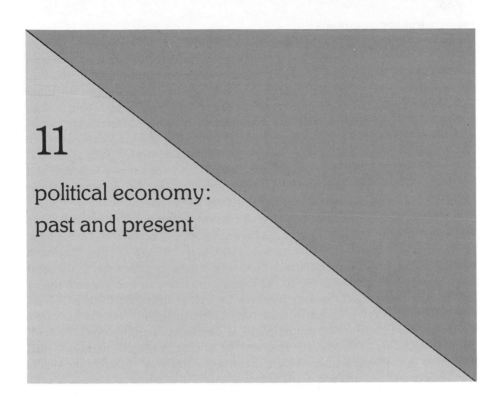

# 11
# political economy:
# past and present

> Speculation about connections between economics and politics becomes much more profitable when one focuses not on the roughest outline, but on the finer features.[1]

In nineteenth-century anthropology, long-term perspectives prevailed which conceived of cultural and civilizational growth in terms of developmental stages much like geological layers. These models were discarded when too few examples could be found to fit the stages meaningfully. Today, anthropologists and scholars in related disciplines are shifting their attention to how systems of meaning shape and are in turn shaped by configurations of power and economic relations in different societies. This has resulted in a renewed interest in long-term perspectives on the societies they study, but with markedly different assumptions than those of the past.

Patterns of trade relations are a case in point. Archaeologists and social historians interested in ancient trade assumed all too readily that in the past the movement of goods followed habitual patterns. More recently it has been argued that patterns of trade, symbiosis and predation often begin and are broken off in "dizzyingly abrupt shifts" in which entrepreneurs and "self-conscious individuals and groups" take advantage of risks and uncertainties rapidly to innovate and to

[1] Albert O. Hirschman, *A Bias for Hope: Essays on Development and Latin America* (New Haven and London: Yale University Press, 1971), p. 9.

adapt to situations not fully known or perhaps unknowable. Instead of gradualist progress along an evolutionary ladder to more complex organization, increases in scale and complexity are seen to depend much more upon reactions to situations and opportunities in which individuals are never fully conscious of where their actions and ideas ultimately will lead. Nonetheless, meaningful correlations can be made between forms of production, political authority, and the ideologies which people use to shape and to make sense of these developments.[2] Such arguments have been most intensively pursued in the contexts of the ancient Near East and medieval Europe, but such a perspective is equally useful in understanding the empires of the medieval Middle East and the states of the present.

In the Middle East as elsewhere in the world, anthropologists have produced valuable studies of local-level politics, administration, and economics. Unlike some other parts of the world, social historical resources are available to place such studies in the broader perspective which is necessary to comprehend just what politics and economics mean today and meant in the past. In studying such topics, the contribution of anthropology has been to look at the "finer features" of the relation, not always a straightforward one, between politics, economics, native concepts of the social order, and programs of development and progress, in short, political economy. This chapter analyzes the approaches which anthropologists have used to make sense of rapid social, political, and cultural change in the Middle East today and to relate them to the historical past.

## MEDIEVAL MUSLIM STATES: PROBLEMS OF AUTHORITY AND INTERPRETATION

As a focus of scholarly inquiry, the medieval Middle East has concerned anthropologists and social historians, even those primarily interested in postmedieval periods, in two principal ways. First, Islamic empires and states have frequently been characterized by historians and sociologists as representing extreme types of political authority. In his analysis of the writings of Max Weber on Islam, Bryan S. Turner concludes that Weber concentrated upon analyzing two aspects of domination in the Muslim world: the charismatic authority represented by the Prophet Muḥammad and *sultanism*, representing for Weber the arbitrary free will of the ruler released from most traditional limitations.[3] The second principal use of

[2] Quoted material is from Robert McC. Adams, "Anthropological Perspectives on Ancient Trade," *Current Anthropology*, 15, no. 3 (September 1974), 239-58; see also Jane Schneider, "Peacocks and Penguins: The Political Economy of European Cloths and Colors," *American Ethnologist*, 5, no. 3 (August 1978), 413-47.

[3] Bryan S. Turner, *Weber and Islam: A Critical Study* (London and Boston: Routledge & Kegan Paul, 1974), pp. 75-92. The following account of Weber's ideas derives largely from Turner's excellent discussion. See also his *Marx and the End of Orientalism*, Controversies in Sociology, 7 (London: George Allen & Unwin, 1978). This short study is essentially a review

the medieval period—"classical Islam" or "the grandeur that was" in the phrasing of some Orientalists—was to serve as a backdrop against which the "decline" of the Middle East could be measured. Coon's mosaic characterization of Middle Eastern polities and other prevailing ahistorical images of Middle Eastern societies derive from the general assumptions made of this period, and the ideological assumption of the decline of the region in many instances provided a convenient justification for colonial intervention.

As Turner indicates, Weber's investigations concerning Islamic society were not as complete as his interpretations of other civilizational traditions and he "often failed to adhere to his own methodological principles" of seeking to understand the motivations and intentions of individuals acting in particular historical contexts. "In Weber's analysis, it was the patrimonial structure of traditional Islam which was incompatible with political radicalism, the freedom of cities, the autonomy of rational law and hence with the emergence of capitalism."[4]

Over a period of several centuries, what Weber and others considered to be the "classical" form of Islamic society emerged based upon a combination of patrimonial politics (as in the social order of cities) and of feudalism. Turner explains in the following manner how these two principles were supposed to combine. A patrimonial ruler (whose rule in its most primitive form is "characteristic of the authority of a lord over his own household") seeks to convert his extended family and others into dependent subjects. A principal way of doing this is through the use of slaves and mercenaries who are dependent upon the royal household. The patrimonial ruler must then seek to minimize the independence of his mercenaries and that of notables and merchants. One technique of doing this was to make official appointments deliberately insecure so that subordinates could be used as scapegoats for popular discontent and the ruler could preserve the "fiction that he is benevolent and concerned for the welfare of his subjects." Turner explains that the paradox of this form of rule and especially of sultanism, its most extreme form, is that "the more a ruler has to rely on his mercenaries or slave army, the more dependent he becomes on their power to subjugate the masses." Soon, mercenary armies are able to extract fiefs and regular advantages from the ruler, forcing him further to pauperize the peasantry while continuing to represent himself as the people's benefactor. The result is two forms of protest: periodic millennial outbursts, usually based upon religious principles, and the "periodic dynastic, political change" which did not result in the change of form of rule but which resulted in prolonged conflicts over succession.[5]

---

essay concerning the major approaches to the understanding of the Middle East in the light of "critical" Marxist theory. Turner's general tone on the state of Middle Eastern studies is dyspeptic; he doubts whether the study of the Middle East has contributed significantly to the analytic development of the academic disciplines involved, although he concedes that anthropology "may be" partially exempt from his negative judgment (p. 1).

[4] Turner, *Weber*, p. 75.
[5] *Ibid.*, pp. 80-81.

This central problem in the succession of dynasties was recognized by medieval Muslim intellectuals themselves, of whom the best known is the North African Ibn Khaldūn (d. 1406). His theories of dynastic succession are worth introducing here because a succession of scholars, including Ernest Gellner, have used Ibn Khaldūn as a point of departure for their own discussions of the nature of premodern political authority.[6] Together with other contemporaries, Ibn Khaldūn acquired an education by traveling to various centers of learning throughout North Africa and the Middle East, serving as counselor of state to a number of North African rulers and to Spanish ones when Spain was still under Muslim domination. Ibn Khaldūn makes for fascinating reading even today, as he had to struggle to create a vocabulary through which he could articulate sociologically the rise and decay of dynasties throughout the Muslim world.

Ibn Khaldūn must have been acutely sensitive to the problems of the decay of dynasties and political domination, for in his lifetime the Spanish Muslim principalities collapsed one after another. One clear threat was from Christian invaders; another was from sudden shifts in the political climate of the Muslim world itself. It has sometimes been argued that Ibn Khaldūn sought to provide a universal model for political developments. I prefer to think that he was primarily concerned with medieval North Africa and southern Spain, from where most of his examples are drawn. His observations on the nature of political domination make more sense in this primary context than if they are made to encompass all forms of domination.

Ibn Khaldūn sees the successive ideal stages of a dynasty as follows. At its inception, it must possess "group feeling" (ᶜaṣabīya), which roughly can be glossed by acting as if compelling ties of obligation bind members of a group together. Such compelling notions of group feeling are more likely to be found in rural or tribal contexts (the notion that group feeling is primarily confined to nomads or Bedouin is, I think, based on a misinterpretation of the Arabic original). Group feeling need not depend upon blood relationships existing between those persons who share it, but the bonds of solidarity must be such that they take precedence over all other bonds of association. The parallels of this notion with the contemporary notion of "closeness," discussed in Chapter 6, are obvious. Such ties imply that persons act together in one another's interests over extended periods of time. Ibn Khaldūn suggests that such solidarity is needed for a dynasty to come into existence, and he gives a number of examples from the North African context. Moreover, he argues that a new dynasty is most likely to be established when it can claim a religious basis of legitimacy: prophecy, reform or some other "religious

[6] Ibn Khaldūn, *The Muqaddimah*, trans. Franz Rosenthal, 2nd ed., Bollingen Series, 43 (Princeton: Princeton University Press, 1967), Vol. I, pp. 249-355; Ernest Gellner, *Saints of the Atlas* (Chicago: University of Chicago Press, 1969); Muhsin Mahdi's *Ibn Khaldūn's Philosophy of History* (Chicago: University of Chicago Press, 1957) remains the best study in English on Ibn Khaldūn; Yves Lacoste, *Ibn Khaldūn: Naissance de l'Histoire passé du Tiers Monde* (Paris: François Maspéro, 1973), is a convenient point of departure for a fresh reappraisal of Ibn Khaldūn's work.

coloring." Only with group feeling can a religious ideology be practically implemented; thus Ibn Khaldūn used the notion to link ideologies to their political
contexts.

Like most political thinkers, Ibn Khaldūn chose a striking metaphor to
depict his view of the nature of political change, the metaphor of the human life
span—growth, maturity, and decay. Each stage of this cycle generated the conditions necessary for the next, and in this sense his theory of dynastic change is
pessimistic because he saw the cyclical succession of stages as inevitable.

The first of his stages was the overthrow of an earlier dynasty and the appropriation of royal authority *(mulk)*. The ruler at this stage appropriates few luxuries
for himself and serves as a model of discipline, nobleness, and restraint to his
followers.

In the second stage of authority, the ruler gains complete control over his
people and appropriates royal authority entirely to himself. Now he is interested
in acquiring adherents and followers in greater numbers and in barring those who
helped him to power from appropriating any of his authority. He spends as much
time in subduing his potential challengers as the first member of the dynasty spent
in the overthrow of his predecessors.

The third stage is one of leisure and tranquility in which the ruler and his
entourage enjoy the fruits of royal authority. Monuments and public benefices
commemorating the dynasty are erected and largesse is distributed to the dynasty's
supporters. The ruler's talents are now directed to bookkeeping and planning. This
stage merges imperceptibly into the fourth, one of contentment and peacefulness,
in which the ruler is satisfied with what his predecessors have built. He relies upon
and imitates the ways of his predecessors.

The final stage is one of waste and squandering. The ruler spends his time in
pleasures and amusements, dissipating the former strength of his regime. To maintain himself in power, he seeks to destroy all those whom he regards as competent
to replace him and thus tends to surround himself with incompetent lackeys. This is
the stage of senility of the dynasty when it is ripe for collapse.

For later generations of Western scholars influenced by Ibn Khaldūn, the
organization and nature of political power within the Ottoman empire has been
a source of fascination and until recently the point from which the "decline" of
Middle Eastern civilization was measured. The Ottoman empire, at its height
in the seventeenth century, controlled a significant part of the Middle Eastern
Muslim world and parts of eastern Europe. Gustave E. von Grunebaum, one of the
best known scholars of the twentieth century, had the Ottoman empire in mind
when he depicted the principles of order in "Islamic" societies in highly formal
terms. These were: the separation of the Muslim from the non-Muslim subject; the
setting apart (and toleration) of a number of different religious groups under the
aegis of Islam in which Christians, Jews, and Zoroastrians possessed a large measure
of internal autonomy for their own communities; the marking off of different
"nationalities" within the Islamic community; and the narrow delimitation of

"social distinctions that assigned people to a more or less definite hierarchy of professions."[7] The mere delineation of these "principles" suggests von Grunebaum's assumption of rigid social hierarchies and distinctions in contrast to the more flexible notions of social order suggested by scholars such as Ira Lapidus and Richard Bulliet, who seek a more thoroughly sociological comprehension of medieval Muslim society instead of a search for a timeless "essence."

A number of analyses exist of the implicit assumptions concerning "oriental" rule made by a prior generation of scholars.[8] The rather contradictory earlier assumptions are characterized as follows by Talal Asad, based primarily upon the influential works of Sir Hamilton Gibb, von Grunebaum, and Snouck Hurgronje:

> An emphasis on the absolute power of the ruler, and the whimsical, generally illegitimate nature of his demands; on the indifference or involuntary submission on the part of the ruled; on a somewhat irrational form of conflict in which sudden, irresponsible urges to riot are met with violent repression; and, finally, an emphasis on the overall inefficiency and corruption of political life.[9]

It is relevant here simply to note these assumptions, not to show how they masked a highly fluid situation, as Roger Owen has sought to do in indicating how a greater knowledge of economic conditions in the period of Ottoman rule, for example, the development of cash crops in the regions of Lower Egypt, Mount Lebanon, and Izmir, the rapid spread of maize cultivation throughout the seventeenth century, and shifting patterns of trade, can be related to specific political and social developments. Earlier scholars tended to disregard the importance of trade and economics in their accounts of Islamic polities.[10] Similarly, many of the "spontaneous" riots in cities and rural regions during Ottoman times are beginning to be studied, like comparable phenomena in Europe, as popular reactions against accepted notions of political and economic justice. If grain was hoarded by merchants and the price of bread became unconscionable, so-called rioters became violent only when authorities refused to enforce prices which were considered just. In some of the Arab Gulf states, merchants and fishermen at the end of the nine-

[7]Gustave E. von Grunebaum, *Medieval Islam,* 2nd ed. (Chicago: University of Chicago Press, 1954), p. 177.

[8]Edward W. Said, *Orientalism* (New York: Pantheon Books, 1978) provides a forceful critique of such studies, although his argument is unfortunately marred by the same sort of ahistorical assumptions which he attributes to Orientalists. For concise analyses of specific Orientalists, see Talal Asad, "Two European Images of Non-European Rule," in *Anthropology and the Colonial Encounter,* ed. Talal Asad (London: Ithaca Press; New York: Humanities Press, 1973), pp. 103-18; Turner, *Weber and Islam,* pp. 122-34; and Roger Owen, "The Middle East in the Eighteenth Century—An 'Islamic' Society in Decline: A Critique of Gibb and Bowen's *Islamic Society and the West," Review of Middle East Studies,* 1 (1975), 101-12. Owen's study is particularly valuable, for it provides an outline of the materials with which revised images of the Middle East's past are being forged.

[9]Asad, "Two European Images," p. 107.

[10]Owen, "The Middle East in the Eighteenth Century," p. 110.

teenth century simply voted with their feet and moved to another city-state if the ruling family sought to make illegitimate exactions. The option of migration effectively provided an informal check on the excesses of rulers.[11] In larger states, the fact that mosques often were the rallying points for demonstrations suggests that "rioters" considered their demands to be moral and just. As with the layout of traditional cities in the Middle East, the imagined "irrationality" of the "crowd" often has been nothing more than a failure on the part of earlier scholars to perceive implicit assumptions of legitimacy and justice. In any case, a convenient excuse for colonial rule was the presumed inability of the "Orient" to govern itself responsibly. As Edward Said has stated, a concrete and conscientious understanding of Middle Eastern societies and civilizations will emerge only when specific societies and problems of the Middle East are studied instead of the "Orient" writ large, or an Islamic "essence," or the "Arab mind."[12]

One of the few anthropologists whose approach is singled out for approval by Said is Clifford Geertz. The latter's analysis of the royal progress in nineteenth-century Morocco can be taken as an example of how popular notions of legitimacy for contemporary or historically known periods can be elicited.[13] A *royal progress* is a journey by a monarch throughout his domain which symbolically establishes or reaffirms possession of the realm. For Geertz, the royal progress is a striking symbolic representation of how political domination is asserted. In fact, he argues that an examination of the symbols of power and the nature of power often shows that both are one and the same thing, a conjunction especially apparent in traditional monarchies as opposed to modern political regimes in which the relation between the symbols of power and men of power is better disguised.[14] In medieval England, the monarch was entertained during the royal progress with public pageants in which subjects dressed up in costumes which depicted the virtues of the realm and the vices which threatened it. In nineteenth-century Morocco, "strength did not have to be represented as other than what it was." Society was "a tournament of wills," and hence so was kingship and its symbolism: "Progresses here were not always easy to tell from raids."[15] Geertz's language is more luxurious than my brief account can begin to suggest, but in essence he argues that the surest sign of grace, *baraka,* was the ability of one man to prevail over another. A number of strongmen—qaids, pashas, marabouts, and others—sought to build and maintain personal configurations of power, with the sultan striving to dominate them all.

In Morocco of the eighteenth and nineteenth centuries, the fertile Atlantic plains and those of the region of Fez and Meknes were firmly dominated by the sul-

---

[11] Peter Lienhardt, "The Authority of Shaykhs in the Gulf: An Essay in Nineteenth-Century History," *Arabian Studies,* 2 (1975), 61-75.

[12] Said, *Orientalism,* p. 326.

[13] Clifford Geertz, "Centers, Kings, and Charisma: Reflections on the Symbolics of Power," in *Culture and Its Creators: Essays in Honor of Edward Shils,* eds. Joseph Ben-David and Terry N. Clark (Chicago and London: University of Chicago Press, 1977), pp. 150-171.

[14] *Ibid.,* p. 153.

[15] *Ibid.,* p. 161.

FIGURE 11-1 Royal *maḥalla,* Morocco, 1911. (From Gaston Doumergue, *Histoire populaire des Colonies françaises* [Paris: Editions du Vélin, 1932] , p. 112.)

tan, but his authority was threatened on all sides by "charismatic adventurers" and periodically had to be reestablished. For the sultan to affirm his *baraka* and hence his "capacity to dominate," he quite simply had to prevail over others. "*[Baraka]* was not a condition, like chastity, or a trait, like pride, that shines by itself but a movement, like will, that exists in its impact."[16]

One way of demonstrating this capacity was through a royal progress *(ḥarka* or *maḥalla),* and Geertz describes in detail the last major one by Sultan Mūlāy Ḥasan I (d. 1894). Mūlāy Ḥasan was usually on the move half of each year, shifting his capital periodically among the so-called imperial cities—Fez, Marrakesh, Meknes, and Rabat. When he moved beyond these capitals, his entourage often numbered between thirty thousand and forty thousand persons. A suitable chastisement for a region unwilling to pay its share of taxes was for the *ḥarka* to stop in one place consuming the grain and herds of the region until tribes and their leaders were worn into renewed submission. Geertz's argument is that the mobility of the sultan was a central element both in his power and, inseparably, in the concept of royal authority in Morocco. "The realm was unified ... by a restless searching-out of contact, most of it agonistic, with literally hundreds of lesser centers of power within it."[17]

The resiliency of the forms in which political domination is expressed is demonstrated by their use throughout the colonial era and after Morocco regained its independence in 1956. In the colonial era, royal progresses included officials of the French *résidence* traveling with the sultan (after 1956 *sultan* was replaced by

[16]*Ibid.,* p. 162.
[17]*Ibid.,* p. 163.

the more modern designation of king *(malik);* in nationalist circles the newer designation was common currency from at least the mid-1940s) and appearing in all formal ceremonials except specifically religious ones. The symbolism of the colonial royal progress also included such features as visits by the sultan to the tomb of the unknown soldier in France and other ceremonies visually suggesting the "protected" status of the royal family. In the current fighting for control and sovereignty in the Sahara, those tribal groups wishing to express fealty to the Moroccan throne continue to do so in the form of the traditional oath of fealty *(bay^c a),* in which tribal delegations offer sacrifices of bulls and sheep to renew their covenant with the Moroccan throne.[18] The "Green March" of King Ḥasan II to the Sahara in 1976 with tens of thousands of Moroccans can also be seen as a classical royal progress. Similarly symbolism prevails in the conduct of monarchies and republics elsewhere.

## THE COLONIAL EXPERIENCE

Many anthropological studies were conducted during the colonial era in the Middle East although, with the exception of French North Africa, these studies were generally not as intensive and thorough as those conducted by English social anthropologists in Black Africa. Many of the contributions to Gellner and Micaud's *Arabs and Berbers* suggest the continuing pervasiveness of the categories initially created by French colonial sociologists: Arabs versus Berbers, town versus tribe, lands of submission (to royal authority) versus lands of dissidence, and other stereotypic representations of North African society.[19] Some of the studies in the Gellner and Micaud volume, notably that of Edmund Burke III, indicate how this "colonial vulgate" came into being; a few merely take the colonial vulgate for granted; others continue to use the colonial vulgate as a scholarly point of departure. Even as late as 1951, when independence movements in the Middle East were rapidly gaining momentum, one of the most distinguished French ethnographers (earlier a military officer) of colonial Morocco could brush aside the delay in publication of a book on Moroccan religious brotherhoods by writing that in Islam "evolution is boundlessly slow. For Islam, even more than for other religions, one has to count not in years but in centuries."[20] These sentiments matched precisely the notion of

[18] The newspaper *al-Muḥarrir* (Casablanca), August 16, 1979, describes the reception of tribal delegations totaling three hundred men and sixty women from the Sahara's Wādī Dhahb region to renew their oath of allegiance to the Moroccan throne. The ceremony involved the sacrifice of sheep and bulls. In the colonial era, similar sacrifices were offered to the French to signify the cessation of hostilities.

[19] Ernest Gellner and Charles Micaud, eds., *Arabs and Berbers: From Tribe to Nation in North Africa* (London: Duckworth; Lexington, Mass.: D. C. Heath and Company, 1972).

[20] Robert Montagne, in his foreword to Georges Drague [Spillman], *Esquisse d'Histoire religieuse du Maroc* (Paris: J. Peyronnet, 1951). (My translation.) Montagne was one of colonial Morocco's outstanding sociologists. For a translation of one of his key works in English, with an excellent introduction by David Seddon, see Robert Montagne, *The Berbers: Their Social and Political Organization* (London: Frank Cass Co., 1973).

the timeless nature of "Oriental" society prevalent in the nineteenth century. Still other studies exist which, like their equivalents in Black Africa, ignored almost completely the impact of colonial administration upon political life. Local disputes were treated as if they had no wider implications and the relations between native officials and foreign administrators, as with the impact of the expropriation of indigenous lands, were mentioned only in passing. One of the few exceptions to these strictures was Evans-Pritchard's study of the Italian colonization of Libya, significantly a study made of the policies of a defeated European power.[21] Evans-Pritchard made no similar analysis of colonial rule in regions under British domination.

At one time or another in the past century and a half, most of the Middle East has experienced colonial domination or, in the case of the Arab Gulf states, decisive foreign influence. This fact is significant in two ways. Colonial society can be studied in itself as a unique, and now passing, social form, as the discussion of colonial urbanization in Chapter 10 has suggested. Secondly, colonial domination has had a formative influence on the shape of the present Middle Eastern polities and societies.

René Maunier, at one time head of the French Academy of Colonial Science, defined colonialism as "occupation with domination and emigration with government."[22] His definition has the advantage of facilitating the comparative study of colonial systems, a field in which Maunier was a leader. His book on the sociology of colonies was for a long time one of the standard texts on the subject, in which Maunier discussed the early Phoenician colonies of the Mediterranean, the Roman Empire, and the more recent experience of European colonial expansion and reactions to it.

The notion of a "colonial science" is of course an indication that colonial rule could be rationalized and systematized and was here to stay, an idea perhaps easy to accept (for Europeans at least) in the early 1930s, when congresses were routinely held in Europe and attended by representatives of various colonial administrations. Jacques Berque, a prominent French social historian of colonial rule in North Africa, suggests that 1930 be taken as its apogee.[23] The year was marked by

---

[21] E. E. Evans-Pritchard, *The Sanusi of Cyrenaica* (Oxford: Clarendon Press, 1949), pp. 90-229.

[22] René Maunier, *The Sociology of Colonies,* trans. E. O. Lorimer (London: Routledge & Kegan Paul, 1949), Vol. I, p. 19. This remains one of the best available accounts of "colonial sociology" and in some ways is all the more valuable for its "insider" perspective.

[23] One of the best accounts of the varieties of North African colonial experience is Jacques Berque's masterly, *French North Africa: The Maghrib Between Two World Wars* (New York: Frederick A. Praeger, 1967). Berque's method is essentially to paint vivid word pictures of tribes, towns, persons, events, and the attitudes of those who experienced them. A more analytical account of comparative colonial rule in North Africa and its impact upon different forms of independent government is Elbaki Hermassi, *Leadership and National Development in North Africa* (Berkeley and Los Angeles: University of California Press, 1972). See also Abdelkader Zghal's excellent "Nation-building in the Maghreb," *International Social Science Journal,* 23, no. 3 (1971), 435-51.

**FIGURE 11-2** Jacques Berque, in uniform, center right, with General Nogues, Resident-General of Morocco and notables of Fez, October 1937. Berque is today one of France's most distinguished interpreters of Middle Eastern civilizations. (Courtesy Jacques Berque.)

an International Colonial Exposition in France, and celebrations took place throughout the year to commemorate the centenary of French Algeria.

The 1918 European armistice is a convenient point from which to survey the extent of colonial dominion in the Middle East. All the Levant except Turkey was firmly occupied by colonial powers, and only stiff resistance by the Turks kept Anatolia as well from succumbing to foreign domination. Syria and Lebanon were under the French, the spoils of the defeated Ottoman empire. Iraq was under the British, who also exercised a major influence over the mini-states of the Persian/ Arab Gulf, with British residents exercising significant control over tribal politics and ordering air strikes when necessary to facilitate accommodation to British imperial interests. Saudi Arabia managed to escape the direct impact of European colonial control, mainly because its autonomy suited the European colonial powers. Both Jordan and Palestine fell within the British sphere of domination. Egypt had been under English domination since 1882, although like the other countries, significant European control over its finances dated from an earlier period. In the Levant as in Egypt, there was virtually no European settlement, although Greeks and others served as artisans in larger cities such as Alexandria, and the British performed many of the higher administrative and military functions, effectively blocking training for Middle Easterners themselves. The prevalent thought of such rule, to paraphrase Lord Cromer, one of the British proconsuls in Egypt, was to do what was good for "Orientals," not necessarily to do what they thought was good for themselves.

Each North African country from Libya to Morocco experienced colonialism

**FIGURE 11-3** British political residents in the Arab Gulf states commonly adopted Arab dress as late as the 1930s. H. R. P. Dickson, British Resident for Kuwait and his wife. (From H. R. P. Dickson, *The Arab of the Desert* [London: George Allen & Unwin Ltd., 1949], opp. p. 48.)

in a different form, but all had a significant population of European settlers. The short-lived Italian colonial experiment in Libya is instructive.[24] In 1911 Italy joined the other European powers in the scramble for power, and by the following year the Ottomans ceded Libya to them. By 1931 a major influx of settlers had begun, each allotted lands, houses, and tools at government expense, the property to become theirs after 20 years of labor. There were only 30,000 settlers in 1921, 50,000 by 1931, and 150,000 by 1940. These settlers were concentrated in the fertile lands of the north. To make room for them, the native population was forced to emigrate to the less productive parts of the country or was confined to camps. At the height of Italy's dominion of Libya, roughly one-fifth of the country was Italian. As with the other countries in the Maghrib, concern for the indigenous population was decidedly secondary.

The rest of North Africa came under French colonial domination, with the exception of Morocco's northern zone and its southern fringes, both of which came under Spanish rule. The earliest French colony in North Africa was Algeria, first occupied by the French in 1830 by means of tactics recognized as brutal even in terms of contemporary standards.[25] Native lands were systematically expropriated, traditional learning and administration were systematically destroyed. Even advocates of French colonial expansion recognized the misrule and brutality experi-

[24] See Evans-Pritchard, *The Sanusi.*

[25] On Algeria, in addition to Berque's *French North Africa,* a good point of departure is Pierre Bourdieu's *The Algerians* (Boston: Beacon Press, 1962). This study was written at the height of the Algerian conflict and should be complemented by his later *Algeria 1960,* Studies in Modern Capitalism (New York: Cambridge University Press, 1979).

enced by the colony. The presence of a large settler class effectively wrested control of the administration from metropolitan France. Between Algerian French and Algerian Muslims there was a marked tradition of violence and mutual incomprehension from the very beginning of colonial rule.

Morocco, in contrast, was the last North African territory to be brought into the French empire (1912), and it was considered by many French to be the jewel of their colonies—an example of "scientific" colonialism at its best. It certainly was the best studied; no Middle Eastern country under English domination has been as thoroughly described ethnographically. One can only concur with Edmund Burke III's judgment that an assessment today of the work of the earlier generation of colonial ethnographers concerned with Morocco can prove to be highly valuable even if one disagrees with the implicit assumptions of their work and the motivation for it. The corpus of ethnographic work is of high quality and the intensity of the work undertaken makes Morocco "a particularly illuminating place to study the ways in which colonial ethnographers went about their business in the generation or so preceding the First World War."[26]

The French intention to colonize Morocco was clear by the end of the nineteenth century, but opposition by the British and the Germans to direct French expansion prevented direct colonization.[27] Nonetheless, clandestine domination took place. One means was by military expansion in Morocco's southeast, where oases were forced to collaborate with the French or risk destruction of their date palms and herds. Another device (used as well throughout the Middle East in various guises) was through control of the police of the major Moroccan ports (together with the Spanish), collection of customs revenues, expansion of commercial operations with extraterritorial protection granted to Moroccans acting in French interests, and from 1907 the creation of the Bank of Morocco to control the country's finances. Ostensibly these measures were to ensure repayment of loans forced upon Morocco by European countries, often at highly disadvantageous terms. By 1907, using as a pretext the struggle over control of the throne between the brothers Mūlāy ᶜAbd al-ᶜAzīz and Mūlāy Ḥafīḍ, three thousand French and five hundred Spanish troops landed at Casablanca and began to occupy the surrounding region to protect the port. The following year the expeditionary force had expanded to fifteen thousand men, and beginning in 1910 Morocco was compelled to indemnify the French for the cost of the force.

[26] Edmund Burke III, "Fez, the Setting Sun of Islam: A Study of the Politics of Colonial Ethnography," *The Maghreb Review*, 2, no. 4 (July-August 1977), 1. See also Burke's excellent *Prelude to Protectorate in Morocco: Precolonial Protest and Resistance, 1860-1912,* Studies in Imperialism (Chicago and London: University of Chicago Press, 1976).

[27] A now-standard French source on this early period and on the Riffian war of the 1920s is Germain Ayache, *Etudes d'Histoire marocaine* (Rabat: Société Marocaine des Editeurs Réunis, 1979); see also Abdallah Laroui, *Les Origines sociales et culturelles du Nationalisme marocain (1830-1912)* (Paris: Librairie François Maspéro, 1977). For a sensitive account of French penetration of Morocco's southeast, see Ross E. Dunn, *Resistance in the Desert: Moroccan Responses to French Imperialism, 1881-1912* (Madison: University of Wisconsin Press; London: Croom Helm, Ltd., 1977).

Finally in November 1911 the French reached an agreement with the other major European powers, and the road was clear for the direct occupation of Morocco. Five thousand troops advanced from Algeria to Fez, where Mūlāy Ḥafīḍ was in his palace. The Spaniards occupied points along Morocco's northern coast. Moroccan ability to resist these incursions was virtually nil. In March, the Minister of France at Tangier (where all embassies to Morocco were situated) set out to Fez on horseback. The sultan briefly considered resistance but finally agreed to sign the treaty of the protectorate after six days of being bullied by the French. He abdicated almost immediately afterward in favor of his younger brother, Mūlāy Yūsif. Formal French domination of Morocco had begun.

Louis Hubert Gonzalve Lyautey was appointed first Résident-Général of Morocco (1912-1925). During the period of his administration he set the tone for what was considered to be an enlightened, "scientific" colonial administration.[28] Lyautey was a champion of "indirect" rule and in fact elaborated an administration which was remarkably economical, requiring only a handful of Frenchmen to supervise vast expenses of territory and which was almost entirely self-financing. He assiduously cultivated ties with Morocco's urban aristocracy and rural strongmen, often overlooking their excesses in exchange for their continued support. Thus

**FIGURE 11-4** Lyautey, Resident-General of Morocco, talks with Berber leaders, c. 1913. (From Doumergue, *Histoire Populaire*, p. 30.)

[28] A sort of colonial vulgate describing the French administrative machinery from the perspective of a former member of the British Colonial Service in West Aden Protectorate is Robin Bidwell's *Morocco Under Colonial Rule: French Administration of Tribal Areas, 1912-1956* (London: Frank Cass, 1973).

during the difficult period of the initial takeover of Morocco, when there was pronounced resistance in many regions, Lyautey sent letters by messenger to Moroccan
notables, an act which in itself indicated the sophisticated French knowledge of
Morocco, stating that their interests would be protected if they proved themselves
to be "friends" of France. France, the letters explained, was in Morocco only to
defend the interests of the sultanate. It is unlikely that many Moroccan notables
were convinced by this claim, but they had the terrifying example before them of
the fate of Algeria's elite. Many leaders visited Lyautey directly; others sent emis-
saries who were reassured of France's intentions. Medical services were made
strategically available and used to further military intelligence, and the French
bought grain and animals at high prices to encourage Moroccans to deal with them.
When such methods failed, dissident tribes were denied access to markets; transhumant groups were denied vital pastures, and in the last resort villages could be
burned and crops destroyed. Most military operations were accomplished with
relatively few losses; in any case, many soldiers fighting for France were from
Senegal and other French colonies. Lyautey's tactics worked so well that when
many French forces had to be withdrawn at the beginning of the First World War
and French control was precarious, there was no major rebellion against French
rule.

Lyautey's patrician image of how Morocco should be ruled prevented the
worst excesses of colonial intervention but by and large prevailed most firmly only
in those parts of the country *not* desired by the growing influx of settlers. For
many colonizers, the so-called "civilizing mission" of France was a mere façade for
the acquisition of land and economic gain. For Lyautey, it was something to be
taken seriously, as indicated by his insistence upon urban planning, the preservation
of Morocco's traditional architecture, and protection of the interests of those
Moroccans designated as notables. He did everything in his power to discourage
the development of a French settler population in Morocco, but it nonetheless
developed, along with the flourishing of large commercial enterprises, banks, railroad interests, agribusiness, and mining companies. By the 1920s, the land grabs of
the settler population and large commercial interests increased, but even in the
expropriation of lands held by Moroccans or in its acquisition by various forms of
fraud or administrative chicanery, the niceties of colonial rhetoric were preserved.
In one case the expropriation of a vast tract of land from a tribe in western
Morocco was claimed to be beneficial for the tribe involved because it would be
"educational" for them to see how European farms were run.[29] This dispossession

[29] For accounts of the impact of colonial penetration in various locales, see Dunn,
*Resistance;* Dale F. Eickelman, *Moroccan Islam: Tradition and Society in a Pilgrimage Center,*
Modern Middle East Series, 1 (Austin and London: University of Texas Press, 1976), pp. 211-
54; and (for the ex-Spanish zone) David Montgomery Hart, *The Aith Waryaghar of the
Moroccan Rif,* Viking Fund Publications in Anthropology, 55 (Tucson: University of Arizona
Press, 1976). Amal Rassam Vinogradov, *The Ait Ndhir of Morocco: A Study of the Social
Transformation of a Berber Tribe,* Anthropological Papers, 55 (Ann Arbor: University of
Michigan Museum of Anthropology, 1974), pp. 79-105, is particularly good in describing the

had serious consequences in turning tribesmen of many regions into a landless, impoverished proletariat.

The impact of French rule in most of Morocco outside of the cities was to freeze a local elite into place. Lyautey's policy had been to select local strongmen and to maintain them in place if they proved good at the job. If certain strong-men such as Pasha Ḥājj Thāmi Glāwi of Marrekesh were notorious for their abuses of power, continued French support for them could be rationalized by saying that Moroccans were used to ruthless officials. The pasha's ability to grasp the nuances of colonial politics meant that he ran Marrakesh and its many lucrative enterprises to his liking until the last days of French rule.

After the 1920s, there were very few changes in local dynasties of privilege and authority until the end of the colonial era. Even then, because of the compe-titive advantage that such individuals and their families had held in the past, a very common pattern was for brothers, uncles, and cousins in a single family to special-ize in the complementary fields of agribusiness, administration, and commerce, thus maintaining their privileged position despite major political and economic changes. It has been argued that until the last days of their rule the French maintained a fragile balance between local elites and the central power at the expense of signifi-cant rural social change. This was managed by a succession of independent Moroccan governments dependent upon French support.[30]

Morocco was "improved" by the French, but the educational achievements of the Protectorate speak eloquently of how little emphasis was placed upon pro-viding Moroccans with the skills necessary for the "evolution" promised by France's civilizing mission. For the French school-aged children in Morocco, educa-tion was virtually universal. The education of Jews was for practical purposes in the hands of private organizations and again was virtually universal in towns and cities. As for Moroccan Muslims, in practice only those recognized as the sons (and

---

social consequences of the expropriation of land for *colons*. For a meticulous study of another locale, see Paul Pascon, *Le Haouz de Marrakech* (Rabat: Centre Universitaire de la Recherche Scientifique, 1977). The best long-term study of the relation between political forms and eco-nomic conditions in North Africa is Lucette Valensi, *Fellahs Tunisiens: L'Economie rurale et la Vie des Campagnes aux 18e et 19e siècles* (Paris and The Hague: Mouton, 1977). See also her *On the Eve of Colonialism: North Africa before the French Conquest, 1790-1830*, translated by Kenneth J. Perkins (New York and London: Africana Publishing Co., 1977 [French orig. 1969]), with accompanying appendices containing interesting primary source materials.

[30]The two best sources on continuity in patterns of the Moroccan elite are John Water-bury, *The Commander of the Faithful: The Moroccan Political Elite* (New York: Columbia University Press, 1970), and R. Leveau, "The Rural Elite as an Element in the Social Stratifica-tion of Morocco," in *Commoners, Climbers and Notables*, ed. C. A. O. van Nieuwenhuijze (Leiden: E. J. Brill, 1977), pp. 268-78. Waterbury's study is perhaps one of the best available to date on the "political culture" of a Middle Eastern country. For one of the rare interpretive essays concerning the sort of men who became colonial administrators in various epochs, see Vincent Monteil (himself a former colonial officer), "Les Bureaux arabes au Maghreb (1833-1961)," *Esprit* (November 1961), 575-606.

to a much lesser extent daughters) of notables had relatively easy access to education. Some primary education was provided for the other students, but in general it was felt that only a modicum of education was "realistic." Moroccans set up their own system of "Free Schools" beginning in the 1930s, so that a "modern" education could be obtained independently from French control, but the standards of these schools were generally mediocre, and they did not provide the certification necessary for governmental and private employment. The educational statistics of the Protectorate almost speak for themselves. Even with a major effort to broaden the educational base after World War II, the results were meager. Of school-age Muslims in Morocco in 1938, only 1.7 percent were in primary school and 0.1 percent in secondary; in 1945 the figures were 2.7 percent and 0.2 percent respectively; in 1950 they were 7.0 percent and 0.6 percent; and in 1955 they were 11.2 percent and 1.2 percent. The dropout rate for primary school alone was 90 percent. As for secondary education, it is sufficient to say that between 1912 and 1956, the years of French rule, only 530 Moroccans had passed the French *baccalauréat* examination, a necessary prerequisite to entering the university.[31]

The ironies of Protectorate government were abundant. The formal fiction of a Morocco simply under the tutelage of France was preserved, but real political power rested with the French. The sultan could still emerge from his palace on feast days to act as head of the Muslim community and slaughter a sheep on behalf of the Muslims in his domain, but access to him was strictly controlled by the French. All messages to his subordinates had to pass through French hands. Appointments at local administrative levels were chosen from lists of nominees approved by the French. In the name of preserving traditional forms, Moroccan ministers were not permitted offices and desks but had to use low-lying benches. Even Qāḍī-s, or religious judges, could not assume office until they passed an examination set by a French Orientalist who advised the sultan's entourage as to whether the candidate possessed an adequate knowledge of Islamic law.

After World War II the colonial system elaborated by the French rapidly disintegrated. Disparities between Europeans and Moroccans had become too pronounced with the dislocation of the wartime black market, the Vichy debacle, the expropriation of tribal lands, rising nationalist expectations, and a monarchy which increasingly asserted its autonomy. The French responded with repression and in 1953 made the decisive error of deposing Sultan Muḥammad V in favor of an ineffective relative. The result was to galvanize Moroccan resistance to French rule. Rural terrorism mounted and bloody urban demonstrations and strikes became routine. The price of maintaining colonial rule became too high, and by late 1955 the French had negotiated the terms of transition to an independent government.

[31] On education, see John Damis, "Early Moroccan Reactions to the French Protectorate: The Cultural Dimension," *Humaniora Islamica*, 1 (1973), 15-31. The cited figures are from Ladislav Cerych, *Européens et Marocains, 1930-1956: Sociologie d'une Décolonisation* (Bruges: De Tempel, 1964), p. 297; and Waterbury, *Commander*, p. 84.

# THE SOCIAL ANTHROPOLOGY
# OF THE NATION-STATE

A map of the Middle East through the 1950s still indicated the presence of colonial powers in a number of settings, or of regimes such as the Egyptian and Iraqi monarchies that were regarded by many intellectuals as too close to the interests of the former colonial power. A map of the region today indicates a very different picture. Virtually the only remaining colonial enclaves possessed by European powers are the Spanish presidios of Ceuta and Melilla on Morocco's northern coast (but considered by Spaniards to be an integral part of their nation). The contemporary balance of forces includes religious fundamentalism, varieties of radical socialism and liberal constitutional regimes, and monarchies, each with particular constellations of internal and foreign support.[32] If colonial regimes are easier to grasp analytically and to oppose given their "external" nature, a measure of the balance of forces in contemporary states is a much more complex task. Many governments seek to exploit potential or real distinctions of class, regionalism, religion, and ethnicity in order to destabilize neighboring states considered hostile to their interests. If some issues such as the Palestine question can galvanize popular opinion in some instances into a unity based upon Arab nationalism and Islamic brotherhood, how such bases for unity figure alongside the wide range of potential bases for social unity and difference is a more difficult issue. What political scientists called "nation-building" in the 1960s is a meaningful point of entry into some of the issues involved, although today most scholars would place a much greater emphasis upon the interconnection between economics and politics than was the case when the concept was first developed.

✓      The work of Lloyd A. Fallers illustrates the distinctive contribution which anthropologists have sought to make to the study of nation-states.[33] He argues that the dilemma of the contemporary nation-state is that it unites what in the past was often diverse and scattered, but at the same time it often creates particularism where formerly there was an attachment to more universal ideals, such as those of religion. Fallers argues that nation-states are popular in the sense that both rulers and ruled lay claim to "qualities which are felt to be ancient, inherent, given, however new they may in fact be: language, territory, culture, race."[34] Whether it be celebrated as the "people's liberator" or condemned as more authoritarian than the older empires which it replaced, "the nation-state within an international system of nation-states remains in our time a fundamental feature of the human condition, in spite of widespread aspiration to a more firmly-based international order."[35]

---

[32] For a preliminary general sketch of some of these cross-currents and the sort of persons who support them, see Abdallah Laroui's *The Crisis of the Arab Intellectual: Traditionalism or Historicism* (Berkeley and Los Angeles: University of California Press, 1977).

[33] Lloyd A. Fallers, *The Social Anthropology of the Nation-State* (Chicago: Aldine Publishing Company, 1974).

[34] *Ibid.*, p. 1.

[35] *Ibid.*, p. 2.

Fallers states that a central issue in the formation of any nation-state is the development of civility, "a tolerant and generous recognition of common attachment to, and responsibility for, the social order, despite diversity."[36] Cleavages of language, religion, and ethnicity rarely coincide fully with the boundaries of nation-states. In ordinary times, the personal ties of neighborhood and workplace, worship and daily activities do not engage such identities in a potentially destructive way. External threats to a nation may allow them to be relegated to the background. But in crisis situations, the ordinarily innocuous acts of daily life can become suffused with larger meaning. A song, an item of clothing, a sporting event, or a funeral may become an incitement to conflict. Fallers writes that such issues are hardly confined to the Third World, as the continuing school busing controversy reminds Americans. Civility is a virtue which must consciously be maintained and which requires the exercise of self-restraint on the part of leaders and intellectuals so as not to appeal to baser sentiments.

An anthropologist can grasp the practical construction and maintenance of civility by using what remains one of the principal techniques of the discipline, the intensive participant-observational study of small groups of men and women in social interaction. As stated in Chapter 1, the fact that such small groups are embedded in much larger entities which are the subject of concern does not in itself create a problem of generalization; as with any other discipline, the issue is how the generalizations are made. By grasping the meaning of civility in particular social circumstances, the anthropologist contributes to the comprehension of how nation-states are elaborated and practically experienced.

The comparative study of nation-building is facilitated by looking at transformations over longer time periods and by evaluating the options of emerging political systems for the integration of their diverse communities, the institutionalization of new forms of social and political identity, economic development, and notions of what Elbaki Hermassi has called "distributive justice."[37] As he writes, foreign economic and political domination, international pressures, and endogeneous and exogeneous factors of change cannot be taken as givens but must be carefully examined in specific instances as to their impact. Even where some of the forces impinging on contemporary societies appear everywhere to be the same, as with international economic pressures, how these are experienced and responded to varies with each society and must be explained in part by its particular historical context. Four contrasting cases are considered here: Turkey, the Sultanate of Oman, Somalia, and Israel. These four examples do not represent the gamut of problems facing Middle Eastern countries or developing nations elsewhere, but each of these countries has significantly transformed its identity or created a new one in the fairly recent past and thus indicates in sharper focus than other possible examples the problems of forging shared identities in a nation-state.

[36] *Ibid.*, p. 5.

[37] Elbaki Hermassi, *Leadership and National Development in North Africa: A Comparative Study* (Berkeley and Los Angeles: University of California Press, 1972), p. 5.

*Turkey.*   Only in the last sixty years could Turkey be considered a nation-state. For more than six centuries before then, it had been at the heart of the polyglot Ottoman empire, controlling a political community that ranged from North Africa and southern Europe to the west and the frontiers of Russia and Persia to the east. This empire was beginning to disintegrate during the nineteenth century, but its demise was hastened by its fateful alliance with the Central Powers during the First World War. In the space of less than a decade after the defeat of 1918, the Turks passed from the status of "faltering imperial overlords to that of nationalist freedom-fighters."[38]

In his studies of Turkey, the late Lloyd A. Fallers sought to analyze the impact of this transformation upon Turkish society. He and his wife spent eighteen months in a provincial town in western Turkey, and a much longer period studying Turkish society. The town in question is Edremit. It has a wholly Turkish-Muslim population of some thirty thousand merchants, artisans, olive growers, wage workers, and small commercial and industrial entrepreneurs and their families. By Turkish provincial standards, Edremit is a prosperous town, and in the 1960s its economy was beginning to diversify from an earlier nearly total dependence upon olive cultivation. All the principal offices of the national government have branches there; there are numerous schools, two hospitals, political party branches, more than a dozen mosques, and an army training base. Its population, says Fallers, has a sense of well-being about it, yet its citizens are profoundly affected by and concerned about Turkey's very real economic and political problems. Mature townsmen personally experienced the turbulent last years of empire and the first years of the republic. Middle-aged people at the time of Fallers's work spoke of themselves as the "fatherless" generation because so many draft-age men were called up for service and never returned. The major battles of the Turkish war of independence were fought elsewhere, but the town experienced two years of enemy occupation with the ensuing consequences of demoralization, collaboration, repression, and revenge.

Kemal Atatürk intended Turkey's war of independence to be a crisis of identity to pave the way for legitimating new forms of authority. The sultanate was abolished in 1922 and the caliphate followed in 1924: Men and women were compelled to choose between ethnic nationalism and loyalty to the vestiges of a theocratic dynasty. Turkish Republican identity did not involve a one-time transformation; it entailed a continuing working out of commitments and personal relationships. Fallers traces these transformations in the context of Edremit so as to give concrete meaning to how the nation-state has been experienced in recent social history. In rapid succession in the 1920s, Atatürk suppressed the dervish (Ṣūfī) orders, substituted European legal codes for Islamic personal law, decreed that the fez could no longer be worn in public (in practice it was replaced by European hats), adopted the Western calendar, decreed that Turkish was henceforth to be

---

[38] Fallers, *Nation-State,* p. 75. The following narrative account of national identity in Turkey is based extensively upon Fallers, pp. 71-116.

written in the Latin alphabet rather than Arabic script (a move which shocked many conservative Muslims because of the association of Arabic script with the Quran), legally emancipated women and gave them access to education, established state banks and industries to stimulate economic growth, and created a new capital, Ankara. Formally, Turkey had become a secular state, although the fact that a Ministry of Religious Affairs was established indicates the continuing interest of the state in religious matters.

During the one-party period of the 1930s and 1940s, most people participated, if not always wholeheartedly, in the new order. A cultural center was created to propagate the new Western life-style, including mixed "ballroom" dancing by the elite on formal occasions. Elite women adopted Western fashions. Islam was not suppressed, but fasting and public displays of piety fell out of style, as was indicated by Atatürk's own ostentatiously secular funeral in 1938.

During the war years of the 1940s, the Kemalist one-party state began to lose its grip. Because of the major economic transformations engendered by the war, salaried workers and entrepreneurs became more numerous and more assertive; they and Turkish intellectuals began to demand greater freedom. From 1950 onward, with several interruptions due to military takeovers of the civilian government, Turkey can be described as a liberal, if turbulent, democracy subject to rapidly shifting forces and combinations and recombinations of power and authority.

Turkish intellectuals characterize the basic issues of politics in terms of an abstract struggle between the forces of religion and secularism. As Fallers explains, these are not disembodied forces in Turkish society; one way of grasping these forces is by seeing what they mean in practice and how they inform and shape the experience of the men and women who created them. Thus those Turks who stress their identity as Muslims adhere to an ideology that has an internal logic of its own which at times contrasts significantly with the secularist ideology of some of the Turkish elite. For such persons, the formal separation which prevails between religion and the state in Turkish society is not easy to comprehend and even is seen to be contrary to the teachings of Islam.

The secular reformist ideology forged by Atatürk maintains its strength especially in industrial centers and among an older generation of educated Turks. For other Turks, from regions with heavy emigration to Europe, leftist ideologies also provide increasingly strong expressions of political identity. The major problem for secularists of Atatürk's generation was to provide Turks with an ideology to enable them to live civilly within their national boundaries. The major ideological problem facing Turkey today is to come to terms with the increasingly critical economic conditions and the consequent internal unrest. As Dubetsky suggests, even when leftist movements in Turkey borrow the vocabulary and policies of the European left to face these issues, in practice both the ideology and the organizational forms have been modified by prevailing regional and religious identities.[39]

[39] Alan Dubetsky (Duben), "Class and Community in Urban Turkey," in *Commoners, Climbers and Notables,* ed. C. A. O. Van Nieuwenhuijze (Leiden: E. J. Brill, 1977), pp. 360-71.

In provincial centers such as Edremit even more than in the major cities, persons of different social types and ideological persuasions are too small in number to exist in closed social groups. The tensions of ideological and political differences are held in check by cross-cutting personal ties. The secular reformists have their public celebrations, such as the fiercely patriotic parades and speeches commemorating Atatürk's death. Religious officials are invited as guests, but the occasion is decidedly nonreligious. Those who emphasize Islam and traditionalism, including a growing number of youth, also have their celebrations: the public prayers on Fridays, Islamic feast days, and the fast of Ramaḍān.

Most Turks seek a compromise among ideological extremes. One result of the growing maturity of the Turkish republic has been a broadening of social and political choices. In the ordinary round of activities, what emerges from the experience of everyday life is a compromise and synthesis, not merely a different mixture of sociocultural elements. The compromise is not always an easy one. Turkey is neither oil-rich nor mineral-rich, and its economy has increasingly weakened, especially as opportunities for labor emigration to Europe are becoming scarcer. Political violence is not unknown on university campuses and elsewhere. Yet the fact that most Turks recognize these problems and seek to resolve them short of violence suggests the resilience and personal courage of many Turks and provides a basis for guarded optimism.

*The Sultanate of Oman.*    The Sultanate of Oman is unique in its nearly total isolation from the outside world until 1970 and the intensity with which its oil resources have been applied to massive economic development since then. In part due to the personal idiosyncrasies of its former Sultan, Saʿīd bin Taymūr (r. 1932-1970), aided by compliant British advisors and military support, Oman was almost as isolated as Tibet until a palace coup in 1970 replaced the Sultan with his son, Qābūs bin Saʿīd.

Before 1970 the country was extremely poor in contrast to most of its neighbors, and the meager revenues derived from British subsidies went mostly for defense purposes and internal security. There were only ten kilometers of paved roads, three primary schools, and one hospital for a population estimated at 750,000. The Sultan felt that higher education only radicalized its recipients, so he allowed few Omanis with more than a primary education to return. Omanis had to tolerate such vagaries as the closing of the gates of Muscat, the capital, three hours after sundown and imprisonment if they did not carry a kerosene lantern on the streets after that time; obtaining the personal permission of the Sultan to make improvements on their houses and to purchase vehicles; and a prohibition against the wearing of Western shoes in Ṣalāla, capital of Dhufar, in the southern region of the country.[40] Even after oil was discovered in 1964 and began to be exported, the

---

[40]This section is based upon J. E. Peterson, *Oman in the Twentieth Century: Political Foundations of an Emerging State* (London: Croom Helm, 1978); John Townsend, *Oman: The Making of the Modern State* (New York: St. Martin's Press, 1977); Fred Halliday, *Arabia With-*

Sultan applied the revenues only in the most grudging fashion to development projects, few of which were under way at the time of his deposition.

By the late 1960s, there were over fifty thousand Omanis living and working in the various Gulf states, with more in other Arab states.[41] Many of these, including members of the Sultan's family itself, were in self-imposed or forced exile and increasingly favored the overthrow of the old Sultan. Open rebellion gained momentum in the southern province of Dhufar in the mid-1960s and by 1968 had become radicalized. Saʿīd bin Taymūr was incapable of meeting this threat effectively, and his obdurate resistance to change or development of any kind increasingly made him an embarrassment to Great Britain. The British Foreign Office may not have directly conspired to bring about the events which led to the accession of Qābūs bin Saʿīd (who had been kept isolated by his father in Ṣalāla and denied access to the palace), but a number of local British officials actively supported the coup.[42]

If most "new" nations face a major challenge in constructing "a civil politics of primordial compromise" as the only alternative to the "forcible suppression of ethnic assertion or a political Balkanization,"[43] the problems facing post-1970 Oman were particularly complex for a country of its relatively small size. Omani government spokesmen are understandably reluctant to speak of the potential lines of division in the country because they have been used in the past as a means of weakening it and to some extent by the former Sultan as a means of ensuring no challenge to his rule. Although Arabic is the principal language of communication, Persian, Baluchi, Sindi, Swahili, several Indian languages, and non-Arabic indigenous languages are known. Especially in the coastal region, many persons are bi- and trilingual. In terms of religious distinctions, there are Sunnī, Shīʿī, and Ibāḍī Muslims and especially in the capital region a considerable number of Banian (Hindu) merchants. There is a similar ethnic and tribal diversity, with Arab, Baluchi, Indian, African, and non-Arab indigenous populations, the disappearing distinction of slave/nonslave origin, and large numbers (approximately forty-five thousand as of 1976) of "temporary" workers from the Indian subcontinent. Additionally, many persons of Omani descent have returned from East Africa over the last decade. Because of conditions prevailing in Oman until 1970, these immigrants have tended to be better educated than native Omanis and have been given responsible posts in government and commerce.

Oman's regional diversity also contributes to its cultural and social richness.

---

out *Sultans* (New York: Vintage Books, 1975) (his figures for Iran and the Arabian peninsula are necessarily outdated, but the study contains data difficult to obtain from other sources); and the Ministry of Information and Culture, Sultanate of Oman, "Facts about Oman" (Muscat: mimeo., 1977).

[41] Peterson, *Oman,* p. 207.

[42] For a concise account of the organization of the coup, see Peterson, *Oman,* pp. 201-3.

[43] Clifford Geertz, "The Integrative Revolution: Primordial Sentiments and Civil Politics in the New States," in *Old Societies and New States,* ed. Clifford Geertz (New York: The Free Press, 1963), pp. 105-57.

Economically and (in the past) politically, the country faces two directions. The culturally and socially complex coastal mercantile community traditionally has faced toward the outside. Through the 1870s, this community conducted a prosperous external commerce. The Sultanate then was comprised of present-day Oman, Zanzibar, enclaves along the East African coast, and Gwadar, an island enclave off Pakistan which was sold to Pakistan in 1958 to help finance a military expedition of Saʿīd bin Taymūr into Oman's interior.[44] The country also faces inward, to the agricultural villages of the mountainous Jabal Akhḍar region of "inner" Oman. Each of these villages was nearly self-sufficient economically, raising a variety of irrigated crops, sheep, and goats but politically integrated into several major tribal units, and religiously united under an Ibāḍī *Imām*. In contrast to the linguistically and religiously complex coastal region, "inner" Oman's potential divisions were primarily tribal. In addition, the southern province of Dhufar has traditionally been isolated from the rest of Oman.

In the late nineteenth century and in the twentieth century the Sultanate suffered serious economic and political decline. The British suppressed the lucrative slave trade, the Sultanate lost its East African possessions, and the coming of steamships seriously affected the key role which Omanis had earlier played in the commerce of the Indian Ocean. By 1920 the highlands had in practice become autonomous under the Ibāḍī *Imām,* leaving Saʿīd bin Taymūr dependent upon the British to administer the remainder of his realm.

The major accomplishment of Saʿīd bin Taymūr's reign was slowly to bring the entire country under his effective control. He was a master of internal politics and adroitly played tribal and other social groups against each other to preserve his own strength. In the late 1940s, he managed to obtain British support (not always willingly offered) to expand the scope of his control and to meet external threats. Because of the country's oil potential, Saudi Arabia supported dissident movements in the Jabal Akhḍar region through the mid-1950s, but Saʿīd became the first Omani Sultan in the twentieth century to bring this region under his control, a control which became increasingly tenuous as Omanis realized that it was not being used for any constructive purpose.

From 1970 to date, the challenges of open rebellion in the south and of creating a better life for all Omanis are being met. The Dhufar rebellion was effectively quelled through a combination of military force and, more importantly for the long term, through the sustained commitment of the government to use the country's resources to improve its standard of living and to involve Omanis from all backgrounds in the country's government and development. Several statistics suggest the scope of what has been achieved. In 1970 there were three schools in the Sultanate and 909 students, all boys. As of 1977, there were 261 schools through the secondary level and 65,000 students, boys and girls, in school. From one hospital in 1970, there were 13 by 1975, with a large number of supplementary clinics and dispensaries. From 10 kilometers of paved roads in 1970, the Sultanate

---

[44] Peterson, *Oman,* pp. 87-88.

possesses roughly 3,000 as of 1979. In practical terms this means that the time for trips to interior points has been greatly shortened. The trip to Nizwa, for instance, which once took two days over rough track, now takes slighty over two hours.[45]

As in all developing countries, disparities inevitably exist between regions and between the capital cities and the hinterland, but Omanis are aware of this and are seeking to mitigate them. The country was dependent upon oil exports for 90 percent of its revenues as of 1978, although the government is actively seeking ways to diversify the economy and to stem the decline of traditional agricultural activities as Omanis find more lucrative careers elsewhere.[46]

Perhaps the most important long-term indices of the country's ability to construct a resurgent and transformed national identity are those which are most difficult to quantify. Sectarian differences within Islam have lost the divisive significance which in the past they sometimes have had. Omanis of non-Arab origin have increasingly made the conscious decision to communicate with their children at home in Arabic instead of Sindi, Baluchi, or other languages, a decision indicative of a renewed commitment to Omani national identity and to the faith placed in education as a means of social advancement. Through the late 1960s, marriages between various sectarian groups were relatively infrequent. Even groups that once had deserved reputations for not tolerating marriages with "outsiders" now encourage intermarriage. Especially in a society in which a large part of social life is carried on within the confines of the extended family, such decisions suggest not only the consequences of recent social and economic change but also a confident self-awareness of many Omanis toward the changed basis of their cultural and social identity. Omanis are actually aware that their future is dependent only in part upon technical and economic resources—Oman's oil reserves are estimated to be much more limited than those of some of its neighbors—and that an even more important consideration is the ability of all Omanis to continue to develop the virtues of civility which have been nurtured over the last decade.

*Somalia: Scientific Socialism.*     Like Oman, Somalia is a small nation, 3.2 million inhabitants as of 1977, but one which traditionally has had a strong sense of ethnic and collective homogeneity. As Ioan Lewis has remarked, Somalis have traditionally tended to see social relations in terms of an expanding universe of kinship.[47] Tribalism for Somalis has traditionally meant ties of kinship and clan. The

---

[45] Ministry of Information and Culture, "Facts about Oman."

[46] "Oman: A Report," *The Economist,* 272, no. 7093 (London: August 11, 1979), 57-68.

[47] The following discussion of "scientific socialism" in Somalia is based upon Ioan M. Lewis, "Kim Il-Sung in Somalia: The End of Tribalism?" in *Politics in Leadership: A Comparative Perspective,* ed. William A. Shack and Percy S. Cohen (Oxford: Clarendon Press, 1979), pp. 13-44. The classic standard work on Somali politics and clan identity is Lewis's *A Pastoral Democracy: A Study of Pastoralism and Politics among the Northern Somali of the Horn of Africa* (London: Oxford University Press for the International African Institute, 1961). See also his "The Politics of the 1969 Somali Coup," *Journal of Modern African Studies,* 10, no. 3 (October 1972), 383-408.

presence of ethnic Somalis beyond the borders of the present-day country has led to a certain political instability in recent years. Roughly 75 percent of all Somalis were nomadic pastoralists until the drought of the early 1970s forced the rapid sedentarization of much of the population.

In 1969 Colonel (now General) Siad Barre successfully led an officers' revolt which resulted in the founding of the Somali Democratic Republic. Somali politics from independence in 1961 until 1969 shared much in common with other recently independent nations. A major organizational problem was integrating the former Italian and British administered zones of the country and operating modern political forms such as a parliament in a milieu in which clan identity remained paramount. Most Somalis presumed with some justification that government officials and their elected representatives acted principally along clan lines.

The revolutionary government aimed to transform Somali identity completely to bring the country into the ranks of "scientific socialism." The use of kinship terms of address was made illegal. Homicides, which previously were regulated by conventions of clan vengeance and blood money, were firmly suppressed with the public execution of violators. The chewing of qāt, a mild narcotic popular with many Somalis and Yemenis, was restricted to the hours between dusk and dawn. The government became highly centralized, with the unemployed youth organized into squads of "Victory Pioneers," or vigilantes, to see that the government's directives were carried out. Even the most remote towns were provided with orientation centers.

The leaders of Somalia's revolution were obliged to create Somali terms to express the goals of the revolution. *Scientific socialism* was translated as "wealth-sharing based on wisdom," a phrase actually first used by the BBC Somali Service. *Jalle,* a Somali term which earlier meant "playmate" or "mate," was used for *comrade.* Posters of Marx, Lenin, Kim Il-Sung of North Korea, and Siad Barre began to emerge everywhere. Kim Il-Sung was especially popular because his country managed to balance itself with relative success between the superpowers of China and the USSR and stressed the virtue of self-reliance *(juché).* Even before their revolution Somalis regarded their own country as delicately poised between East and West and placed a high value upon their own autonomy.

In October 1973 Somalia adopted the Latin script; government officials were given two months to learn the new script. Somali had until then been an unwritten language, and there were stiff debates as to whether Arabic script (favored by the religiously traditional) or Latin script should be adopted. Traditionalists objected to Latin script on the grounds that it was areligious and to indicate their sentiments pronounced Latin as *lā dīn,* which in Arabic means "no religion." The strength of Siad Barre's government allowed the reform to be effectively imposed. Later, in 1974-1975, all schools in the country were closed so that students could teach the rest of the largely illiterate population to read and write. This movement emerged as one of the world's more successful mass literacy campaigns.

The way in which these reforms were popularly interpreted demonstrated how even "scientific socialism" had to accommodate implicitly popular notions of legitimacy and how much the revolution as practiced owed to a continuity of cultural form. The banning of kinship terms of address was intended as a break with the prerevolutionary past, although in government propaganda, the Head of State is often referred to as the father, the revolution as the mother, and the people as the issue of the two, with the orphans and unemployed, the "flowers of the revolution," receiving particular attention of the state. *M.O.D.*, a code name for the revolution which in Somali means *hail* (as in a greeting), is interpreted by many Somali as an acronym for the three important clans bridged by General Barre's own kinship ties. Although the state seeks to separate itself from religious traditionalism, it uses the imagery of Islam as locally understood to win popular support for many of its programs. General Barre allows himself to be compared with Muḥammad ᶜAbdille Ḥassan, a Somali religious leader who in the 1920s led an almost successful revolt against the British and whose kinship ties, like those of Barre, bridged Somalia's most important clans. Scientific socialism is repeatedly claimed to be compatible with the Quran, and the Quran is regularly broadcast by Somali radio with commentaries on it being used in subtle ways to win popular acceptance of governmental reforms. Most innovations are introduced in the form of "crash" programs, most of which are labeled as *jihād*-s, or holy struggles.

*Israel.*    The anthropological literature concerning Israel as a nation-state and an emerging nation is extremely rich, so that here it is possible only to indicate some of the principal approaches that have been used in its study. One of the major points of departure concerns the changing position of Arab Palestinians, both Muslim and Christian, and their class situation vis-à-vis the Jewish population. A second approach has been concerned primarily with the "ingathering of the exiles" and the forging of a Jewish/Israeli national identity in the context of immigrants with highly disparate backgrounds and skills. The first approach entails understanding the patterns of Jewish settlement in Palestine prior to the foundation of the state of Israel.[48] From 1882 to 1903, a small number of Jewish settlers arrived from eastern Europe, and the rate of arrivals increased somewhat for the period 1919-1931. By 1931, there were 175,000 Jews in Palestine, both indigenous and nonindigenous, out of a total population of 1,036,000. Jews thus constituted 17 percent of the population. The period of 1932-1939 was marked by outbursts of violence between the Jewish population on the one hand and Palestinian Christians and Muslims on the other. The British Mandate authorities sought to limit the potential for violence in part by placing immigration quotas on Jewish settlers, but these restrictions were largely ineffective. On May 14, 1948, the Mandate was terminated and the State of Israel came into being. The population of Palestine has

---

[48]Two succinct and readable accounts of these developments are Peter Beaumont, Gerald H. Blake, and J. Malcolm Wagstaff, *The Middle East: A Geographical Study* (London and New York: John Wiley & Sons, 1976), pp. 404-25, and Nicholas S. Hopkins, "The Evolution of Palestinian Arab Society," in *Arab Society in Transition: A Reader*, eds. Saad Eddin Ibrahim and Nicholas S. Hopkins (Cairo: The American University in Cairo, 1977), pp. 418-39. The statistics in the following paragraph are based upon Beaumont, Blake and Wagstaff, pp. 414-20, where full bibliographical references are provided.

been estimated to be 2,065,000 as of May 1948, of which 31 percent (or 650,000) were Jews. Jews owned 6 percent of the total area and 15 percent of the cultivable land. By November 1948 in that part of Palestine which became Israel, 82 percent of the population of 873,000 was Jewish. This dramatic increase in the proportion of the Jewish population was due in part to the flight or expulsion of an estimated 650,000-700,000 Arabs and the accelerated immigration of over 100,000 Jews in the months following independence.

The new state gave priority to the problems of assimilating massive numbers of Jewish immigrants of diverse backgrounds. For this reason and for reasons of security, restrictions were placed upon the movements and labor opportunities of the Arab population. The consequences of these restrictions and their effect upon the Arab population are documented by studies such as Cohen's *Arab Border Villages* and Emanuel Marx's *Bedouin of the Negev*, the latter of which describes the economic and political life of the Bedouin during a period when Israeli military rule still applied to them.[49] Other anthropologists and political scientists have adopted the complementary perspective of studying the economic status of various groups in Israeli society and relating the class situation of the Arab and Jewish population to recent political history. Joel Migdal has linked the lack of a growth of class consciousness among Palestinian Arabs in the 1930s to the fact that no specifically urban Arab political elite had emerged. Rosenfeld has dealt with the same issue but over a longer time span which includes the thirty years since the founding of the state of Israel.[50]

Many of the studies concerning Israel as a nation-state and the politics of assimilation began as part of the Bernstein Israel Research Project, initiated at the University of Manchester in 1963 by Max Gluckman and Emrys Peters.[51] The intent of this project was to undertake comparative studies of family and kinship among Israel's different ethnic groups, to analyze varieties of leadership and local political organization, and to assess the changing relations between ethnic groups, including comparative studies of Jewish and non-Jewish communities. In practice,

---

[49] Abner Cohen, *Arab Border Villages in Israel* (Manchester: Manchester University Press, 1965), pp. 22-23; see also Talal Asad, "Anthropological Texts and Ideological Problems: An Analysis of Cohen on Arab Villages in Israel," *Economy and Society*, 4, no. 3 (August 1975), 251-82; and Emanuel Marx, *Bedouin of the Negev* (Manchester: Manchester University Press, 1967), pp. 37-39, 46-47.

[50] Asad, "Anthropological Texts"; Joel Migdal, "Urbanization and Political Change: The Impact of Foreign Rule," *Comparative Studies in Society and History*, 19, no. 3 (July 1977), 328-49; and Henry Rosenfeld, "The Class Situation of the Arab National Minority in Israel," *Comparative Studies in Society and History*, 20, no. 3 (July 1978), 374-407.

[51] For a complete description of this project, from which my following comments are derived, see Emanuel Marx, "Anthropological Studies in a Centralized State: The Bernstein Research Project in Israel," *The Jewish Journal of Sociology*, 17, no. 2 (December 1975), 131-50. Some of the studies which resulted from the Bernstein Research Project, including those by Deshen, Shokeid, and Marx, are discussed in Chapter 7 of this book. See also Marx's "Introduction" in *A Composite Portrait of Israel*, ed. E. Marx (London: Academic Press, 1980). This work is the tenth and concluding volume of the Bernstein Research Project and launches out into new fields such as slums, factories, ports, and old-age homes among other topics.

the resulting studies concentrated upon only a few aspects of Israel society such as cooperative rural villages *(moshavim)*, collective settlements *(kibbutzim)*, and the newer towns which contain higher proportions of recent immigrants.

If the first generation of these studies has concentrated upon particular communities within Israeli society, later essays have sought to interpret major trends in Israeli society on the basis of detailed prior research. One such seminal study is Deshen's "Israeli Judaism."[52] Deshen sees two major trends in the varieties of patterns of religious observance and nonobservance among Israel's Jews. One is the emergence of the "new" ethnic/religious category of "Oriental" Jew, formed as Jews of Middle Eastern origin have come to realize how their divergent heritages differ substantially from that of Jews of European origin. Secondly, Deshen suggests that one of the reasons that Israel's orthodox Jews have a political significance far beyond their numbers (less than 5 percent of the population) is because of the religious basis of Israeli national identity. Although orthodox Jews have not always offered viable solutions to Israel's major political and economic crises, no other version of Judaism has been identified as closely with the symbols of tradition and religious legitimacy. Deshen sees the continuing debate among Israelis as to the meaning of Jewish tradition as one of the keys to understanding Israeli society today.

## DEVELOPMENT IN PERSPECTIVE

The Middle East contains a range of state forms—the traditional monarchies of Morocco, Jordan, and the Arabian peninsula, democracies, such as Turkey and Israel, and one-party or military regimes in countries such as Syria, Iraq, Algeria, and the People's Democratic Republic of Yemen. Some of these states advocate radical political doctrines; others are profoundly conservative. A major feature of all of them is a professed commitment to development, an improved life for their citizens, and either a popular participation in government or the state's claim to speak "for the people." Whether the states are devoid of major economic resources, such as Turkey, Jordan, and the two Yemens, or possess major oil reserves, as do Algeria and many states of the Arabian peninsula, they seek to provide services such as schools, hospitals, roads, and other community improvements within the limits of their resources. Especially as oil revenues have increased massively in recent years, the pace of development has had a profound impact upon many Middle Eastern societies.[53] In many instances the efforts to bring about economic, administrative, and in some cases political reform have led to profound social transformations of Middle Eastern political and economic life.

In seeking to understand these transformations, some anthropologists have

[52] Shlomo Deshen, "Israeli Judaism: Introduction to the Major Patterns," *International Journal of Middle East Studies*, 9, no. 2 (May 1978), 141-69.

[53] See Halliday, *Arabia Without Sultans.*

emphasized how, despite changes in economic opportunities and patterns of political action, locally held conceptions of power and authority often suggest major continuities with those of the past.[54] Other studies of political activity, including those of Peter Gubser and Richard T. Antoun on Jordanian communities, place greatest emphasis upon the rapid economic and political change of the last thirty years.[55] Gubser, a political scientist who conducted a field study in Al-Karak, stresses the increased differentiation of townsmen in socioeconomic status, especially over the decades since the Second World War. One result of this is that an educated middle stratum of townsmen, teachers, government officials, and others has drawn away from the mass of the population and is in a position to express dissatisfaction with the traditional tribal political leaders. He documents how changing economic patterns have diminished the role of traditional leaders, how the growth of the central government and increased socioeconomic differentiation has created new cleavages between nation-state and province, although the government has sought to mitigate these cleavages through agricultural cooperatives and expanded social services. Antoun traces a similar development in his two studies, especially in *Low-Key Politics.* He writes that village life, both in the past and today, has been characterized by considerable economic mobility and social differentiation. The shortage of land has acted as a constant pressure toward emigration, both in the form of military service and in wage labor elsewhere. In terms of long-term change, Antoun sees a shift in the way that day-to-day village issues are intertwined and resolved. Villagers who in the past were tied to lineage and tribal leaders now have a greater individuality and freedom to switch alliances, although their leaders enjoy no comparable flexibility. Even given these shifts, personal interrelationships remain so complex that with the exception of politicized schoolteachers and other persons not intimately tied to village politics, confrontations rarely involve overt challenges with the ensuing risk of total disruption of social and economic life.

A trend in virtually every Middle Eastern country has been toward more centralized state control and allocation of major resources: The consequences of investment in development are not always as intended by planners. The experience of many countries with schooling is highly significant in this respect. We have already seen how education was highly valued during the colonial era in Morocco. Relatively few persons received education and a diploma was almost a guarantee of significant employment. One of the first commitments of the independent Moroccan government was to expand the school system dramatically. In the early

[54] For example, see Lawrence Rosen, "Rural Political Process and National Political Structure in Morocco," in *Rural Politics and Social Change in the Middle East,* eds. Richard Antoun and Iliya Harik (Bloomington and London: Indiana University Press, 1972), pp. 214-36; Leveau, "The Rural Elite"; and Michael E. Meeker, "The Great Family Aghas of Turkey: A Study of Changing Political Culture," in *Rural Politics,* eds. Antoun and Harik, pp. 237-66.

[55] Peter Gubser, *Politics and Change in Al-Karak, Jordan* (London: Oxford University Press, 1973); Richard T. Antoun, *Arab Village: A Social Structural Study of a Trans-Jordanian Peasant Community* (Bloomington and London: Indiana University Press, 1972); and also his *Low-Key Politics: Local-Level Leadership and Change in the Middle East* (Albany: State University of New York Press, 1979).

years after independence, students and parents in many parts of the country enthusiastically assisted in the building of schools. The Moroccan government has continued to build schools but has been unable to keep pace with the rapid population growth. Of those who can attend school and graduate—the dropout rate at all levels hovers near 90 percent—the government and the nearly stagnant private sector of the economy have been able to absorb only a few. Rapid expansion has entailed lower educational standards, so that those who can afford to do so send their children to private schools or pay for tutoring. This trend in turn encourages the poorly paid teachers to reserve their best efforts for students who can pay private tuition, a trend already prevalent for several decades in Egypt. Hence education now more than ever tends to reinforce disparities between those who can pay and those who cannot, and the initial promise of "progress" through education has abated.[56] In other countries, such as those of the Arabian Peninsula, educational facilities have been expanded only in recent years, salaries are high enough to attract competent teachers from other countries, and recent graduates are rapidly employed. In such cases, the hope placed in education as a vehicle for social change remains unshaken.

The nether side of expanded governmental services has been the expanded opportunities for corruption. In an unusual essay, John Waterbury has sought to assess systematically various patterns of corruption, using Egypt and Morocco as examples. He distinguishes three major types: endemic, planned, and developmental corruption, all of which are inherent in and exacerbated by the processes of economic development. *Endemic* corruption "is the abuse of public office that occurs to varying degrees in any system."[57] When civil servants are poorly paid and there is more demand for government services than can be fulfilled, access to services often can be had only upon payment of an extralegal fee. This may be for medical attention, housing, documents such as passports and driving permits, or for the tutoring offered by teachers at all educational levels which is necessary for students to pass critical examinations. Promotions may also hinge upon payment of such fees. Such practices are not condoned in either Egypt or Morocco, but Waterbury reports that their existence is widespread and known. So long as such exactions are kept within tolerable limits, public protest is negligible. When it reaches too high a level, resentment often takes a violent turn.

*Planned* corruption occurs when political leaders find it desirable to achieve a certain level of short- and medium-range control of subordinates. There are three short-term advantages to planned corruption over the distribution of rewards by

---

[56] For a highly readable account of the initial popular enthusiasm for education in Morocco and the reasons for later disenchantment, see Thomas W. Dichter's excellent, but unfortunately unpublished, "The Problem of How to Act on an Undefined Stage: An Exploration of Culture, Change, and Individual Consciousness in the Moroccan Town of Sefrou—With a Focus on Three Modern Schools," Ph.D. Dissertation, Department of Anthropology, University of Chicago, 1976. Dichter, initially a Peace Corps volunteer teaching in a secondary school in Sefrou, later returned as an anthropologist to study education more systematically.

[57] John Waterbury, "Corruption, Political Stability and Development: Comparative Evidence from Egypt and Morocco," *Government and Opposition*, 11 (1976), 428, 437.

objective needs or merit: The principal distributor of spoils guarantees his indispensability to the system; it undercuts the emergence of too rigorous a meritocracy, which in the case of "kings in particular, but many republican heads of state as well," might lead to questioning the competence of the ruler. With a spoils system, rewards come from loyalty to the boss, and officials are rewarded for concentrating on their narrow self-interest. Finally, Waterbury argues that planned corruption mitigates class and social cleavages by building vertically integrated clientele through which spoils are distributed.[58] The result is to encourage a dependency and subservience toward central authorities and to dilute the ideological content of politics. Waterbury argues that this form of corruption exists both in Egypt and in Morocco but is more extensive in Morocco, where the political elite's comparatively small size makes it easier to control. If the short-term gains are considerable for rulers, in states with limited resources such as Egypt and Morocco, the negative consequences are to squander public resources and to increase the cynicism of the elite and the masses toward governmental initiatives.

*Developmental* corruption occurs in situations in which the state owns or controls most of the major resources and makes most major new capital investments.[59] In the overall context of low standards of living and low literacy rates, no group except the state can play a major role. In this context there are opportunities for "brokerage" fees, noncompetitive contracts, the siphoning of foreign aid for black-market use, the evasion of currency and import regulations, and other practices which enable elements of the governmental elite and poorly paid bureaucrats at lower levels to make fortunes or at least to live more tolerably. In countries rich with oil or other resources, the consequences of such discriminatory awarding of services and favors are sometimes less damaging, but in countries where resources are meager, as in Egypt and Morocco, they reinforce "the resentment and suspicion on the part of the great mass of the poor citizenry towards the civil service and public authorities in general" and "have pernicious effects on the will of a national collectivity to work toward developmental goals."[60]

While Waterbury's focus is upon a prevalent yet unfortunate byproduct of development, several anthropologists have sought to evaluate the long-term implications of developmental schemes. As Nicholas S. Hopkins explains, a manifest function of development is to improve the income, the health, and the educational standards of the poor. Indirectly, development projects function to reinforce the authority of the central government and its scope of control, consequences regarded by the political elite as desirable.[61] He reviews the developmental trans-

---

[58] *Ibid.*, 432-34.

[59] *Ibid.*, 438-39.

[60] *Ibid.*, 444.

[61] Nicholas S. Hopkins, "Development and Center-Building in the Middle East," paper presented at the conference on "Strategies of Local Development in the Middle East," University of Maryland, Baltimore County, September 20-23, 1978 (mimeo.). Used by permission. A discussion of this issue is also contained in the "Introduction to Part III: Agrarian Transforma-

formations of Egypt over the last two centuries. In the early nineteenth century, Sultan Muhammad ᶜAlī Pasha introduced new agricultural techniques and the cultivation of cotton as a major cash crop. Annual basin irrigation in the Nile valley was increasingly replaced by perennial canal irrigation, and a small rural elite eventually managed to acquire control of much of the best agricultural land.

This technological and economic pattern remained relatively constant until the Egyptian revolution of 1952. One of the goals of the revolution was to maintain the technical advantages of the first agricultural transformation but to neutralize its built-in tendency toward social inequality. The size of rural landholdings was limited; large estates were broken up as part of a program of extensive land reform; and cooperatives were established in an effort to retain the economic advantages of large estates. The declared policy of the government was the mobilization of the peasantry, but despite these intentions major decisions were made by an administrative elite that often looked with disdain upon peasants and regarded them as incapable of acting in their own best interests. Nonetheless, Egyptian land reform was undertaken in earnest and had a major social impact.[62]

**FIGURE 11-5** Mechanization of agriculture has led to major social changes in the rural Middle East. Combine harvester, Tunisia. (Courtesy Nicholas S. Hopkins.)

---

tion and Rural Values," in *Arab Society in Transition,* eds. Saad Eddin Ibrahim and Nicholas S. Hopkins, pp. 179-82. See also Hopkins's "Modern Agriculture and Political Centralization: A Case from Tunisia," *Human Organization,* 37, no. 1 (Spring 1978), 83-87.

[62] Hopkins, "Development," p. 8; for a critique of Western studies of Middle Eastern politics and an analysis of why many governments are reluctant to involve the bulk of the population in political discussion despite their declared commitment to political mobilization, see R. M. Burrell, "New Questions or Old: Tradition and Modernity in the Middle East," *Encounter* 39, no. 5 (July 1972), 69-73. For discussions of landownership and land reform elsewhere in the Middle East, see Nur Yalman, "On Land Disputes in Eastern Turkey," in *Islam and Its Cultural Divergence,* ed. G. L. Tikku (Urbana: University of Illinois Press, 1970), pp. 180-218, and Robert A. Fernea, "Land Reform and Ecology in Postrevolutionary Iraq," *Economic Development and Cultural Change,* 17, no. 3 (April 1969), 356-81.

Hopkins describes a third transformation of agricultural technology which is now under way. Part of it has been engendered by the "green revolution," new high-yield seeds and agricultural techniques, dam building, the use of computers, and intensive mechanization. The land reform of the "second transformation" created holdings too small to make mechanization pay. Effective use of the new technology requires the coordination of large numbers of peasants and the coordination of many of these holdings. Despite the effort to achieve these goals through cooperatives, the government was not wholly successful. Moreover, the expense of developing the new technology requires the central government to extract a maximum surplus from rural areas. Hopkins's argument is essentially that the prior transformations of agricultural technology and landownership had major consequences upon social differentiation and that the present one is having equally profound, if not fully predictable, implications.

Other anthropological studies confirm the unintended consequences of economic development and planned change. David Seddon describes recent economic change in an impoverished Riffian village in northern Morocco.[63] He reports that the great majority of the active population is involved in agriculture but that only a few persons find farming sufficiently productive to live from it. Many people are compelled to emigrate in search of work, although it is increasingly hard to obtain. At the same time, farming as a way of life and wage labor in agriculturally active seasons are becoming increasingly indistinguishable. Sharecropping arrangements, which in the past provided a modicum of security for poorer families, have become rare. Labor is now treated as a commodity, and landowners find daily salaries to be a more "economic" arrangement.

Jon Anderson's account of the introduction of tractors to tribal Afghanistan traces the social consequences of technological innovation in particular detail, especially as it has affected the relations between *khān*-s and their supporters.[64] He writes that *khān* in Turkic means "lord" or "chief" of a tribe or component of it, but that in highland Afghanistan the term merely "denotes big men who are economically and politically prominent in their communities." *Khān*-s develop leadership through patronage: gifts, favors, even regular stipends in return for support; locally, they are known for their ability to "feed their people." Supporters are not considered employees or dependents, but as "equals" who "just miss having the wherewithal to actualize this equality in a politically meaningful way."[65] If they were fully dependent, there would be no prestige to be gained by having them as followers. Major *khān*-s are distinguished from lesser ones by their ability to

[63] J. David Seddon, "Aspects of Kinship and Family Structure among Ulad Stut of Zaio Rural Commune, Nador Province, Morocco," in *Mediterranean Family Structures,* ed. J. G. Peristiany, Cambridge Studies in Social Anthropology, 13 (New York: Cambridge University Press, 1976), pp. 173-94. See also his companion study, "Economic Anthropology or Political Economy? Approaches to the Analysis of Pre-capitalist Formations in the Maghreb," in *The New Economic Anthropology,* ed. John Clammer (New York: St. Martin's Press, Inc., 1978) pp. 61-109.

[64] Jon W. Anderson, "There Are No *Khāns* Anymore: Economic Development and Social Change in Afghanistan," *The Middle East Journal,* 32, no. 2 (Spring 1978), 167-83.

[65] *Ibid.,* 168-69.

mediate disputes between tribesmen and to represent their group to those outside of it.

Beginning in 1966, tractors were introduced in the region and cultivation was markedly increased. Planners intended the tractors to be purchased collectively, but in practice they ended up in the hands of the wealthier individuals. Anderson explains that Pakhtuns favor personal autonomy and prefer not to participate in corporate ventures they cannot personally control. Moreover, the cost of tractors was too high for all but the most wealthy (which Anderson calculates in terms of 350,000 pounds of bread at retail prices or nearly twenty brides in 1973).[66] Only the wealthy purchased the machines, but rather than use the expensive technology for developing unimproved land, they not surprisingly used the tractors to bring the most immediate return. This was the cultivation of wheat on rainfall irrigated lands, which previously were regarded as a supplement to crops grown on stream-fed lands. These "supplemental" lands now were commercially plowed. Owners of tractors rented them out by the hour at a rate which was eight to ten times the going daily wage of an unskilled laborer. Tractors became strictly economic investments for "quick return and high profit" and had the consequence of diverting the investment of *khān*-s in maintaining their followings. Perennially irrigated lands of the Pakhtun require intensive labor which often is secured through sharecropping ventures among relatives and fellow community members. As economic interest has shifted to rainfall-fed lands and to crops such as wheat which require only short periods of intensive labor, long-term economic relationships such as sharecropping have declined and have been replaced by short-term migrant workers paid by the day.[67]

The social consequences of this economic shift have been dramatic. Social relations have become more strictly economic. Anderson reports that the rich tend to get richer by diverting the proceeds of their agricultural production to non-agricultural investments. Marginal landowners are unable to generate the capital needed for agricultural production and are being squeezed out, while poorer tribesmen, whose social status was traditionally ambiguous, are becoming peasants.

> Like the "green revolution" elsewhere, introducing tractors into Pakhtun farming is nothing more than the spread of agribusiness with its high technology of hybrid seeds, chemical fertilizers, mechanical cultivation and commodity markets which, by dismembering an integrated enterprise, reduced labor as well to a commodity, usually the one that "costs" the least. Paradoxically, it is not a rising standard of living and greater security that is purchased by increased production but increased dependence on larger and more diversified spheres of exchange and an overall diminution of security.[68]

---

[66] *Ibid.*, 172-73.

[67] *Ibid.*, 176.

[68] *Ibid.*, 181-82. For other studies of economic development, see Dawn Chatty, "Leaders, Land, and Limousines: Emir versus Sheikh," *Ethnology*, 16, no. 4 (October 1977), 385-97; and (for one of the few studies by a sociologist ever turned into a film), Jean Duvignaud, *Change at Shebika: Report from a North African Village* (Austin and London: University of Texas Press, 1977).

# CONCLUSION

The emphasis which I have placed on the unplanned consequences of technological innovation and economic change implies a vision of the social sciences at marked variance with some popular conceptions of it. The French social historian Marc Bloch made the profound comment that new social forms are not usually consciously intended, but usually occur "in the process of trying to adapt the old."[69] There is a strain of reform and idealism which has characterized social science since the nineteenth century: an attempt to assess social forms "scientifically," to assure social progress, and even to plan it. One theme of this book has been to stress the inadequacy of simple formulas to account for the direction and consequences of social and cultural change, and instead to seek to *interpret* events and their significance. Many countries in the Middle East and elsewhere face profound challenges in development, including incorporation in a world market economy, technological and organizational innovations which permit a centralization of states that would have been unimaginable in earlier epochs, and a quantum leap in the size of populations. Egypt is typical of many countries in this regard. Its population was 38.5 million in 1976, and current estimates expect this figure to double within thirty years, with no major expansion of cultivable land or of other economic resources.[70] Such challenges may be common to many countries, but each adapts to these developments and alters its direction in the light of its own history and long-established practices. The Iranian revolution of 1978-1979 serves as a poignant reminder that the direction of change cannot be "read" or predicted from general indicators and that popular notions of legitimate authority, like other fundamental cultural values, are often much more stable and enduring than the massive technological, economic, and political transformations of recent years initially suggest and have profound consequences for the direction of change.

A second theme of this book has been to seek to compare a wide range of more specialized studies of the Middle East. The comparison of specialized studies and the particular topics and contexts which they interpret are used to sharpen our understanding of distinctive Middle Eastern cultures and societies, not to seek an illusory overall synthesis. Such comparison is used to sharpen qualitative judgments and interpretations of evidence for such general issues as the nature of legitimate authority, social inequality, conceptions of family, community, and state and how these are affected by economic and political development, the significance of transnational identities such as Muslim, Jew, and Arab, and of religious belief and practice past and present.[71] The initial questions posed must be broad enough to permit meaningful comparison, but significant interpretation involves using these

[69] Marc Bloch, *Feudal Society* (Chicago and London: University of Chicago Press, 1961, p. 148 [French orig. 1939]).

[70] "Egyptian Census Foretells Doubled Population in 30 Years, Negating Economic Gains," *New York Times,* April 26, 1977, p. 8.

[71] This formulation is strongly influenced by discussions with Clifford Geertz and the late Lloyd A. Fallers and their writings.

concepts in such a way as to clarify particular historical and contemporary developments. This interpretative vision of anthropology and related disciplines is necessarily complex and requires a sensitivity to particular cultural and historical details. Yet its rewards for those interested in the main issues of social thought and a greater understanding of their own and other cultures and societies are also substantial.

Two recent studies, one on Islam, the other on a small country on the Arabian Peninsula, conclude with similar images. Geertz's *Islam Observed* concludes with what the author calls the "human metaphor" of a traditionally raised but French-speaking Moroccan student on an airplane bound for New York to study at an American university. It is the student's first trip away from home, and Geertz writes that "he passes the entire trip with the Koran gripped in one hand and a glass of scotch in the other." The second book describes an Omani who carries a dagger but adorns it with a wristwatch, who holds a camelstick in his hand but travels by Datsun, who dresses in *dishdāsha* and skullcap but conducts business in English and spends holidays in London.[72]

Both "human metaphors" describe real comportment (although the student passing the *entire* trip from Morocco to New York grasping a Quran and a scotch is difficult to accept), and they are contrived to suggest strikingly contradictory and ambivalent elements of comportment. There is an element of perhaps inescapable caricature in both metaphors. I am writing the conclusion to this book in a small provincial center on the Arabian peninsula. A group of young officials has just paid me an unexpected visit. I translated the passages containing the human metaphors described above for them. They were uneasy with them, and we sought to find out why.

My friends acknowledged that the comportment described in the metaphors was probably realistic but that the choice of images was wrong because they implied a contradiction of thought and action which they found inaccurate and misleading. Our discussion led us to suggest the following description of their present situation as a more satisfactory one, although admittedly less visually striking. Intellectuals in the Middle East have often used ideological models borrowed from the West to explain developments in their countries and their aspirations. This is probably an inescapable phenomenon given world historical developments. At the same time, in the name of what the West (especially the French) calls *authenticity* and the Arabs call *aṣāla*, Middle Easterners seek to cultivate or to revive native traditions and ideals and to achieve international recognition and respect. Middle Easterners and those of other traditions interested in comprehending Middle Eastern developments must admire the efforts, often courageous and resourceful, and at other times unavoidably hesitant and faltering, of persons and nations seeking to renew long-standing values and traditions in the exigent context of modern political and economic developments.

[72] Clifford Geertz, *Islam Observed* (New Haven: Yale University Press, 1968), pp. 116-17; Peterson, *Oman*, p. 213.

# glossary

Terms are defined here according to local usages. Many terms, especially those used in religious contexts, appear in slightly different forms in each of the major languages of the Middle East; not all of these variants are given here. (P = Persian; A = Arabic; T = Turkish; H = Hebrew.) The spellings given here often reflect local usages and not the conventions of written Arabic.

Āl (A): family, clan, people

ᶜAlāwī (A), Alevi (T): Shīᶜī religious sect found in Turkey, Iraq, Syria, and Lebanon

ᶜālim, pl. ᶜulamā' (A): religious scholar

amīr, pl. umarā' (A): prince or tribal chief

ᶜār (Mor. A): conditional supernatural curse or compulsion

ᶜaṣabīya (A): "group feeling" (Ibn Khaldūn)

asāla (A): authenticity

āyatullāh (A and P): principal Shīᶜī religious leader

ᶜaynayn (Saudi A): "eyes," tribal leaders

baraka (A): supernatural blessing; abundance

bayt (A): house; household

bayᶜa (A): oath of fealty; homage

bin ᶜamm (A): father's brother's son (for a full listing of kinship terms, see Chapter 6, note 2)

dam (A): blood

dār (A): house; tribal territory

darb (Mor. A): quarter, neighborhood

dawra (P and A): circle; discussion group

dawwār (Mor. A): rural local community

dhikr (A): Sufi term for repetition of certain words or phrases in praise of God

dishdāsha (A): a long, flowing garment, usually white for men, worn in Eastern Arabia

diya (A): blood money; recompense for bodily injury

dürüstlük (T): trustworthiness

fakhda (A): subdivision of a tribe; thigh

falaj, pl. aflāj (A): irrigational canal, partially underground (Oman)

fqīh (cl. faqīh), pl. fuqahā' (A): a person who knows Islamic law; a Quranic teacher

ghaṭṭāra (A): irrigation canal, partially underground (Morocco)

ḥabus, pl. aḥbās (North African A): religious bequest; same as waqf

ḥajj (A): pilgrimage to Mecca

ḥājj (A): a pilgrim, also the title assumed by one who has made the pilgrimage

ḥakim (A): ruler or judge; arbiter in pre-Islamic times

ḥāl (A): Sufi term for mystic exaltation

ḥamūla (A): kinship group (esp. Arabs in Israel)

ḥaqq (A): obligation; share or right; truth

ḥaram (A): religious sanctuary; that which is sacred or forbidden

ḥarka (Mor. A): royal progress; movement

hijra (A): emigration; Prophet's emigration from Mecca to Madina in 622.

ḥillūla (Mor. A): festival for a Jewish saint

ḥshūmīya (A): propriety; deference

ᶜīd al-Kabīr (A): the Great Feast, or Feast of Abraham

iḥrām (A): white seamless garment worn by pilgrims to Mecca

ijāza (A): teaching license

ijmāᶜa (A): concensus

ᶜilm, pl. ᶜulūm (A): religious knowledge; religious scholarship

imām (A): spiritual leader; prayer leader

jāhilīya (A): the pre-Islamic time of ignorance

jalle (Somali): comrade; playmate

jihād (A): religious struggle or endeavor

jinn, pl. jnūn (A): a form of supernatural being

juché (Somali borrowing from Korean): self-reliance

Kaᶜba (A): sacred enclosure at Mecca

kāhin (A): soothsayer

khān (P): tribal leader

khānqah (P): religious lodge

khayma (A): tent

khūwa (A): brotherhood; tax paid for protection to a more powerful tribal group

kibbutz, pl. kibbutzīm (H): collective settlement

kizb (A): lie; lying

kunya; pl. kunan (A): surname

laqab; pl. alqāb (A): nickname

madīna, pl. mudun (A): town

maḥalla (Mor. A): royal encampment or progress

mahdī (A): the rightly guided one; religious leader

makrūh (A): reprehensible

maktūb (A): that which is written, foreordained

malaka l-ḥifḍ (A): mnemonic domination; the faculty of memory

malik, pl. mulūk (A): king, sovereign

mallāḥ (A): Jewish quarter

marabout: a person, living or dead, thought to have a special relation toward God which enables him to ask for God's grace on behalf of his clients and to communicate it to them (North Africa)

maᶜrifa (A): secular knowledge

maᶜrūf (A): known; used with reference to distinguished or noble families

moshav, pl. moshavim (H): agricultural colony

muḍīf (Iraqi A): guest house

mujtahid (A and P): Shīᶜī religious leader

mulk (A): royal authority; sovereignty

mullah (P): village preacher

murīd (A): Sufi term for student or disciple

mushāᶜ (A): collective landownership

mūsim (Mor. A): a periodic festival in honor of a marabout

nafs (A): the self; the passions

nazdīk (P): nearness or closeness

nisba, pl. nisab (A): name derived from occupation or origin

nīya (A): faith; intent

niẓām (A): order; organization

pīr (P): Sufi master

qbīla (Mor. A), gabīla (Saudi A), pl. qabā'il or gabā'il: tribe

qāḍī, pl. quḍā (A): religious judge

qā'id, pl. qāda (Mor. A): tribal chief appointed over a tribe or small town during the protectorate; now a ministry of interior official

ᶜqāl (A): reason

qanāt (A and P): irrigation canal, partly underground

qarāba (A): nearness or closeness

qaṣba (A): citadel or fortress

qāt (A): mild narcotic plant, the leaves of which are chewed in Somalia, Djibouti, and the Yemen

qawm (A and P): people or nation; kinship term in Afghanistan

qudrat Allāh (A): God's will

rakᶜa (A): a bending of the torso from an upright position, followed by two prostrations in Islamic prayer

Ramaḍān (A): lunar month of fasting

rasūl (A): messenger; envoy

rūḥ (A): spirit

rukn, pl. arkān (A): pillar or principle

ṣafāyi bāṭin (P): integrity and inner purity

sajᶜ (A): rhymed prose

salafīya (A): Islamic reform movement

ṣalāt, pl. ṣalawāt (A): Islamic prayer ritual

Sanūsīya: North African religious order

ṣawm (A): fast

sayyid, pl. sāda (Iraqi A): descendants of the Prophet

ṣdāq (A): bridewealth

shahāda (A): declaration of faith

Sharīᶜa (A): the revealed, or canonical, law of Islam

sharīf, pl. shurafā' (A): descendant of the Prophet through his son-in-law, ᶜAlī, and his daughter, Fāṭima

shaykh, pl. shuyūkh (A): tribal or religious leader

Shīᶜa: major subdivision of the Islamic community

silsila (A): chain; patrilineal genealogy

ṣūfī: Islamic mystic

Sunnī: major subdivision of the Islamic community

sūq, pl. aswāq (A): market

taᶜāruf (A and P): etiquette

tafsīr: sciences of interpreting the Quran

taḥrīk (Mor. A): competitive display of horsemanship

taqīya (A): concealment

ṭarīqa, pl. ṭuruq (A): religious order

ṭaṣawwuf (A): mysticism; Sufism

ṭāṭā (Berber): contractual ritual alliance

ṭawāf (A): act of circumambulating the Kaᶜba

taᶜzīya (A): mourning

tekke (T): religious lodge

thiqa (A): confidence

umma (A): Islamic community

wālī, pl. awliyā' (North African A): saint

waqf, pl. awqāf (A): pious endowment

zaᶜīm, pl. zuᶜamā' (A): leader or strongman

zāwiya, pl. zāwāya (A): religious lodge

zawwār, pl. zawāwir (Mor. A): a visitor; a maraboutic descendant who acts as intermediary between clients and his maraboutic ancestor

zakāt (A): alms tax

zerangi (P): cleverness; insincerity

# index

RECEIVED
MAR 1994
Mission College
Learning Resource
Services

RECEIVED
MAR 1984
Mission College
Learning Resource
Services